MEDIA COMPOSER® 6:

PROFESSIONAL PICTURE AND SOUND EDITING

Woody Lidstone

Course Technology PTR
A part of Cengage Learning

COURSE TECHNOLOGY
CENGAGE Learning®

Australia, Brazil, Japan, Korea, Mexico, Singapore, Spain, United Kingdom, United States

COURSE TECHNOLOGY
CENGAGE Learning®

Media Composer® 6:
Professional Picture and Sound Editing
Woody Lidstone

Publisher and General Manager,
Course Technology PTR:
Stacy L. Hiquet

Associate Director of Marketing:
Sarah Panella

Manager of Editorial Services:
Heather Talbot

Senior Marketing Manager:
Mark Hughes

Acquisitions Editor:
Dan Gasparino

Development Editor:
Bryan Castle Jr.

Project Editor:
Kezia Endsley

Technical Reviewer:
Trevor Boden

Copy Editor:
Kezia Endsley

Interior Layout:
Shawn Morningstar

Cover Designer:
Mike Tanamachi

DVD-ROM Producer:
Brandon Penticuff

Indexer:
Valerie Haynes Perry

Proofreader:
Sue Boshers

Printed in the
United States of America
1 2 3 4 5 6 7 14 13 12

Library of Congress Control Number: 2012930802

ISBN-13: 978-1-133-60195-1

ISBN-10: 1-133-60195-2

Course Technology, a part of Cengage Learning
20 Channel Center Street
Boston, MA 02210
USA

Cengage Learning is a leading provider of customized learning solutions with office locations around the globe, including Singapore, the United Kingdom, Australia, Mexico, Brazil, and Japan. Locate your local office at:
international.cengage.com/region

Cengage Learning products are represented in Canada by Nelson Education, Ltd.

For your lifelong learning solutions, visit **courseptr.com.**

Visit our corporate Web site at **cengage.com.**

This book includes material that was developed in part by the Avid Technical Publications department and the Avid Training department.

For the storytellers.

Acknowledgments

Many thanks to the companies and individuals who provided us with the footage used in this book: The Upper Ground Enterprises/*Hell's Kitchen* post team for the *Hell's Kitchen* footage, and the *Agent Zero* footage (© Brian Barnhart and Thomas Graham 2010).

Special acknowledgment to the Avid personnel who've worked on previous versions of the course materials for the contribution it made to this book.

Thanks to my Splice co-instructor, Aaron Collier, for being a sounding board for Lessons 10 and 11. His knowledge and expertise in all things sound proved instrumental.

Thanks over at Cengage Learning to Kezia Endsley for helping me break some bad writing habits (rather, poor writing habits) and to Dan Gasparino and Stacy Hiquet for keeping things organized and moving through the pipeline.

And a final thanks to the crew at Avid who directly participated in this book, by helping me to make it better through their edits, page shuffles, and re-ordering: Trevor, Mary, Patty, and of course Bryan.

About the Author

Woody Lidstone is a trainer, editor, and consultant specializing in workflow for post-production and broadcast. He has worked with Avid's professional services team and worked in industry as an editor, as well as a visual effects compositor for a SciFi series.

Woody is the principal instructor at Splice Training, Canada's Avid Training Partner, where he teaches Avid Certified Training courses and iOS App Development courses in Vancouver, Toronto, and Halifax. When not in the classroom, he provides on-site training throughout North America and Europe.

Chat with the author by emailing woody@splicetraining.ca or by tweeting @splicetraining.

Table of Contents

Lesson 1
How Workflow Makes, Manages, and Moves Media 1

Exercise 1
Exploring Projects, Clips, and Bins   47

Lesson 2
Professional Acquisition   51

Exercise 2
Professional Acquisition   115

Lesson 3
Advanced Picture Editing   119

Exercise 3
Editing and Refining Your Sequences   157

Lesson 4
Play Together   167

Exercise 4
Using Markers and Comments   195

Lesson 5
Multicamera Editing   201

Exercise 5
Editing a Scene from Hell's Kitchen   231

Lesson 6
Script Integration and ScriptSync   235

Exercise 6
Using Script Integration and ScriptSync   259

Lesson 7
Advanced Dialogue Editing   267

Exercise 7
Performing Advanced Editing   289

Lesson 8
Working with Multichannel Audio   293

Exercise 8
Working with Multichannel Audio   321

Lesson 9
Fundamentals of Audio Mixing   327

Exercise 9
Working with Sound
351

Lesson 10
Adjusting Audio EQ
355

Exercise 10
Equalizing Audio   385

Lesson 11
Real-Time AudioSuite (RTAS)   389

Exercise 11
Working with Real-Time AudioSuite Effects   407

Lesson 12
Wrapping Up a Project   413

Exercise 12
Preparing for the Online Editing Stage   435

Lesson 13
Mastering the Media   441

Exercise 13
Managing Media
491

Appendix A
Technical Reference
499

Index
507

Introduction

Welcome to *Media Composer 6: Professional Picture and Sound Editing* and the Avid Learning Series. Whether you are interested in self-study or would like to pursue formal certification through an Avid Learning Partner, this book is a key step toward developing your core skills and introduces you to the power of Media Composer 6 advanced techniques. In addition, *Media Composer 6: Professional Picture and Sound Editing* is the first course of study for those pursuing Media Composer Professional certification.

The material in this book covers the advanced techniques for picture and sound editing, with particular attention to managing media and understanding Media Composer at an in-depth level. Whether your work involves editing corporate industrials, television programming, Web programming, or independent films, *Media Composer 6: Professional Picture and Sound Editing* will teach you what you need to know to take your career in Avid storytelling to a higher level.

Using This Book

The goal of this book is to give you the capabilities to excel in the field of post-production as an Avid Professional. Particular attention is paid to concepts and workflows relating to larger productions.

This book begins with an examination of projects, clips, media, and codecs so that you will learn to see Media Composer projects as a complex set of interrelated files on your computer. You'll learn advanced offline editing techniques, including Trim techniques, Replace Edit, Sync Point Edit, Multicam, and script-based editing. The book progresses to sound, with four lessons ranging from mixing and EQ to real-time AudioSuite. The final lessons tie back to where you started: understanding Media Composer at an in-depth level for workflow and media and how the two relate.

As one of the technical reviewers wrote, "If I was opening a post-production company, and someone knew Lessons 1, 2, 12 and 13, I would hire them on the spot." Those lessons might not be as fun as multicamera editing, but they are mission-critical.

Using the DVD

The DVD-ROM included with this book contains projects and media files for the exercises in the book. These must be installed before you can use them.

Some exercises present the choice of using short clips included on the DVD, or longer clips that are only available by download.

If you purchased an ebook version of this book, or would like to obtain the supplementary media files, you can download the contents from www.courseptr.com/downloads. Please note that you will be redirected to the Cengage Learning site.

Installation Instructions

Please follow these installation instructions exactly or you may not have access to all the project files and media associated with this course.

1. Make sure Media Composer 6 is installed and that you have opened the application at least once. Opening the application creates important folders that you will use during this installation.

2. Insert the accompanying DVD into your Windows or Macintosh computer's disc drive.

3. View the contents of the DVD. There are three folders on the DVD, and each folder must be copied to specific locations.

4. Drag the STUDENT MATERIALS (201) and PP&S AVID PROJECTS folders to your desktop.

5. The Avid MediaFiles folders on the DVD contain the individual media files you'll use for this book. This folder should be copied to the top level of your hard drive. If you've already used Media Composer on this system, it is possible that you have an existing Avid MediaFiles folder, which you should not delete.

6. Navigate to the root level of the hard drive where you want to store the media files. This may be your internal drive, in which case navigate to C: DRIVE:\ (WINDOWS) or MACINTOSH HD (MAC). If you have a locally attached external hard drive you want to use, navigate to the root level of the external hard drive.

Note: The root level of a hard drive is also called the *top level*. It is the highest level in the hierarchy of folders on your computer.

7. Make sure at the top level of your hard drive that there is no existing Avid MediaFiles folder. If there is no existing Avid MediaFiles folder, drag the entire AVID MEDIAFILES folder from the DVD onto the top level of your hard drive. If an Avid MediaFiles folder does exist on the top level of your hard drive, double-click it to reveal the MXF folder.

8. On the DVD, double-click the Avid MediaFiles folder, and then double-click the **MXF** folder.

9. Inside the DVD's MXF folder are eight folders in a series, such as 1201, 2301, 5201, and so on. Drag all of the numbered folders from the DVD into the MXF folder on your hard drive.

Caution: Do not rename the folders named OMFI MediaFiles or Avid MediaFiles located on the media drive. Media Composer uses the folder names to locate the media files.

Prerequisites

This book is designed for editors who have been cutting on Media Composer for a while and want to take their skills to the next level. It's expected that you have already taken or read *Media Composer 6: Part I–Editing Essentials* and *Media Composer 6: Part II–Effects Essentials*. Ideally, you have obtained Media Composer 6 User Certification.

This book is also suitable for technical professionals who seek to achieve the Avid Certified Support Representative certification and require advanced understanding of Media Composer prior to engaging in further study.

System Requirements

This book assumes that you have a system configuration suitable to run Media Composer 6. To verify the most recent system requirements, visit www.avid.com/US/products/media-composer and click the System Requirements tab.

Becoming Avid Certified

Avid certification is a tangible, industry-recognized credential that can help you advance your career and provide measurable benefits to your employer. When you're Avid certified, you not only help to accelerate and validate your professional development, but you can also improve your productivity and project success. Avid offers programs supporting certification in dedicated focus areas including Media Composer, Sibelius, Pro Tools, Worksurface Operation, and Live Sound. To become certified in Media Composer, you must enroll in a program at an Avid Learning Partner, where you can complete additional Media Composer coursework if needed and take your certification exam. To locate an Avid Learning Partner, visit www.avid.com/training.

Media Composer Certification

Avid offers two levels of Media Composer certification:

- Avid Media Composer User Certification
- Avid Media Composer Professional Certification

User Certification

The Avid Media Composer Certified User Exam is the first of two certification exams that allow you to become Avid certified. The two combined certifications offer an established and recognized goal for both academic users and industry professionals. The Avid Media Composer User Certification requires that you display a firm grasp of the core skills, workflows, and concepts of non-linear editing on the Media Composer system.

Courses/books associated with User certification include the following:

- *Media Composer 6: Part 1–Editing Essentials* (MC101)
- *Media Composer 6: Part 2–Effects Essentials* (MC110)

These User courses can be complemented with *Color Grading with Media Composer 6 and Symphony 6.*

Professional Certification

The Avid Media Composer Professional Certification prepares editors to competently operate a Media Composer system in a professional production environment. Professional certification requires a more advanced understanding of Media Composer, including advanced tools and workflows involved in creating professional programs.

Courses/books associated with Professional certification include the following:

- *Media Composer 6: Professional Picture and Sound Editing* (MC201)
- *Media Composer 6: Professional Effects and Compositing* (MC205)

These Professional courses can be complemented with *Color Grading with Media Composer 6 and Symphony 6.*

For more information about Avid's certification program, please visit www.avid.com/US/support/training/certification.

How Workflow Makes, Manages, and Moves Media

This lesson introduces editing workflows that bring a video from raw materials to a finished show. Almost everything you do creatively in Media Composer—from building a sequence to applying effects—is possible because Media Composer keeps a clear distinction between clips in a bin and the media files referenced by those clips. This first lesson begins with workflows and concludes with an exploration of the relationship between clips and media files.

Understanding that relationship is key to understanding other lessons, including Lesson 7, "Advanced Dialogue Editing" and, of course, Lesson 13, "Mastering the Media."

Media Used: Picture and Sound

Duration: 60 minutes

GOALS

- Differentiate between offline and online workflows
- Learn video and audio encoding/compression techniques
- Become comfortable choosing the appropriate media resolution and type
- Identify what a media file is
- Differentiate between types of media files
- Understand how clips locate their media files
- Learn how subclips and master clips differ
- Recognize the elements of metadata and essence in a media file

Understanding Workflow

Editing is one stage of a broad, three-staged pipeline for creating broadcast content. That pipeline consists of acquisition, editing and distribution, as shown in Figure 1.1.

Figure 1.1
Three stages of creating content for broadcast.

"Workflow" is the management of media as it moves through the stages of that pipeline. There are various ways to acquire footage, ranging from animation to stereoscopic recording. The distribution stage also has many workflows of its own, from YouTube to theatrical release and every screen size in between. But it's the editing stage that is likely most interesting to readers of this book.

Workflows are the backbone of an efficient post-production process. They move the footage from acquisition to distribution. To move up in the industry, you need to know workflows. Not just one, but a bunch.

Consider this analogy: You land at JFK Airport in New York City. You hop in a cab, and tell the driver that you want to go to the Empire State Building. The taxi begins the journey but then encounters road construction. Most cars are detouring through a side street. You ask the taxi driver to take the alternate route, but he declines because he isn't comfortable, having never travelled it.

A taxi driver who knows only one route from point A to Z is not as versatile nor as adaptable to changing conditions as one who knows many routes. Given the choice, you'd prefer the taxi driver that knows a few different routes. Likewise, producers prefer editors who know different workflows. You will not be an adaptable, versatile, and sought after editor if you don't know the workflows that keep the media moving through your edit suite.

Goals of Great Workflows

A good post-production workflow will help you deliver an on-time final product that looks and sounds great. A bad workflow, on the other hand, could result in your show being rejected by the broadcaster, if you manage to deliver it at all.

How do you tell a poor workflow from a great workflow? Here're some things to watch out for. You've got a bad workflow if:

- The footage looks or sounds worse after editing than it did when it was shot.

- Footage is not available on-demand. It must be ingested, restored, or recaptured before the editor can see it.

- More time is spent copying/moving or deleting media than is spent actually editing.

The first sign of a bad workflow, having degraded images or sound, is one of the most horrible things imaginable. It's your duty as the editor to protect the fidelity of the picture and sound quality.

The Big Picture

Before delving into post-production workflows specifically, let's examine the three broad stages of creating broadcast content. That's the "big picture." Editing is not an isolated stage. Some choices you make in post-production are the result of decisions made during acquisition—the choice of project format and raster size. Other choices you make are limited by the intended distribution—YouTube vs. network television, or perhaps both.

Acquisition

Content, anything you can see and hear, has to come from somewhere. Either it's generated in computer software, like scenes in *Toy Story*, or it's shot using film or video cameras. Generating that raw, uncut, original content is the end result of the *acquisition* stage, and that content becomes your source material in the editing stage.

As the editor, it's important for you to know how the source material was created.

Consider a TV show using the following acquisition formats: The main production unit records Sony XDCAM video at 1280×720 pixels at 60 frames per second (fps). The show uses extensive use of animation, which the 3D animators render into sequential image files having a resolution of 1920×1080 at 24fps. A separate camera unit is shooting secondary footage (b-roll) using HDV camcorders.

That's three different frame sizes and frame rates (HDV uses 1440×1080 at 29.97fps), as shown in Figure 1.2. You need this information to make informed decisions when you begin the editing stage.

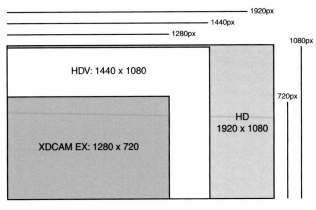

Figure 1.2
Acquisition may produce footage with varying formats.

Editing

In the editing stage, your goal is to transform the bits of source footage into a final piece and prepare it for the distribution phase. Footage will be combined (dissolves, superimposes); luminance and chrominance will be altered (color-correction); clips will be re-processed for smooth playback on your computer (rendering) and possibly reformatted to suit different screen sizes (16:9 vs. 4:3). Finally, the editing system may re-encode the picture and sound to suit the output format.

There are plenty of opportunities for picture and sound quality to be accidentally degraded. You must be mindful to choose the right workflow based on your acquisition and delivery formats.

Distribution

In the late 1990s, Avid coined the term *universal mastering*. It means to edit content once, and repurpose it for multiple mediums: PAL, NTSC, 720p, 1080p, 1080i, YouTube, iPod, Stereoscopic 3D, and many more.

You may look at a project and think, "This is only going to cable, it won't be repurposed for other formats," but you never know. The 1950s TV show *I Love Lucy* was repurposed more than 30 years after its initial airing, on VHS, then DVD, and it'll probably be repurposed again for distribution through digital download or Blu-ray.

If your footage is acquired in the best quality, and if suitable workflows are chosen for post-production, you'll deliver great looking picture and brilliant sound for each of your distribution methods.

Summary

The right workflow will preserve the integrity of the picture and sound quality all the way through the pipeline: great images in, great images out.

Understanding Offline and Online Procedures

The terms *offline* and *online* mean different things in different scenarios. The terms can relate to the quality of media files, or the stages of the editing process, or even different roles that editors take: the offline editor vs. the online editor. In this section, you'll learn what the words mean in different situations.

Stages in the Creative Process

They say that editing is like sculpting: You start with a mound of clay, from which you carefully remove unwanted material until a finished shape emerges. So it is with editing: You start with lots of footage, and you whittle it down until a story emerges.

Offline Editing

When you assemble the story from the raw source footage, you are an offline editor, performing offline editing. You are the storyteller: As the offline editor, your juxtaposition of shots creates or alters the meaning of the scene. You choose the shots, and you advise the director when you determine a shot is required to tell the story but doesn't exist. Offline editing is a creative process.

Online Editing

The online editing stage follows the offline stage. During online editing, the attention shifts from storytelling to the technical aspects of creating content for broadcast.

An online editor's checklist may include:

- [ ] Are picture and sound within legal broadcast ranges?
- [ ] Has the content been spaced appropriate for the insertion of commercials?
- [ ] Have the opening and closing titles been added?
- [ ] Are bars, tone, and a slate present at the beginning of the piece?
- [ ] Does the story begin at the right timecode? (such as 10:00:00:00)
- [ ] Has the video been color-corrected?
- [ ] Has the finished soundtrack been inserted?
- [ ] Are there bumpers before and after commercials?
- [ ] Is the video and audio of the highest technical quality?

- ☐ Have effect shots been incorporated?
- ☐ Have drop-outs and dust/hair (from film scans) been removed?
- ☐ Is the video formatted properly for the output medium (letterboxed or pillarboxed, as needed)?

The Changing Role of the Online Editor

The technical role of online editor doesn't traditionally offer the opportunity for creativity that the offline editor role does. That's changing, particularly in areas involving effects, sound, color-correction, and motion graphics. Those three areas previously involved other staff using specialized software and specialized workstations. As Avid editing systems gain greater capabilities in effects, sound, and color-correction, more tasks are assigned to the online editor, and there is greater opportunity for the online editor to be creative. One such area is in color-correction.

Color-correction can be used to fix problems from the acquisition phase: wrong filters or lenses on the camera, wrong lights on set. But color-correction can be a very creative device in the storytelling process: it can indicate time and place. Without color-correction, an offline editor would indicate time and place through establishing shots: an exterior of an office building before dissolving to the interior shot.

Shows like *24* and *CSI* and the film *Traffic* are all able to convey their location through color-correction performed in the online editing stage. In *CSI* and *24*, you know you're in the lab or Counter Terrorism Unit offices, respectively, when there are excessive blue highlights. You know the *CSI* scene is outside in Miami when there are greens and oranges, and you know *24* is outside in LA when there is washed-out orange.

It's not uncommon for one person to be asked to perform both roles of offline and online editor, despite the skill sets being so very different (artistic vs. technical). That's the result of software like Media Composer being equipped to handle aspects of offline and online equally.

Tip: To learn about color-correction, consider taking the *MC239 Color Grading on Media Composer and Symphony 6* course at an Avid Learning Partner.

Offline and Online Roles in Broadcast News

In the broadcast news industry, the separation of offline and online video editing exists for news stories too—Journalists are often expected to be the offline editors, cutting their story on Avid NewsCutter and choosing the images and adding their voice-over. They then send their stories to a *craft editor* (synonymous with online editor) for finessing and the technical check, after which the story is inserted into the newscast and encoded for the broadcaster's website.

Summary of Offline and Online Editing as Stages in the Creative Process

Hopefully, you now understand the differences between offline and online editing: One emphasizes the creative shot selection, whereas the other emphasizes technical skills. With different jobs come different needs in the edit suite: An offline editor needs access to all of the source footage, which might be 10–20 or even 100 hours of footage. The online editor, however, only needs the footage chosen by the offline editor. That could be just 22 minutes of the original 10 hours.

Let's now take a look at another use of the terms offline and online: media quality.

Quality of Media

First of all, the term *media*: It's anything you can see or hear and place in your timeline. Media includes video, still images, sound effects, music beds, voice-overs, logos, graphics you imported, and QuickTime movies created in other programs.

The Name "Media Composer"

Even the name of the editing system, Media Composer, harkens back to what your ultimate goal is—creating a composition of images and sound.

A musical composer creates a composition by creating tracks of complementary melodies and counter-melodies for the percussive, woodwinds, strings, and brass ensembles within the orchestra. A media composer (as a person, an editor) also creates tracks of media that, when played together, are better than when they were solo tracks.

Media is big. Storing it takes up space on a storage device, and space is limited. See Figures 1.3 and 1.4.

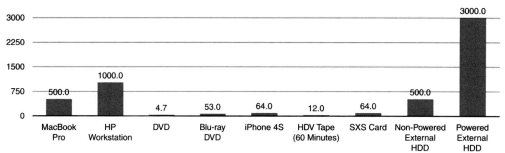

Figure 1.3
Storage capacities of selected devices in gigabytes.

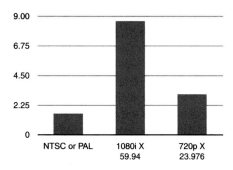

Figure 1.4
Amount of storage (GB) required
per minute of uncompressed video.

One of the key differences between offline editing and online editing, as discussed in the previous section, is that the offline editor needs access to all of the source footage in order to choose the best shots.

Shooting ratio is a term that becomes useful here. It's a way to express the ratio of the amount of source footage to the amount of footage in the finished piece. The higher the shooting ratio, the more footage the offline editor has to review. (And the longer it takes to edit.) The more source footage, the more space, because footage takes up space on a storage device. This creates a problem because, as shown in Figure 1.4, a lot of space is required to store even a minute of HD uncompressed video.

Shooting ratios vary between genres. Documentaries have a greater shooting ratio than soap operas, and sitcoms fall in between.

Ratio	Genre
10:1	A documentary
3:1	A sitcom
1.5:1	A soap opera

Documentaries are often created in the offline edit: The editor and producer/director identify themes from interviews and weave a story. That requires lots of raw source material, and results in high shooting ratios. For every 10 hours of interviews, there might be only one hour of footage used in the finish product. That's a shooting ratio of 10:1.

Soap operas, on the other hand, must fit almost 44 minutes of new content through their pipeline every day. There isn't time during acquisition for an actor to try for a great performance; it's often enough just to get the footage. A shooting ratio of 1.5:1 means the editor only gets a choice of takes half of the time. Unless the director and actors record a take twice, there isn't anything for an offline editor to select, other than the angle. That could be a good thing, because with fewer decisions to be made, offline editing will go quicker. Then again, it could be bad if the only footage available isn't a good take.

Note: Sitcoms and soaps often use multicamera setups, which further contribute to the space required for storing video, but don't typically contribute to editing time due to Media Composer's strength in editing multicamera footage, as you'll see later in this book.

How do you solve a problem like the documentary editor who wants to fit 10 hours of high-definition media onto a laptop? You compress the footage.

Video Compression

You compress video for the same reason you compress anything—to make it smaller. Once it's smaller, you can fit more of it in the same space. That means fewer hard disks, so storage costs decrease, or storage capacity (when expressed as hours of footage) increases. However, video quality decreases when you significantly compress your files, as illustrated in Figure 1.5.

Compression   Video Quality and
                   Storage Requirements

Figure 1.5
Video quality decreases as you compress footage.

Lossless Spatial Compression

You can possibly fit one or two filled balloons in a cupboard, but you can fit thousands of them in the same space if you remove the air. That would work, because you know you can put the air back in them later and they'll look roughly the same as they did originally. There is no visible difference as a result of the compression. That's lossless compression, it is without video quality loss.

Lossless compression in video is rare, although there are some techniques for lossless compression with audio, which are based on research that certain frequencies are outside the human hearing range, and therefore can be eliminated.

Lossy Spatial Compression

Lossy compression is akin to taking a piece of paper, crumbling it up into a tiny ball, and then later spreading it back out. No matter how hard you try, the paper will still have wrinkles: quality has been lost, so it's lossy.

JPEG compression is a form of lossy compression. It's used a lot in video codecs although it's better known for being used in still pictures. Given that video is a series of still images, it makes sense that it can be applied to both.

Adjacent pixels in an image are often similar—the same red/green/blue (RGB) values. Instead of uniquely recording the RGB values for a bunch of adjacent pixels, lossy compression will take up less space to record the values for one pixel, and then include an encoded direction in the image that says, "Repeat the previous pixel 200 times." The reason JPEG is lossy is because of those 200 original pixels—some could have been slightly darker or lighter than the original one, and those differences are lost when the image is encoded. The more you compress the image, the wider the range of acceptable loss of quality, as shown in Figure 1.6.

Figure 1.6
The left side of this image has been compressed.
Compare it to the right side, which has no compression.

Both lossy and lossless compression are a form of spatial compression. They can be applied on each frame video, making the frame smaller, but they do not consider the previous or next frames in the series of frames that make up the video. Well, there's a compression technique for that, too.

Temporal Compression

Aside from spatial compression, the other big kahuna in compression techniques is *temporal compression.* The underlying theory is this: Pixels don't frequently change from frame to frame, and even when they do, they tend to all shift in a similar offset. An interview with a CEO discussing his company will consist of the person and the backdrop. The thing that moves the most in each frame of video is the CEO's mouth, while the backdrop might not change at all.

"Why bother recording the pixel values of the background for every frame," a temporal compression algorithm might ask itself. "Instead, I'll record them once on the first frame and make a note for the next frame to reuse the ones from the previous. And the next one, and the next one." If the pixels of the backdrop represented 25 percent of the image, a significant reduction in storage requirements has been achieved!

In actuality, the temporal compression algorithm will typically refresh the whole image, including the backdrop, after a predetermined number of frames. For HDV footage, refresh is once every 15 frames. If you've ever watched a satellite feed during a storm and noticed part of the image freezes into a mosaic/square pattern, and then the little squares went away, that's the result of a transmission error between full-frame refreshes.

That's your primer on compression. You have spatial compression, affecting pixels within a frame (JPEG uses it), and temporal compression, which reduces pixels between sets of adjacent frames. Both techniques can be used at the same time, for a significant reduction in media file size. With those two techniques, you can solve the problem of getting hours upon hours of footage onto a 500GB laptop hard disk, enabling the offline editor to edit from Starbucks or, as I'm doing with this section of this book, from an airplane.

Footage Needs of the Offline Editor

As an offline editor, you want instant access to all the source footage for your project. You don't care how technically good the image quality is, all you need is to be able to make out the performance of the actors, so you may choose the best shot. For this reason, you make a trade-off: It's better to have all the footage available, but at a lower image quality, than to have only a portion of the footage available at the highest image quality. To do that, you compress the footage during ingest. (Reminder: Ingest is when you take the footage from the original medium—tape, P2, SxSs—and put it onto your Avid's storage.)

Media that has been compressed for offline editing is called *offline quality* media. The original media is never compressed, it's always a copy of the original media that is compressed during ingest.

Determining Your Storage Requirements for Offline Storage

The amount of storage needed for offline is really a product of how much source footage you have, and how much you are willing to compress it.

Avid has a storage calculator available on their website. Tell it how much footage you have, either in time or in film frames/feet, and then pick three different compression levels (codecs). The calculator will tell you the amount of required space (see Figure 1.7).

Access it from http://www.avid.com/US/resources/avid-storage-calculator.

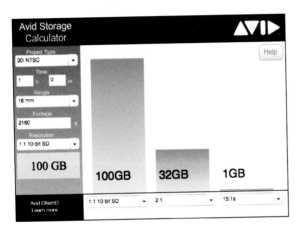

Figure 1.7
The Avid storage calculator, from Avid.com.

Footage Needs of the Online Editor

The online editor prepares the finished product for broadcast. That's hard to do with compressed footage from the offline stage, for a few reasons:

- Broadcasters want great looking footage. Compressed footage isn't great looking.

- It's challenging to remove dust, scratches, and other artifacts from the footage if you can't see them clearly.

- Color detail (chrominance) is lost when media is compressed, making it hard to create good chroma keys (green screen–style effects).

Compressed footage is bad for online editing. There are a few solutions, which you learn about next.

Offline to Online Conform

The process of conforming a finished sequence involves deleting the highly compressed offline quality media, and then re-ingesting it with less compression, which yields better looking pictures. It's called *conforming* because you need to verify that the re-ingested sequence visually conforms to the offline editor's sequence: No shots are missing or were captured incorrectly, which would be the case if you accidentally inserted the wrong memory stick.

As you'll learn in the next lesson, the sequences you cut and the media used by those sequences live separate lives and are stored in different locations on the computer. You can delete the clips and the media remains, you can delete media and the clips remain. In an offline to online conform, you delete the highly compressed (low-quality) media, leaving the metadata-rich clips and sequences behind. The metadata includes source information, such as the original tape name and timecode, or the path to the original media files.

Media Composer then uses the metadata in the clips to re-ingest the media a second time, but with less (or no) compression. You get great looking images, and because you only conform the media that was used in the final sequence, you can fit more of it on your storage device without having to compress it (or compress it as much).

Let's say you were cutting that documentary with a 10:1 shooting ratio. Originally you had 10 hours of raw source footage to ingest, but now you only need 1 hour of it. Since you only need one hour's worth of footage, you don't need to compress it: One hour of footage is enough.

Realistically, one hour of uncompressed high-definition footage will still take up considerable space, so you may choose to apply compression again. You just won't apply as much of it. Avid has an excellent compression codec called Avid DNxHD. It's a good choice for online editing because it shrinks HD video from approximately 1185Mb/s to 145–220Mb/s, a savings of 80 percent. It retains an image quality still suitable for broadcast.

Caution: Failure to name your sources properly during the offline editing can wreak havoc during the online editing. Save the project, and your reputation, by being careful to use labels and tape names from the start!

AMA Relinking with XDCAM

Another technique you can use for conforming involves content shot on XDCAM. XDCAM is a Sony video recording format in which the camera writes two versions of the video to the XDCAM disc:

- A high-quality video, compressed in either DV or IMX format.
- A low-quality video, compressed in an MPEG4 format. The quality is akin to video recorded on an older mobile phone.

When you ingest XDCAM footage using Avid Media Access, you can edit using the low-quality version of the media. When moving to online, you can re-insert the XDCAM discs and instruct Media Composer to relink to the high-quality media (see Figure 1.8).

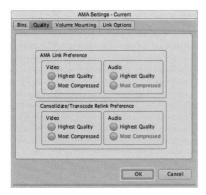

Figure 1.8
AMA allows relinking based on quality.

In Lesson 13, you'll learn the Relink tool and how it can be used in workflows to relink a sequence to media of various compression levels.

Understanding Media and Clips

Media is anything you can see or hear in your timeline, excluding items generated in real-time like some effects. Transforming raw footage into finished shows involves workflows in which media is copied, moved, deleted, transcoded, played, and exported. Before learning workflow recipes, you need to understand how clips, bins, projects, and media files work together under the hood.

You will be differentiated from many Avid editors when you understand why Media Composer behaves the way it does. Perhaps even more importantly, you will be on your way to troubleshooting and resolving issues that arise during those 4 AM editing sessions, when there is no technical support staff available on-site.

Clips versus Media Files

Clips and media files may seem like the same thing because playing a clip in the Source monitor results in the media being played, but there is a distinction between clips and media that is the basis for almost all of the post-production workflows: Clips don't contain any picture or sound. Clips only contain metadata, such as the clip name and timecodes, and data that Media Composer uses to identify the associated media files. It's those media files that contain the picture and/or sound.

Clips in Bins, Bins in Projects

A *bin* is a file that contains clips. *Clips* are anything that you can see in a bin—sequences, master clips, subclips, titles, and an assortment of other kinds of items.

Each bin is a single file on your hard drive, which contains clips when viewed from within Media Composer as shown in Figure 1.9. If your project has 15 bins, you have 15 bin files in your project folder on your hard drive.

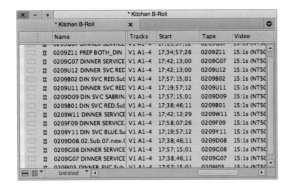
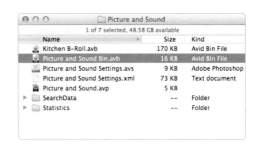

Figure 1.9
A bin as viewed within Media Composer (left) and within the file system (right).

Bins Contain Clips

The bin files have a file extension of .avb, which is an abbreviation for Avid bin. By comparison, JPEG images have .jpg as their extension, QuickTime movies use .mov, and Avid bins are recognizable by their .avb extension.

If you delete the Avid bin, either by using the Windows Explorer or OS X Lion Finder, you're also deleting all the clips inside the bin, but you are not deleting the media. Bins and media are separate.

Note: Clips are stored in bins. Bins are stored in your project's folder.

Bins tend to be quite small. The bin in Figure 1.9 is only 16KB. An unusually large bin, perhaps containing a feature film sequence, might be 5–10MB (megabytes). Bins are small precisely because they only contain clips, and clips only contain text such as:

- Start and end timecodes
- Source tape names
- Clip name

- Creation and modified dates
- Anything else that you see when you look in a bin, excluding the thumbnail image

Bins are small because they contain only metadata, not the actual media files, as shown in Figure 1.10.

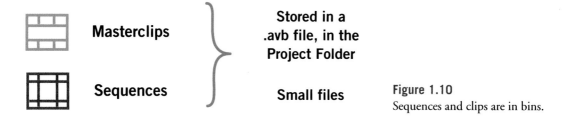

Masterclips

Stored in a .avb file, in the Project Folder

Sequences

Small files

Figure 1.10
Sequences and clips are in bins.

Although bins tend to be small, do not underestimate the importance of the content they contain. Every decision an offline editor makes in the timeline is saved in a sequence, which is saved in a bin. The small size makes it easy to back up the bin and even email the bin to another editor. Just keep in mind that bins contain no media, so if you did email a bin, the other editor wouldn't see the picture or hear the sound unless he also had access to the media files.

The Project Folder Contains Bins

Bins in Media Composer are grouped together in the Project window. On your hard drive, bins are grouped together in a folder, along with a few additional files. That folder is called your *project* folder. Figure 1.11 illustrates a folder called Picture and Sound when viewed from within Media Composer (left) and the file system (right).

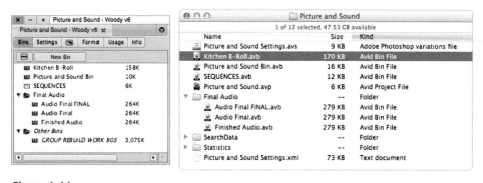

Figure 1.11
The project folder viewed within Media Composer (left) and as viewed on the hard drive (right).

The project folder also contains additional files, including the project settings (.avs files) and a file that identifies the folder as being an Avid project (.avp file) in contrast to a regular folder. Without the Avid project file (.avp), the Select Project window would not list the folder as an available project, even if it were a folder that contains bins.

Your project folder is usually located within a folder called Avid Projects (or Shared Avid Projects). The Avid Projects folder can be located anywhere you choose, from the internal hard drive to a flash memory stick, to a network location. The rule of thumb, however, is never store your media files and the project folder on the same drive. Storing the project folder and the media files on the same drive puts you at risk—if the drive dies, you lose both the project and the media. It's like keeping your spare key on the same key ring as your normal key: an unwise and unsafe move.

As you'll learn, there are ways to recover some of your losses in the event that you lose media or the clips, but not if you lose both. Clips can be recreated using the Media tool, and media can be re-ingested using the metadata contained in clips.

Locating the Project Folder

To locate your project folder, look no further than the top of the Select Project dialog box, as shown in Figure 1.12.

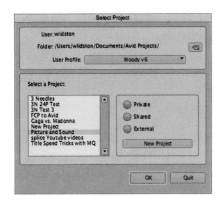

Figure 1.12
Select Project dialog box indicates
the location of the project folders.

The Select Project window appears when you launch Media Composer, as well as when you close the Project window from within Media Composer.

Notice that the location of the Avid Projects folder is different depending on whether you have selected Private, Public, or External. The Private selection allows only the currently logged in user to see the projects, whereas the Public selection means anyone who can log in to the computer can see the projects. External is used when the projects are in any other location, including on Avid Unity or even an external hard drive.

How Private Are Private Projects?

The ability to set projects as public or private should be considered a convenience, not an enforcement of a security protocol. The *private* selection results in Media Composer placing your project folders into a location that is not expected to be readable by other users of the computer, but that could be overridden. Furthermore, regardless of whether you choose private or public, media files on connected hard disks are available to all users and will appear in the Media tool.

If you need to restrict media files from being accessible by everyone, you should place media on different hard disks, which you can disconnect. Avid Unity also allows administrator-defined access to network-based storage workspaces, which is an effective way of implementing private/public projects and media.

Standard Locations for Media Composer 6's Project Folder

Aside from referring to the Select Project window, the following table documents the default locations for Private and Public project folders with Media Composer:

Private	(Windows) *drive:\Documents* and Settings\Windows *login name\My* Documents\ Avid Projects
	(Macintosh) Macintosh HD/Users/Mac *login name/Documents/Avid* Projects Shared Projects
Public	(Windows) *drive:\Documents* and Settings\All Users\Shared Documents\Shared Avid Projects
	(Macintosh) Macintosh HD/Users/Shared/Avid *editing application/Shared* Avid Projects

As for external projects, they can be located anywhere else.

Locating a Specific Bin

From the project window's Fast menu, you can perform a few file-level operations such as creating folders and opening bins. You can't, however, drag bins from the project window onto a memory stick or into an email to send them as an attachment. Those tasks require you to use the Avid bin file from your computer's file system.

The Fast menu has a command that makes it easier to discover the location of a selected bin. It's called Reveal File.

To reveal the location of a bin:

1. Right-click the bin in the PROJECT window.

2. Select REVEAL FILE, as shown in Figure 1.13.

   Windows Explorer or OS X Lion's Finder will open with the bin file selected.

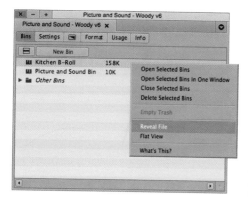

Figure 1.13
The contextual menu for a bin in the project window.

 Take a moment to complete Exercise 1, Part 1.

Media Drives Contain Media Files

Media files contain the actual video images and audio samples that you see and hear during playback. Video media files are typically larger than audio files, the difference being gigabytes compared to megabytes, as shown in Figure 1.14.

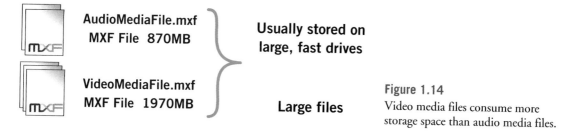

AudioMediaFile.mxf
MXF File 870MB

Usually stored on large, fast drives

VideoMediaFile.mxf
MXF File 1970MB

Large files

Figure 1.14
Video media files consume more storage space than audio media files.

Because they take up such large quantities of space, media files are typically stored on separate, large-capacity, high-speed storage devices called *media drives.*

You should know how to choose a media drive suitable for use with Avid Media Composer, which is the next topic. Afterward, you'll read how the media actually is stored and organized on the media drives.

Tips for Choosing a Media Drive

A media drive is any drive on which media is stored. Your internal hard drive could be a media drive if you use it to store media, as often happens with laptop computers. You can also use external storage for a media drive. Avid recommends that media drives are used exclusively for media and are not used for program files or documents. You should also ensure your projects and your media are not on the same drive, because losing that drive would affect both projects and media, which is worse than losing just one or the other.

When choosing external additional storage, you should consider the bus speed, drive speed, and drive redundancy. If you have a laptop computer, you should also consider whether or not the drive needs external power.

Fast Buses Move Quicker

The *bus* is the connection between the drive and the computer. You can think of it as the cable, although it's technically the cable and chips located in the hard disk and in the computer. The faster the bus, the quicker the media can be moved.

There are different kinds of buses—USB, Firewire, eSATA—and each move media at different speeds and use proprietary cables. When choosing an external drive, ensure the drive and your computer have the same bus. Cheaper drives will have a single bus, more expensive drives will offer multiple bus types, so with those drives, you can choose the fastest bus that your computer supports. If you move the drive to another computer, you have the comfort of knowing that with multiple bus types on the drive, the drive will likely be compatible.

Universal Serial Bus (USB)

USB connectors are popular, it's a safe bet that your computer has a USB port, so a USB drive will likely work. There are two common speeds of USB, called USB2 and USB3. USB2 is slower but more popular, whereas USB3 is beginning to increase in popularity with PCs, but no Mac (as of January 2012) ships with USB3 support.

You can interchange USB2 and USB3. If your computer isn't USB3 capable, the drive will transfer data at the slower speeds of USB2. You might choose a USB3 drive anyway, so when you upgrade to a newer computer with USB3, your drive will be ready. An add-on card can be purchased to provide USB3 for most workstations.

1394 (Firewire, iLink)

1394 ports are popular on Macs, and are less popular on PCs. However, in the absence of a factory-supplied 1394 port, they can easily be added to PCs through an expansion card costing typically less than USD $100. 1394 comes in two speeds: 400 megabits per second and 800 megabits per second (Mb/s).

If your producer is fussing about paying extra for the 800Mb/s drive, ask him if he's willing to pay you twice as much per hour, because a 400Mb/s drive will take twice as long to transfer the data. The amount of time (and money) he saves in just an hour of using an 800Mb/s drive should more than compensate for the additional cost of the drive.

(Then again: If you're being paid by the hour, perhaps a 400Mb/s drive is the way to go!)

External SATA (eSATA)

External SATA is one of the fastest bus types for external drives as of this writing. Most computers don't have the eSATA port, so you would need to add it as an add-on card. Speeds are typically 3,000Mb/s, which is more than triple of 1394 800, which makes it super for video editing.

Thunderbolt

The newest bus to the block is Thunderbolt. An innovation of Intel, it's not expected to be on PCs until mid-2012, although Apple has made it standard on all Macs introduced from the spring of 2011 onward. Thunderbolt transfers data at 10,000Mb/s, which is 12.5 times faster than the fastest 1394. It's an exceptional choice for high-definition video editing. It's also priced accordingly: quite higher than any of the other formats, but it's also new and as with all technology, likely to come down in price with time.

Rotational Speed

The bus speed moves the data between the drive and the computer, whereas the rotational speed is a measurement of how fast the disk is physically spinning. Traditional hard drives have one or more spinning discs inside. The faster they spin, the faster the data can be read. It's no good to have a very fast bus, like eSATA, but a very slow drive. Choose a 7,200RPM drive, or faster, when possible. Most external hard drives are 5,400RPM, so be aware of the rotational speed, especially on lower-priced drives.

It's also possible to find drives that spin at 15,000RPM. Avid used to manufacturer and sell these, although they no longer sell standalone external drives.

Power Requirements

If you're editing on a laptop computer, be mindful that larger-capacity external drives will usually need to be connected to a power outlet. Smaller-capacity (and often slower) drives don't require their own power adapter. Faster, bigger drives take more power than smaller, slower drives.

If your goal is to move freely between Starbucks, a public park, and an airplane, you'll need to go with a non-powered external drive. Or, use the workflows in this book to shuttle media between your external drive and your laptop's internal hard drive before taking that transcontinental flight.

Tip: There is an extra option for laptops that is becoming popular: Remove the optical drive and replace it with a second internal hard drive. Other World Computing (OWC) makes a frame called an *OptiBay* that permits this kind of retrofitting into a standard MacBook Pro. It's a handy way to get 1,500GB onto your laptop with no external drives in sight.

Redundancy (RAID)

Some external drives provide redundancy by actually being an enclosure that contains two individual hard drives. It's called a *redundant array of independent drives*, or simply a RAID. Data is automatically mirrored from one disk to the other, so that in the event of a disk failure, the data is protected and still available.

You might pay a few hundred dollars more for a drive with built-in RAID, but weigh that against how much you will lose if the drive containing all your media dies.

Scalable, Centralized Storage: Avid Unity

Avid Unity allows a facility to have centralized storage that is simultaneously available to all their editing workstations throughout their facility. The workstations are connected to the Unity storage using standard Ethernet cables, which allow for long distances between the storage and the actual editing workstations.

Post-production and broadcast facilities tend to choose Avid Unity storage because it makes more administrative and financial sense than maintaining a collection of external hard drives for each editing workstation, and allows the editing staff to more easily collaborate and share media.

Note: Unity MediaNet was a model of Unity that used fibre channel cables. After 12 years of empowering post-production facilities, it was discontinued at the end of 2011.

The Avid Unity administrator can then divvy up the storage to particular editing suites on-demand, changing the allotted storage as the needs of the project changes. It's very efficient, but does come with the expectation that the edit suite will be attached to the network. Using workflows covered later in this book, you will learn how to move projects and media between Unity workspaces and media drives.

You've learned about clips, bins, projects and media drives. You're now ready to hone in on the core of this lesson: understanding media files.

Understanding Media Files

As mentioned earlier, a *media file* is a file containing something you can see or hear. They are linked to clips, which are in your bin, and usually end up on your timeline.

Even if you're quite new to Avid Media Composer, you're likely not unfamiliar with media files.

Popular Media File Formats

Do you listen to music digitally or watch videos online? If so, you've already experienced MP3s, QuickTime movies, and Windows Media files, which are three types of consumer media files.

These three formats share some common features:

■ They all may be played back using specialized software called *players*, such as QuickTime and Windows Media.

■ They embed *metadata*, including the song title, author, artist, genre, and more.

QuickTime movies and Material Exchange Format (MXF) files are a special kind of media file called a *container file*.

Container Files Are Content Independent

Container files act like jars: They have contents and a label identifying those contents. Jars hold whatever you want, be it pens, flour, coins, or juice. To know what's inside, you label the outside. A container file is similar: it can contain any kind of data—video, audio, still pictures—and it contains a digital label called metadata. The metadata labels the container's contents, as illustrated in Figure 1.15.

Video and audio in container file can be encoded in any format—JPEG, MPEG, DV, AIFF, DNx, Apple ProRes, M-JPEG, H.286—it really doesn't matter. Technically, a developer could even encode a Microsoft Word document and stash it in a QuickTime file. The key word is *encode*: the video is encoded and to decode it, you need the digital equivalent of a secret decoder ring. That's another bit of computer code called a *codec*.

The metadata specifies the encoding of the video and/or audio. Media Composer reads the metadata to determine which of its many codecs it should use to properly decode the contents of the file.

At this point, it's sufficient to recognize that container files store any kind of data, and require additional software called a codec to make them usable. There's more on codecs coming up. (See "Codecs Are Secret Decoder Rings" on page 30.)

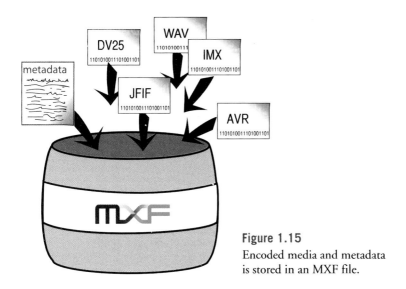

Figure 1.15
Encoded media and metadata
is stored in an MXF file.

Media Composer's Media Files

Media Composer is capable of editing many different types of media files and the list continues to grow. Broadly speaking, you can break down the supported types into two categories: Managed Media Files and AMA linked media files.

Managed Media Files

Media files tightly controlled by Media Composer are called *managed* media files.

Managed media files are kept only in specific locations on your hard drive. Media Composer maintains a database of those files, and they'll work with Avid's media management tools, including the Media tool, Avid Interplay, and Avid Unity.

Media Composer supports two file formats for managed media: MXF and OMFI files.

The MXF Container Format

Material Exchange Format (MXF) is a container file format that's purpose-built for digital storytelling workflows. It is a file format intended to be created at acquisition and move all the way through the pipeline to broadcast. MXF files created natively by professional cameras are edited by Media Composer and played to air by broadcast servers.

MXF files are rich in metadata. Their design allows them to retain their metadata even if a system that's using them doesn't understand the metadata that's present, allowing for longevity without loss of metadata as the file moves through the acquisition, editing, and broadcast stages.

MXF files can be uniquely identified. The MXF media file contains a Media Object Identifier, which is a 128-bit number that—in theory—is unique across space and time. There should never be two MXF files with the same Media Object ID. This significantly improves Media Composer's ability to manage and track the media file even if the file is renamed. QuickTime files do not have a unique internal identifier, which is one reason why they are not used as the format of choice for professional acquisition, editing, or broadcast.

The Pro MPEG Forum governs MXF's development. SMPTE ratified MXF as standard 377M, ensuring its specification is documented and belongs to no individual organization.

On the Web

Learn more about the MXF at the Pro MPEG Forum at http://www.pro-mpeg.org.

An MXF Technology whitepaper is available from Avid at http://www.avid.com/static/resources/common/documents/mxf.pdf.

MXF enables other workflows, too. MXF is written to storage in a way that allows the file to be read while it is being written. For editors using Avid Unity, a clip can be ingested by one editing system, whereas an editor simultaneously uses bits of the clip in a sequence. This MXF capability allows for rapid turnaround of news stories and is referred to as *frame chase editing*.

Variations of MXF

Not all MXF files are equal, nor are they necessarily interchangeable. By design, and as part of the standard, there are specific flavors of MXF for specific scenarios. The way MXF is used in a camera might be different than how it is used by an editing system. The different flavors are standardized as a collection of *operational patterns* (OPs).

Avid Media Composer's managed media conforms to the MXF OP-Atom standard. Any MXF file that also conforms to the OP-Atom standard should be usable by Avid without plug-ins or conversion. For example, Panasonic's P2 cards contain MXF OP-Atomic files. Media Composer can natively handle those files without requiring an AMA plug-in.

Sony's XDCAM, however, creates MXF files based on Operational Pattern 1A (OP-1A). Media Composer uses OP-1A MXF files with assistance from an AMA plug-in. Those OP-1A files are converted to OP-Atomic files when the media is ingested using the Consolidate tool, which is covered in the next lesson.

Location of MXF Media Files

The MXF media files are stored in a subfolder called \Avid MediaFiles\MXF\. Usually the subfolders are named sequentially beginning with 1, as shown in Figure 1.16.

Figure 1.16
Managed MXF media is stored in \Avid MediaFiles\MXF\[#], whereby [#] is any number.

The OMFI Container Format

The Open Media Framework Interchange (OMFI) format was created by Avid in the early 1990s. Both versions, OMFI1 and OMFI2, use the .omf file extension. OMF interchange files were the native managed media file format prior to the introduction of MXF in 2004. Media Composer v6 can read OMF interchange files from as far back as the early 1990s, although the format is deprecated and there has been no further development with it since the introduction of support for the Material Exchange Format (MXF) file.

Location of OMFI Media Files

Avid Media Composer looks for OMF interchange files in a folder called \OMFI MediaFiles, as shown in Figure 1.17.

Figure 1.17
Managed OMF interchange media is stored in \OMFI MediaFiles.

If Media Composer is storing files on Avid Unity, there will be one or more subfolders within the OMFI MediaFiles folder. Otherwise, all of the media is simply within the \OMFI MediaFiles folder.

There is no requirement for your editing system to have an OMFI MediaFiles folder. It is present only to support legacy media.

Organization of the Managed Media Folders

Media Composer has been designed to manage the contents of \Avid MediaFiles\ MXF\ and \OMFI MediaFiles on its own. These folders are a bit like the elephant graveyard in *The Lion King*. You must never go there, editor Simba. They are no-go zones and only the bravest (or most knowledgeable) of editors go there.

The managed media folders have no subdivision by project name or any other kind of organized folder hierarchy. The filenames don't exactly match the name of the clip in a bin. They contain a kind of serial number, making it less obvious as to what they are, and harder to manage directly.

Without third-party software, you can't even view the files in the QuickTime Player, nor can you inspect their properties to determine the Avid project to which they belong. That's because the managed media folders were not designed to be managed by the user. They were designed to be managed from within Media Composer. Their structure and naming convention make them most suitable for Media Composer to manage.

> Note: The folder names aren't case sensitive, but you do need to be mindful of the
> space character: One space character after MXF or OMF and no spaces in
> MediaFiles. Furthermore, the managed media folders are expected to be
> found at the top (root) level of the hard drive (or Unity workspace). If you
> move or rename the folder, Media Composer will ignore it.

In opposition to the tightly controlled managed media files, Media Composer also supports another kind of media called Avid Media Access (AMA). AMA is a newer technology that flips the controlled world of managed media files its side.

Avid Media Access (AMA)

Footage that you record today is probably saved as a file onto a flash memory device or hard drive inside the camera, as opposed to being saved to videotape. Camera manufacturers frequently release new cameras with better quality recording, higher resolution images, or better compression, which means longer recording time. Often, these changes result in changes to the format of the media file created by the camera.

This previously created a tricky situation for the Avid engineers: If the engineers had to implement support for every new camera format, they wouldn't get much work done implementing other new editing features. Furthermore, what would happen if Avid released a new version of Media Composer on February 1st, and then on February 5th, Sony released a new camera that writes to a new file format? Productions that invested in the new camera format would insist that Avid release a new version of Media Composer immediately, even though the next planned release might be months away.

The solution is AMA. AMA is a plug-in architecture that allows the camera manufacturers to write software, including codecs, that will enable Media Composer to understand and decode their files. When Sony revises their cameras, they can revise their AMA plug-in and you can download the update to gain support for the new camera types.

Tip: As of Media Composer v5.5, AMA plug-ins are not installed with Media Composer. They are a free download at http://www.avid.com/ama. This allows the plug-ins to be updated without Avid having to repackage the Media Composer software.

AMA linked files are *unmanaged* media files. That is, they are not managed by Media Composer. You edit them and they play back from their original locations (the memory stick, a folder on your desktop—wherever you originally put them). They don't appear in Media Composer's Media tool. There are no guarantees about playback performance with unmanaged media because you could be playing back from a very slow memory stick instead of a very fast hard drive.

Editors like AMA linked files because they can directly and immediately begin editing them. No copying them to a media drive. No capturing. No importing. Just improved productivity over the alternative method, as covered in the next section.

The AMA workflows typically go in two stages:

Step 1: Cut a sequence using AMA-linked clips.

Step 2: Copy the media that you used from the original location to a managed folder, converting or transcoding if necessary.

Compare the AMA workflow of the previous two steps with the traditional workflow, using managed media files instead of AMA files:

Step 1: Copy the media from the original location to an Avid managed folder, converting or transcoding if necessary.

Step 2: Cut a sequence using the managed clips.

The process is flipped: In the former, cutting happens first, in the later, cutting happens second. Editing with AMA is faster than the traditional workflow because when the copy stage begins, in which media is copied into the managed folder, the AMA method involves only the media that you used in the sequence.

Identifying Media Related to a Clip

The Reveal File feature, located on Media Composer's File menu, allows you to select a clip in a bin and cause your computer to automatically highlight the related media files in the file system. This is useful if you want to delete, move, or label the media file. You can also use it to locate *precomputes* (rendered effect media) created with imported graphics, motion effects, and titles.

To find a related media file:

1. Select the clip in a bin for which you want to find the media files.

2. Choose FILE > REVEAL FILE.

The system searches all available drives and opens one or more folders and selects the related media files. On Windows systems, Windows Explorer appears with the related media file highlighted. On OS X Lion, the Finder does the same task.

 Take a moment to complete Exercise 1, Part 2.

Media Files Summary

The previous few sections had a lot of information. To summarize:

■ Media Composer supports a variety of professional media file formats through AMA plug-ins, which are free at avid.com/ama.

■ AMA plug-ins edit content in-place, without copying it or transcoding it.

■ AMA plug-ins do not ship with Media Composer; you need to get them as a separate download. It's possible they will be updated periodically, even between releases of Media Composer software.

■ Media provided by an AMA plug-in is referred to as *non-managed media*. You cannot use the Media tool to view/locate/edit/delete such media.

■ AMA is fantastic because it allows you to begin editing instantly. No copying the media into a managed folder first.

■ Media Composer's built-in media-management tools act on MXF and OMFI media stored in specific folders at the top level of your hard drives (or Unity workspaces).

- MXF is a modern, SMPTE standard container file format.

- Managed media files contain the name of the project that was active when they were created.

- Media Composer's managed MXF media is of the OP-Atom variety.

- Container file formats contain media plus metadata that describes the media's encoding.

Codecs Are Secret Decoder Rings

(They're also secret encoder rings. That didn't fit in the headline, but it's true.) A reminder from earlier in this lesson: MXF files are container files. Container files have raw picture or audio data and metadata that identify the specific kind of picture or audio data they contain.

When Media Composer begins playing a clip, it uses metadata in the clip to determine the location of the associated media file. It retrieves the media file and examines the file's metadata to determine the encoding of the contained video or audio data. In its encoded, stored state, the media is unusable. You could say it has been freeze-dried.

To make the media usable, Media Composer has to reconstitute the media by decoding it. After locating the source media, Media Composer reads the metadata of the file and then attempts to load a suitable codec to convert the encoded frames to their un-encoded state, which makes the frames ready for use. This happens for every frame Media Composer plays back on all types of media, except for uncompressed (1:1) media, which, by its nature, is not encoded. (Technically, there is some encoding, although there is no compression, so the image quality is unaffected.)

> ## Etymology of Codec
>
> Codec is a compound of the words *coder* and *decode*. It dates back to the 1960s, when codecs were initially created to reduce the size of data for transmission, as opposed to storage.

Media Composer will often refer to the technology of codecs by the term *resolutions*, as shown in Figures 1.18 and 1.19.

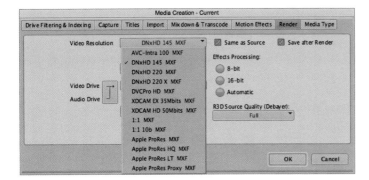

Figure 1.18
Media Creation tool specifies the codec for rendered media (HD codecs shown).

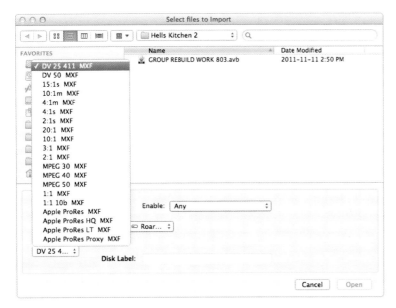

Figure 1.19
Pictures/movies are encoded during the import process (SD codecs shown).

Available Video Codecs

An "uncompressed" codec (or "resolution") is one that encodes and decodes the video but doesn't compress it. The ratio 1:1 indicates that the image you put in is the same as the image you get out. Because there is no compression, there are no compression artifacts and therefore no loss of image quality.

Uncompressed codecs are a good choice for media used during the online editing stage. Provided your storage is able to move the large, uncompressed files quickly, Media Composer also performs better with uncompressed media because the video can be decoded quicker in the absence of the unneeded decompression steps.

Standard Definition Uncompressed Codecs

Media Composer supports the following standard-definition uncompressed codecs for its managed media files:

1:1 MXF	8-bit 4:2:2 $Y'C_BC_R$ uncompressed MXF media
1:1 10b MXF	10-bit 4:2:2 $Y'C_BC_R$ uncompressed MXF media (see the 10-bit vs. 8-bit sidebar for more details)
1:1 OMF	8-bit 4:2:2 $Y'C_BC_R$ uncompressed OMF media; OMF only supports 8-bit media; there is no support for creating 10-bit OMF files

Avid Media Composer also supports Avid JFIF (from Meridien-based or later Avid systems), DV25, DV50, and IMX media. All resolutions can be freely mixed in the timeline, even if the clips have different frame sizes and play back at different rates.

High-Definition Uncompressed Codecs

Media Composer supports uncompressed and compressed high-definition media. Depending on your requirements, you may find that compressed media is more than sufficient. However, if your project contains extensive keying and compositing, you may prefer to work with uncompressed high-definition media.

All high-definition media is stored in the MXF format and is stored in the Avid Media File folders on your media drives.

The following high-definition uncompressed media types are available:

1:1 10b HD	10-bit 4:2:2 Y'CBCR full raster (1920×1080 or 1280×720) uncompressed media
1:1 HD	8-bit 4:2:2 Y'CBCR full raster (1920×1080 or 1280×720) uncompressed media

---

10-Bit versus 8-Bit. Just Two More Bits?

You may have noticed a few of Avid's codecs are labeled as 10-bit. It's either written as 10b or x, with x being the Roman numeral x, as in DNxHD 220x. If a codec doesn't specify otherwise, it's 8-bit.

10-bit video has two more bits per channel than 8-bit video.

That works out to an additional 768 values for red, green, and blue (or their color-difference variations). The image from a fax machine is usually 1-bit, with values being black or white. Then consider the difference between a fax machine and regular video: that's an additional 255 shades of red/green/blue. When you move to 10-bit video, you have three times more shades than you had from fax machine to 8-bit video. That's a lot of color and Luma detail.

If your source material is 10-bit, choose a 10-bit codec to preserve that detail. Otherwise, you'd be creating 10-bit media, which is four times larger than 8-bit media, and takes considerably longer to render and more processing power to play.

Number of Bits	Number of Distinct Values
1	2
2	4
3	8
4	16
5	32
6	64
7	128
8	256
9	512
10	1,024
11	2,048
12	4,096
13	8,192
14	16,384
15	32,768
16	65,546

DNxHD: Beauty over Bandwidth

Avid created its own open-sourced codec, called Avid DNxHD. It's a mastering-quality, compressed, high-definition codec purpose-built for post-production. In its first year, it was picked up by *American Idol* and was used by NBC for the 2005 Olympics.

The DNxHD family of resolutions provides both 8-bit and 10-bit, extremely high quality, full-raster compressed media. Multiple compression levels are provided for each high-definition format. Some DNxHD compression and decompression is performed by Avid's DX line of digital nonlinear accelerators.

I Don't See the Difference. Can You See the Difference?

I once took DNxHD on a tour around the United Kingdom with Avid. I had a timeline of three identical clips, stacked on top of each other. I used a vertical wipe effect to split screen the images, so you could see a third of each image. The media files for each clip were 1:1 HD, DNxHD 220x, and DNxHD 220. I'd pull up to broadcasters in a kind of tour bus and would demonstrate the technologies. When I'd show DNx to engineers, I'd point out that DNxHD 220 is 1/5th the size of uncompressed HD, and then I'd play the video on a loop and ask them to tell me which third was uncompressed, and which was compressed. A couple people got it right once, but they could never get it right two times in a row. I figure if broadcast engineers with decent eyes for video can't tell the compressed from the uncompressed, it's a pretty remarkable codec.

DNxHD media is named by its data rate in megabits/second instead of the compression level. As the data rate varies based on the high-definition format and frame rate, the specific numbering of DNxHD media varies from one format to another.

For reference, the following resolutions are available in the 1080i/59.94 format:

DNxHD 220x	10-bit 4:2:2 Y'CBCR full raster (1920×1080 or 1280×720) 220Mb/s compressed media. The compression ratio is approximately 5.7:1 for 1080i and 2.5:1 for 720p.
DNxHD 220	8-bit 4:2:2 Y'CBCR full raster (1920×1080 or 1280×720) 220Mb/s compressed media. The compression ratio is approximately 4.5:1 for 1080i and 2.0:1 for 720p.
DNxHD 145	8-bit 4:2:2 Y'CBCR full raster (1920×1080 or 1280×720) 145Mb/s compressed media. The compression ratio is approximately 6.8:1 for 1080i and 3.1:1 for 720p.
DVCPRO HD	8-bit or 10-bit 4:2:2 Y'CBCR subsampled raster (1280×1080 or 960×720) 100Mb/s compressed media.

Media Composer 6 introduced support for creating media in Apple's Pro Res formats, HDV, XDCAM, and AVC-Intra.

Available Audio Formats

In most cases, the audio specifications will be determined before the program reaches the online stage. At this stage, it's sufficient for you to know that Media Composer supports multiple audio sample rates and bit depths.

Four lessons within this book are devoted to working with audio, in which sample rate and bit depth are covered in greater detail.

Sample Rate

Media Composer supports 32kHz, 44kHz, 48kHz, and 96kHz audio sampling rates, provided those rates are supported by the hardware.

Bit Depth

Media Composer supports both 16- and 24-bit audio samples.

Note: Digital Betacam only stores 20 bits of audio information but accepts a 24-bit signal.

Because it is natively supported on Digital Betacam, HD CAM, and other popular tape formats, the majority of your conforms will probably use 24-bit, 48kHz sampling. In addition, the 48kHz rate allows you to embed the audio in either the SD or HDSDI bitstream.

Now that you know more about media than you ever thought possible, it's time to focus on the other side of the relationship: clips.

 Take a moment to complete Exercise 1, Part 3.

Clips Are Linked to Media Files

There are multiple types of clips that can be stored in a bin, as explained in Table 1-1.

Table 1-1 Available Clip Types

Clip Type	Description
Master clips	Master clips are created:
	● During capture
	● When logging
	● When importing an ALE
	● When consolidating

Continues...

Table 1-1 Available Clip Types (continued)

The unique property of master clips is that a master clip points back to a media file, and that media file has a duration equal to the duration of the master clip.

Clip Type	Description
Subclips	Subclips reference a portion of a media file. Because a master clip is of equal length to a media file, it is easy to think of subclips as being a bookmark or a shortcut to a subsection of a master clip.
Sequences	Sequences are built from a series of subclips, effect clips, and title clips. When you open a master clip in a Source monitor, mark IN and OUT points and insert the material into the timeline, Avid Media Composer is placing a subclip into the sequence. The subclip is also made in the bin, but under normal circumstances it is hidden from view.
Title clips	Title clips are generated by the Title tool or the Marquee Title tool. They point to two media files: One that indicates the portion of the title that should be transparent (the alpha channel) and another that points to the media file containing the graphic fill data of the title. A title clip's metadata tells Media Composer how to recreate the title, enabling you to edit it after the fact.

Essence Is the Core of a Media File

Aside from metadata, media files also contain *essence*. Essence is the part of the media file that is not metadata—it's the actual audio or video data.

The MXF OP-Atom standard specifies that each audio and video track be contained in a separate file: one media file for each channel of audio, and another media file for the video essence. This is called *separation of essence*.

A master clip having the tracks V1 and A1-2, therefore, would reference three media files when all the media is online, as shown in Figure 1.20.

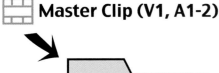 **Master Clip (V1, A1-2)**

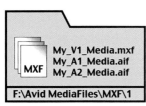

My_V1_Media.mxf
My_A1_Media.aif
My_A2_Media.aif
MXF
F:\Avid MediaFiles\MXF\1

Figure 1.20
Each master clip track points
to a separate media file.

The Perks of Separate Media Files

There are two significant performance and practical benefits relating to the separation of tracks into separate files, discussed next.

Unity Performance

Avid Unity uses network cables to connect the editing system to the storage. The network infrastructure has limits to the amount of data that can be moved at once. If your sequence is using only the audio component of a clip that was captured with video and audio, by separating the audio tracks, it's feasible to transmit just the audio portion. There is no requirement to consume valuable bandwidth transferring the non-required video media.

This leaves more Avid Unity bandwidth for other attached client workstations and improves workgroup performance.

Media Management

Media Management is easier when the media is in separate files.

Consider a scenario whereby a producer is using the camera microphone to record ambient sound. You accidentally capture the video along with the audio, even though the lens cap was on and the video is black. Video takes up more space than audio, so you want to delete the video but not the audio.

It's easier and faster to delete an accidentally captured track when that track is in a self-contained file. Had the video and audio media been combined into a single file (as with QuickTime), Avid Media Composer would have to extract the video and audio media into a new file, delete the original file, and re-link the original clip to the new file.

This would not be nearly as quick as simply deleting the unwanted media file.

Deep Dive into Media Files and Clips

Media Composer uses a database to connect clips and media files. It also uses metadata to connect master clips, subclips, and sequences. It's useful for you to understand how these relationships work, as it will make consolidating and relinking easier in later lessons.

Media Object Identifiers

Master clips have metadata, and media files have metadata. Aside from well-known metadata, such as the clip name, source tape, date modified, and color, there are internal bits of metadata that you would not normally see in a bin.

Each managed media file has a unique serial number called a Media Object Identifier (MOB ID). The metadata of a clip stores the MOB ID of the clip's associated media files. This is how clips are linked to managed media, which is the MXF or OMF interchange files located in one of Media Composer's managed folders. (See "Managed Media Files" on page 24.)

Avid Media Access clips don't use MOB IDs to link themselves to media files. Instead of MOB IDs, AMA stores the path to the file in the clip.

Structure of a Master Clip

A master clip, shown in Figure 1.21, contains all of the statistical, factual metadata that you see in a bin, along with internally used metadata such as the MOB ID or path to the AMA linked file.

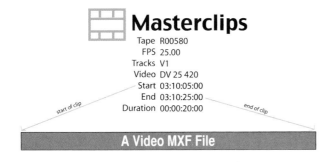

Figure 1.21
Structure of a master clip.

Subclips Specify a Range of Frames

A subclip is similar to a master clip, in that it contains statistical metadata that appears in a bin, and contains a MOB ID or path to the associated media files. The difference between a master clip and a subclip, other than the icon, is that a subclip contains a reference to the original master clip and has additional metadata called *frame offsets,* as shown in Figure 1.22.

Subclips reference a range of frames within the media file, unlike master clips, which always reference the entire media file, from the first frame through to the final frame.

In order to know which portion of the media file is referenced, a subclip stores the first frame to use and the number of frames to use. From this information, the last frame to use can also be calculated by adding those two numbers together.

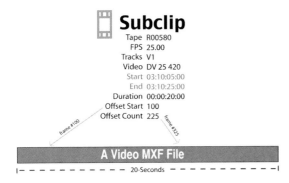

Subclip

Tape R00580
FPS 25.00
Tracks V1
Video DV 25 420
Start 03:10:05:00
End 03:10:25:00
Duration 00:00:20:00
Offset Start 100
Offset Count 225

A Video MXF File

20-Seconds

Figure 1.22
A subclip indicates a range
of frames in a media file.

When a subclip is loaded into the Source monitor, Media Composer only shows the range of frames from the *offset start* until the calculated last frame. Notice in Figure 1.22 that the subclip is still pointing to the original media file shown in Figure 1.21.

If you delete the original master clip and its associated media, you will also delete the subclip.

A Sequence Is a Series of Subclips

Technically, a sequence does not contain master clips; it contains subclips. Master clips have the same duration as their media files. If a sequence contained master clips, the entire master clip's footage would be present, and that's not what happens in a sequence. The clips in a sequence show the marked duration from the clip when it was in the viewer. *Marked duration* should sound familiar. It's what a subclip is. A sequence is a series of subclips.

When you mark a five-second region of a master clip and perform an insert or overwrite edit, Media Composer creates a subclip using the IN and OUT marks, and then places that subclip into the timeline. It's important that subclips are used, because subclips are designed to reference a portion of a media file.

As shown in Figure 1.22, a subclip contains all of the original metadata as the original master clip. That additional metadata is part of each clip in the sequence and can be quite useful, as covered in the following section.

 Take a moment to complete Exercise 1, Part 4.

Showing Reference Clips

A sequence contains a series of subclips, even though when displayed in a timeline, they are often called *segments*.

Avid bins have a handy trick that relies on the fact that a sequence contains sub-clips that contain all of the information of their original master clips. A bin can be configured to display the original master clips that are referenced by any of the bin's sequences. This is extremely useful if someone gives you a bin containing only a sequence, and you need information on, or want to recapture, a specific source clip.

In a normal scenario, a bin is configured to display clips created by the user. To have it display reference clips, you need to set the bin display.

To show reference clips:

1. Use the FAST menu in the lower-left corner of a bin, and choose SET BIN DISPLAY.

2. Select SHOW REFERENCE CLIPS.

Avid Media Composer will show you all the clips that were placed into any sequences in that bin.

Media File Databases

As covered in the preceding sections, Media Composer has multiple types of clips, all of which are contained in bins, and the clips are connected to individual media files on the media drives. How do clips find their managed media files? How does the pointing actually work? The secret lies in the Media Object Identifier (MOB ID).

You might be tempted to think that each clip contains the path and filename of the actual media file, such as e:\Avid MediaFiles\MXF\1\V1E039129M.MXF. That's how many non-linear editing systems work, including Adobe Premiere and Apple Final Cut Pro 7, and it's true of AMA-linked clips, but it's *not* true of managed media files. (Reminder: "managed" media files are ones in the OMFI or MXF media file folders.)

Question: If media file paths were contained in the clip, what would happen if you moved the clip's managed media files? What would display in the Source monitor?

Answer: Media Composer would use the file path to try to locate the file, and the file wouldn't be there. Instead of the clip's video, Media Composer would display the message "Media Offline." You would then need to tell the editing system where the new file is located.

The Avid solution for managed media is to track media files, their locations, and their metadata using a database. It's called a *media files database*, and you get one in every managed media folder.

A media files database tracks all of the media within its managed media folders. The media object identifier (like a unique serial number) in the metadata of the managed clips also exists in the media files, as shown in Figure 1.23. This is the common element that provides the connection between the clips in the bin and the managed media files.

When you open a clip in Media Composer, it reads the MOB ID from the clip, checks the database for the location of the related media files, and loads those files.

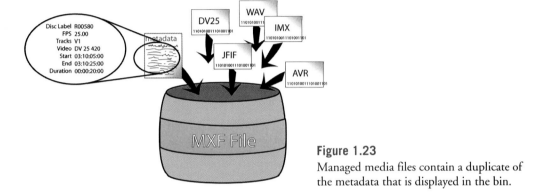

Figure 1.23
Managed media files contain a duplicate of the metadata that is displayed in the bin.

The Media File Database's Files

The media file database is updated when Media Composer detects that the contents of the folder have been changed. This should happen even if Media Composer wasn't running at the time that the files were moved, such as if you moved the files yourself from one drive to another using the Windows Explorer or OS X Lion Finder.

There are two files that make up a media file database, and you will find both of these files in each managed media file folder. The role of each file is not too important, but it's provided in Table 1-2 for your information.

Table 1-2   Media Database Filenames

Filename	Description
msmFMID.pmr	The index file containing a quick look-up table of MOB IDs and filenames.
msmFMDB.mdb	An aggregate copy of all of the metadata for each media file.

It's easier and quicker to search the index file, msmFMID.pmr, than to open each media file and check the metadata for a match when Media Composer is attempting to locate a file that contains the same MOB ID as a clip.

Each media file has embedded within it the same metadata that exists in its original master clip, and msmFMDB.mdb contains a copy of all the metadata for all the files managed by that media files database.

Corruption of Media Files Databases

Sometimes the database might get corrupt. A power failure, bad cabling to an external drive, an unexpected power surge, or just plain bad luck might cause your media files database to become corrupted. When one or more of your databases becomes corrupt, Media Composer can't make the connection between clips in a bin and the media files. What happens when Media Composer can't locate the media files? Clips will appear offline even though the media is there.

Note: You have one database (consisting of two files) per managed media files folder. If you have 10 volumes (drives or workspaces), you'll likely have 10 media file databases (consisting of 20 files).

In the event that clips are showing as offline, even though you know they exist, or in the event that a sequence is reporting media errors, you can safely quit Media Composer, delete the two media file databases referenced in Table 2-2 from your managed media files locations, and then restart Media Composer.

Upon detecting the absence of the media files databases, Media Composer will iterate through each media file, reading the metadata and rebuilding the database files. In an Avid Unity environment, there should be no clients accessing the workspace. If you have any doubts, verify with your Unity Administrator first.

   Take a moment to complete Exercise 1, Part 5.

Playback: Under the Hood

The previous sections discussed media files and master clips, subclips and sequences, as well as the link between them: the media file databases.

Let's consider a practical example and see how it all fits together: Playback of a master clip in the Source monitor.

You load a clip into the Source monitor.

Although you are not playing back yet, Media Composer needs to display a frame from that media file. It needs to locate the media file containing the video essence. As you are not playing the footage (nor scrubbing), Media Composer does not require the audio media files.

Media Composer's master clips point back to a media file for each track. For a master clip of a managed media file having tracks [V1, A1-2], that master clip will contain three MOB IDs. In this example, Avid Media Composer retrieves the MOB ID referenced by the video track for the clip in the Source monitor. It takes that MOB ID and asks the database:

"Where is the file corresponding to MOB ID 3E2039102aF02?"

The media file database responds with f:\Avid MediaFiles\MXF\1\1013e10293.mxf.

Armed with that filename, Media Composer then retrieves the video frame from that file. It displays a single frame of that video essence in the Source monitor, and remembers the path to the video essence so that it does not need to requery the database for each additional frame requested when you play or step-through the footage.

Media Offline

When Media Composer can't find a media file, either because it's genuinely deleted, the drive isn't mounted, the workspace isn't connected, or the database file is corrupt, it refers to the media as being offline. In this context, "offline" means "unavailable."

Here are some other notes about media that's offline:

- After deleting audio and video media files, the associated clips and sections of sequences play silence and display the *Media Offline* frame.

- Offline audio-only clips will display a gray frame and play without sound. They will not display the *Media Offline* message.

- You can add the Offline heading to a bin view to quickly determine which tracks or clips are offline.

- To prevent accidentally deleting important media files, such as imported graphics, lock the clip in the bin by selecting it and choosing CLIP > LOCK BIN SELECTION.

Review/Discussion Questions

1. How do the roles of offline and online editors differ? (See "Stages in the Creative Process" on page 5.)

2. How does offline and online media differ? (See "Quality of Media" on page 7.)

3. What are two ways that video can be compressed? (See "Video Compression" on page 9.)

4. Why would you create an online project? (See "Online Editing" on page 5.)

5. If you had to choose between being an online editor or offline editor, which would you prefer to be? (See "Understanding Offline and Online Procedures" on page 5.)

6. What technical issues is an online editor concerned with? (See "Online Editing," page 5.)

7. How would the role of an offline editor be different when cutting a documentary compared to a scripted sitcom? (See "Stages in the Creative Process" on page 5.)

8. What kind of additional tasks might an online editor expect if she is editing programs with a significant proportion of historical footage (1930s–1950s), as opposed to a big-budget science fiction TV series? (See "Online Editing" on page 5.)

9. What's the difference between a clip and a media file? (See "Clips versus Media Files" on page 14.)

10. What's the relationship between clips and projects? (See "Clips in Bins, Bins in Projects" on page 15.)

11. There is a sequence in a bin called FINAL SEQUENCES. How do you make a backup of that bin? (See "Locating a Specific Bin" on page 18.)

12. You've finished the offline edit of a project and now want to send a copy of the project to the online editor. How do you locate the project? (See "Locating the Project Folder" on page 17.)

13. The folder in Figure 1.24 is not being displayed in the Select Project dialog box as an Avid project. What are some possible explanations? (See "The Project Folder Contains Bins" on page 16.)

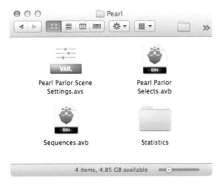

Figure 1.24
A suspicious project folder.

14. You inform your post-production supervisor that you need additional storage capacity. Your editing system has 1394 800Mb/s and USB2. Which kind of drive will you recommend that your producer buy, and how do you justify the additional or lower price compared to other drives? (See "Tips for Choosing a Media Drive" on page 20.)

15. Compare and contrast external hard drives and Avid Unity storage. (See "Scalable, Centralized Storage: Avid Unity," on page 22.)

16. What's the difference between a managed media folder and an AMA linked volume? (See "Media Composer's Media Files" on page 24.)

17. Name the two of Media Composer's managed media formats. (See "Managed Media Files" on page 24.)

18. What is the difference between DNxHD and HD? (See "Available Video Codecs" on page 31.)

19. What is the advantage of encoding video into the DNxHD format, in contrast to leaving it in the uncompressed high-definition format? (See "DNxHD: Beauty over Bandwidth" on page 33.)

20. Another editor couriers you a USB hard disk containing her Avid project and media files (material exchange format). She requests the hard disk be returned immediately. How do you incorporate her files onto your Media Composer system? (See "Locating the Project Folder" on page 17.)

21. Your producer insists that you ingest video material in a 10-bit format. Your source material is AVC-Intra (8-bit), and your delivery format is HDCAM (8-bit). Do you object to his request? Why or why not? (See "10-Bit versus 8-Bit. Just Two More Bits?" on page 32.)

22. How does a subclip differ from a master clip? (See "Structure of a Master Clip" on page 38.)

23. How does Media Composer locate the media for an AMA-linked clip? (See "Media File Databases" on page 40.)

24. How does Media Composer locate the media for a managed media file, such as an MXF file? (See "Media File Databases" on page 40.)

25. What is a "media database" and where would you find a media database file? (See "Media File Databases" on page 40.)

Exploring Projects, Clips, and Bins

This exercise explores the relationship between clips and media files. You'll explore how bins are organized within projects from the perspective of the file system on the computer. You'll also compare how a subclip and a master clip are different, and by examining the raw, unadulterated media files, you'll get a glimpse into how Media Composer's managed media works under the hood.

Note: The exercise files are sometimes revised after the DVD media is created.
Please be sure to check Cengage's website for an updated file for download.
Visit http://www.courseptr.com/ downloads and then enter the book's title or
ISBN to find out of there is any updated information.

Media Used:
Project: Hell's Kitchen
Bin: Picture and Sound

Duration:
40 minutes

Exercise 1.1:
Revealing Bins: Which Final Is Final?

You have multiple copies of a bin in a project you're taking over. You can't tell which one is the one that is likely the most recent bin. Use REVEAL FILE to find out.

As you collaborate with other editors, you may find that you have a few copies of the same bin; such is the case in the Lesson 1 > Finals folder, in the Picture and Sound project.

To determine which bin of three is the most recently modified bin:

1. Open the PRO PICTURE & SOUND project. There are three bins in the folder LESSON 1 > FINALS.

2. Determine which bin is newest, by using REVEAL FILE, and then right-click the file and choose PROPERTIES (Windows) or GET INFO (Mac).

3. Rename the older bins to include the word OLDER. When you return to Media Composer, it updates the bin's names in the Project window.

Exercise 1.2: Viewing the Media Files

An editing system with multiple drives (or Unity workspaces) may have media for the same project spread across different drives. In this exercise, you'll modify a bin to show the drive that media is on, and then reveal the media to see the file directly.

1. Open LESSON 1 > LESSON 1.

2. Add the DRIVE column if it is not already available in the bin view.

3. Note the drive on which the green clip, **0209A02 WHERE AM I?**, is located.

4. Right-click the clip and click REVEAL FILE to identify the media file(s) associated with this clip.

Exercise 1.3: Exploring Resolutions (Codecs)

Various video resolutions encode the video with different levels of compression. In this exercise, you'll examine two identical clips that differ only in their Avid resolution. You'll inspect the size of their associated media files and see the trade-off for compressing footage.

1. Open Lesson 1 > Resolution Comparison. The bin contains two clips: one red, the other blue.

2. Examine the two clips by loading them into the Source monitor. Which clip do you think is more compressed?

3. Reveal the source media files for the two clips and determine their file sizes. How much more storage is required for the better-looking clip?

4. Add the Video column to the bin and note the Avid resolutions (codecs) used for each clip.

When would you choose the resolution that resulted in the smaller clip? Can you think of an example where you might use it even for an online edit?

Exercise 1.4: Understanding Subclips

Subclips point to the same media files as the master clip from which the subclips were created. You'll confirm that in this exercise.

To better see how subclips work:

1. Open Lesson 1 > Lesson 1.

2. Load the yellow clip, called I am a Master clip, into the Source monitor.

3. Mark a range in the clip and create a subclip called I am a subclip.

4. Reveal the source media of the master clip and that of the source.

How do the media files differ for the subclip in comparison to the master clip?

Exercise 1.5: Media File Folders and Databases

Media Composer searches for managed media in two very specific locations on each drive, as covered in "Location of MXF Media Files" on page 26. In this exercise, you will change the name of the folder and observe how Media Composer behaves.

1. Play a clip from the Lesson 1 > Lesson 1 bin.

2. Open the Windows Explorer or OS X Lion Finder and locate the drive containing your media.

3. OS X Lion may not display the drives in the Finder. If that is the case, use Go > Computer and select your media drive from the resulting window.

   Windows 7 has a shortcut key for displaying the Windows Explorer: ⌨ +E.

4. Rename the Avid MediaFiles folder xAvid MediaFiles.

5. Return to Media Composer and play the clip.

Explain what you see in the Source monitor. The ability to rename a managed media folder and have Media Composer ignore the contents is one of the fundamental concepts when troubleshooting corrupt media files.

Note: You would normally rename media folders while Media Composer is open. But for this lesson, it's fine and saves time since you do not have to wait for Media Composer to launch.

Professional Acquisition

Many upcoming editors have not encountered videotape, owing to the low cost and high availability of file-based recording cameras. This lesson covers why tape is encountered in a professional edit suite, some techniques for capturing and logging footage, and an audit of settings that impact the capture process. It concludes with an exploration of Avid Media Access.

Media Used: None

Duration: 75 minutes

GOALS

- Understand why videotape is sometimes used in professional environments
- Understand the benefits of videotape compared to file-based media
- Gain awareness of popular tape formats, including the Betacam series, HD-CAM series, and DV series
- Learn the options for connecting videotape equipment to your computer
- Understand the differences between capturing on-the-fly and capturing from IN to OUT, and learn the technique of logging clips for the purpose of batch capture
- Understand selected items in Capture settings, Audio Project settings, and Media Creation settings
- Learn to add markers and create subclips while capturing
- Use the Console during capture and after capture to summarize a bin's selected items
- Understand how a plug-in architecture allows for timely updates to Media Composer
- Differentiate between capturing and Avid Media Access as techniques for acquisition
- Compare the differences in performance and media management for AMA-linked footage and managed media

Tape: It's Alive

The death of magnetic videotape has been predicted for almost as long as there have been alternative recording formats, such as the original XDCAM which recorded on Blu-Ray discs enclosed in a caddy, and flash-memory formats like P2, MicroSD, and XDCAM SxS, which record onto non-volatile memory chips that don't lose their contents when they lose power.

Despite the alternative formats and claims to the contrary, tape isn't dead yet. You're likely to encounter tape when working in professional post-production environments, where clients may arrive with almost any format and expect you to handle it in stride. Tape isn't for just legacy formats, such as Panasonic's DVCPro, it's also actively used for new and emerging formats, like Sony's HDCAM SR.

Tape is an inexpensive way to record a lot of data. It's still used in the data archival and backup industries, and by camera manufacturers where there is a lot of data to record, such as high-definition video in the RGB color space.

Some of the reasons why you'll still encounter videotape include:

- Many organizations have shelves upon shelves of archival and stock footage stored on videotape

- Tape, compared to hard drives and flash-based memory, is relatively inexpensive when you compare the formats in terms of cost per gigabyte

- HDCAM SR cameras, a high-end HD RGB format, records to videotape

It's important for professionals to know how Media Composer captures from videotape. To not know how to deal with tape is to have a gap in your knowledge and skill set as an editor or assistant editor.

This section covers two topics: popular videotape formats, and technology that physically connects the videotape player to your editing system.

Close Encounters of the Magnetic Kind

There are a variety of videotape formats that you may encounter. For a while in the 1990s, it seemed as though every year there was a new tape format. Many formats have come and gone, but there are some formats that have persevered in popularity, if only for archival purposes.

This section introduces some popular tape formats, although it is by no means an exhaustive review of the formats available.

Decks, VTRs, and Cameras

Two terms that are used almost interchangeably are deck and VTR. A tape-based camera can also be used as a deck, although that's not as ideal as using a genuine VTR, for reasons about to be unveiled.

A Video Television Recorder, VTR, is a standalone unit that's essentially a professional VCR, having professional-grade connectors at the rear and is typically automatable. VTRs are often rack-mounted in an equipment room and connected to an editing system's video I/O hardware either directly or through a patch-panel.

A camera is exactly that. It can also play and record videotapes, but a camera lacks the professional variety of connectors found on a VTR. When you don't have a VTR, you can often use a camera for playback of videotape.

The "transport mechanism" of a camera—the internal mechanical parts that are used to shuttle the videotape—are optimized for forward playing in a camera, while the transport mechanism in higher-end VTRs is optimized for highly accurate and rapid forward and reverse movement, such as would be ideal for use with the Clip > Batch Capture feature of Media Composer.

The term "deck" is generic and typically means VTR, but can also mean the tape-deck that's built into a camera.

HDCAM SR

HDCAM SR is the 2004 successor to Sony's HDCAM from 1997. The SR is an acronym that stands for "Superior Resolution," which makes sense given the qualities of the original HDCAM format. Table 2-1 compares the two.

Table 2-1   HDCAM SR Compared to HDCAM

Characteristic	HDCAM SR	HDCAM
Year of introduction	2004	1997
Cassette identification	Cyan lid	Orange lid
Sampling	4:4:4 or 4:2:2	3:1:1
Data rate (Mb/s)	440 (YUV) or 880 (RGB)	135
Raster	1920×1080	1440×1080
Bit depth	10-bit	8-bit

Table 2-1 illustrates that the original HDCAM had 1¼ the luma and chroma range just by being 8-bit instead of 10-bit. Only 75% of the luminance was preserved, and only 25% of the chrominance was preserved (that's 3:1:1 sampling). Furthermore, HDCAM uses a sub-rastered format (1440×1080) instead of the full HD 1920×1080 raster. By designing the format in this way, Sony achieved a data rate of 135Mb/s, and was first to market with an HD product that fit on the standard 1/2" tape format.

The 1/2" tape was already used by Sony for their other popular professional formats: BetacamSP, BetacamSX, and Digital Betacam. By fitting the HD image onto a 1/2" tape format, Sony maintained physical compatibility with their standard definition tapes and were able to introduce VTRs capable of playing both high-definition and standard-definition tapes.

HDCAM SR allows recording in two formats: YUV (440Mb/s) and RGB (880Mb/s). It can also record in a dual-YUV mode, which still uses 880Mb/s, although it's essentially two independent video streams being recorded simultaneously to the same tape. Kind of like what you might want if you were recording stereoscopic HD content.

RGB Encoding

A camera's electronic sensor is made up of a raster of pixels. The sensor will sample the levels of red, green, and blue (RGB) for each pixel and pass those levels onto an electronic processor. If a camera is capable of recording in RGB, the RGB values are written to storage as the sensor sampled them. If the camera is not capable of recording the raw RGB values, image conversion will occur, which is described in the next section about YUV encoding.

In a 1920×1080 raster, there are 2,073,600 pixels. RGB encoding has a high data rate because there is a unique trio of values (the red, green, and blue color values) that are recorded for each pixel.

When the sampled RGB levels are recorded for every pixel, the format is described as being a 4:4:4 format. In this system, 4 is the best and 0 is the worse. It's sort of like figure skating scores: You might expect the scale to go 1-10, but it goes 0-6. For video image sampling, the scores are 0-4. It means Red gets a 4, Green gets a 4, and Blue gets a 4. (Go team RGB! Perfect scores!)

Perfect scores require lots of processing power and the ability to move data quickly between the storage subsystem, the memory subsystem, and the video hardware. For these reasons, RGB encoding is rare compared to YUV encoding, which is covered next.

Media Composer only gained RGB support with release 5, although Avid DS has supported RGB for eternity. When working with Media Composer in RGB mode, you must set the Project Format to HD and RGB. There are only a few Avid resolutions (codecs) that permit encoding the RGB 4:4:4 image data.

YUV Encoding

Images are captured by the camera's sensor as RGB color values for each pixel, as described in the preceding section. The difference between RGB and YUV color encoding modes occurs when the RGB pixel data is sent to the processor inside the camera. YUV encoding reduces bandwidth requirements by using algorithms based in theories that the human eye is sensitive to luminance (Y) more than chrominance (UV), and the eye is more sensitive to red and blue than it is to green.

With that observation in mind, YUV encoding will record the full spectrum of the luminance (a grayscale image), and will then encode blue and red by using a color-difference formula.

Color difference works sort of like this: If you know that I have three numbers that add up to 100, and you know the first number is 25 and the next number is 50, you can figure out the third number. This is a gross simplification of the technique, but it'll suffice to explain that green doesn't need to be recorded, it can be determined if the value of red and blue are known. By not encoding green distinctly, the data rate can be reduced.

Note: There's a legacy reasoning to YUV encoding, too. Black-and-white TVs of the 1950s only understood a Y (luminance) signal. When color was added to the broadcasts, by separating it from the luminance, black-and-white TVs would still interpret the Y signal and display a black-and-white image, while newer TVs would also interpret the UV signal, mapping color on top of the grayscale image, allowing for cross-technology compatibility as color broadcasting was rolled out.

When a YUV signal is converted into a digital signal, it's sampled using 4:2:2 encoding. This means all of the luminance (Y) is preserved, and half of the two color-difference channels are preserved. This is an accepted practice across all aspects of the post-production industry. Although the color data is only half-sampled, the eye does not tend to notice it because the luminance channel is fully sampled, which results in sharpness. If you were to view the color channels independent of the luminance channel, you would find them blurry by comparison.

Almost all of the Avid resolutions (codecs) will record in YUV.

880Mb/s Compared to 440Mb/s Encoding for HDCAM SR

HDCAM SR is a particularly interesting and flexible format because at 440Mb/s, it will record a YUV 4:2:2 signal. Yet when the data rate is doubled to 880Mb/s there is enough bandwidth to record full RGB. The trick with 880Mb/s, is that it's so intensive, it can't "fit" through a standard HD-SDI cable, the HD-SDI standard wasn't designed to send a digital signal at 880Mb/s. How do you solve that problem? Use two HD-SDI cables.

Sony HDCAM SR decks (VTRs) have dual HD-SDI spigots, which are ganged together to provide enough bandwidth to move an RGB signal. The use of two HD-SDI connectors to move RGB image data is called RGB Dual-Link.

In an RGB Dual-Link scenario, one spigot will output the 4:2:2 signal, and the other will output the remaining data: think of it as the 0:2:2 that's missing. Dual-Link creates both challenges and opportunities.

On the challenges side, you need I/O hardware that has two HD-SDI inputs, and you need software that's capable of controlling both HD-SDI inputs simultaneously. Avid Mojo DX hardware cannot do this, but Avid Nitris DX hardware can.

There are plenty of opportunities. Sony HDCAM SR decks have two HD-SDI inputs that can be enabled simultaneously and recorded to the same tape, which records them in sync with each other. When the same tape is played back, whatever was fed in is then fed out. You can record two separate feeds to each of the spigots, such as the left-eye camera and right-eye camera of a stereoscopic recording. You could have two entirely separate YUV HD images being recorded, with the VTR operating at the 880Mb/s recording mode.

RGB Dual-Link Support

Media Composer supports RGB Dual-Link capture using the Avid Nitris DX hardware. This hardware has two sets of HD-SDI inputs and outputs, labeled set A and set B, as shown in Figure 2.1.

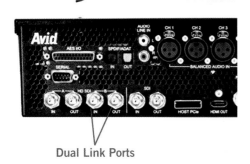

Dual Link Ports

Figure 2.1
Nitris DX HD-SDI input/output B is used for RGB dual-link capture.

Avid Resolutions (Codecs) for HDCAM and HDCAM SR

When choosing the best Avid resolution (codec) for HD media, look up the data rate of the HD camera format, and pick a DNxHD resolution that is closest to that data rate.

For example, HDCAM has a data rate of 135Mb/s, so you could choose DNxHD 145. HDCAM SR 880 4:4:4 RGB has a data rate of 880Mb/s, but DNxHD 350 X is able to compress it to 350Mb/s, which is unlikely to be noticeable, or you could use the 1:1 10-bit RGB resolution, although that codec will uncompress the spatial compression in the image and bloom the data rate to almost 2000Mb/s.

Betacam Family

Sony's betacam family may have lost the consumer war, but they fared well in the professional space. Sony has released a variety of standard definition 1/2"-tape formats, both digital and analog, summarized in Table 2-2.

Table 2-2   Selections from Sony's Betacam Family

Format Name	Encoding	Compression	Bit Depth	Target Market	Identifying Color
Betacam SP	Analog				Black cassette, black or grey lid
Betacam SX	Digital	5:1 MPEG2	8-Bit	News	Yellow cassette
IMX	Digital	30, 40 or 50Mb/s	8-Bit	Corporate/industrial	Green cassette
Digital Betacam	Digital	2:1 proprietary MPEG2	10-Bit	TV and professional mastering	Grey cassette, blue case

All of the formats listed in Table 2-2 use the same physical cassette sizes: large or standard size. The larger the size, the more tape, and the more recording time.

Sony has a variety of VTRs, some are able to play all, or a mixture of, these formats. Some VTRs can also play a combination of these formats plus HDCAM/HDCAM SR. Some VTRs shipped with support for a specific format, like IMX, and then the owner could upgrade the VTR by adding internal circuit boards that extended the codecs recognized by the deck.

When you are new to a facility that has Sony or Panasonic VTRs, it is worth asking a technician which formats are supported by the VTRs. You can't always tell, by looking at the front of a VTR, which tape formats it supports because it may have been upgraded after purchase.

DV Family

The DV family of formats includes DVCAM, DV, DVCPRO, and HDV. You should recognize the difference between the DV codec and DV cassette tapes, as the two are distinct but people often mistake one for the other.

DV Is Standard Definition Digital Video

The DV codec is a standard method of encoding and decoding standard definition digital video (DV). It's used by many manufacturers, from Panasonic to JVC and Sony, from Avid to Apple.

The codec specifies the following:

- Raster size in NTSC 720×480 (six lines fewer than D1)

- Intraframe compression of 5:1

- A bit rate of 25Mb/s

- Sampling of 4:1:1 (NTSC) or 4:2:0 (PAL)

The tape format specifies the following:

- 1/4" tape

- Mini-cassette size (45-60 minutes) or full-cassette size (2–3 hours)

With those two specifications, a MiniDV tape is simply a small-cassette tape with media recorded in the DV codec. A DV tape could be a mini-sized cassette, or a full-sized cassette. Full-sized cassettes can record up to three hours and typically fit in shoulder-mounted news-style cameras. Mini cassettes typically fit in hand-held "handcam" style camcorders.

Media Composer has a resolution (codec) called DV25, where the 25 refers to the data rate: 25 megabits per second (Mb/s). There is also a DV50 codec and a DV100 codec for Panasonic's enhanced DV codecs, which improve image quality by reducing compression and, as a result, increases the data rate from 25Mb/s to 50 or 100Mb/s.

HDV Is High Definition on a 1/4" Tape

The goal of HDV is to take a high-definition signal and encode it onto the same physical media as DV, and at the same data rate as DV: 25Mb/s.

Consider this, for a moment: The goal of HDV is to take a tape format designed for standard definition digital video, and make a codec that compresses HD so well that it can fit high definition onto the same quarter-inch tape, at the same data rate.

That means that if a tape holds 60 minutes of DV, the same tape will hold 60 minutes of HDV. That's what happens when the data rate is the same. It's an amazing accomplishment. But how was it achieved?

The HDV codec was created with the goal of compressing high-definition video to a data rate of 25Mb/s. The codec's specification follows:

- Sub-rastered frame size of 1440×1080 or 1280×720

- Long group of pictures (Long GOP) compression

- A bit rate of 25Mb/s

- Sampling of 4:2:0

There are some notable items:

- **Storage space:** HDV and DV take the same space on a tape, and they will take the same quantity of storage space on your media drives. If your media drives can hold two hours of DV, they can also hold two hours of HDV.

- **Temporal compression:** HDV uses an encoding method called Long GOP. In this temporal encoding technique, the video stream is broken up into 15-frame "groups" (although JVC uses six-frame increments). Within that group, the first frame is a full frame, whereas each subsequent frame contains just the differences from the previous frame to the current frame.

Long GOP compression creates some challenges for nonlinear editing, as the odds are 1 in 15 that when you move the current position indicator, you'll actually select a naturally full frame. When you place the current position indicator (blue line) on any of the other 14 frames, Media Composer needs to build that frame by adding all the previous frames from beginning of the current group of pictures (GOP) to the current frame.

Capturing from DV and HDV Sources

When you capture from a DV/HDV source, there is an ideal workflow for preserving image integrity. It's based in the fact that the footage is already encoded in the DV/HDV codec in the camera, and that Media Composer also includes native DV/HDV codecs. To preserve image quality, you want to avoid generation loss, which occurs when video is decoded, transferred and then re-encoded.

To prevent generation loss when acquiring footage from a DV/HDV source:

1. Use an **OHCI** (Firewire) cable to connect the VTR/camera to Media Composer.

2. Set the **AVID RESOLUTION (CODEC)** of the Capture tool to be the same codec as was used in the camera: DV25 or HDV.

With a Firewire cable in use, and the same codec used on both ends, Media Composer is able to perform a digital copy of the media from the tape to the media file. That means no decoding and re-encoding, and no generation loss. Just a perfectly accurate, pristine digital copy of the DV-encoded data.

No Dropouts

Magnetic tape is composed of a base ribbon (the tape) onto which metallic particles are stuck using an adhesive. As the tape rolls over the heads of the VTR or camera's transport mechanism, particles might flake off and stick to the playhead. This creates two problems: Dropouts and dirty heads.

Dirty playheads are bad because the particles that are stuck to them will act as an abrasive surface, resulting in more particles being removed as more tape passes over the head. The head becomes a kind of SOS or scotch-pad, like the kind you might use to clean pots. Abrasion is good for dishes, but bad for tape.

Dropouts are when part of the image data is missing on the tape, and appear as thin black horizontal lines or black squares when the video is played. The portion of the frame has literally "dropped" in the form of particles being dropped from the tape. You can often repair these using Avid IntraFrame Effect techniques with effects such as Scratch Removal and Paint.

In the Avid Learning Series

For more information on Media Composer's Scratch Removal and Paint Effects, consider purchasing *Media Composer 6 Professional Effects and Compositing*, or taking MC205 from an Avid Learning Partner.

To improve the longevity of your tapes, do the following:

- Rewind all cassette tapes to prevent creating slack in the middle of the tape

- Store tapes in their manufacturer-provided cases

- Store tapes "standing up" as opposed to lying flat

- Have your VTR and camera heads professionally cleaned by a manufacturer authorized technician

As you'll see in the section "Capture Settings > Batch" on page 84 of this lesson, Media Composer can assist you with this list by automatically rewinding the tapes after a batch capture.

Video I/O and Monitoring Options

Computers have USB ports, they have Display Port or DVI or VGA ports for monitors, and they have 1/8" headphone jacks. A computer might have an OHCI (Firewire/iLink) port. Those are fine for general-purpose computing, but not for video editing.

Computers do not have HD-SDI ports, or YCbCr analog inputs and outputs, nor do they have RS-422 deck control serial ports. VTRs and some professional cameras do have those ports, but don't have USB ports, and may not have OHCI (Firewire/iLink) ports either.

When performing an online edit, many online editors find it useful to have a set of external monitoring scopes connected to their editing system. Those scopes typically take a SDI or HD-SDI signal and display the signal levels.

Editors often want to hear a surround mix, which requires connecting six or seven discrete speakers to their editing system, as opposed to the more typical computer output of stereo (2-channel) audio.

It's also useful to have the contents of the Record monitor fed to a large in-room TV, so the producer can sit on that comfortable producer-couch, eat her intern-prepared producer sandwiches, drink her latte (skinny, no-fat, soy), and judge your work on the 50" flatscreen.

You need additional hardware for monitoring and for capturing. There are a variety of options expanding the connectivity of your Media Composer 6 editing system. Avid designs and manufactures a couple options, and established industry technology companies also make hardware you can use. You may even be surprised to learn that many of the hardware purchases you made for the now discontinued Apple Final Cut Studio can live on with Media Composer 6.

Avid Options

Avid designs and manufactures two I/O options for Media Composer: Avid Nitris DX and Avid Mojo DX. When you use a genuine Avid I/O device with Avid Media Composer, you have hardware that's able to fully exploit the capabilities of the Media Composer software. You also have a single point of contact when there is a technical issue to resolve.

The Avid Nitris DX and Mojo DX hardware is also capable of doing some tasks that the non-Avid I/O hardware is not yet able to do (as of February 2012), such as support Universal Mastering and use hardware codecs to accelerate performance when used with specific media encodings, such as DNxHD.

The following is a high-level comparison between the Nitris DX and the Mojo DX:

Feature	Nitris DX	Mojo DX
Portability	Not realistically portable. Intended for rack mounting.	Can be rack mounted, but intended to be portable. Take it in your carry-on luggage.
Ports	Multiple HD-SDI, SDI, and analog video ports. Multiple analog and digital audio (AES/EBU, RCA, optical) ports, plus LTC timecode	One set of Video I/O and Audio (1/4") ports
Expandability	Can be upgraded with two additional hardware codecs	No upgrading to support hardware codecs
Dual-Link	Supports RGB Dual Link	No support for Dual Link nor RGB
Price	More expensive than Mojo DX	Less expensive than Nitris DX

Nitris DX

The Nitris DX is Avid's high-end I/O hardware, with multiple dedicated-purpose rear connectors allowing it to be suitable for rack mounting in a broadcast facility with other equipment routed to it using a patch-bay or switchers.

The ability to expand Nitris DX by adding two hardware codec chips means your computer's CPU doesn't have to do the heavy lifting of decoding video, and can allocate its resources to other tasks, like real-time effects processing. You can add either two DNxHD codec chips, or two AVC-Intra codec chips, or one of each. Having two codec chips of the same kind will allow two streams of video to be decoded or encoded simultaneously, which particularly benefits a stereoscopic workflow. In a stereoscopic workflow, Media Composer is usually processing the left- and right-eye images as two separate streams.

Figure 2.2 is an illustration of the back of an Avid Nitris DX.

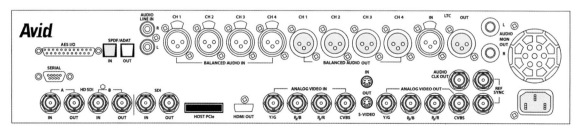

Figure 2.2
I/O connectors for the Avid Nitris DX.

Mojo DX

The Avid Mojo DX is based on the same underlying technology as the Nitris DX, but it emphasizes portability. Mojo DX is an ideal I/O and monitoring solution for companies and individuals that do not need a wide variety of simultaneously connected devices, but do need to ingest HD-SDI and provide monitoring to external speakers and a client viewing monitor.

Mojo DX is YUV only and doesn't support dual-link RGB connections, 4:4:4 mode on a HDCAM SR deck, or the addition of hardware codecs.

Figure 2.3 is an illustration of the back of a Mojo DX.

Figure 2.3
Connections for the Avid Mojo DX.

Avid Open IO

Avid Media Composer 6 introduces Avid Open IO. Open IO is a technology that allows third-party manufacturers to create I/O and monitoring hardware that works with Media Composer. Prior to Media Composer 6 and Open IO, only Avid-designed hardware could be used, along with a few exceptions with Media Composer 5.5, such as the Matrox 02 and AJA IO HD.

Open IO is implemented by third parties as a software update to their existing hardware. This creates a significant advantage for any facility that has I/O and monitoring hardware previously used on other editing systems, as they can check with the manufacturer of that hardware and often obtain updated drivers to allow that hardware to be used with Media Composer.

Capabilities and Limitations of Open IO

The initial release of Open IO in Media Composer 6 doesn't yet support some capabilities that are supported by Avid-designed IO hardware, such as the Nitris DX and Mojo DX. Some items not supported at the initial release of Open IO include:

■ Ancillary data

■ LTC I/O (timecode over RS-422 *is* supported)

■ Audio punch-in

- Full frame stereoscopic 3D simultaneous capture/digital cut

- Hardware codec encode/decode

- Multiple I/O hardware support in CPU

- Universal mastering

- Thin raster timeline modes

Avid has indicated their intent to enhance Open IO to support additional capabilities over time.

On the Web

The list of features is from the Avid Knowledge Centre, filed under article 422991. By the time you read this, the list may have changed. For the latest information on the capabilities supported by Open IO, check Avid's Knowledge Centre at the following URL: http://avid.custkb.com/avid/app/selfservice/search.jsp?DocId=422991.

Third-Party Companies Supporting Open IO

Companies offering Open IO solutions include:

- AJA Video Systems

- Blackmagic Design

- Bluefish444

- Matrox Digital Video Solutions

- MOTU

More information on supported third-party hardware is available at: http://www.avid.com/US/products/media-composer/hardware-options.

On the Web

Workflows for Capturing

There are three workflows that you are likely to use when capturing from tape: Capture on-the-fly, Capture from IN to OUT, and Logging Before Capturing. This section explains each of those workflows, from how you perform the task to why.

Capture On-the-Fly

Capturing on-the-fly refers to using the Capture tool without pre-determining the IN and OUT timecodes. You configure the Capture tool, click the Record button, and Media Composer captures the incoming signals. It stops when one of the three following situations occurs:

1. You press the **RECORD** button again (or F4), which completes the capture.

2. You press the **ABORT CAPTURE** button (the icon is a trashcan) (or press Escape), which aborts the capture.

3. The duration of the capture exceeds the value set in **CAPTURE SETTINGS > MEDIA > MAXIMUM (DEFAULT) CAPTURE TIME**, at which point Media Composer completes and stops the capture.

There are a few scenarios when capturing on-the-fly is particularly valuable, aside from capturing the entire tape, such as when you want to efficiently capture a live performance and when you want to quickly bring in a clip or two. These two scenarios are described next.

Live Venue Recording

Consider the normal procedure for capturing footage from a camera: The camera operator goes to a venue or studio, shoots the video, returns to the edit suite, and gives you the tape. You capture it.

If you can get a feed from the camera into your editing system, you can record the live feed directly to your media drives at the same time as the camera records it to tape. It could be that your editing system is on a laptop and you take it on-set, or in studio you may be able to run a trunk-line between master control and your edit suite, allowing you to capture the image live.

In this scenario, the tape in the camera is a back-up just in case something goes wrong during the capture. If all goes well, when the performance has completed, you can begin cutting without having to capture from the tape. You can even sub-clip and add markers live during the recording, as covered in "Capture Settings > Keys" in this lesson, on page 90.

Technical tips for live venue recording:

■ An SDI or HD-SDI cable can transmit audio and video. This simplifies the connections and reduces the potential points of failure.

■ Analog cables tend to suffer from signal attenuation and increased noise over longer distances and may not be sufficient for long runs from studio to edit suite.

- The Capture tool can be configured to use external longitudinal timecode (LTC), which is connected using an analog XLR cable from the source camera to the Nitris DX hardware. (Neither the Mojo DX nor the Open IO third-party hardware supports external LTC input as of this writing.)

- In the absence of LTC, the Capture tool will record time of day timecode using the clock in the computer. You can later modify the start timecode of the clip using the recorded image of a slate (if available) or the timecode from a synchronization frame from the recorded tape.

- An OHCI (Firewire/iLink) cable can transmit video, audio and timecode, although Firewire is not as easily routable as SDI, nor are the cable runs as long. An OHCI connection would be ideal for a DV/HDV camcorder recording into a laptop-based Media Composer system.

Technique for Live Recording

To record live, follow these steps:

1. Connect the camera to the editing system.

2. Open the Capture tool.

3. Disable DECK CONTROL.

4. Select EXTERNAL TIMECODE (if available).

5. Confirm your Capture settings for RESOLUTION (CODEC) and TARGET DRIVE.

6. Right-click and choose CAPTURE SETTINGS > MEDIA FILES. Ensure the maximum (default) capture time exceeds the expected length of the performance or tape.

7. Begin recording.

Upon completion, press the RECORD button again to complete and save the recording.

Figure 2.4 indicates the locations of the items referenced in the previous steps.

Note: If Media Composer is capturing to Avid Unity and the clip is being checked-in to Avid Interplay, you can benefit from Frame Chase Capture and Editing. In this workflow, you capture with one editing system and begin editing the footage from another, whereas the capture is on-going. (See "What Is Frame Chase Capture?" on page 88.)

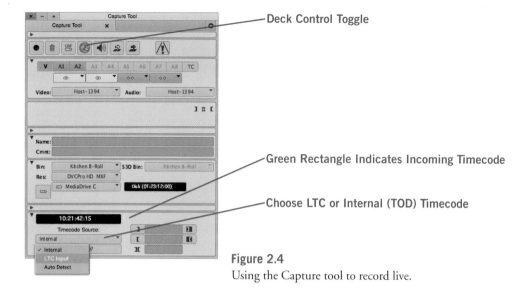

Deck Control Toggle

Green Rectangle Indicates Incoming Timecode

Choose LTC or Internal (TOD) Timecode

Figure 2.4
Using the Capture tool to record live.

Capture from IN to OUT

Capturing from IN to OUT on a videotape requires that you know two of the following three timecodes: IN Mark, OUT Mark, or Duration. It also requires that Media Composer can remotely control your deck, in order to instruct the deck to cue to specific locations on the tape.

Command and Control

Media Composer needs to issue commands to a deck in order to control that deck. The commands range from "Cue to Timecode 04:10:01:24," to "Record Now," to "Play at 2x Speed," as well as a few polling questions, such as "What is the current timecode?"

The generally used set of commands is described in a protocol called the Sony Deck Control Protocol. These commands are often issued over a Firewire Cable or RS-422 Serial cable. An RS-422 serial cable is capable of transmitting command and control but no audio/video, whereas a Firewire cable can transmit audio and video and can be used for deck control.

You may encounter a situation where Media Composer is unable to control a deck that previously was controllable. This problem is often caused by a Remote switch or toggle on the deck, or in the deck's menu.

Decks can also have their Remote switch set to Local, which is analogous to it being a teenager, as the deck will not respond to commands and is not controllable by any external force. When the deck is in Local mode, Media Composer indicates this by writing Remote! instead of the deck's timecode in the Capture tool.

A deck set to Remote mode will often disable the controls and buttons on the front of the deck. For this reason, operators in a machine room will often change the deck to Local in order to use it. This is why your decks will often be uncontrollable and require a visit to the machine room for re-enabling the remote control.

You prepare for capturing from IN to OUT by entering timecodes in the deck control area of the Capture tool, as shown in Figure 2.5.

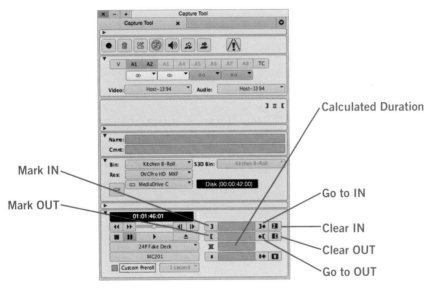

Figure 2.5
Mark a clip on a tape by specifying the IN and OUT marks.

As you enter timecodes, the status area of the Capture tool updates to indicate that marks will be used when the record button is pressed.

Consider using Capture from IN to OUT in the following scenarios:

- Your producer has performed a paper edit and knows the start timecode of the clip, and the approximate duration or the OUT point.

- You want a clip of a specific duration, such as a five-second clip and want that clip to automatically be cut into the timeline using the Edit to Timeline feature of the Capture tool. (See "Enable Edit to Timeline" on page 86 of this lesson.)

Tip: The contents of a bin will print exactly as they appear on screen. After you've captured or logged a tape, you could print the contents of the bin in Text View, fold the hardcopy, and insert it into the sleeve of the tape: it'll serve as a table of contents for the tape. Years later, when the tape is pulled from a shelf, the editor can review the print-out of the bin to see what clips are on the tape and their timecodes without having to screen the tape, or even track down a deck capable of playing the tape. That editor could then quickly bring a clip in from the tape by entering the timecodes from the print-out instead of shuttling through the tape.

The Capture tool normally does what it says: Captures media. But the Capture tool lives a dual life, and also serves as a Log tool. When it is configured as a Log tool, it does everything almost exactly the same as when it's in Capture mode, except for actually capturing media. You can still remotely control the deck, you can set IN and OUT points as described in this section, but instead of the red Record button, there is a button with an icon of a pencil, shown in Figures 2.6 and 2.7.

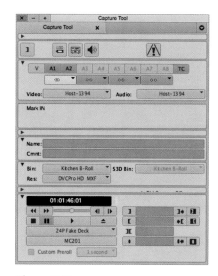

Figure 2.6
Capture tool set to Log mode (left).

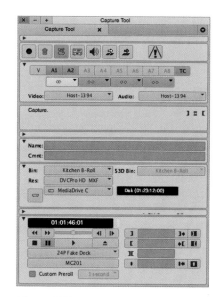

Figure 2.7
Capture tool set to Capture mode (right).

This allows you to log shots to a bin first, and capture them later, as described in the next section.

Logging Before Capturing Footage

An efficient way to input media into Media Composer is to log all your clips (shots) first, and then use Clip > Batch Capture to capture material automatically. This section covers two topics:

- What footage you will log
- Whether you will log shots individually or in groups

Logging All or Selected Shots

In the world of handwritten logs, the logger generally sits down at a tape deck, watches the footage, and takes notes on each shot. You usually log everything, because the written log serves as a key tool in the edit, and it's easy enough just to keep writing. During the edit, if you need to find (just for example) a rock climbing shot to use as a transition, you can look through the paper logs and locate it. When you work with electronic logs, you might be tempted to be more selective, and log only the shots you intend to use in the video. Then, if you need a rock climbing shot, you might not have a log entry for that shot.

In the long run, it is less aggravating and less time-consuming to log all the footage. You can indicate the shots to be captured in a custom column.

Tip: Creating custom columns is covered in Lesson 4, "Play Together."

Logging Individual or Groups of Shots

Do you log each shot individually, or log groups of shots together? Here are three options with an evaluation of each:

Option 1: Log Each Shot

Each shot is logged into a separate clip.

- Advantage: Log is the most accurate representation of the shot.
- Advantage: Best method for sorting and sifting, so you can easily locate clips in the bin.
- Disadvantage: Capturing is slow because of separate tape preroll for each clip.
- Disadvantage: May input extra material, because overlap may be logged for each clip.

Option 2: Log Groups of Shots

This option logs groups of shots into a clip. It is useful for logging multiple takes of a scene, multiple shots in a sequence, or shots of short duration.

- ■ Advantage: Capturing is faster, because you reduce preroll and record overlap.

- ■ Disadvantage: Log is not as detailed as option 1.

Option 3: Log Each Shot and Groups

Logs each shot, as done with option 1. When you discover a group of consecutive shots to input in Media Composer, create a single clip for this series of consecutive shots. In your Capture custom column, note to capture the group shot instead of each individual shot.

- ■ Advantage: The group of shots is captured, but individual clips are available for sorting and sifting.

- ■ Advantage: You conserve an accurate log but reduce the capturing time.

- ■ Disadvantage: It takes longer to log.

Avid MediaLog Workflows

Avid MediaLog is a bare-metal software application that resembles Media Composer, but handles only offline clips, bins, and projects. It can't perform editing tasks, but it does have the Capture tool although it's permanently set to Logging Mode.

You can use Media Log to log clips to a bin, either through deck control or manually entering timecode. A common workflow would be to configure a Media Log workstation in a screening room, where a producer could review a tape and log footage. The Avid bin (.avb file) could then be delivered to a full Media Composer suite, along with the source tape, where the editor would perform a Batch Capture on the contents of the bin.

That workflow allows the producer to review and log, whereas the editor is available to cut other material. It also means a full Media Composer suite with video I/O and monitoring hardware isn't being tied up while someone reviews a tape and logs clips to a bin.

No MediaLog? No problem. Use a text editor or even Microsoft Excel and save a text file that you can import directly into a bin after a small bit of preparatory editing in a text editor. Search Media Composer's help for "Avid Log Specifications" for importing shot logs.

Preparing to Ingest from Tape

The first step in editing is capturing your tape or file-based footage elements. The basic steps of ingesting footage with the Capture tool is covered in the appendix of Media Composer 6, "Editing Essentials."

This section reviews some of those steps and elaborates on professional features to help you become more efficient at ingesting footage. Before any capturing can take place a project has to be created to match the tape format, or the current project's format has to be adjusted to match the tape format.

When you create a new project, you need to specify the format and raster of the project. By specifying the format, Media Composer will create either HD or SD media, such as HD1080p media or SD 720i media. The raster size is used to specify variations of the HD frame width, such as 1920 pixels for HDCAM SR media or 1440 pixels for HDV media. Lesson 12, "Wrapping Up a Project," covers the project formats and raster in detail.

Media Composer uses Raster, Project Format, and the Color Space settings to configure the Capture tool, as well as the Video Input and Video Output tools.

There are a few guidelines when it comes to preparing to ingest from tape:

1. If you are creating a new project, use Project settings (format, raster, color space) that match the majority of your source material.

2. Before opening the Capture tool, verify that your Project settings (format, raster, color space) match the material you are about to capture.

3. You can change your Project format, at any time, to other Project formats with compatible frame rates, as shown in "Table A-1: Available High-Definition Project Formats," in the appendix.

There will be occasions when you want to use footage that has a frame rate that is not compatible with your project, such as capturing and mixing 30P, 50i, and 23.967 footage in the same timeline. That's really easy to do in Media Composer using the following technique:

1. Create a new project using the Project settings (format, raster, color space) of the material you want to capture. This project exists only to ingest the non-standard material.

2. Ingest the material as normal.

3. Close the project and re-open your main project.

Refer to "Setting the Project's Format" in Lesson 12 on page 415 for recommendations on creating the project and choosing the format.

Available Resolutions Are Determined by the Project Format

A Media Composer project can be configured in the Project window to be either an HD or an SD project. Further, when Media Composer is configured as an HD project, it can be an RGB or YUV HD project. HD YUV projects can further be configured with a choice of raster formats.

The selection of SD/HD and RGB/YUV, and raster format settings will alter the Avid resolutions (codecs) that are available when using the Capture tool. The list of codecs will be further altered depending on the I/O and monitoring hardware connected to the computer.

Figures 2.8 to 2.11 show how the available resolutions (codecs) in the Capture tool change given various combinations of Project window settings.

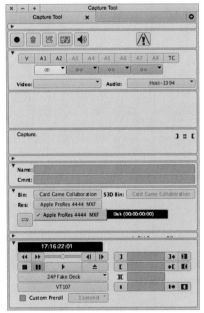

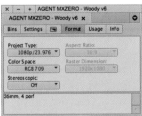

Figure 2.8
RGB capture with Pro Res 4:4:4.

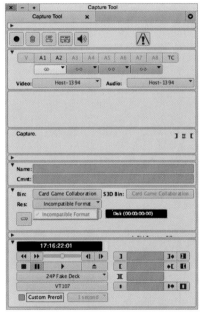

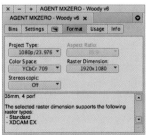

Figure 2.9
1080P 23.976fps project with 1920×1080 raster but without suitable video I/O hardware.

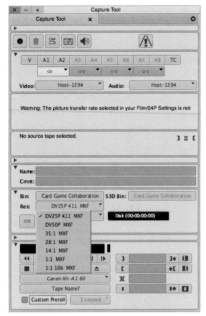

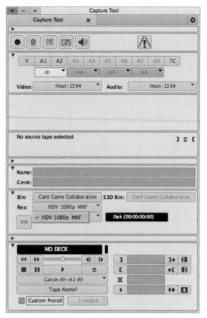

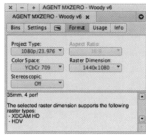

Figure 2.10
NTSC 23.976fps project with
compatible video I/O hardware.

Figure 2.11
1080P project with 1440×1080 raster.

Raster Dimensions Impact Playback Performance

The Raster Dimension impacts playback performance. When choosing your Raster Dimension, use the list in the bottom half of the Format tab that shows the supported formats for your choice.

When working with a variety of raster sizes, you should set the raster to its smallest resolution size to optimize Media Composer's playback performance; scaling down the raster is easier than scaling up. For example, if you're mixing 1920×1080 and 1440×1080 footage, set the raster to 1440×1080 while playing back as part of the editing process. Prior to rendering or any other task that generates media, switch the raster back to the higher setting so that media will be created at the more detailed raster setting. When you change the project format, the hardware input and output, resolutions, and new sequences change to support the new project.

> Situations where this feature is useful:
>
> ■ You are working with downconverted HD material in an offline-to-online workflow. You can offline edit using the equivalent SD format.
>
> ■ You are working in an HD project and need to capture SD material to include in your sequence. You can capture the material you need, then change back to the HD project and work with both SD and HD clips.

Suggested Settings for Ingesting from Tape

The following section lists the settings that you may want to review and adjust prior to capturing footage from tape. These settings ensure the media is created in a form that retains optimal picture and sound quality and ensures compatibility with your project.

Using the Media Creation Tool

The Media Creation tool allows you to set resolutions (codecs) for all the scenarios where Media Composer can generate media: capturing, importing, creating titles, rendering and creating video or audio mixdowns. It also enables you to assign media drives or Unity workspaces for each type of media. You can use this tool, for example, to switch all media to your finishing compression at once, or to specify that no additional compression should be applied when rendering by using the 1:1 resolution.

The Media Creation tool is available from Tools > Media Creation. It is also available from the Settings tab of the Project window. It doesn't matter how you access it, the result will be the same. There is a benefit in realizing that it is a project setting, however, because project settings can be converted into site settings, which establishes new default settings for all future projects.

Media Creation > Drive Filtering and Indexing

The Drive Filtering and Indexing tab is used to exclude specific kinds of storage. It's shown in Figure 2.12.

Figure 2.12
Drive Filtering and Indexing tab of the Media Creation tool.

Filter Out System Drive

The system drive is the drive that contains the operating system: Windows 7 or OS X Lion. When the system drive becomes full, the operating system grinds to a halt. By selecting this option, you prevent Media Composer from accidentally filling the system drive while creating media, which reduces the likelihood of a system freeze.

Select Filter Out System Drive when:

- You have other media drives that you intend to use for storage.

Don't select Filter Out System Drive when:

- You only have one drive, such as when Media Composer is on a laptop without additional storage.

Filter Out Launch Drive

The Launch Drive contains the Media Composer application. This may be the system drive, or it may be some other drive. Some Media Composer systems ship with two internal hard drives, one for the system and one for Media Composer plus audio media.

As much as it's undesirable to have Media Composer accidentally fill the system drive, it's also undesirable to have Media Composer fill the drive that contains the Media Composer software. That's because the title tool and other portions of Media Composer need to create temporary files, and a full drive would prevent them from so-doing and potentially cause unexpected behavior.

Select Filter Out Launch Drive when:

- You have other media drives that you intend to use for storage.

Don't select Filter Out Launch Drive when:

- You only have one drive, such as when Media Composer is on a laptop with no additional storage.

Caution: Your Media Composer system may display additional auto-index options that apply only to systems connected to an Avid Interplay workgroup. They control how local media is indexed by the Interplay Media Indexer. If you are not connected to an Interplay workgroup you can ignore these options. If you are on an Interplay workgroup, you should consult with your on-site Avid Certified Support Representative for Avid Interplay before modifying these settings.

Media Creation > Capture Tab

The Capture tab of the Media Creation tool, shown in Figure 2.13, allows you to specify the resolution (codec) that will be selected by default when the Capture tool is opened. This is only a default, it is not an enforced requirement: You can choose another resolution (codec) at any time while the Capture tool is open.

Use this tab to set a default resolution (codec) to reduce the potential of accidentally recording hours of footage for your online edit at an offline resolution such as 15:1s.

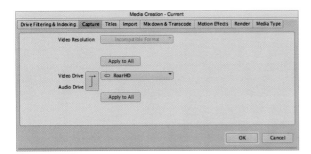

Figure 2.13
Capture tab of the Media Creation tool.

Video Resolution/Apply to All

These two options allow you to specify the default resolution for the project. Clicking the Apply to All button applies your selection to the other tabs of the Media Creation tool: titles, import elements, mixdowns, motion effects, and renders.

If desired you can click on the specific tabs and specify unique resolutions for each media type.

Video and Audio Drive/Apply to All

These options allow you to specify the media drives for video and audio media. Clicking the Apply to All button applies your drive selection to captured media, titles, import elements, mixdowns, and motion effects.

Note: Why separate video and audio? These days, it's uncommon that you would have Media Composer put audio on one drive and video on another, owing to the speed of modern day storage. In past years, however, drives were more expensive and not nearly as fast as modern drives, so the high-speed drives would be reserved for video and slower drives would contain audio media.

Fewer Problems and Faster Captures: Capture Settings

Tape is mechanical: the physical tape has to glide over playheads in a compartment of the VTR or camera called the "transport mechanism." Not all transport mechanisms are created equal: some are very efficient and accurate, and some are...not.

Typically, the transports used in cameras and entry-level VTRs are designed for recording and moving the tape forward at a constant rate.

The transport mechanism used in a professional VTR is designed to rapidly shuttle the tape in both directions at various speeds with accuracy. Accuracy in this scenario means that given a particular timecode, the deck can quickly shuttle the tape to that timecode.

In a professional online environment, it isn't advisable to use a camera as a VTR, except when there are only a few short shots to acquire. The difference a professional VTR's transport mechanism makes in capturing can save considerable time compared to using a camera's transport mechanism. If your facility does not have a professional-grade VTR for a given tape format, you should consider renting one. If you have numerous tapes to ingest, there may be a cost savings in renting a deck as opposed to struggling with using a camera as a deck.

Note: Avid's Hardware Qualifications Team verifies compatibility between Media Composer and a variety of decks and cameras. The team will often write a short note about the performance of verified hardware. The note may indicate known issues, or perhaps give a positive review. You can review by selecting the deck in Deck settings.

Capture Settings > General Tab

Capture settings is available from the Project window, as well as from the contextual menu in the Capture tool. It's shown in Figure 2.14. The settings on the general tab are focused on optimizing Media Composer's interaction with the tape transport: how it finds coincident points (specific frames on the tape) and how it handles the tape after capture is complete.

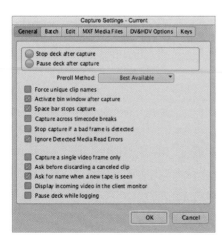

Figure 2.14
Choose the Capture settings > General tab.

Stopping versus Pausing a Deck

A deck's transport mechanism can be told to stop or pause. In Media Composer, stopping or pausing the playback of a clip is the same thing, but to a deck, those are two different things. The following is a comparison of Stop and Pause.

When you use Stop:

- Playheads are removed from the surface of the tape

- No image is output from the deck

- Longevity of the playheads is increased because the heads are not making contact with the tape

When you use Pause:

- The VTR's playheads remain in contact with the surface of the tape

- An image is output from the deck

- Heads will require cleaning or replacement sooner, because they are in use while paused

There are three settings on the General tab that relate to pausing or stopping. When a deck switches from stop to pause, the transport mechanism raises the heads to the tape and threads the tape around the heads. That process takes a couple seconds. If that happened for a capture of 30 clips, you'd add almost two minutes to your capture time while the deck threads the tape.

Set the deck to Pause when you're capturing a series of clips. If you are bringing in just a single clip (or the entire tape in one pass), then you could set it to Stop. You could also set it to Stop if you know your deck heads have to be cleaned soon and want to do everything you can to decrease wear on them, at the cost of it taking longer to capture.

Activate Bin Window After Capture

Clips are always captured into a bin, and for the purpose of organizing your project, every clip should have a descriptive name. Activate Bin Window After Capture causes the bin to become active (just like the command says), and then selects the name of the clip so you can type a new name. You do not have to select the name first or backspace the existing name, you just start typing a new name.

This feature appears convenient, but has drawbacks: You need to reactivate the Capture tool. Each time you switch from a bin to the Capture tool, Media Composer re-initializes the Record monitor to use it to monitor the incoming signal, and this process takes a couple seconds, which means it slows you down. There is a method of naming clips that is more suitable for professionals.

When the Capture tool is ingesting, start typing. You won't see a flashing I-beam cursor, and there is no on-screen indication that you can or should type, but once you start typing, Media Composer will put the words you type into the Name field of the Capture tool, shown in Figure 2.15. When the ingest has completed, the clip will be saved to the bin using the name you gave it during capture. There is no need to bring the Bin window to the front, and no need for Media Composer to re-initialize the Record tool for displaying the timeline contents. It's faster.

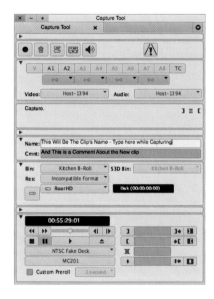

Figure 2.15
The Capture tool's Name and Comments fields.

After entering a clip name, and while the ingest is still on-going, you can press Tab and enter a comment.

Timecode and Preroll

The Capture tool sends deck control messages to the deck through the RS-422 or Firewire cable connected between your computer (or Video I/O hardware) and the deck itself. There is a standard list of commands that can be sent, including a series of commands that instruct a deck to cue a deck to a specific frame, also known as a coincidence point.

The Capture tool has two broad recording modes: on-the-fly and using marked timecode. Both of those methods were covered earlier in this lesson.

Timecode-based recording occurs either as a result of Clip > Batch Capture, or by entering timecode into the Mark IN and Mark OUT fields in the Capture tool. In timecode-based recording, Media Composer will capture the footage from the specified In-Mark.

The procedure is *almost* as follows:

1. Capture tool commands the deck to advance to the start timecode (the coincident point).

2. Capture tool commands the deck to play.

3. The Capture tool begins recording the incoming signal.

There is a missing step. The missing step stems from the fact that tape is mechanical and the tape has to be moving at a certain speed before an image can be properly output from the deck. Depending on the deck, it may take 1–10 seconds for a deck to get up to speed before it outputs usable video. The amount of time it takes for a deck to get up to speed is called Preroll. When a deck is configured in Media Composer, the preroll value of the deck is also configured. You can override the preroll value at the bottom of the Capture tool.

If you enter an IN Mark of 05:25:30:00 in the Capture tool and press Record, the Capture tool will command the deck to cue to that frame, and then instruct the deck to rewind by the preroll amount. Challenges can occur when a timecode break on the tape prevents the deck from locating the preroll point.

A timecode break occurs when the timecode is no longer consecutive. Figure 2.16 illustrates a tape with a timecode break.

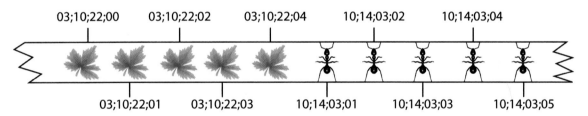

03;10;22;00   03;10;22;02   03;10;22;04   10;14;03;02   10;14;03;04

03;10;22;01   03;10;22;03   10;14;03;01   10;14;03;03   10;14;03;05

Figure 2.16
A timecode break is the result of nonconsecutive timecode.

What Causes Timecode Breaks?

A timecode break occurs when adjacent frames have discontinuous timecode.

Tapes that are recorded in one uninterrupted pass have consecutive, unique timecode with no timecode breaks. You put a blank tape into a camera, press Record, and after an hour or so, the recording is finished when the cassette reaches the end of the tape. The beginning of the tape has timecode 01:00:00:02 and the end of the tape has a timecode of 02:03:00:00 or a similar number.

Continues...

A timecode break can occur when the recording is stopped before the tape has been entirely used. In this case, the camera operator reviews the footage, allowing the tape to play beyond the end of the recorded content, where nothing has been recorded yet. When the camera continues recording, it checks the tape to see if there's any timecode under the record-head already, and when it finds none, it restarts the timecode from a preset value. Now there's not only a break in the timecode, but there are also two frames that start at 01:00:00:02.

Another scenario that causes timecode breaks is when the camera is set to free-run timecode generation instead of record-run timecode generation. Record-run is the setting that causes the camera to pick-up the existing timecode on the tape and continue with that timecode when recording new footage. Free-run timecode generation continues incrementing the timecode even when the camera is not recording. When recording is paused and continues, there will be a timecode break on the tape.

As shown in Figure 2.17, you can select one of four preroll methods, which affect how the Capture tool and the deck work to locate the coincidence point.

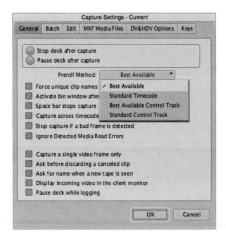

Figure 2.17
The Consolidate/Transcode tool.

- **Standard Timecode**: Instructs Media Composer to always seek the preroll point by direct access. This is done by subtracting the specified preroll duration from the IN point timecode. If the preroll timecode does not exist, the clip is not captured and an error is reported.

- **Standard Control Track**: Instructs Media Composer to always seek the pre-roll point by control track access, which is an alternative method of locating frames on a tape located before or after any other given frame. This is done by first seeking the IN point then switching the deck to Control Track Offset mode and rolling backward by the specified preroll duration. If sufficient continuous control track does not exist prior to the IN point, the clip is not captured and an error is reported.

- **Best Available Control Track:** Instructs Media Composer to seek first using Standard Control Track. If a control track break is encountered, the system will shorten the preroll to the amount of continuous control track available. If there is not enough control track prior to the IN point, the clip is not captured and an error is reported.

- **Best Available:** This option instructs Media Composer to try the following options, in order:

  1. Standard timecode

  2. Standard control track

  3. Best Available control track

The default option, Best Available, provides the greatest chance to capture the material but can take longer, in some instances, than other methods if chosen directly. For these reasons, it's recommended that you do the following (in conjunction with other Capture settings options):

- Choose Standard Timecode first when capturing material previously captured in the offline. This is the fastest capture method.

- After batch capturing a reel, if clips still remain offline, change the Preroll method to Standard Control Track to capture the remaining clips.

Capture Across Timecode Breaks

The Capture Across Timecode Breaks option instructs Media Composer to watch for irregularities in the timecode, which suggest a timecode break. When it detects a break during capture, it stops the recording, finishes writing the media file, and creates a master clip in the bin. It then commands the deck to seek to the first frame after the timecode break and it prerolls and starts capturing a new clip.

This feature is useful because:

- Timecode breaks don't cause a capture to be aborted

- The clips can still be batch captured at a later time

Ask for a Name When a New Tape Is Seen

This is an option that's selected by default and you should think twice about ever turning off. The functionality is as it says: When you change tapes, Media Composer asks you to identify the tape. If you've ever worked as an online editor using Final Cut Studio, you'll understand why this is such an important feature—it prevents you from having a box of tapes, all identified by the editing software as Reel 001.

When you recapture footage, Media Composer will ask you to insert a tape, as shown in Figure 2.18. It only knows the name of the tape because you tell it. If you turn this feature off, you will likely capture media and it will be associated with the previously named tape. This will become a major problem if you ever have to recapture the clip. The more tapes you have, the more problematic it will be.

Do everyone three favors:

■ Leave this setting enabled, regardless of the temporary inconvenience it may cause.

■ Always label your tapes.

■ Use the same label when Media Composer prompts for the tape name.

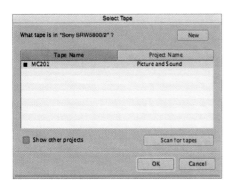

Figure 2.18
Media Composer tracks the tape so it can use the tape name in the clip's metadata.

Capture Settings > Batch

Batch Capture is used when you have clips in a bin but do not have the associated media files. That may be the result of using a workflow where footage is first logged and captured after. You would also batch capture when you've deleted media in preparation for recapturing at an online quality resolution (codec), or even in a scenario where your media drive crashed and you need to recapture your footage. (Once again, this is why it's important to back-up your bins and to keep your bins and media on separate drives, when possible.)

The settings on the Batch Settings tab, shown in Figure 2.19, allow you to automate tape handling functions, such as automatic rewind, and allow you to control how the Capture tool behaves when the logged settings for a clip do not match the current settings of the Capture tool.

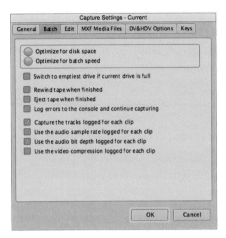

Figure 2.19
The Capture Settings > Batch tab.

Optimize for Disk Space or Batch Speed

Enable this option to potentially speed up the capture process. If this option is active, and the distance between the OUT point of one clip and the IN point of another is five seconds or less, the deck will not pause between the two clips and will roll forward to the next clip. Since this is not an uncommon occurrence when batch capturing, enabling this option can save a significant amount of time (and wear on the deck's transport) that would otherwise be spent seeking and prerolling.

Switch to Emptiest Drive if Current Drive Is Full

Although this option may be useful in some local-storage-only configurations, it is generally better to manually manage your storage and specify in Media Composer which volumes you would like to use when capturing.

Rewind Tape When Finished

Tapes last longer when rewound and are stored vertically. With this option selected, Media Composer will be kind and rewind. That will contribute to the health and longevity of the tape.

Eject Tape When Finished

If enabled, the tape will be ejected after the last clip from that reel is captured. Ejecting the tape is a useful prompt for the editor, assistant editor, or tape operator that the system is ready for the next tape. This option is particularly helpful when working with machine rooms, and is often used with Rewind Tape When Finished.

Log Errors to the Console and Continue Capturing

It is strongly recommended that this option is enabled when batch capturing. If an error, most likely a *coincidence* error, is reported by the deck, the system will note the error and proceed to the next clip. If this option is not selected, the system will pause capture and display a dialog box every time an error is encountered.

You should enable this option if you leave Media Composer batch capturing unattended, perhaps while you go for lunch. With this option enabled, Media Composer will do its best to bring in the clips while you are away. With it disabled, Media Composer will stop at the first problem, presenting an error message and waiting for you to dismiss the message.

Capture Settings > Edit

Compare Figure 2.20 and Figure 2.21, both of which are images of the Capture tool's toolbar. Do you see the difference?

Figure 2.20
The Capture tool's default toolbar.

Figure 2.21
The Capture tool with Edit-Ready toolbar.

Enable Edit to Timeline

You must first enable this option in Capture Settings > Edit > Enable Edit to Timeline, which causes the Splice and Overwrite buttons to appear, as was shown in Figure 2.21.

Once Edit to Timeline is enabled, you can capture footage directly from tape to a sequence loaded in the Timeline in one step, bypassing several steps such as organizing and reviewing clips, marking edit points, and performing edits.

This is a powerful feature that lets you place footage quickly into the timeline. Once in the timeline, you can top/tail the shots; change their order using the Smart Tool and even add dissolves between all the shots using Quick Transitions > Apply to All Transitions from IN to OUT.

By default, your Avid editing application edits the tracks you select for capturing to the corresponding tracks in the Timeline. You can patch the captured footage to any track in the Timeline by using the track selector panels located to the left of the tracks in the timeline.

Handle Length

Setting a handle length causes Media Composer to place the footage in the timeline with the IN point and OUT point offset by the value of the handle length. For example, if you set the handle length to 30 (frames) the IN point would be 30 frames from where the clip began, and Media Composer would capture an additional 30 frames at the end of the clip, but not place those frames in the timeline, thus giving you handles.

Capture Settings > Media Files

The Media Files tab allows you to customize how Media Composer writes the media files on the media drive. The Media Files tab is shown in Figure 2.22.

Figure 2.22
The Capture Settings > Media Files tab.

Maximum (Default) Capture Time

The Maximum Capture Time helps Media Composer anticipate how much media you will be capturing. You can never capture more than this amount without stopping the recording and then continuing it with a new clip.

When Media Composer begins capturing, it first reserves enough space on the media drive to accommodate a media file of this duration at the Capture tool's current resolution (codec). There is a brief delay when you press record, during which Media Composer reserves the space on the drive. When using codecs that consume more space, the delay is longer than when using highly compressed codecs, which don't use as much space.

Why is this important? If you set this value to 70 but try to record a 90-minute tape, you will find the recording stops prematurely. You need to change this to 90, perhaps even 95 to give yourself some extra leeway. (Professional video tapes are usually a few minutes longer than is indicated on the cassette.)

On the other hand, if you are only recording 30-second clips, you'll find that you can reduce the reservation-delay by changing this setting to 1 minute.

If you are using Frame Chase Capture, described in the following section, the value of Maximum (default) Capture Time is also used to predict the final length of a clip while the capture is in-progress.

What Is Frame Chase Capture?

Frame Chase Capture is a feature of Media Composer that's only available when you are using Avid Unity and Avid Interplay. Avid Unity, as covered in an earlier lesson, is Avid's shared storage solution, for sharing media. Avid Interplay allows sharing of clips and items similar to bins and projects.

Frame Chase Capture writes the media to Unity and creates a special kind of clip called an in-progress clip, which exists as long as the capture is on-going. In-progress clips will become master clips once the capture has been successfully completed.

An in-progress clip and associated media files can be used by other workstations before the capture has been completed. For example, you could begin capturing a two-hour tape using one Media Composer, and from another Media Composer you could begin viewing and cutting the media that has already been captured.

At certain time intervals, Media Composer updates Interplay and informs it that additional media has been captured, and that extra media is appended to the in-progress clip.

When you capture in this way, the media becomes available for viewing and editing from any applications in the Interplay workgroup while the capture is still in progress.

The process works like this:

1. You begin capturing to a Unity workspace on an Interplay-connected system.

2. After a specified number of minutes of media has been captured, your Media Composer checks the in-progress clip with Interplay. (By default, it's a 10 second turn-around time from the beginning of the record to the initial check-in.) The in-progress clip is now available for other editing workstations.

3. Another editing workstation uses the clip and can access the captured media.

4. At specific intervals, Media Composer updates the in-progress clip in Interplay. Other editing workstations get access to the additional media.

5. Your Media Composer finishes the capture and closes the media file. It performs one final update in Interplay in which the in-progress clip is changed to a master clip.

During Capture, Clip Is Updated in Interplay: When this option is selected, Frame Chase capture is enabled. An initial check-in takes place 10 seconds after a capture begins. Subsequent Interplay updates occur at intervals defined by the Update Interval option.

Update Interval: Select an update interval from the menu to determine how frequently updates to Interplay occur during the capture. In most circumstances it is preferable to keep the update interval low (1 minute or 2 minutes). This ensures that information added during capture (for example, comments or markers) is available as quickly as possible.

Capture Settings > DV & HDV Options

A time-saving feature is located on the DV & HDV Options tab, called Scene Extraction, shown in Figure 2.23. You can capture an entire tape, and Media Composer will either create subclips or create markers automatically at all the locations where the recording was paused and then resumed. Since stopping and starting the recording often indicates a scene change, or another take, this feature is quite effective.

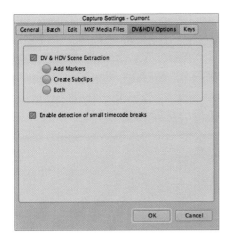

Figure 2.23
The Capture settings > DV & HDV options.

Without this feature, you'd have to capture separate clips, or create the subclips or markers yourself.

To understand this feature, you must first understand that a DV/HDV camcorder records digital video, audio and also the date and time into the digital data stream. The extra data that is recorded into a digital stream is called *ancillary data.*

With this feature enabled, Media Composer watches the ancillary data for inconsistencies in the time and date in the incoming DV/HDV data stream during capture. Each time the time or date jumps, the recording must have been paused, and Media Composer starts a new subclip or adds a new marker (or both).

Notes about this feature:

- The date and time are stored differently than timecode, so this feature has nothing to do with timecodes or timecode breaks

- The full DV/HDV data stream is preserved when there is an OHCI/Firewire cable between the editing system and the deck, but it is not preserved when other methods are used, such as SDI or Analog Component, because those methods discard the ancillary data.

Capture Settings > Keys

In the Keys tab of Capture Settings, shown in Figure 2.24, you can map markers to function keys.

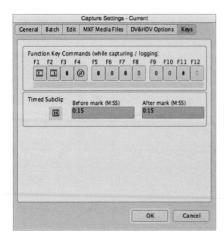

Figure 2.24
The Capture Settings > Keys command.

Creating Subclips While Capturing

Editors can take advantage of the real-time nature of the capturing process to perform organizing tasks such as subclipping and adding markers. You can create as many as twenty subclips while capturing a single master clip.

Note: You cannot create subclips during a batch capture.

To create subclips while capturing:

1. Start capturing as usual, with or without marked IN and OUT points.

2. To begin the subclip, press the **F1** key. This highlights the subclip IN mark in the Capture tool, shown in Figure 2.25.

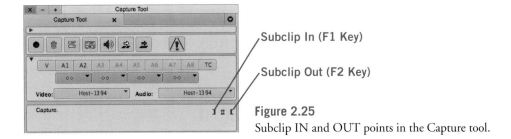

Subclip In (F1 Key)

Subclip Out (F2 Key)

Figure 2.25
Subclip IN and OUT points in the Capture tool.

You can press the **F1** key again if you want to change or update the start point of the subclip.

3. Type a name for the subclip. The information you type will not appear in the bin until you complete capturing.

Note: Stopping capturing without pressing F2 to end the previous subclip results in an OUT point for the subclip identical to the OUT point for the master clip.

4. When you want to close, or end the subclip, press F2. This highlights the subclip OUT mark in the Capture tool. A subclip's IN point remains open to change until you press F2.

You can press the **F2** key again to change the subclip's OUT point if you decide to close the subclip at a later point in the footage.

5. Press F1 to create the first subclip and simultaneously open the next subclip. The interface of the Capture tool will update to indicate the current subclip number and that a subclip OUT point has not yet been specified, as shown in Figure 2.25.

Mapping Markers to Different Function Keys

You can map the multi-colored marker keys to different function keys. These function keys are activated when the Capture tool is recording, and temporarily override any other commands that you may have mapped to the function keys using the Keyboard Settings.

1. Open **CAPTURE** settings, **KEYS** tab.

   The Capture Settings window appears as shown in Figure 2.26.

2. Click on a marker, and in the menu that appears, choose a different marker color.

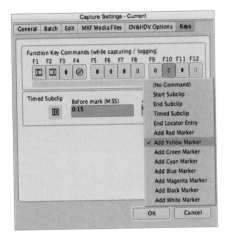

Figure 2.26
Changing the marker assigned to a function key.

3. Click **OK**.

The new color is applied to the function key.

Adding Markers During Capture

You can add a virtually unlimited number of markers to a master clip or a subclip during capturing. You can use these markers during the edit as multiple IN and OUT marks, or to hold descriptive content-related text. You can also sort them by color, name and so on.

To add a marker during capturing:

1. Start capturing as usual, with or without marked IN and OUT points.

2. Press the appropriate function key wherever you desire a marker.

These are the color markers and their corresponding default Function keys. During capturing, the markers override any other functions mapped to these keys. See Table 2-3.

When the captured clip is loaded into the Source monitor, the markers appear in the position bar. These markers carry over to the Record monitor if you do not change the Copy Source Markers Composer setting, shown in Figure 2.27. If you do change this setting, they will remain with the Source clip only.

Table 2-3   Markers Mapped to Function Keys

Color Marker	Function Key
Red	F3 and F5
Green	F6
Blue	F7
Light blue (cyan)	F8
Magenta	F9
Yellow	F10
Black	F11
White	F12

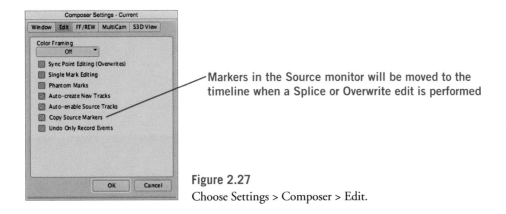

Markers in the Source monitor will be moved to the timeline when a Splice or Overwrite edit is performed

Figure 2.27
Choose Settings > Composer > Edit.

Adding Markers During Batch Capture

Using the marker function keys, you can add multi-colored markers, with marker comments, during batch capturing. These markers are particularly useful if the first step in the process was to scan through footage and log IN and OUT points. You can add markers while watching the material in real time during the batch capture process. You might perform this action after you add the clip's name and a clip comment.

1. During capture, press one of the marker function keys.

2. (Optional) Type a marker comment.

3. Press **F4** to end the marker comment.

Deck Settings

You use Deck settings to configure a default preroll for your camera or VTR. You also use Deck settings to confirm that Media Composer knows which manufacturer and model of deck you have. Also, your deck might have notes provided by the Avid Hardware Qualification Team, which are available from Deck Settings, shown in Figure 2.28.

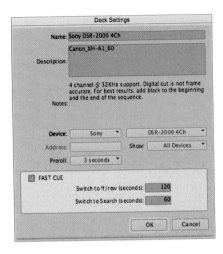

Figure 2.28
Choose Settings > Deck Settings.

Preroll

Sets the deck's default preroll duration. This value defaults to five seconds for most decks. Well-maintained modern digital decks such as the Sony DVW-A500, Sony HDV-F500, Sony HDW-M2000, and Panasonic AJ-HD3700 can get to speed and lock in less than a second. Reducing this preroll duration to one or two seconds can slice minutes or even an hour or more off the time required to recapture a long-form program with a lot of edits.

The Deck Settings dialog box is accessed via the Deck Configuration setting as follows:

1. Open the DECK CONFIGURATION setting.

   The current deck patch will be displayed, showing the control port and deck. If this dialog box is empty, you should first connect the deck and select AUTO-CONFIGURE.

2. Double-click the deck on the right side of the patch to open the DECK settings.

Note: The Deck Configuration setting applies for all users and all projects. It is a
       site-wide setting, although "site" refers to the editing system and not the
       company or facility.

Audio Project Settings

After preparing the Media Creation tool for the types of visual media settings
required, the Audio Project settings must be established. Project Window >
Settings > Audio Project Settings is where you select the sample rate, reference
levels, and type of audio files.

Establishing Audio Input Quality

Depending on the facility and type of work, audio formats and sample rates can vary from
project to project.

Often a post house or broadcast facility will have specific requirements for their audio standards. Some facilities may want to have all of the audio at 44.1kHz. A broadcast facility may
require audio at 48kHz to meet airing standards. If you work in one of these scenarios where
workflow is consistent and project deliverables seldom vary, you can save your Audio Project
setting as a site setting.

To save your Audio Project setting as a Site setting, which establishes the default setting for
new projects, while not altering other existing projects, do the following:

1. Open **SPECIAL > SITE SETTINGS**. The Site Settings window appears. It may be
    empty if no site settings have been established for your Media Composer System.

2. From the list of settings, drag **AUDIO PROJECT** to the **SITE SETTINGS** window.

3. Close the **SITE SETTINGS** window.

If you work on diverse projects that range in scope with different audio requirements always
ask your clients what is required.

It will save you time, energy, and embarrassment in the long run.

Consider the following when determining how to capture your audio media.

■ The preferred sample rate for a project is set in the Audio Project settings.

■ Digital information is not susceptible to the same kind of noise that analog audio
   signals are susceptible to.

Audio Project Settings > Main Tab

The Main tab of Audio Project Settings is where you configure how the audio media will be created, captured, and converted during playback. It's shown in Figure 2.29.

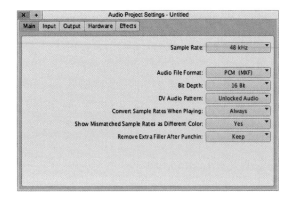

Figure 2.29
Choose Audio Project Settings > Main tab.

Sample Rate and Sample Bit Depth

Set as required by the project. In most cases, if you are mastering to Digital Betacam, HD CAM, or a similar format, these should be set to 48kHz and 24-bit, respectively.

If you're working on a Unity system, avoid mixed sample rate. It's much better to get sample rates corrected early if the finished sequence will be sent to an on-air playback device. In addition, deletion of original media may not be possible, depending on the Unity workspace permissions.

Note: The DV codec permits audio at 32, 44.1, and 48kHz. 32kHz is lower than other recording formats, but by dropping the audio samples to 32000 per second, the DV codec is able to encode four discrete channels of audio, whereas it is only able to encode two channels of audio at 44.1 or 48kHz.

Audio File Format

Both OMF and MXF media formats are available and can be freely mixed in a sequence. Let's look at the three available options:

- WAVE (OMF): The media is packaged using the Wave format, which is readable by nearly all Windows applications that support sound. This media is stored in the *OMFI MediaFiles* folders on your media drives.

- AIFF-C (OMF): The media is packaged using the Audio Interchange File Format, which is readable by most computer sound applications. This media is stored in the *OMFI MediaFiles* folders on your media drives.

■ PCM (MXF): This media is packaged using the industry-standard Pulse Code Modulation format. This media is stored in the *Avid MediaFiles* folders on your media drives.

The reason you would change this depends on your workflow, and what happens to the audio media beyond your edit suite. If you'll be sending your audio to a digital audio workstation, speak to your audio engineer and determine what format of media he or she would prefer.

Show Mismatched Sample Rates as Different Color

This enables you to visually identify audio clips with the incorrect sample rate in the Timeline.

Note: You must enable Audio Waveforms to see the mismatched rates indication.

It's useful to know when you have mismatched audio clips on the timeline, because Media Composer must resample those on-the-fly in order to play them. That resampling takes some processing power that could be better allocated to effects or compositing, and real-time resampling uses a procedure may produce audio that is not of the highest quality.

Convert Sample Rates When Playing

When Media Composer converts audio sample rates during playback, the audio quality may not be as optimal as it would be if you pre-converted the audio sample rates. However, if you set this to Never, Media Composer will output mismatched audio as silence.

Which scenario would you prefer?

A) To accidentally output a sequence with missing audio clips

B) To output a sequence with the audio you intended, even if some audio clips might not be as pristine as they could be?

If you answered A, set this option to None.

If you answered B, set this option to Always and allow Media Composer to convert the mismatched audio on-the-fly.

Note: Don't procrastinate by leaving the audio sample rate conversion to the last minute. By converting it in advance, you'll not only reduce the demands on the processor during playback, but you can also choose a high-quality algorithm that can result in better sounding audio than the real-time method.

Right-click a sequence and then choose Change Sample Rate.

Audio Project Settings > Input Tab

The Input tab of Audio Project Settings allows you to configure the audio input hardware. It's shown in Figure 2.30.

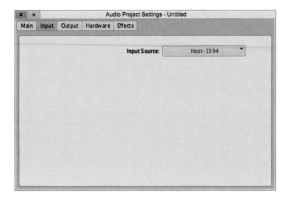

Figure 2.30
Choose Audio Project Settings > Input tab.

Note: You can create multiple Audio Project settings and switch between them on-the-fly by selecting them under the Settings tab in your Project window. For example, you might want to create one for analog audio sources and one of AES/EBU digital audio sources.

Input Source

Set to match the audio input you are using. If you are using the analog inputs, set the appropriate level (Pro vs. Consumer) and, if desired, enable the Soft Clip in the Options for Analog input dialog box.

Sample Rate Conversion

This option allows you to convert mismatched sample rates (from digital audio sources) on-the-fly as they are being captured. For online conforms, I recommend that you set this option to Never and convert the sample rates, as required, after capture.

Audio Project Settings > Hardware Tab

The Hardware tab, shown in Figure 2.31, allows you to verify the audio hardware that's detected and in-use by Media Composer. You can also adjust the Hardware Calibration of the Media Composer software to match the calibration of the hardware.

HW Calibration

Set to the level the finishing system's audio interface is calibrated to. The Avid Media Composer Nitris DX arrives from Avid calibrated to –20dBFs (decibels, full scale) to match most professional audio equipment.

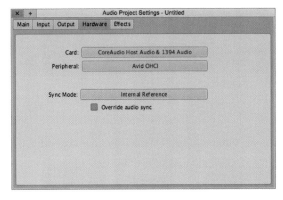

Figure 2.31
Choose Audio Project settings > Hardware tab.

Caution: If you change the HW Calibration setting from the default (–20) you must recalibrate the analog outputs on the Avid Nitris DNA. Refer to the system's online help for information on calibrating the Avid Nitris analog audio inputs.

 Take a moment to complete Exercise 2, Part 1.

Extra Audio Setup

There are a couple extra items to keep in mind prior to capturing, and those deal with configuring or using audio.

Capturing Multi-Track Audio Clips

Media Composer 6 is capable of recording up to eight audio tracks simultaneously, provided that your Video I/O and Monitoring hardware supports it. The optical connector on the Nitris DX supports eight channels of audio, as does the Nitris DX's AES/EBU connector. Some digital decks will also record eight-channels and embed it in the HD-SDI signal.

Media Composer supports four different kinds of audio clips:

- **Mono:** A mono track contains a single audio channel.

- **Stereo:** A stereo track contains two audio channels. You can pan between the two tracks, and when you adjust the level of a stereo clip, both channels are affected together. A stereo clip can be placed on a Stereo Audio track in a sequence.

- **5.1 Surround:** Contains six discrete audio channels: three in the front, two in the rear and a subwoofer.

- **7.1 Surround:** Contains eight discrete audio channels: three in the front, two in the middle, two in the rear and a subwoofer.

When preparing to capture, you enable audio inputs by selecting them, and you can also group the audio inputs to create a stereo or surround clips by using the options located under the audio inputs of the Capture tool, as shown in Figure 2.32.

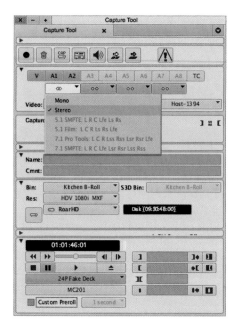

Figure 2.32
The Capture tool configured to record a clip with stereo audio tracks.

When a clip is captured with a specific audio track configuration, that clip can only be placed onto similar timeline tracks: Stereo Clips go on Stereo Tracks; 7.1 Surround Clips go on 7.1 Surround Tracks.

Tip: For more information on multi-track audio clips, refer to Lesson 8, "Working with Multichannel Audio."

Using Calibration Tone from a Tape

If the head of the tape includes 0dB tone, you should use it to set the reference level for audio on the tape. To do that, adjust the pots on the front of the deck so the audio levels peak at 0dB (analog). Although this is a best-practice, keep in mind that you cannot assume that the audio levels on the tape matches the tone.

While capturing the footage, you should check the input levels to ensure that audio peaks are no more than +6dB as measured on the analog scale. This ensures there will be plenty of audio headroom to use when mixing and equalizing the audio.

Many broadcasters will only accept a maximum peak of +8dB over reference.

Analog and Digital Audio Levels

Systems that use digital audio (including all Avid products and digital tape decks) use digital audio levels that are measured differently than analog levels. Absolute peak in digital audio is assigned a value of 0dB. Unlike analog audio, there is no headroom above the 0dB peak. Therefore, the reference level for digital audio is assigned a certain number of decibels below peak. Reference levels of –14dB, –18dB, and –20dB are the most common, with –20dB rapidly becoming an industry standard.

Digital audio systems usually contain two sets of meters—digital meters with an absolute peak of 0dB and analog meters that are designed to display the analog equivalent. If the digital system has a –20dB reference, then –20dB digital is equivalent to 0dB analog. The different digital reference levels allow for different amounts of signal headroom before absolute peak is reached. Regardless of the reference level you are using, always measure the audio signal using the analog meters as most broadcast specifications define their limits in terms of analog decibels.

For more information, see Lesson 9, "Fundamentals of Audio Mixing."

Importing Audio from CD

Whenever possible, convert audio tracks from CDs into electronic files and then import them into Avid Media Composer or Avid Symphony. By converting the music or sound effects into digital files, you make the capturing process a simple transfer of digital 1s and 0s. There should be no degradation or compromises in quality. The audio should sound the same on Avid Media Composer or Avid Symphony as it does on the CD.

When you capture digital audio using audio clocking, you need to change the video sync to AES/EBU or the audio will drift. Open the Audio Project settings and change the Input Source to AES/EBU. The Sync Mode entry will automatically change to AES/EBU, and the Sample Rate entry will change to 48kHz.

Audio imported from a CD is often louder than audio imported through other means. You can reduce the level of the audio during the import by adjusting settings on the Import Settings > Audio tab, as shown in Figure 2.33.

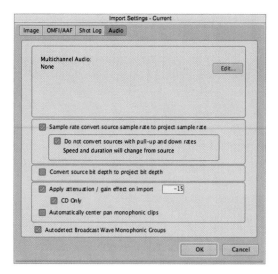

Figure 2.33
Attenuating (Reducing) the CD audio levels during import.

Extra Features of the Capture Tool

There are a few extra features in the Capture tool that can help you get through your edit quicker. Those features relate to managing the tape and specifying the drive on which the media will be recorded, and they are discussed in the following sections.

Using Tapes from Other Projects

The Select Tape dialog box can give you access to tape names from additional projects.

1. Click the **TAPE NAME** button in the Capture tool.

    The Select Tape dialog box opens, as shown in Figure 2.34.

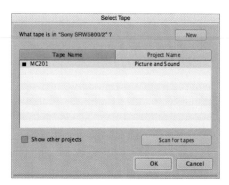

Figure 2.34
The Select Tape dialog box.

2. Press **CTRL/CMD+N** if you want to create a new tape name. (Remember: N for New.)

3. Select the option called **SHOW OTHER PROJECTS** to display the tape names and associated project names for other projects on your system.

4. If the tape you want still is not displayed, click the **SCAN FOR TAPES** button. This option scans the system to update the project list. It will display tape names and associated project names for all online media files.

If you want to capture media from tape 001Sam into Project B, and you had previously captured from that tape into Project A, do not create a new tape using the same name, 001Sam. You should instead choose the 001Sam tape that's associated with Project A. This will obey the most important tape naming rule: give each tape a unique name.

Each tape assigns project ownership, although you can modify the project ownership through consolidating. This is covered more in Lesson 13, "Mastering the Media."

Selecting a Target Drive

When selecting target drives for capturing, some general guidelines may improve play performance. In using these guidelines you should be aware of the difference between drives and partitions. When you mount a hard drive on your system it may appear as several different Drive icons in My Computer (Windows) or on the desktop or Finder's sidebar (OS X). These are called *volumes*. See Figure 2.35.

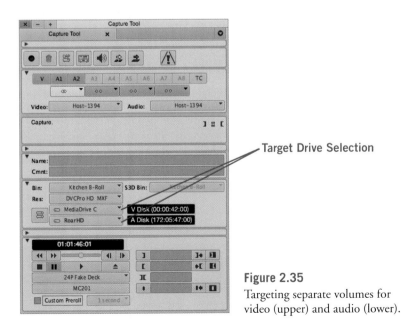

Figure 2.35

Targeting separate volumes for video (upper) and audio (lower).

Follow these drive selection guidelines:

- If you need to target audio and video to separate drives, make sure you target separate physical drives—not separate volumes on the same drive. This might improve playback performance when working with multiple streams of high resolution, uncompressed, or marginally compressed media.

Tip: Targeting audio and video to separate volumes on the same drive or striped drive set is less desirable than targeting all tracks to the same volume.

- A straightforward numbering scheme for drives simplifies target selection. It is difficult to identify which partitions are on the same drive when they are named "Little Ricky" or "Spock" as opposed to "Video A" or "Audio C."

It is also a good idea to target all the media for a specific project to specific drives, particularly if you are going to move the media to another system.

Relogging a Clip

After you capture a clip, you may want to change its IN or OUT point.

To reload the clip's timecode back into the deck controller in the Capture tool:

1. Connect the deck. (This procedure will not work unless you do this.)

2. Open the CAPTURE tool.

3. Drag a clip from a bin into the timecode IN and OUT boxes in the deck controller.

Now you can either relog the clip as is, or change its IN or OUT point. Either way, the system will create a new clip distinct from the original when you capture it.

Mounting a Tape

You can also use this technique to quickly identify a tape needed to capture a clip.

Drag the clip you want to capture from the bin into the Timecode IN and OUT boxes. The system prompts you to load the clip's tape into the deck.

Using the Console While Capturing

The Console creates a text record during capturing. You can use this record to keep track of drive space and as a diagnostic tool. For example, repeated messages like "Unable to find coincidence point" might indicate that the wrong tape was in the deck, or that the preroll needs to be modified. The Console is particularly helpful during batch capturing. It displays drive consumption and any errors.

To log errors to the Console, select the option in the Batch Capture settings called, Log errors to the Console and continue capturing.

To use the Console window while capturing:

1. Select a bin and enter **CAPTURE** mode.

2. Select **TOOLS > CONSOLE** or press **CTRL+6** (Windows) or **K+6** (Macintosh).

The Console opens, as shown in Figure 2.36.

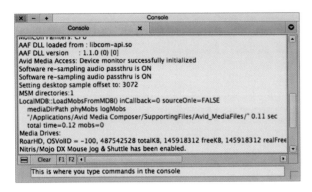

Figure 2.36
The Console window.

Caution: Exercise caution when the Console is open. Do not enter text at the Console cursor unless you are instructed to enter a specific text string by Avid Customer Support. Close the Console when not in use. Entering incorrect text in the Console can cripple Avid system operation.

3. Size the Console so that both the target bin and the Console are visible in the Bin monitor.

4. Proceed with capturing.

The Console will update as each clip is captured. It will report drive space consumption for the clip and any errors that occur.

Checking the Number and Duration of Clips in a Bin

You can use the Console to quickly ascertain the number of clips in a bin and their cumulative duration. This is helpful when capturing to determine if the duration of clips selected for a batch capture will all fit in the estimated remaining space on the target drive.

To check the number and cumulative duration of selected clips in a bin:

1. Open the bin you want to check.

2. Select the clips you want to check.

3. Right-click and choose **BIN > GET BIN INFO**.

The Console opens as shown in Figure 2.37. It displays the cumulative duration of all the selected clips as well as the total number of clips selected.

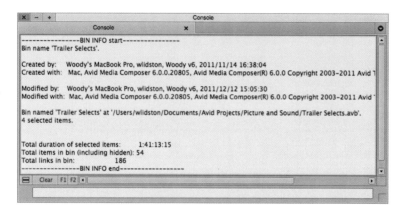

Figure 2.37
The Console window displaying bin info.

File-Based Acquisition Using Avid Media Access

Although tape isn't dead yet, file-based formats are the dominant way of acquiring footage from modern equipment. Avid Media Access, AMA, is a technology featured in Media Composer that allows direct, immediate access to unmanaged media. You may recall that *managed media* refers to the MXF files in the *Avid MediaFiles/MXF/* subfolders. Unmanaged media files are any files that exist outside of those folders, and are typically from a camera's hard disk, flash-memory stick, SxS card, P2 card or any other such file-based storage device. (Hereafter it'll be simplified as "flash-memory based storage.")

AMA allows Media Composer to create a clip that links to an unmanaged media file and read it in its native format. Media Composer will store the location of the file in the clip's metadata. AMA is implemented partially in Media Composer, and partially in downloadable third-party plug-ins, which are used to support specific kinds of flash-memory based storage formats.

AMA Is Similar to Other Technologies

You may be thinking that AMA sounds similar to Avid Pan and Zoom, or perhaps to how Final Cut Pro 7 links to files. It is and it isn't. Pan and Zoom is just for still images, not video, while Final Cut Pro 7 can link to, and immediately use, a media file as long as it's in the QuickTime format. Avid Media Access's plug-in architecture allows it to link to a variety of media file formats, including QuickTime, XDCAM, P2, AVCHD, and Red.

Note: For detailed information about working with each of the formats supported by
AMA, go to Media Composer Help > Editing Guide > File-Based Media-AMA.

Keeping Up with the Jonys

And the Panasonics. And the Sonys. And the REDs. Avid faced a problem of keeping up with the camera manufacturers, who have been transitioning from traditional tape-based cameras to flash-memory based storage. The team responsible for creating Media Composer has a schedule of the planned updates to Media Composer. If the next planned update is in November but a camera manufacturer has a new format available in April, customers who buy-in to the new format get upset when they can't edit the footage using the world's best editing system. Customers would demand that Avid update Media Composer to support the new format, and that meant releasing updates earlier than planned and it meant allocating software engineers to the task of implementing support for the new format instead of implementing tools for the editors.

The solution was to design Avid Media Access as a plug-in architecture, as shown in Figure 2.38. The plug-ins are updated by the camera manufacturers instead of by Avid, and the plug-ins can be padded to Media Composer by the editor: No intervention from Avid is required. This totally puts the onus on the camera manufacturers to develop their own plug-ins, and it leaves Avid to focus on productivity and performance-enhancing tools. It's a great solution.

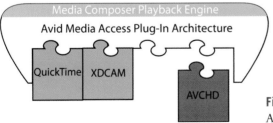

Figure 2.38
Avid Media Access's plug-in architecture.

BYOP: Bring Your Own Plug-Ins

Media Composer ships with one AMA plug-in: QuickTime. It doesn't ship with any other AMA plug-ins, so if you want to link to media on a flash-memory based storage device, you need to obtain the plug-ins. This is particularly important for freelancers to note, as you may be working on an editing system with no plug-ins. Facility technicians who have not earned the Avid Certified Support Representative (ACSR) designation are likely unaware that they must install plug-ins separately.

Which Plug-Ins Do You Have?

Media Composer's Console (Tools > Console) provides a quick way to determine which plug-ins are installed.

 Complete Exercise 2, Part 2 now and determine which plug-ins your Media Composer has.

Obtaining the Plug-Ins

There are different versions of each plug-in, and each version of a plug-in is intended to be used with a specific release of Media Composer. Ensure you choose the version of plug-in intended for your version of Media Composer. If you update or upgrade your copy of Media Composer, you should also come back and check for revised versions of the AMA plug-ins.

Tip: You can download plug-ins from Avid.com/ama, which is a very easy link to remember. You can also access the link to the AMA website from the AMA Settings.

The steps for installing a plug-in are relatively straightforward:

1. Download the plug-in.
2. Quit Media Composer.
3. Install the plug-in by double-clicking it.
4. Launch Media Composer.

Tip: Download all the plug-ins and install them. It doesn't hurt to have extra ones installed, as they are not loaded until they are needed. Further, freelancers should download all the plug-ins, including all the versions, and keep them organized on a memory stick so they can be easily retrieved in an editing suite that might not have Internet access.

 Take a moment to install a plug-in by completing Exercise 2, Part 3.

Using the AMA Workflow

You use an AMA workflow because it gets you editing quicker. Eventually the media will be copied into the managed media folder, it's just that the copying usually happens later when you use AMA compared to when you ingest from tape or import from a file.

The actual process of editing AMA footage is not overly different from the process of editing managed media.

Traditional Ingest Method

When you capture from tape (or import from a file), the original frames of video are read from the incoming video stream (or file) and they are copied onto the media drive into a new MXF file. The clip in the bin points to that managed file.

If you have a 60-minute QuickTime file, you would need to import the entire 60-minute file and then choose the portion that you want to use. Likewise for capturing, you need to capture the material first before you can put it into the timeline.

AMA reverses the order, so the copying of the video is deferred to a later time.

AMA Method

When using AMA, you edit first, then copy. When you copy, it's usually just the frames you edited into a sequence, not the entire source clip, although you certainly can copy the entire source clip. The idea behind AMA is that you should be able to begin cutting as soon as the dailies are delivered to your suite, without needing to capture first. When you link to the clips using AMA, the footage is available immediately. Instantly.

You then do your edit as normal, and later in the process, you'll consolidate the sequence (or source clips). Consolidating is the process of copying the frames from the original media files into new files in your managed media files folder. If you select a sequence, you'll consolidate (copy) just the frames referenced in the sequence, plus some additional frames, for a bit of extra flexibility later. If you consolidate source clips, the whole source clip is consolidated.

The point to remember is that when you use AMA, you will still eventually copy the source material from its native format and location onto the media drive, you'll just do it later. And you'll often consolidate (copy) just the frames you referenced, which is quicker than copying the entire clips.

Linking to Volume versus File

Media Composer's File menu allows AMA linking to a file or to a volume. A file is one specific file, often a QuickTime file. You would use AMA Link to File to relink AMA clips that are already in a bin, or to create a new link to a single file.

A volume is either a flash-based memory device, or a folder that contains the items originally written to a flash-based memory device. Media Composer is capable of automatically creating a bin containing AMA-linked clips as a result of you plugging-in a flash-based memory devie, such as an SxS or P2 card. You can configure Media Composer's behavior from the AMA Settings of the Project window. Alternatively, you can use File > Link to AMA Volume to specify a folder on a hard disk containing the copied contents of a flash-based memory device.

Since flash memory is expensive compared to video tape, camera crews often have a limited number of flash memory devices. When the camera fills one, an assistant will copy the files onto an external hard disk and prepare the memory stick for re-use by erasing it. At the end of the day, the production has a hard disk with many folders, one for each filling of the flash memory device. A sample folder is shown in Figure 2.39.

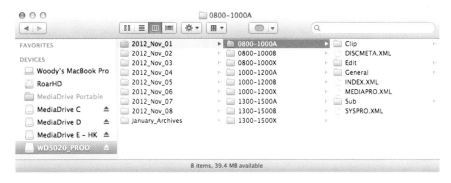

Figure 2.39
Sample folder hierarchy of a hard drive to which a camera operator has copied a day's contents of XDCAM media.

The sample folder in Figure 2.39 shows one folder for each production day at the top level of the hard disk. Within each day folder are sub-folders for each block of shooting hours, which in Figure 2.39 is two hours, the limit of the SxS flash memory units used in this production. There were three cameras on set, so there are three folders for each block of time, each differentiated by the camera identifier, such as A, B, and X. Within each camera's folder are the contents of that camera's SxS flash memory media.

If you were using AMA Link to Volume with Figure 2.39, you would select 0800-1000A, but not the individual items within that folder. Always select the top level of the folder that contains the copied media from the original flash memory.

Linking to QuickTime

You can AMA Link to a QuickTime file. Changes made to that QuickTime file will be reflected by Media Composer. This creates some options for file-based workflows, particularly when using QuickTime content generated by a third-party program where the file is updated throughout the production process.

For example, you may be editing a show that uses QuickTime content created by Adobe After Effects. The animator in After Effects creates a rough render of a shot and you cut it into the timeline to ensure it works with the other items in its scene. Then the animator creates an updated version of the QuickTime. If the original QuickTime was linked using AMA, you can overwrite the original file and the changes will be reflected in Media Composer. If the visual element was a lower-third background (for placement behind a title), overwriting the source file on the hard disk will result in all instances of it being updated in any sequence that references it.

The only trick is that you need to ensure the length of the file doesn't change, or Media Composer won't link to the file. As of this writing, you also can't AMA Link to clips with alpha channels.

Caveats of AMA

Avid Media Access opens the door to many new workflows and decreases the turn-around time for your videos. With all that it provides, there are a few things of which every AMA-using editor must be aware.

Performance Is Not Optimal

Playback of AMA linked media requires more system resources than playing managed media files. You may notice stuttered playback if your system is at the low end of the system requirements.

Additionally, plug-ins incorporate codecs that may not be as optimal as the ones used for managed media that are included with Media Composer. AVCHD is a particularly challenging format to process using AMA and often must be consolidated first to achieve real-time results.

Files Shouldn't Be Moved

Managed media files are always stored in the *Avid MediaFiles* folder, so Media Composer always knows where to locate them. Avid Media Access media can be in any location, from an external hard disk to your desktop or a USB memory stick. If you move the files, unplug the memory stick or re-organize your desktop, the files will be in a different location and Media Composer will be unable to locate them. The clips will appear as *Media Offline*.

You can put the clip back in the original location, and it'll be found. Furthermore, Media Composer stores the Universal Network Client paths (UNC), which doesn't store the drive letter, allowing drives to be moved from Mac to PC. Remember that the goal with AMA is to defer the consolidation of the media to the managed media folders. You should consolidate the media before making significant changes to the location of the source media files.

 Take a moment to complete Exercise 2, Part 4 and experience what happens when AMA linked media is moved.

Review/Discussion Questions

1. Your friend tells you "tape is dead." Do you agree or disagree? Explain your reasoning. (See "Tape: It's Alive" on page 52.)

2. What are some of the differences between RGB and YUV encoding? (See "RGB Encoding" on page 54.)

3. You're preparing to edit a show recorded on HDCAM SR. What additional hardware, aside from a computer, might you need? (See "Video I/O and Monitoring Options" on page 61.)

4. Describe some differences between HDCAM SR and HDCAM. (See "HDCAM SR" on page 53.)

5. What are the advantages and disadvantages of recording HDCAM SR in 440Mb/s mode compared to 880Mb/s mode? (See "HDCAM SR" on page 53.)

6. When would you prefer to edit with a Mojo DX as opposed to a Nitris DX? (See "Avid Options" on page 61.)

7. Why and how can you expand the capabilities of a Nitris DX? A Mojo DX? (See "Avid Options" on page 61.)

8. What's Avid Open IO? (See "Avid Open IO" on page 63.)

9. List some scenarios where it would make sense to consider Capture on-the-fly. (See "Capture On-the-Fly" on page 65.)

10. What is live venue recording? (See "Live Venue Recording" on page 65.)

11. What are the steps for performing a Capture from IN to OUT? (See "Capture from IN to OUT" on page 67.)

12. How can the process of logging clips result in saving time and money? (See "Logging Before Capturing Footage" on page 70.)

13. You open the Capture tool and the resolution you want to choose is not listed. Why? (See "Available Resolutions Are Determined by the Project Format" on page 73.)

14. What is a timecode break? (See "Capture Settings > General Tab" on page 78.)

15. Describe two scenarios where a timecode break will occur. (See "Capture Settings > General Tab" on page 78.)

16. What's the difference between using timecode and using Control Track for pre-roll? (See "Timecode and Preroll" on page 80.)

17. How can Media Composer help improve the longevity of your tapes? (See "Stopping versus Pausing a Deck" on page 79, and "Rewind Tape When Finished" on page 85.)

18. You are capturing a 90-minute tape but Media Composer stops after 70 minutes. Why? (See "Capture Settings > Media Files" on page 87.)

19. Describe a scenario where it would be advantageous to use Frame Chase Capture. (See "What Is Frame Chase Capture?" on page 88.)

20. How can you organize and annotate clips during capture? (See "Capture Settings > Keys" on page 90.)

21. Why are you discouraged from having audio clips of different sample rates on the same timeline? (See "Convert Sample Rates When Playing" on page 97.)

22. Which keys start and end a subclip while capturing? (See "Creating Subclips While Capturing" on page 90.)

23. If your tape has timecode breaks, which Capture settings will enable you to batch capture most efficiently? (See "Capture Across Timecode Breaks" on page 83.)

24. How can you apply the same resolution (codec) to both media that you capture and media that you create in making titles? (See "Video Resolution/ Apply to All" on page 77.)

25. How can you check the number and duration of clips in a bin? (See "Checking the Number and Duration of Clips in a Bin" on page 105.)

26. When would you convert audio sample rates on-the-fly, and what option must you select in the Audio Project Settings to enable this feature? (See "Convert Sample Rates When Playing" on page 97.)

Professional Acquisition

In this set of exercises, you will try some of the techniques found in this lesson. If you do not have access to video I/O and monitoring hardware, or a compatible tape deck, you will be somewhat limited in your ability to perform the tasks.

Media Used:

Picture and Sound

Duration:

60 minutes

Exercise 2.1: Exploring Tape-Based Capture

Perform the following tasks:

- Capture on-the-fly

- Live Capture (capture on-the-fly without deck control, and using Time of Day timecode)

- Capture from IN to OUT

- Provide a clip name and comment during capture

- Log clips (with or without deck control)

- Batch capture of logged clips

- Capture five clips with edit to timeline, then top/tail and re-order them, and finish it by adding transitions to each edit

- Remap the keyboard so F5 is a blue marker and F6 is a yellow marker

- Capture a clip with stereo audio while subclipping on-the-fly

- Capture one clip at 44.8kHz, another at 48kHz, and place both in the time-line

  - Configure the timeline to show mismatched sample rates.
  - Convert the sample rates of the clips in the timeline to be a uniform sample rate of 48kHz at Highest Quality

- Select a set of master clips in a bin and determine the sum of their durations

Exercise 2.2: Checking the Installed Plug-Ins

You can use Tools > Console to determine which plug-ins are recognized by Media Composer. This is easier than browsing the hard disk looking for the plug-in files, and it's more effective because simply having the files in the right place doesn't mean the plug-ins are of a compatible version. If the plug-ins don't show up in the Console, Media Composer doesn't recognize them.

Follow these steps to confirm the plug-ins that are installed:

1. Open TOOLS > CONSOLE.

2. Click in the text field located at the bottom of the Console.

3. Type AMA_LISTPLUGINS and press ENTER.

Media Composer will report the plug-ins it finds and their versions.

Exercise 2.3: Installing an AMA Plug-In

Avid Media Access plug-ins are downloaded from avid.com/ama and installed separately from Media Composer. If a plug-in is already installed, there should be no problem with installing it again, which is what you'll do in this exercise.

The plug-ins are not provided with the book's materials because they would become out of date as new versions are released. You can obtain the plug-ins from avid.com/ama, or in a classroom environment, your instructor will direct you to their location.

Use the following steps to install each AMA plug-in:

1. Quit Avid Media Composer.

2. Double-click one of the plug-in files.

3. Follow the prompts to proceed through the license agreement and accept the default options, if any are presented.

4. Restart Avid Media Composer upon completion of the plug-in installation.

5. (Optional) Use the instructions from Exercise 2, Part 2 to confirm that the plug-in is installed.

Exercise 2.4: AMA Linking to a File

Media: **Picture and Sound**

Bin: **Student Materials > Lesson 2**

In this exercise, you will link to a video recorded using an iPhone. iPhones have unusual recording properties, because their aspect ratio correlates to the shape of the phone—tall and thin, or wide and narrow, depending on whether the device is in portrait or landscape orientation.

As mobile phones and DSLR cameras evolve to record video, you'll more frequently encounter scenarios where you need to incorporate footage from an iPhone, and then need to position it next to footage from a high-end format like HDCAM SR.

1. Open Picture and Sound > Lesson 2.

2. Select File > AMA Link to File.

3. Navigate to your Student Materials > Lesson 2 folder.

4. Select TakeOffYHZ_A330.mov.

5. Play the clip in the Source monitor.

   Media Composer will link to the H.264 encoded video clip, and even recognize the unusual aspect ratio of 3.16.

6. Create a new sequence containing the clip.

7. Apply the **RESIZE** effect (choose **EFFECT PALETTE** > **IMAGE** > **RESIZE**).

8. Restore the proper aspect ratio by setting the **SCALE** > **X** value of the **RESIZE** effect to 32. See Figure EX2.1.

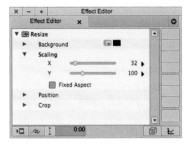

Figure EX2.1

Resize effect used to restore the aspect ratio of an iPhone 4 video clip.

Next, you'll move the TakeOffYHZ_A330.mov file from its original location, which will break the link between the clip in Media Composer and the media.

9. Use the Windows Explorer or OS X Finder to navigate to the **STUDENT MATERIALS** > **LESSON 2** folder.

10. Drag the **TAKEOFFYHZ_A330** clip into the **FLIGHTS** folder.

11. Switch to Media Composer and notice that the clip is no longer online.

   If you were to move the clip back to the original location, the clip would come online again. If you genuinely wanted to move it in order to better organize the contents of a drive, however, you can update the link within Media Composer using the following steps.

12. Right-click the **TAKEOFFYHZ_A330** clip in the Media Composer bin.

13. Select **RELINK TO AMA FILES**.

14. Navigate to **STUDENT MATERIALS** > **LESSON 2** > **FLIGHTS** and select the **TAKEOFFYHZ_A330** clip.

Media Composer relinks the clip with the QuickTime movie and updates the sequence that uses it.

Advanced Picture Editing

This lesson begins by introducing powerful techniques that enhance features that you may already use in Media Composer. The enhancements will increase your productivity and they're often just one modifier key away. Also, there are many makes and models of cameras in the world, with as many different frame rates and frame sizes. More and more devices are gaining the ability to record HD video, including tablets, and mobile phones. As your acquisition methods evolve, you'll be presented with myriad sizes of video and you must be able to efficiently incorporate them into your sequence. Media Composer's Open Timeline is able to seamlessly integrate footage of various frame rates and of various frame sizes. This lesson concludes with the techniques you need for mixing media in Avid Media Composer.

Media Used: Agent MXZero

Duration: 45 minutes

GOALS

- Learn techniques for selecting, renaming and organizing multiple tracks
- Efficiently remove match frame edits
- Find and manage black holes and flash frames
- Enhance editing functions using modifier keys
- Understand the information provided by phantom marks
- Know when to use Sync Point Edit (SPE) and how it is different from Replace Edit
- Repurpose 16:9 content in a 4:3 sequence and vice-versa
- Learn how to reformat material to exclude letter- and pillarboxing
- Be able to convert a sequence from one frame rate to another

Working with Multiple Tracks

Media Composer supports 24 video, 24 audio, and 24 metadata tracks, plus one data track, one filmstrip track, and multiple timecode tracks. With those numbers, you could have over 70 tracks in a sequence. Multi-channel audio tracks, such as the 7.1 surround audio track, can further support up to eight channels of audio. Given that you could have 24 of those tracks, you could have 192 discrete audio channels in your timeline. Video tracks support a collapse/nesting technique. Through nesting of video tracks, an unlimited number of tracks can be nested, and those can also be nested, and those can also be nested and so on. With that consideration, Media Composer can support an infinite number of video tracks. That should suffice for even the most complex of visual stories.

This part of the lesson is about efficiently managing multi-track sequences.

Selecting Multiple Tracks

Perhaps the slowest way to change your track selection is to use the mouse to click each track selector button. Track selection is such a frequent task in editing that learning to quickly select and deselect the tracks of interest can help speed your edit process.

Tip: **The more tasks you can perform using your keyboard, the more proficient an editor you'll be.**

There are several ways to select or deselect multiple tracks in the timeline:

■ Shift+drag across track lights in the Track Selector panel to turn on and off multiple tracks. The setting of the first track (on or off) is applied to the other tracks.

   This method is useful for turning on or off only the video or audio tracks.

■ Drag a lasso starting above the Track Selector panel across the track lights to reverse the selection: turn off those tracks that were on, and turn on those that were off.

   This method is useful because you do not have to be as accurate with the mouse as you do in the previous method. Simply position your cursor in the gray-space above the Track Selector Panel, drag all the way down and through the existing tracks, and the selected tracks will invert.

■ Alt+drag (Windows) or Shift+Command+drag (OS X) a lasso from anywhere in the Track Selector panel across the track lights to do a reverse selection: turning off those tracks that were on, and turning on those that were off.

What Are Meta and Data Tracks?

You're familiar with video and audio tracks, but chances are that you're less familiar with Meta and Data tracks. Indeed, many editors never need those tracks, but for those who do, they are a compelling reason to choose Media Composer over other nonlinear editing systems that lack those tracks.

A Meta track works in conjunction with the Avid MetaSync software to allow synchronization of content in your timeline with external presentation equipment. It may be made clear with some examples. Consider a 3D ride at an amusement park like Universal Studios, the kind of ride where you and 30 others sit in a car mounted on a hydraulic platform. The movement of the platform, creating a realistic experience with motion, augments the stereoscopic projection in front of the audience along with the 7.1 surround sound.

Media Composer already handles 7.1 surround sound tracks, and stereoscopic clips on the video tracks, and the movement of the hydraulic platform would be synchronized using the Meta track. The designers of the ride would create "enhancement object clips," which you import into a bin and then edit into your sequence just like any other clip—you can trim them, cut them, and splice them.

In this example, the ride designers might create enhancement objects such as Roll Left, Roll Right, Tilt Back, Tilt Forward, and perhaps Rumble. The creation of the enhancement objects is done using Avid MetaSync. You cut those clips into the Meta track to describe how the hydraulics should move the ride. If the V1 track has a clip of a rollercoaster slowly going up the initial incline, you'd add a Tilt Back clip. As the coaster moves over the cusp of the inline, you'd edit-in the Tilt Forward enhancement object clip, trimming it to be short, so the ride would quickly transition from being tilted back to forward.

After you've edited the tracks, you export the Meta track and import that data into the computer that controls the hydraulics of the ride.

Meta tracks can also be used to synchronize closed captioning data with an external, third-party closed captioning controller.

The Data track is also useful for closed captioning, particularly when editing content that has already been close captioned. Here's the problem and how the Data track provides a solution: You capture a previously edited montage with voiceover and closed captioning. You need to change the order of the shots, but the voiceover and closed captioning must stay the same. How do you preserve the closed captioning and not change the order of the words?

You first extract the closed captioning data using Clip > Extract DNxHD Data. This creates a new clip in the bin that's just the data portion of the clip, which contains the closed captioning data.

You then edit the video, audio, and data onto V1, A1-2, and D1. Then you can edit the three components of the content (picture, sound, and closed captioning) separately. You can lock A1-2 and D1 to prevent modifications, and focus on editing just the picture.

- Multiple Track selector buttons on the keyboard can be toggled on or off simultaneously. It is not necessary to click them one at a time. All 24 tracks can be mapped to keys, for both audio and video, as shown in Figure 3.1.

- Press Ctrl/Cmd+A to select all tracks when the Timeline window is active.

- Press Shift+Ctrl/Cmd+A to deselect all tracks when the Timeline window is active.

  The shortcut key to make the Timeline window active is Ctrl/Cmd+0.

Tip: The ability to deselect all tracks is particularly useful when the sequence contains tracks that are not visible in the Timeline window. Deselecting all, making a specific track selection, prevents unwanted changes in unseen tracks.

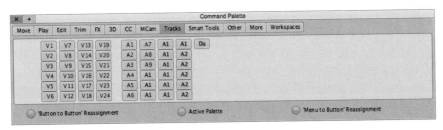

Figure 3.1
Video, audio, and data tracks can be mapped from the Command palette to the keyboard for quick toggling.

Creating Tracks Out of Order

When you create a new track, Media Composer numbers it incrementally based on the existing tracks. For example, if you have a timeline with V1 and V2, and you then create a new video track, it will be named V3. If you have a timeline in which you deleted a track, such as a timeline having V1, V3, and V4, the next video track will normally be named V2.

You can create tracks with any track number by holding the Alt/Option key while you create the new track:

- If you normally create a track with Clip > New Video Track, hold Alt/Option before you create selecting Clip > New Video Track.

- If you normally create a track with Ctrl/Cmd+U, add Alt/Option to the Mix: Cmd/Ctrl+Alt/Option+U.

Media Composer will present the Add Custom Track dialog box as shown in Figure 3.2.

Figure 3.2
The Add Custom Track dialog box.

Note: The track number sets the position of the track in the processing pipeline. The position of the track in the processing pipeline is not determined by the order in which the tracks were created.

Lowered-numbered tracks are processed first and upper-numbered tracks are processed later. If your timeline has V1 and V24, and you later create V2, Media Composer will process the clips on V1 as the background, then add V2, then add V24.

Inserting Tracks

You can create new tracks and insert them between existing tracks. For example, you might have a sequence with tracks V1–V10 and then decide you need a new track between V1 and V2. You could select all the clips and move them up using Lift/Overwrite tool (red arrow), but an easier way is to simply insert a new track after V1.

To insert a track:

1. Create a new track using the out-of-order technique described in the previous section.

2. Select a track number that already exists, such as V2 in this example.

Media Composer will then confirm that you want to insert a new V2 track. If you click Insert, the clips on track V2 and higher are moved up to make room for the new track.

Renaming Tracks

Video tracks are named V1–V24 and audio tracks are named A1–24. This is how it has always been, but it isn't as it must be—you can rename your tracks, which is a useful technique to keep them (and you) organized.

Some examples of why you might rename tracks include:

- Your audio editor wants you to separate your audio elements to different tracks. Giving those tracks specific names will make this easier for you to remember, as shown in Figure 3.3.

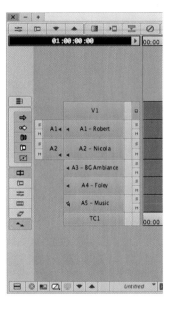

Figure 3.3
Renaming audio tracks makes it easier to organize content.

- You want to reserve some "upper" video tracks for utility functions. Upper video tracks are any tracks toward the upper end of the possible track range, such as V20–24. (See the previous section, "Creating Tracks Out of Order.") Using a track for a utility feature involves placing an effect on the filler of an otherwise empty track in order to affect all the video beneath the track, as shown in Figure 3.4.

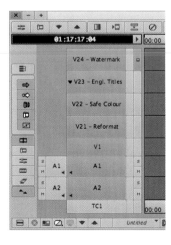

Figure 3.4
Renaming upper-level video tracks makes it clear they are performing a useful task.

■ You are editing a show with many visual effects and want to ensure you place the effect elements on the appropriate tracks, as shown in Figure 3.5.

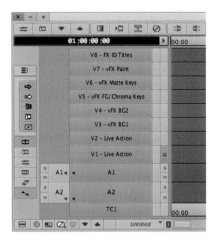

Figure 3.5
Complex effect-based sequences, like science fiction TV shows, can be better organized with renamed tracks.

To rename a track, right-click the Track Enable button and choose Rename Track.

After you rename a track, Media Composer will not display the track's original name, such as V1 or V2, unless you include that name when you rename the track. This will become important when you export the track or use some multi-track effects, such as Timecode Burn-In, because some features of Media Composer will still refer to tracks by their original names. It will be clearer for you if those original names are still referenced in the timeline.

Note: Renaming tracks has no effect on their processing order. Tracks internally remember their original position in the processing pipeline and will always be processed in that position. Renaming V10 to V1 will have no effect in the processing of the items in the timeline.

Moving Tracks

You can reposition tracks in the timeline. Repositioning tracks does not affect how the tracks are processed. Repositioning tracks is a convenience feature, enabling you to work more efficiently in a multi-track sequence.

Scenarios where it might be useful to move tracks:

■ You are synchronizing items on a video track to music on an audio track. It is easier to align the video edits to the audio beats by positioning the video track directly above the audio track, as opposed to having numerous video and audio tracks separating the video and audio tracks of interest.

■ You prefer to have the timecode track separating the video and audio tracks.

To move tracks:

■ Hold Alt/Option and drag a Track Selector up or down.

Cleaning Tracks

As you edit and refine your timeline, debris may be left in your wake. Small, barely noticeable gaps may exist between adjacent clips when the Ctrl/Cmd key was not used to enable segment snapping. You might have broken up an audio voiceover using Add Edit, only to put the pieces back together and now your timeline has unnecessary edits, called *match frame edits*.

Media Composer contains some useful housekeeping tools for cleaning up your timeline, reducing track clutter. This section introduces you to tools for removing the match frame edits, black holes, and flash frames.

Removing Match Frame Edits

Adding artificial edit points to sequence material is a common action. These edit points between adjacent frames are called *match frame edits*. The Add Edit command, shown in Figure 3.6, is an easy way to add edits, which, like a razor blade, divides one segment into multiple segments, which can then be repositioned using the Smart Tool.

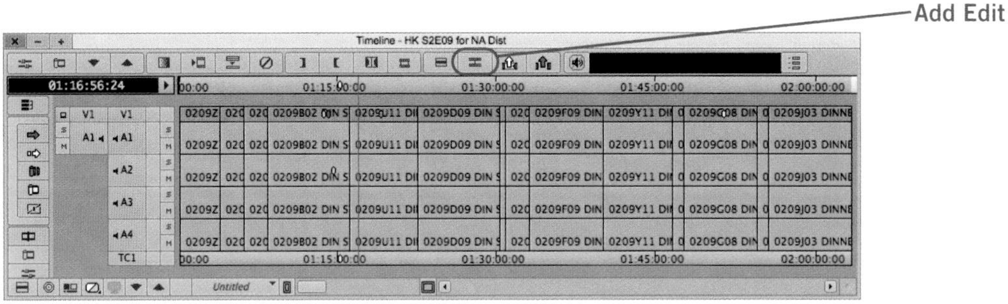

Figure 3.6
Add Edit slices segments for easier repositioning with the Smart Tool.

After some time, you may find that your sequence has become so cluttered with match frame edits that it can be confusing to look at. Worse, these can clutter an EDL list generated from the sequence.

There are two kinds of match frame edits: continuous and discontinuous. A continuous match frame edit that has a white "equals" symbol (=) on the edit means the clips on either side have no differences, while a red "equals" symbol means there is a difference between the two sides.

Differences that cause the equals sign to be red include:

- An effect on one side that doesn't exist on the other

- The same effect is on both sides, but the parameters or keyframes are different

You cannot remove a match frame edit unless there is a white equals symbol on the edit. If there is a red equals sign, you will need to correct the difference between the two clips first, usually by removing an effect.

Note: If you are removing a customized effect in order to remove a match frame edit, consider saving it as an effect template so you can easily re-apply it after the match frame edit has been removed.

There are several easy ways to remove match frame edits.

To remove match frame edit(s) at one location in the timeline:

1. Enter trim mode at a match frame edit.

2. Press the **DELETE** key on the keyboard.

To remove match frame edits from a range in the sequence:

1. Set an **IN** and **OUT MARK** around the range you want to affect (or the entire sequence).

2. Select the tracks you want to affect.

3. Do one of the following:

- Select **CLIP > REMOVE MATCH FRAME EDITS**.

- Right-click in the timeline and choose **REMOVE MATCH FRAME EDITS**.

Finding Black Holes

To err is human. And the faster you edit, the more "human" you may find yourself. It is not uncommon that while cutting, an editor will inadvertently create "black holes" or "flash frames."

Black holes are segments of the sequence that consist of one or more frames of filler. Use the Find Black Holes command to help you quickly find these within your sequence.

To find black holes:

1. Click the timeline to activate it.

2. Select the tracks you want to search.

3. Move the position indicator to the beginning of the sequence or before the part of the sequence you want to search.

4. Select CLIP > FIND BLACK HOLES.

The position indicator moves to the first segment that contains filler. You can then edit or delete the filler, if necessary.

To find the next segment that contains filler, select Clip > Find Black Holes again.

Finding Flash Frames

Flash frames are clips that have an extremely short duration, for example, fewer than 10 frames. They tend to appear as almost subliminal because they appear for a fraction of a second, and you may not notice them without watching your sequence in full screen or on an external client monitor.

Use the Find Flash Frames commands to help you quickly find these within your sequence.

To find flash frames:

1. Set the maximum frame length that you want to detect:

   a) In the Project window, double-click the TIMELINE setting.

      The Timeline Settings dialog box opens.

   b) Click the EDIT tab.

   c) In the FIND FLASH FRAMES SHORTER THAN option, type the maximum number of frames you want to detect. The default value (10 frames) indicates the system will detect clips with nine or fewer frames.

   d) Click OK.

2. Click the timeline to activate it.

3. Select the tracks you want to search.

4. Move the position indicator to the beginning of the sequence or before the part of the sequence you want to search.

5. Select CLIP > FIND FLASH FRAMES or RIGHT-CLICK and then choose FIND FLASH FRAMES.

The position indicator moves to the first flash frame.

To find the next flash frame, select Clip > Find Flash Frames again.

 Take a moment to complete Exercise 3, Part 1.

Enhancing Functions with Modifier Keys

Aside from the standard alphanumeric keys that every keyboard has, keyboards also have modifier keys: Shift, Control, Alt/Option and the Windows key or the Macintosh Command key.

A modifier key doesn't do much on its own: pressing Shift by itself doesn't normally do anything. Modifier keys are used in conjunction with other keys: Press Shift and an alpha character, and the character becomes uppercase. Modifier keys are the keys that modify, or change, the functionality of the standard keys.

This section describes how and when to use modifier keys to enhance Media Composer's features.

Match Frame

Match Frame is a Media Composer feature that allows you to quickly locate a master clip that was used to create a subclip or motion effect.

Some uses of Match Frame include the following scenarios:

- If a subclip is in the Source monitor, the Match Frame command loads the original master clip into the Source monitor.

- If a motion clip is in the Source monitor, the Match Frame command loads the original master clip that was used to create the motion effect.

- If the timeline is active, Match Frame will load into the Source monitor the master clip associated with the clip under the Current Time indicator (the blue line). (Remember from Lesson 1 that a sequence is a sequence of subclips, so this behavior is consistent with subclips being in the Source monitor.)

When a master clip is opened as a result of the Match Frame command, the following operations happen:

- The original master clip is loaded.

- Previously set IN and OUT marks are cleared.

- A new IN mark is added to the master clip at the frame that corresponds to where the Current Time indicator was located in the subclip.

Modified Match Frame

You can use Match Frame with the Alt/Option key to maintain the source clip's original IN and OUT marks. In this scenario, the original master clip is loaded and its original IN and OUT marks are retained.

The Match Frame icon is shown in Figure 3.7.

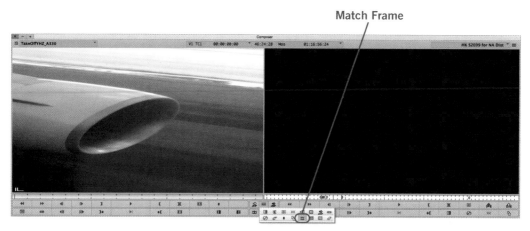

Figure 3.7
Match Frame and Reverse Match Frame icons resemble a master clip icon.

To use Match Frame with the Alt/Option key:

1. In the sequence, move to the frame that you want to match.

2. Turn on the record track that you want to match.

    Match Frame matches from the highest active track in the TRACK SELECTOR panel.

3. ALT/OPTION+CLICK the MATCH FRAME button.

The source footage for the frame currently displayed in the Record monitor is loaded into the Source monitor, and the clip's original IN and OUT marks are maintained.

Reverse Match Frame

You can also do a reverse match frame. In this case, Media Composer locates the currently displayed frame in the Source monitor and displays it in the sequence. If the frame on the active source track is not in the sequence, Media Composer beeps.

The Reverse Match Frame icon is shown in Figure 3.7 along with the normal Match Frame.

Reverse Match Frame is a fast way to determine whether you have used a specific frame of source material somewhere else in the sequence.

1. In the Source monitor, move to the frame that you want to match.

2. Do one of the following to perform a reverse match frame:

   ● Map the REVERSE MATCH FRAME button from the OTHER tab in the COMMAND palette to a button or key. Use the button or key.

   ● Open the COMMAND palette and select ACTIVE PALETTE. Then use the REVERSE MATCH FRAME button from the OTHER tab.

Match Frame Track

Normally the Match Frame command acts upon the top-most enabled track. In a scenario where you have many tracks and the one you want to match frame is at the bottom of the list, it can be tedious to disable all tracks first. Match Frame Track is a better way.

You can use the Match Frame Track command to quickly locate a source frame regardless of track selection. Follow these steps:

1. In the sequence, move to the frame that you want to match.

   You don't need to select the track you want to use.

2. In the TRACK SELECTOR panel, RIGHT-CLICK (Windows) or SHIFT+CONTROL+CLICK (Macintosh) the track you want to match and choose MATCH FRAME TRACK.

The matched frame for that track appears in the Source monitor.

Note: This feature is particularly useful when you have a complex sequence with lots of tracks.

Find Bin

Related clips are typically stored in the same bin. Be it a bin of shots for a particular scene, or a bin of exterior shots of a building, the contents of a bin are usually related. When you're working in the timeline and want to find shots that are similar to the current shot, you can probably find them in the same bin as the current shot. (Current shot refers to the clip under the Current Time indicator for the top-most enabled track.)

Find Bin can be helpful in that scenario. The icon for Find Bin is shown in Figure 3.8, and it's located under both the Source and Record monitors (unless, of course, you remap the buttons and remove it).

When a clip is loaded in the Source monitor, and you want to find the bin in which it is stored, you can use the Find Bin button. This button finds and/or opens the bin and highlights the clip within it.

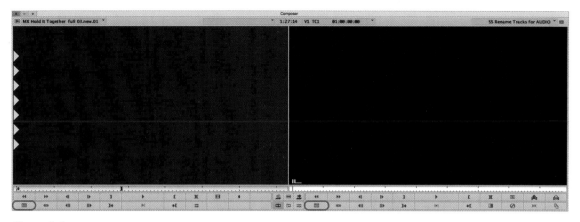

Figure 3.8
Rapidly locate the bin containing the content in the monitor.

When the Record monitor is active, Find Bin also works for the content of the Record monitor: sequences. With the Alt/Opt modifier key, it can be used for clips within sequences.

To find the bin for a clip in the Source monitor, or for a sequence in the Record monitor:

1. Load the clip into the Source monitor or load the sequence into the Record monitor.

2. With either the Source or Record monitor active respectively, choose FIND BIN from the Monitor's unscrewing buttons.

    The system locates and/or opens the bin, and highlights the clip or sequence within it.

Sometimes you would rather find the bin that contains the clip under the Current Time indicator in the timeline, as opposed to finding the bin that contains the sequence.

To find the bin for a specific clip in a sequence:

1. Place your current time indicator on the clip in the timeline.

2. Enable the appropriate record track.

3. Hold the ALT/OPTION key and select the FIND BIN button below the Record monitor.

The bin containing the clip comes to the front in the Bin monitor with the clip highlighted.

Lift and Extract

Lift and Extract do not normally use the Source monitor. By using the Alt/Option key, you can have the Lift and Extract commands place the material between the IN and OUT points into the Source monitor. Once the material is in the Source monitor, you can retarget the source and record track selectors and splice or overwrite the content back into the timeline.

Command	Without Alt/Option	With Alt/Option
Lift (Shown in Figure 3.9)	Removes content, leaves a gap	Moves content from timeline to Source monitor, leaves a gap
Extract (Shown in Figure 3.10)	Removes content, closes the gap	Moves content from timeline to Source monitor, closes the gap

Tip: Because the Source monitor and its Clip Name menu only hold 20 items at a time, you should subclip this material to a bin if you want to guarantee yourself access to it later.

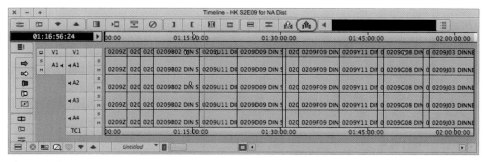

Figure 3.9
Lift icon: Red means it leaves filler and does not alter timing.

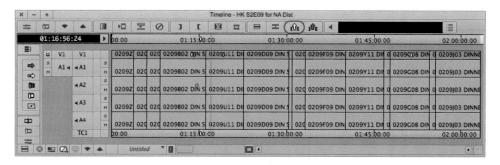

Figure 3.10
Extract icon: Yellow alters timing by closing the gap.

Copy to Clipboard

As with the Lift and Extract commands, Copy to Clipboard can also be used with the Alt/Option key to load the contents from IN to OUT into the Source monitor. Unlike the Extract and Lift methods, Copy to Clipboard does not remove content from the timeline. Copy to Clipboard is shown in Figure 3.11.

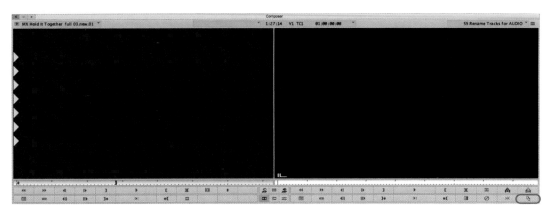

Figure 3.11
The Copy to Clipboard icon.

The Clipboard allows you to quickly restore lifted or extracted segments when you have performed several edits since removing the material. Unlike the Undo function, the Clipboard restores the lifted or extracted material while maintaining subsequent edits.

When you Copy to Clipboard, you create a subsequence for the marked segment. You can view the subsequence as a source timeline by clicking the Toggle Source Record in Timeline button, as shown in Figure 3.12.

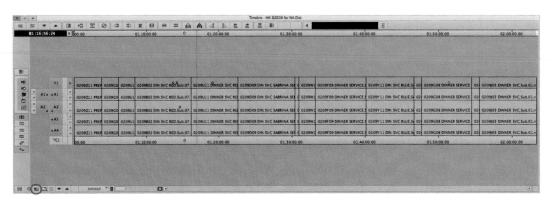

Figure 3.12
The Toggle Source Record in Timeline button.

Note: The Toggle Source Record in Timeline feature switches the timeline to display the contents of the Source monitor instead of the Record monitor. While this mode is enabled, the Current Time indicator in the timeline is displayed in green instead of blue, and the Toggle Source Record in Timeline button is also displayed with a green highlight.

Clip Name Menu

There is a Clip Name Menu located above the Source monitor, and also one located above the Record monitor. They are shown in Figure 3.13. Aside from displaying the name of the item loaded into the associated monitor, they are also menus with commands that affect the contents of the monitor, and they contain a quick access list of the last 20 items located into the monitor.

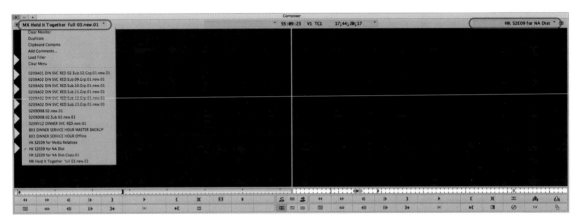

Figure 3.13
Clip name menu locations.

Normally the list of the previous 20 items is sorted alphabetically, with the As on top and the Zs on the bottom. To sort the list chronologically instead of alphabetically, hold the Alt/Option key and click the Clip Name menu. The clips are then displayed in the order in which they were loaded into the monitor or in which they were used, instead of alphabetically.

Mark Clip

The Mark Clip command, shown in Figure 3.14, marks the nearest edit to the left and right of the blue position indicator by searching for common edit points on all enabled tracks.

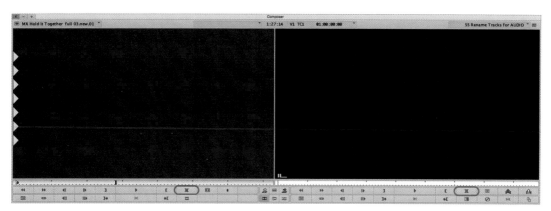

Figure 3.14
Locations of the Mark Clip command.

Adding the Alt/Option key causes Mark Clip to select the nearest edits regardless of track selection. Figure 3.15 shows how the Alt/Option modifier key affects Mark Clip's behavior.

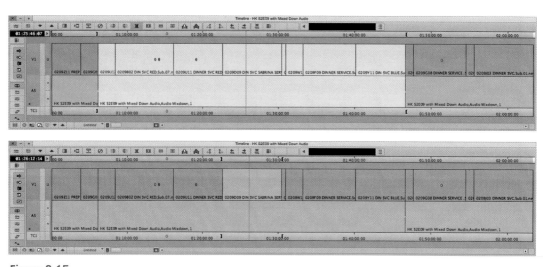

Figure 3.15
Top: Mark Clip without a modifier. Bottom: Mark Clip with the Alt/Option modifier.

Note: You can also press T instead of using the Mark Clip button. If you select segments in Segment mode, pressing T will add a Mark IN on the first frame of the leftmost selected segment and a Mark OUT on the last frame of the rightmost selected segment. Adding Alt/Option to the Mark Locators command achieves the same behavior, setting marks at the closest locators regardless of track selection.

Play IN to OUT

Play IN to OUT (keyboard shortcut: 6) does what it says—it plays from IN to OUT. You can also loop playback between IN and OUT marks. This can be particularly useful when playing a logo or element live to air, or when recording a short segment to a long videotape, perhaps when preparing a reel for a tradeshow display. Without the ability to loop from IN to OUT, you would need to duplicate the timeline contents over and over until your timeline reached the same length as the output format.

To continuously loop playback between IN and OUT marks:

1. Mark an **IN** and **OUT** in the sequence or on the source clip.

2. ALT/OPTION+CLICK the PLAY IN TO OUT button, or press ALT/OPTION+6.

   You can change the IN or OUT mark on-the-fly while the marked material is looping. However, this will not affect the playback, which will continue looping the same range as was originally selected from IN to OUT when the looped playback began.

3. To stop, press the SPACEBAR, or click the PLAY IN TO OUT button again.

Summary of Alt/Option Modifications

Many of the buttons and menu items you just went over have a modified function when used in conjunction with the Alt/Option key. Table 3-1 presents a summary of the modifier keys.

Table 3-1	Using Commands with the Alt/Option Modifier
Feature	**With Alt/Option Modifier**
Match Frame	Retains the clip's original IN and OUT marks
Find Bin	Finds the bin for a clip in the sequence
Lift, Extract, Copy	Places lifted, extracted, or copied material between IN and OUT points into the Source monitor
Mark Clip	Marks the nearest edit to the left and right of the position indicator, regardless of track selection
Play IN to OUT	To loop play between IN and OUT marks
Clip Name menu	Displays the clips in the order in which they were loaded into the monitor
Audio tracks	Toggles solo monitoring for all tracks (up to 16)

Continues...

Table 3-1   Using Commands with the Alt/Option Modifier (continued)

Feature	With Alt/Option Modifier
J-K-L keys	Enables J-K-L speed ratcheting
IN/OUT marks	(Source and Record monitors only) Moves the IN or OUT mark when you Alt/Option+drag the mouse right or left
Lasso tracks to enter Slip trim mode	Allows you to lasso tracks into Slide Trim
Go to Previous Edit (S) or Go to Next Edit (A)	Enters Trim mode at the previous or next transition regardless of the selected track
Re-enter Trim mode	Re-enters Trim mode with the trim rollers restored to their last positions
Create a Timeline View	Replaces a Timeline view with the current configuration
In Frame view, click the name under a Frame	Displays the tracks for the clip
Add Edit	Adds an edit to all empty/filler tracks; tracks containing clips are not affected

Tip: The Alt/Option modifier can be added to an existing button or keyboard shortcut by assigning it from Tools > Command Palette > More. If there is a technique in the previous section that you think you will use frequently with the
modifier key held, it may be convenient to build the Alt/Option functionality
into the button or keypress.

Three-Point Editing Power User Tricks

One of the golden rules of nonlinear editing is this: You need only three edit points
to describe a splice or overwrite edit. You can have two IN marks and one OUT
mark, or one IN mark and two OUT marks, but you must have three marks.

When you have four marks, such as an IN and OUT mark in the Source monitor, as well as an IN and OUT mark in the Record monitor, the OUT mark of
the Source monitor is disregarded.

Note: The OUT mark of the Source monitor is the least significant mark. In the
presence of four marks, it will be ignored.

When you have three marks, the monitor with a complete set of marks is used to determine the duration of the edit, and the two marks that are the same (both IN or both OUT) are used to set the alignment point, which determines if the edit is a forward edit or a reverse (back-timed) edit.

There are scenarios where you have fewer than three marks, and Media Composer is still able to perform the overwrite by using the Current Time indicator as an IN mark in the absence of a real IN mark, and using the end of the clip as an OUT mark. In this scenario, though, the result of the overwrite operation is not obvious to the editor. It is also often unclear as to whether there is sufficient media to perform the edit.

Using Phantom Marks

Phantom marks provide visual guidance when editing according to the three-point rules.

Phantom marks will answer the following questions:

- Do I have sufficient media to perform the edit?
- Precisely where is the footage coming from?
- Exactly where is the footage going, and what footage will be overwritten in the case of an Overwrite edit?

The following examples illustrate two typical phantom mark scenarios.

Setting One Mark

In this example, you set only the mark IN on the source side. By default, Media Composer uses the location of the position indicator as the mark IN for the sequence and calculates both OUT points based on the length of the source clip, as shown in Figure 3.16.

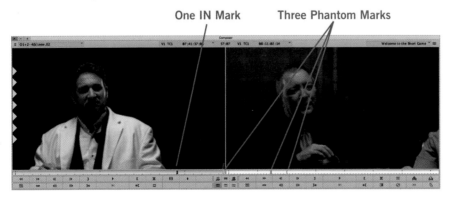

Figure 3.16
You can see the system calculations instantly and can make the edit after setting just one mark, when appropriate.

Adding a Second Mark

If you decide that a mark OUT is required—to shorten the source clip, for example—the system recalculates and displays new phantom marks, as shown in Figure 3.17.

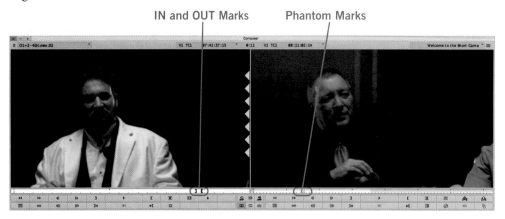

IN and OUT Marks   Phantom Marks

Figure 3.17
Phantom marks immediately reflect the calculated IN and OUTs in the absence of real IN and OUT marks.

If phantom marks are enabled and you have an IN or OUT mark added, yet no phantom marks are visible, it indicates that you do not have sufficient media to perform an edit. This is a fantastic use of phantom marks for avoiding the "insufficient media" errors prior to overwriting or splicing footage.

Note: The Go-To-In (Q) and Go-To-Out (W) commands recognize the phantom marks.
        If you want to see the exact last frame that will be used for an overwrite, you
        can go to its phantom mark and preview the final frame of the edit prior to
        performing the cut.

Enabling Phantom Marks

Phantom marks appear under the Source or Record monitors, which are part of the Composer window. The setting to show or hide the phantom marks is therefore part of the Composer settings, which is a user setting and saved with your user profile.

To enable phantom marks:

1. **DOUBLE-CLICK COMPOSER** in the **SETTINGS** list of the **PROJECT** window.

   The Composer Settings dialog box opens.

2. Select the **PHANTOM MARKS** option in the **EDIT** tab.

3. Click **OK**.

You can also toggle phantom marks using one of the following methods:

- Choose **SPECIAL > SHOW PHANTOM MARKS**.

- **RIGHT-CLICK** in the **COMPOSER** monitor and choose **SHOW PHANTOM MARKS**.

- **CTRL/CMD+=** in the **COMPOSER** monitor and choose **EDIT > SHOW PHANTOM MARKS**.

Replace Edit

Media Composer has an edit command called Replace Edit, which is similar to an Overwrite Edit with the significant exception that it does not obey the rule of three-point editing. In fact, if you specify three points and try to perform a Replace Edit, you'll be told that you have too many marks.

Replace Edit is located in the toolbox located between the Source and Record monitors. It's also available by choosing Tools > Command Palette > Edit. Both locations are shown in Figure 3.18.

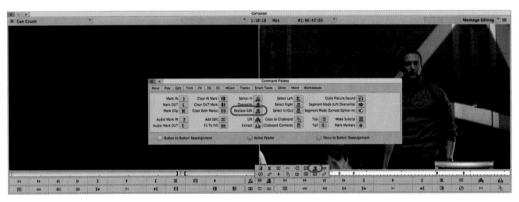

Figure 3.18
Location of the Replace Edit command.

Replace Edits are useful when you have an alternate take of a shot already in your timeline. You want to overwrite the shot in the timeline into the space currently occupied by the existing shot.

A Replace Edit determines the IN and OUT positions in the timeline by referencing the shot under the top-most enabled track in the timeline. The IN mark it uses is the edit to the left of the current position indicator, and the OUT mark it uses is the edit to the right. You don't specify any marks in the Source monitor: The Replace Edit synchronizes the Current Position indicators (blue lines) in the Source and Record monitors and takes as much footage before and after the indicator in the Source monitor to meet the edit boundaries of the clip in the timeline.

The footage that you use in a Replace Edit works best if it's very similar in timing to the footage that's already in the timeline. That way, the edits that are in the timeline are more likely to be suitable edits for the new clip.

Using Sync Point Editing (SPE)

Sync Point Editing is a specialized version of the Overwrite function. When enabled, Sync Point Editing (SPE) allows you to overwrite material in such a way that a particular point within the source material is aligned, or "synchronized," with a particular point in the sequence, much like Replace Edit.

SPE requires two pieces of information:

- **The sync points.** These are the source and record frames that you want to sync up, and are determined by the position of the Current Time indicators in the Source and Record monitors.

- **The duration of the relationship.** This is determined by IN and OUT marks. Both marks can be in one monitor, or one mark can be in one monitor and the other mark in the other monitor. It is important that the duration of the material being edited into the sequence be sufficient for the size of the edit. It is helpful to use phantom marks to determine this.

Sync Point Edit (SPE) versus Replace Edit

Sync Point Editing is similar to Replace Edit in that they both use the Current Time indicator as the sync point. Replace Edit, however, uses a clip (or marked segment) in the sequence to determine the amount of footage to use from the source clip. Sync Point Editing always determines the duration based on the IN and OUT marks you set. Without IN and OUT marks, Sync Point Editing won't work.

A basic rule of thumb: With Replace Edit you cannot mark IN and OUT points in the source clip. Therefore, SPE is preferable when you want to add a timed cutaway to the sequence.

Using Sync Point Editing

Sync Point Editing must be enabled before you can use it. There are several ways to enable Sync Point Editing. The most efficient is to map it to a key on the keyboard to enable the feature as needed. It can also be enabled by right-clicking on the Composer Monitor, and choosing Sync Point Editing from the contextual menu, or through the Composer setting.

When Sync Point Editing is enabled, the arrow on the Overwrite button is orange, and the line below the arrow now has a small orange mark on it, as shown in Figure 3.19.

Sync Point Editing Indicator: Orange Highlight

Figure 3.19
An orange mark indicates you are set up for Sync Point Editing.

To perform a Sync Point Edit:

1. Activate the source and record tracks that you want to use for this edit.

2. Mark an **IN** and **OUT** in the Source monitor, or an **IN** and **OUT** in the Record monitor. Or mark an IN point in one monitor, and mark an OUT point in the other monitor.

3. **SHOW PHANTOM MARKS** to see where the material will overwrite.

4. Move the Source monitor's blue position indicator to the sync frame in the clip. This establishes the source sync point.

5. Move the Record monitor's position indicator to the sync frame in the sequence.

6. Select **SYNC POINT EDITING** from the **COMPOSER SETTINGS** dialog box.

7. Click **OVERWRITE**. The sync point edit is made.

Note: If you have more than two **IN** or **OUT** marks, the system will prompt you with a message indicating there are too many marks for the Sync Point edit.

8. Turn off **SYNC POINT EDITING** when you're finished.

EXERCISE   *Take a moment to complete Exercise 3, Part 2.*

Integrating Mixed Media

There are many makes and models of cameras in the world, with as many different frame rates and frame sizes. More and more devices are gaining the ability to record HD video, including tablets and mobile phones. As their acquisition methods evolve, editors are presented with myriad sizes of video and they must be able to efficiently incorporate them into their sequences.

Media Composer's Open Timeline is able to seamlessly integrate footage of various frame rates and of various frame sizes.

This section is about the techniques you need for mixing media in Avid Media Composer.

Frame Rates and Sizes Are Mixable

Video can be recorded in a variety of frame rates and sizes. A common example is NTSC compared to PAL video.

NTSC, mostly the standard in North America and some other parts of the world, has a frame rate of 29.97 frames per second (fps) and has a frame size of 720×486. PAL, the standard in Europe mostly, has a frame rate of 50fps and a frame size of 720×586, meaning it has fewer frames per second but more lines of image detail.

HD has a variety of frame widths: 1920, 1440, 1280, and 720, and even more frame rates.

Media Composer can mix any of them in the same timeline, at the same time, and it'll take care of making it just work. There's nothing you have to do. That is, nothing you have to do, normally. But there are things you can do to improve the image quality when you mix media, and you need to know how to convert a sequence to one format or the other, as you may be expected to produce a video in both a 16:9 and a 4:3 aspect ratio.

Mixing Frame Sizes

A sequence adopts the raster and frame size of the project. If a project's raster, as set in the Project window, is 1440×1080, so are all the sequences in the project. When you change the raster or project format, the sequences are adjusted automatically to match.

It's easiest to see this when you mix HD and SD video in the same sequence. If the project format is HD, then the SD clips in the sequence are scaled (up-converted) to HD in order to match the project format. The opposite is true too: If you place HD clips into a sequence while the Project window is set to SD, the HD clips in the sequence will be scaled down to fit the SD frame size.

The automatic scaling is very important because without it, you would need to adjust every clip individually, otherwise a portion of the clip would be cut off or a black border would be visible, as shown in Figure 3.20.

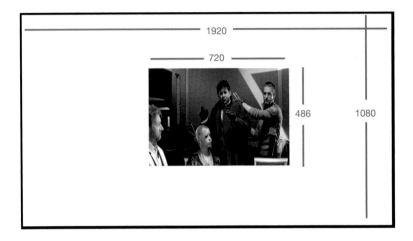

Figure 3.20
SD clips do not fill HD frames without being scaled.

When Media Composer reformats a clip to match the project settings, the original media is never adjusted. The conversion happens as though a hidden resize effect has been applied to the segment in the timeline: It only affects the segment in the timeline.

Aside from mixing NTSC and PAL, and HD and SD, you can also mix 3-perf and 4-perf film, and 8, 16, 35, and 70mm film.

There is a Reformat column in the bins that is used to control how Media Composer reformats video when the clip's native dimensions do not match the current project settings. Use of that column is discussed later in this lesson, in a section called "Changing the Aspect Ratio" on page 148.

Mixing Frame Rates

When you add a clip to a sequence and the clip's frame rate is not compatible with the project format, Media Composer applies a *motion adapter* to the clip. A motion adapter is a kind of private, internal timewarp effect that speeds up or slows down the clip so it matches the project rate and ultimately plays back as it would if the project rate and the clip rate were the same.

The automatic addition of motion adapters is very important because without it, non-conforming clips would play back at different speeds. A 60fps clip in a 30fps timeline would either play back at twice the speed, or it would play back at half the speed for twice as long.

Clips with motion adapters appear in the timeline with their original frame rate in brackets. When un-rendered, they also have a green dot/square, as shown in Figure 3.21.

Original Frame Rates of These Clips

Figure 3.21

Frame rates indicate clips with motion adapters applied; the green square indicates the motion effect is unrendered.

Modifying Motion Adapters

Motion adapters are automatically added to clips when you cut them into a sequence. As with timewarps and motion effects, there are different render methods that can be used to affect how Media Composer processes a clip having a motion adapter.

Changing the Interpolation Method of a Motion Adapter

The interpolation method of a motion adapter is changed using the Motion Effect Editor. The only option you can change is the render method. All other methods are disabled.

To change the interpolation method of a motion adapter:

1. Place the **Current Time indicator** over the clip having a motion adapter.

2. Click the **Motion Effect Editor**.

3. Change the **Render** method, as shown in Figure 3.22.

You might change the render method to remove jitter or improve the quality of the effect after it has been rendered.

Figure 3.22
Changing the Render method
of a motion adapter.

**In the Avid
Learning Series**

For more information on timewarp render methods, consider purchasing *Media Composer 6, Part 1—Effects Essentials* or taking MC110 from an Avid Learning Partner.

Promoting Motion Adapters to Timewarp

A motion adapter is an automatically applied timewarp, preset to make the source clip work in the timeline's play rate. You may want to use the motion adapter as a starting point, and then further customize or tweek the position of the frames or the speed of the clip. To do that, you need to promote the motion adapter to a timewarp.

The Promote button unlocks the other settings in the Timewarp Editor, making them available for modification. It is available for motion effects and motion adapters.

Reformatting Media

There are two approaches to reformatting a clip to fit the project format and raster:

- **Source-side reformatting:** This is the automatic method that uses the setting of the Reformat column in the bin.

- **Record-side reformatting:** This uses an effect in the Reformat category of the Effect Editor.

Source-side reformatting has been more recently added to Media Composer and is good for general purpose, day-to-day use. Record-side reformatting allows you to customize the reformat by animating pan and scan effects and setting very specific picture extraction areas.

These two methods are discussed in the following sections.

Changing the Aspect Ratio

The clip's width to height is referred to as its *aspect ratio*. 16:9 is an aspect ratio that indicates there are 16 pixels across the image for every 9 pixels up/down the image, whereas a 4:3 aspect ratio indicates 4 units across and 3 up/down, as shown in Figure 3.23.

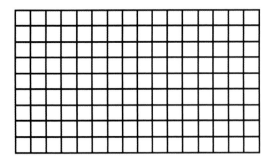 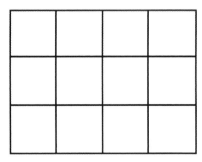

Figure 3.23
16:9 and 4:3 aspect ratios.

When a clip having a 4:3 aspect ratio is placed in 16:9 sequence, it doesn't fit perfectly because of the difference in aspect ratios. There are three accepted ways to handle the scenario, each of which is easily supported by Avid Media Composer: Stretch, Crop (shown in Figure 3.24), and Letterbox/Pillarbox (shown in Figure 3.25).

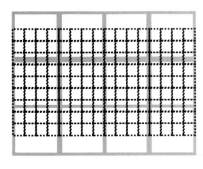

Figure 3.24
A 4:3 in a 16:9 frame. Cropping allows the 4:3 image (dark lines) to fill the 16:9 frame (gray lines) but the 4:3 image is cropped.

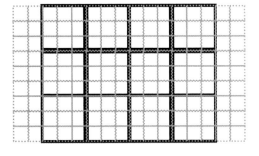

Figure 3.25
A 4:3 in a 16:9 frame: pillarboxed content preserves the 4:3 aspect ratio.

In choosing one of these methods, you need to consider the following questions:

- Is it acceptable to have letterbox or pillarbox, as shown in Figure 3.25?

- Is it acceptable to lose some of the image by cropping it, as shown in Figure 3.24?

- Is it acceptable to distort the image by stretching it?

These three choices correspond to the three choices of the Reformat column in a bin, which is the basis for source-side reformatting.

Source-Side Reformatting

When a clip is added to a sequence, Media Composer compares the clip's dimensions with that of the project to determine whether they are different. If they are different, Media Composer then consults the value of the clip's reformat attribute to determine how it should reformat the clip to compensate for the difference.

Source-Side Reformat Options

The value of the reformat column, shown in Figure 3.26, indicates how Media Composer should reformat the clip when it is added to a sequence having an aspect ratio.

Figure 3.26
Reformat column in a bin.

The default setting is Stretch for managed media, and AMA linked files, while it is set to Center, Keep Size for AMA linked volumes. Stretch causes a clip to either become taller or wider than it would naturally be, neither of which are often desirable effects, as shown in Figure 3.27.

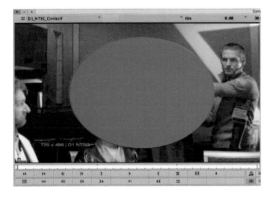

Figure 3.27
Stretching distorts the image: This oval is not a circle because it's stretched wide.

Other options for the Reformat column include Pillar/Letterbox (Preserve Aspect Ratio), Center Crop (Preserve Aspect Ratio), and Center Keep Size. These options result in the original aspect ratio being preserved by either introducing letterboxing or pillarboxing to pad the image to the new aspect ratio (shown in Figure 3.28), or by scaling the image to fill the frame, which results in some of the image being cropped, as shown in Figure 3.29.

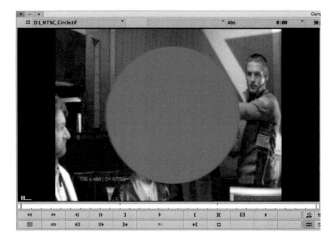

Figure 3.28
Letterboxing preserves aspect ratio by padding the image with inactive pixels.

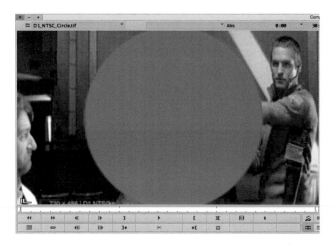

Figure 3.29
Cropping preserves aspect ratio but cuts off part of the image.

Changing the Reformat Setting

The value of the Reformat column is only considered at the instant the clip is added to the sequence. Subsequent changes to the Reformat column have no effect on clips already added to sequences. That's beneficial because you wouldn't want to inadvertently have clips in your final, finished sequences accidentally gaining letterboxing when you originally wanted them to be cropped...or would you?

Sometimes you might want a sequence to adopt the changes you've made to a clip's Reformat setting. For example, your documentary incorporates archival footage originally shot in 4:3, and when it was added to your timeline, the default setting of Stretch was set in the Reformat column. This has resulted in the 4:3 image being stretched to fill the 16:9 frame, which has the undesirable effect of making people appear heavier. You catch the problem during a screening and change the Reformat value for each clip to Letter/Pillarbox, but the clips are already added to the sequence so they are not changed.

The new Reformat values will only affect the clips when they are added to sequences, not when they are already in sequences. That's for the safety and security of all timelines. But you can override it. You can tell Media Composer "Run through every clip in this sequence, and double-check the clip's Reformat setting in the original bin, refreshing it as needed" and Media Composer will do just that, but only if you explicitly request it to do so.

To refresh the reformat setting of clips in a sequence:

1. Right-click the sequence in its bin.

2. Select REFRESH > REFORMATTING.

Ta'da. The clips in that specific sequence have been refreshed to incorporate any changes that have been made in the source clips (hence source-side reformatting), but any other sequences using the same clips are still unaffected.

Tip: The items in the Refresh submenu can be used for more than just updating a sequence with source-clip format changes. You can also refresh the Field Motion column's contents with Refresh > Motion Adapters/Timewarps. When using RED camera footage, you can revise the source settings for the RED clips and apply the changes to the sequence with Refresh > Source Settings. You can also apply stereoscopic 3D correction to source clips in a bin and refresh sequences that use those clips by using the Refresh > Stereo Correction Effects.

Record-Side Reformatting

The Reformat effect palette category, shown in Figure 3.30, contains effects that assist in compensating for differences in aspect ratios. Unlike source-side methods, the record-side methods are applied like any other effect: by dragging and dropping the effect onto the clip in the timeline, after which they can be adjusted using Media Composer's Effect mode.

Figure 3.30
Reformat category of the Effect palette.

The record-side reformatting effects are typically used when the value of the Reformat column in a bin is left at Stretch. The letterbox and sidebar (pillarbox) effects restore the original aspect ratio of a clip by padding the frame, and provide similar results to the Letterbox/Pillarbox setting in the bin. Pan and Scan, however, solves a problem that crops up when using the Center Crop (Preserve Aspect Ratio) source-side setting.

As discussed in the previous section, "Source-Side Reformatting," when Center Crop (Preserve Aspect Ratio) is selected, the center of the image is retained while the sides or top/bottom are cropped. The benefit of Center Crop is there are no black bars, but the downside is that part of the image is cropped, and you have no control over the cropping. There could be an object significant to the story at the top of the frame and that might be cropped. That's the problem solved by Reformat > Pan and Scan.

Pan and Scan allows you to choose the part of the frame that is retained by using the Effect Editor, as shown in Figure 3.31. You have fine control down to the pixel level. You can have a little bit of the top and a lot of the bottom, or a lot of the left and none of the right, the choice is yours.

Figure 3.31
Effect Palette > Reformat > Pan and Scan in the Effect Editor.

To use Pan and Scan:

1. Ensure the clip's source setting is set to **Stretch**.

   If the clip's source **Reformat** setting in the bin is not set to **Stretch**, change it back and either refresh the sequence, or recut the clip into the timeline.

2. Apply the **Effect Palette > Reformat > Pan and Scan** to the clip.

3. Open the **Effect Editor** and set the **Source** and **Target** settings. Set **Source** to what you have: the native aspect ratio of the clip in the timeline. Set **Target** to what you want: the project's aspect ratio.

   The options for **Target** will change depending on what you select for **Source**, so always set **Source** first.

   The Record monitor will show the effect with a white box representing the area to be extracted.

4. Drag the white box in the Record monitor to specify the area to extract.

   Anything outside of the white box will be cropped. Keyframing is available, so you can introduce faux camera movements if you like.

The ability to keyframe Pan and Scan is also useful when you need to show both edges of the frame in the same shot instead of just one side, such as the shot in Figure 3.32 that would otherwise only show one of the characters or just the center of the frame.

EXERCISE *Take a moment to complete Exercise 3, Part 3.*

Figure 3.32
Center extraction includes the white-boxed area but excludes the character at frame right.

Review/Discussion Questions

1. Media Composer is limited because it only supports 24 tracks of video and 24 tracks of audio." Do you agree or disagree with this statement? Why? (See "Working with Multiple Tracks" on page 120.)

2. What are three of the six ways to select multiple tracks? (See "Selecting Multiple Tracks" on page 120.)

3. Why might you want to create A5 and A6 without creating A3 and A4 first? (See "Creating Tracks Out of Order" on page 122.)

4. You tell your co-worker that you intend to reserve the "upper tracks" for utility purposes. Your coworker doesn't understand. How do you explain this to him or her? (See "Renaming Tracks" on page 123.)

5. Why is it important to retain the original name of the track when renaming tracks? (See "Renaming Tracks" on page 123.)

6. A coworker has a sequence with five video tracks. He has moved the tracks on the timeline such that the bottom-most track is V5, then V4, V3, V2, and V1, which puts them reverse of their natural order. Despite this, the clip on V5 continues to appear on top of the clip on V1 during playback. Why is this? (See "Moving Tracks" on page 125.)

7. When are match frame edits created? (See "Cleaning Tracks" on page 127.)

8. What is the difference between a black hole and a flash frame? (See "Cleaning Tracks" on page 127.)

9. Your broadcaster airs 1080i footage at 60fps. They reject all clips that are shorter than half a second. How can you re-configure a tool covered in this lesson to help you quickly locate any clips that would be rejected? (See "Cleaning Tracks" on page 127.)

10. You have a sequence with eight video tracks, all of which are enabled. You want to match frame the clip located on track A2. How can you efficiently do this? (See "Match Frame Track" on page 131.)

11. What two keys can you use to quickly load material from a sequence into the Source monitor and how do they function? (See "Enhancing Functions with Modifier Keys" on page 129.)

12. What is the function of reverse match frame and how do you execute the command? (See "Reverse Match Frame" on page 130.)

13. True or False. You must set at least two marks in order for the system to calculate and display the additional phantom marks. (See "Using Phantom Marks" on page 139.)

14. What is the primary difference between Sync Point Editing and Replace Edit? (See "Using Sync Point Editing (SPE)" on page 142.)

15. The Project window is currently active. You want to deselect all tracks in the timeline using only the keyboard. What two keyboard shortcuts do you use to select the timeline, then deselect all tracks? (See "Selecting Multiple Tracks" on page 120.)

16. Why is it useful to mix frame rates in a sequence? (See "Frame Rates and Sizes Are Mixable" on page 144.)

17. How does the use of the Reformat column in a bin differ from use of the Reformat effects? (See "Record-Side Reformatting" on page 151 and "Source-Side Reformatting" on page 149.)

18. When would it be more appropriate to use a record-side reformat than a source-side reformat? (See "Reformatting Media" on page 147.)

19. Why would you set a clip to Letter/Pillarbox instead of Center Crop? (See "Changing the Aspect Ratio" on page 148.)

20. What is a motion adapter? (See "Mixing Frame Rates" on page 145.)

21. How do you add motion adapters? (See "Mixing Frame Rates" on page 144.)

22. How do you customize a motion adapter's render method? (See "Modifying Motion Adapters" on page 145.)

23. What visual clue exists on the timeline to indicate that a clip has a motion adapter and has been rendered? (See "Mixing Frame Rates" on page 145.)

24. You've changed the value of the Reformat column for some clips in a bin, but the changes are not reflected in the sequences. Why is that, and how do you resolve it? (See "Changing the Reformat Settings" on page 150.)

Editing and Refining Your Sequences

In these exercises, you will practice the techniques you've read about in this lesson, including cleaning up your sequences, Sync Point Editing, and using mixed media in your sequences.

Media Used:
Agent MXZero

Duration:
50 minutes

GOALS

- Practice cleaning a sequence by removing flash frames and black holes
- Use phantom marks
- Use Sync Point Editing
- Practice using source-side reformatting
- Adjust the Render method on a motion adapter
- Fix a frame composition problem by using Pan and Scan
- Convert a sequence from one frame rate to another

Exercise 3.1: Sequence Cleaning

In this exercise, you will tidy a sequence that has unnecessary match frame edits and unexpected flash frames and black holes.

To clean the sequence:

1. Open the AGENT MXZERO > 201 > LESSON 3 - ADV. PIC > LESSON 3 MATERIALS. Load the sequence called DIRTY SEQUENCE.

2. Watch the sequence through.

   You should notice numerous flash frames and black holes.

3. Return to the head of the sequence. Use the command FIND BLACK HOLES to find the black hole.

4. Trim all tracks to close up the black hole while maintaining sync.

5. Find and fix any flash frames in the sequence.

6. Clean up the sequence by removing all match frame edits.

Practice both methods of removing add edit points, individually and over a range.

As you work, try the following Alt/Option key modified functions.

Feature	With Alt/Option Modifier
Match Frame	Retains the clip's original IN and OUT marks.
Find Bin	Finds the bin for a clip in the sequence.
Lift, Extract, Copy	Places lifted, extracted, or copied material between the IN and OUT points into the Source monitor.
Mark Clip	Marks the nearest edit to the left and right of the position indicator, regardless of track selection.
Play IN to OUT	Loops play between the IN and OUT marks.

Exercise 3.2: Sync Point Editing

In this exercise, you will practice using phantom marks and the Sync Point Editing feature to perform an advanced edit.

To perform these advanced edits:

1. Open the AGENT MXZERO > 201 > LESSON 3 - ADV. PIC > LESSON 3 MATERIALS > POWER USER TECHNIQUES.

2. Review the sequence, paying particular attention to the area marked using green markers.

   The clip with the resize effect—located at timecode 01:07:04:17—has the Agent staring in response to the villain's offer to play poker. In Walter Murch's "In the Blink of an Eye," Mr. Murch explains that one use for an eye-blink is to show recognition: The moment that someone registers an idea, he writes, the person will blink. When he chooses reaction shots, he will prefer footage in which the actor blinked because he says performance will appear more natural.

3. Review the footage again and notice that the Agent does not blink. Then open **Agent MCU** from the **Lesson 3 Materials** and locate the footage of the Agent blinking at approximately nine seconds from the head of the shot.

   There is no marker for you this time, and you are free to use another section of footage in which the character is blinking.

Sync Point Editing requires two marks and proper positioning of the Current Time indicators:

1. **Mark IN** and **Mark OUT** in the **Montage Editing** sequence at the locations of the green markers.

   Unlike Replace Edit, Sync Point Editing lets you overwrite a range from IN to OUT, instead of overwriting between the enclosing edit marks. You will be overwriting the clip with the resize effect, as well as a portion of the clips on either side. Three clips in total will be affected.

2. Ensure only the V1 track is enabled for both **Source** and **Record monitors**.

3. Enable **Sync Point Editing** using a method described earlier in this lesson.

4. Ensure there are no **IN** or **OUT** marks in the Source monitor.

   The IN and OUT marks are set in the Record monitor, and no marks are set in the Source monitor. The last step is to position the two Current Time indicators, which determines the synchronization point.

   The footage taken from the Source monitor will be as much footage as is required to back-time from the timeline's Current Time indicator, and to forward-time from the timeline's Current Time indicator. This can sometimes be hard to visualize, so you will enable display of the phantom marks, which will show the range of frames coming from the Source monitor.

5. Enable phantom marks using a method described earlier in this lesson.

Figure EX3.1 reveals the relationship between the Timeline/Record monitor and the Source monitor when Sync Point Editing and phantom marks are enabled.

The Source monitor is displaying phantom marks.

The number of frames selected in the Source monitor is determined by the number of frames in the timeline between the CTI and the timeline's OUT mark.

The number of frames selected in the Source monitor is determined by the number of frames in the timeline between the CTI and the timeline's IN mark.

Current Time indicators indicate the sync point. The two visible frames in the Record and Source monitors will be aligned.

Figure EX3.1
The exercise with phantom marks enabled.

Look at the timeline in Figure EX3.1 and notice that the Current Time indicator is about 25 percent of the way between the timeline's IN and OUT marks. Then look at the Source monitor and see the same relative positions for the phantom marks and the Source monitor's Current Time indicator.

6. Scrub the CURRENT TIME INDICATOR in the SOURCE MONITOR.

Notice that the phantom marks keep their relative distances before and after the Current Time indicator, which always matches the real IN and OUT marks in the timeline.

7. Scrub the CURRENT TIME INDICATOR in the SOURCE MONITOR to the beginning or end of the Source monitor's scrub area. What happens to the phantom marks?

8. Reposition the CURRENT TIME INDICATOR on the Agent's blink and perform the Sync Point Edit.

9. Review the sequence. Does his reaction seem more or less believable?

You may want to undo and redo the Sync Point Edit to compare the impact the new footage has on the story.

Sync Point Editing is also useful for aligning sound effects with visual elements, particularly sound effects where the sound fades up and down, and the most interesting part of the sound effect is in the middle, like any sound effect being affected by the Doppler effect, such as a locomotive.

10. Review the sequence again, noting the clip at 01:06:52:12 in which a man clenches his fist.

11. Open the **CAN CRUSH** clip.

12. Play the **CAN CRUSH** clip.

    You should notice that the Can Crush effect is three separate takes of a similar sound effect. This is typical for some sound effect libraries, particularly ones originally distributed on CDs, where a CD can only hold 99 tracks, so multiple related effects were placed onto the same track.

    To make it easier to visualize the audio, you'll have the timeline display the Source monitor contents, and enable audio waveforms.

13. Click **TOGGLE SOURCE RECORD IN TIMELINE**. (See Figure 3.12 earlier in this lesson.)

14. Enable audio waveforms—choose **TIMELINE FAST MENU > AUDIO > AUDIO WAVEFORMS** to do so.

15. Mark **IN** and **OUT** around one of the three sound effects.

16. Determine the sync point by placing the **CURRENT TIME INDICATOR** at the position between the IN and OUT marks where the sound effect is at its apex.

17. Click **TOGGLE SOURCE RECORD IN TIMELINE** to restore the timeline to showing the contents of the Record monitor.

    You now have an IN and OUT mark in the Source monitor, and possibly still have an IN and OUT mark in the timeline. Sync Point Editing only uses one IN and one OUT mark, so you must clear the IN and OUT marks in the timeline.

18. Press **CTRL/CMD+O** to select the timeline. (Or click in the timeline.)

19. Press **G** to remove the IN and OUT marks in the timeline.

20. Place the **CURRENT TIME INDICATOR** on the frame where the character is halfway through his fist-squeeze. (01:06:52:12 or the frame of your choice.)

21. Verify that your necessary audio tracks are selected, that the video is deselected, and perform the Sync Point Edit.

You may need to attenuate (reduce the volume of) the Can Crash clip using techniques learned during your previous experiences with Media Composer.

Exercise 3.3:
Using Mixed Media in a Sequence

In this exercise, you will create an NTSC 4×3 sequence of the Agent Zero sequence. There are many screens still using the 4×3 aspect ratio, such as the in-flight entertainment systems of some airliners. The original Agent Zero footage is 23.967 footage, so Motion Adapters will be used as well as source and record-side reformatting.

1. Create and open a new project called **AZ In Flight** with the following settings: **30i NTSC 4:3**.

2. Choose **File > Open Bin** and open **Agent MXZero > 201 > Lesson 3 > Lesson 3 Materials.avb**.

3. Set the bin view to **Format**.

   The **Lesson 3 Materials** bin now displays the **Format** column, which indicates the **Montage Editing** sequence is HD 1080p/23.976, clearly a mismatch from the format of the current project.

4. Open the **Montage Editing** sequence by double-clicking it.

   Media Composer recognizes the difference in the two formats and proposes a solution: It will convert the sequence to match the current project's frame rate, as shown in Figure EX3.2.

Figure EX3.2

Sequences will be converted to match the Project format.

5. Verify that the conversion has worked by examining the new sequence in the bin, as shown in Figure EX3.3.

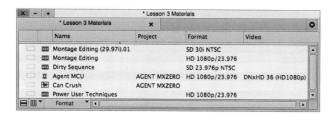

Figure EX3.3

Media Composer has converted the original sequence to match the format of the current project.

6. Play the converted sequence. The timeline should indicate the original frame rate of the clips (23.98fps). Notice that both video and audio have been adapted, but the frame size has not been adjusted to properly fit the 4×3 aspect ratio. The 16×9 clips are being stretched to fill the 4×3 frame, resulting in an incorrect, if not flattering, distortion of the image. Characters and objects are taller and thinner than they would normally be.

    You will next perform a source-side reformat by adjusting the value of the bin's **Reformat** column for the original master clips, followed by refreshing the sequence so it will adopt the changes from the bin. This project does not contain the original master clips, but you will configure the bin to display them.

7. Rename the converted sequence to **AZ Airline NTSC 4x3 Letterbox** and move it into a separate bin.

8. Close the original bin.

9. In the new bin, choose the **Fast** menu and then choose **Set Bin Display > Show Reference Clips.**

    Media Composer uses the metadata in the sequence to display master clips that correspond to the clips in the sequence.

10. Set the bin view to **Format** and then add the **Reformat** column.

11. Open one of the clips into the Source monitor and observe that it is being stretched, as per the setting in the **Reformat** column.

    Some clips will not have video media online. Be sure to choose one that does.

12. Select all the clips and change the value of **Reformat** from **Stretch** to **Letterbox/Pillarbox.**

    The clip in the Source monitor will adjust to the new Reformat setting. Letterboxing should be visible and the aspect ratio of the clip has been restored. The image is no longer distorted.

13. Map the **Reverse Match Frame** command to the Source monitor.

    Reverse Match Frame is located in **Tools > Command Palette > Other.**

14. Use **Reverse Match Frame** to locate the Source monitor's frame in the sequence.

    You may have to try a few times after moving the Current Time indicator, as the source footage has handles that will not be referenced in the sequence.

    Notice that the change in the bin has not propagated to the sequence: The clip in the sequence is still stretched.

15. Select the **AZ In-Flight NTSC 4x3 Letterbox** sequence. Choose **Clip > Refresh Sequence > Reformatting Options.**

    Media Composer updates all clips in the sequence to use the new Reformat setting of Letterbox/Pillarbox, and all clips now fit in the 4×3 frame with letterboxing.

You have successfully converted an HD 1080 project to NTSC, including frame rate and frame size conversion. When selling content, as with clothing, cars, and any other material good, it's helpful to have a variety of selections to appease the various buyers. Some airlines might not want letterboxing because the screens are already small, and letterboxing makes the active picture area even smaller.

You will make another version of the sequence, this time using 4×3 Center Crop:

1. Duplicate the sequence and rename it from **Letterbox** to **Center Crop.**

2. Select all the clips and set their **Reformat** value to **Center Crop.**

3. Select the **Center Crop** sequence and refresh it using **Clip > Refresh Sequence > Formatting Options.**

4. Open the **Center Crop** sequence and confirm that you have now created a non-distorted, non-letterboxed version of the sequence.

5. (Optional) Drag the letterboxed version of the sequence into the Source monitor and position the Current Position indicator at the head of the sequence. Place the timeline's Current Position indicator at the head of the sequence too. Click the Gang icon located under either one of the monitors and scrub through the sequence. You can compare both versions to determine if an important part of the frame is being cropped. (Gang is covered more in Lesson 5, "Multicamera Editing.")

    The **Center Crop** version is okay but there are a couple shots that are cropped too much. You can manually adjust the crop through use of the **Pan and Scan** tool.

6. In the timeline, place the Current Time indicator at 01:07:07:01.

    This is a three-up shot where Turk is mostly cropped out of the frame.

7. Note the name of the clip, U2+5A-1(b).new.01, and find it in the bin.

    Normally you could **Alt/Opt+click** the **Find Bin** button, located under the Record monitor, to find this clip, but that won't work this time because the bin that contains the original clip is not in this project. You are using the **Show Reference Clips** trick to get the clips to appear in the same bin as the sequence, but **Find Bin** doesn't consider those clips.

That is why you must locate the clip yourself. You could, remember, use **BIN > CUSTOM SIFT** to assist you.

You will change the **REFORMAT** setting for the clip back to stretch and then perform a record-side reformat.

8. Change the clip back to **STRETCH**. Refresh the **CENTER CROP** sequence so this change takes effect.

9. From the **EFFECT** palette, apply **REFORMAT > PAN AND SCAN** to the clip at 01:07:07:01.

10. Use the **EFFECT** palette and set **SOURCE** to 16:9 **ANAMORPHIC** and **TARGET** to 4:3.

11. Adjust the white box that appears in the Record monitor. Drag it to the right in order to incorporate more of Turk and less of the dead space at the left of the frame.

12. Play the sequence and confirm that the shot has been corrected by the **PAN AND SCAN** effect.

If time permits, use the **MOTION EFFECT EDITOR** on a few clips and note that the settings are locked off other than **RENDER** method. You can improve the rendering by changing the **RENDER** method. You can also set a default method from the **RENDER** settings.

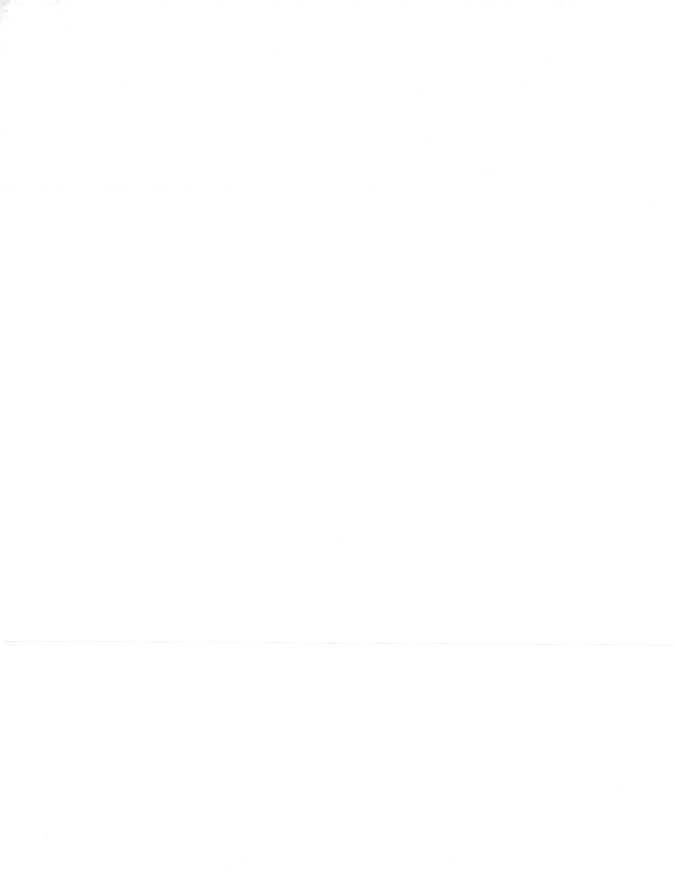

Play Together

This lesson extends the media management topics to include collaborative workflows.

Media Used: Agent Zero

Duration: 45 minutes

GOALS

- Use markers, colors, and comments to communicate with others
- Become familiar with techniques for collaborative editing
- Learn to safely share projects and media with Avid Unity

The Editor's Dialogue

Creating a finished show may involve the skills of an offline editor, online editor, and sound editor. Those could be the same person, or they could be different people in different cities. Regardless, there needs to be a way to communicate the intended vision of one editor to another.

In the case that you're doing all of it, you might have a great idea for a clip today, but three weeks from now have no recollection what the idea was. You can use these techniques to document and manage your own work.

The offline editor needs to ensure that his vision can be accurately communicated to the online editor and sound editor, because he's relying on them to add elements that are not part of the offline, but are needed for the story. He may have an idea for a non-obvious sound effect, or perhaps an idea for a specific color treatment, as in *Schindler's List* where the little girl had a red coat while everything else remained black and white.

Markers and comments are two features of Avid Media Composer that allow such communication and note keeping.

Markers Are Post-It Notes

A marker is like a 3M Post-It note attached to a specific frame and specific track of a source clip or a sequence. It appears as a colored dot on the track and it also appears below the Source or Record monitors, as shown in Figure 4.1.

Markers can be one of eight different colors, all of which are available in the Command Palette (choose Tools > Command Palette), as shown in Figure 4.2.

Within your post-production department, you might consider defining a standard color scheme for markers, where you apply specific meanings or messages to specific colors. For example:

Color	Meaning
Green	Needs "dream-like" color correction.
Yellow	This shot is coming from a visual effects house.
Blue	Unwanted background sound; please remove.
Magenta	Dust/scratch/drop-out located on this frame. Please clean.
White	The problem on this frame has been fixed.

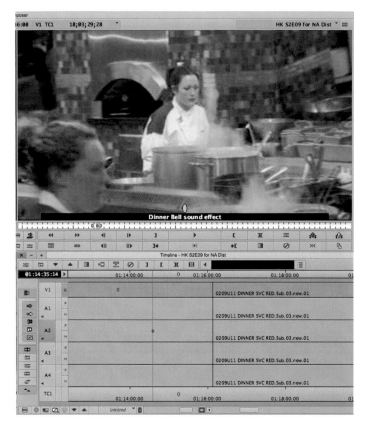

Figure 4.1
A timeline with three markers, which are on the TC, V1, and A2 tracks, and the green marker from the A2 track also appears in the Record monitor.

Figure 4.2
The Command Palette has eight colored locators.

If all editors use the same table, additional comments will rarely be needed, which means less typing and more speed and productivity. Using the preceding table as an example, a green marker will be recognized by the online editor as an instruction to make a sequence dream-like, perhaps by desaturating the image and adding a blue tint.

The Markers tool (Tools > Markers), shown in Figure 4.3, is a centralized location for viewing all the markers in a sequence, which makes it suitable as a kind of "To-Do" list. The Markers tool indicates the location of the marker (timecode), the name of the user who added the marker, and the description of the marker, as provided by the original editor.

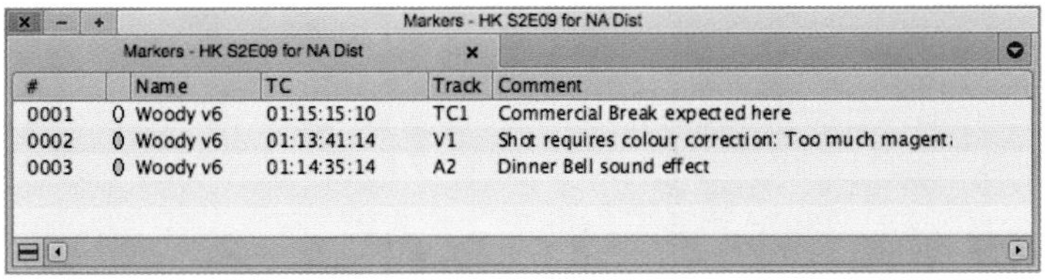

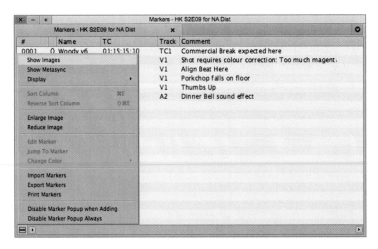

Figure 4.3
The Markers tool, available from Tools > Markers.

Markers Automate Task List Creation

The Markers tool can be used as a task list, allowing you to easily jump to different markers by double-clicking them. You can also change the marker's color, and assign tasks (markers) to other editors.

Displaying Marker Thumbnail Images

You can configure the Markers tool to display thumbnail images.

To configure the Markers tool to display thumbnails:

1. Open the MARKERS tool (choose TOOLS > MARKERS).

2. Enable the images' display by choosing SHOW IMAGES from the FAST MENU of the MARKERS tool, as shown in Figure 4.4.

Figure 4.4
Image thumbnails are enabled from the Marker window's fast menu.

Images make it easier to identify the shot, but their larger size results in fewer markers being visible in the Markers tool, as shown in Figure 4.5.

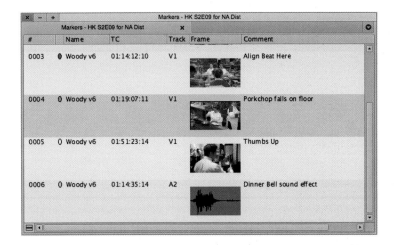

Figure 4.5
Markers tool with image thumbnails.

Sharing the Task List (Markers Tool)

The contents of the Markers tool can be printed with true what-you-see-is-what-you-get fidelity. You can print the contents of the Markers tool (choose File > Print) and distribute it to your assistant editor, or perhaps share it with the producer.

Tip: OS X Lion includes the PDF Printing and PDF Print to Email options, allowing you to print the contents of the Markers tool to a PDF that will be attached to an email. Similar software is available for Windows 7.

Editing Markers

You can edit a marker by doing one of the following:

1. Click the colored dot in the **RECORD** monitor.

2. Right-click a marker in the **MARKERS** tool, and then select **EDIT MARKER**.

    After doing either of these methods, the **MARKER** window appears, as shown in Figure 4.6.

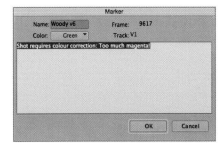

Figure 4.6
Markers can be edited after they have been added.

When editing a marker, you can:

- Change the color
- Change the comment
- Change the assignee's name

Consider a scenario in which you are working with a couple of other editors. You have a marker that defines a specific task, and you want to assign it to the editor on the nightshift, David. You would just type over the existing name, as shown in Figure 4.6.

Now when David arrives for his shift and opens the Markers tool, he'll see a marker has been assigned to him with a specific task. When he finishes the task, your organizational policy might dictate that he revise the marker description to include the completion date and any further comments about the challenges encountered in performing the task.

Note: Unlike previous releases of Avid software, markers added in Media Composer 6 will be recognized by Pro Tools 10. This ensures markers are an effective way for an offline editor to communicate with both the online editor and the sound editor.

   Take a moment to complete Exercise 4, Part 1.

Comments Appear in Bins

Each clip in a Media Composer bin has a column called *comments*. You can use it for whatever comments you'd like, such as "Good clip" or "Can't use this clip," or even to write the voiceover that your talent will read when that clip is visible. Because comments are visible from the bin, unlike markers, they are useful for annotating sequences at a bin level. Annotations might include comments like "16:9 for Luftansa" or "4:3 for Pan Am Airways," thus allowing you to differentiate between different versions of a sequence.

The Comments column in a bin is normally only visible from Script view, as shown in Figure 4.7, but it can be manually added to Text view, as shown in Figure 4.8.

   Take a moment to complete Exercise 4, Part 2.

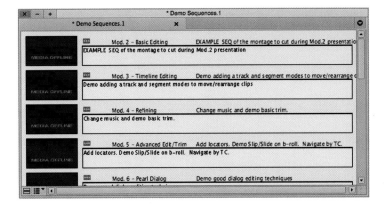

Figure 4.7
A bin in Script view displaying the Comments column.

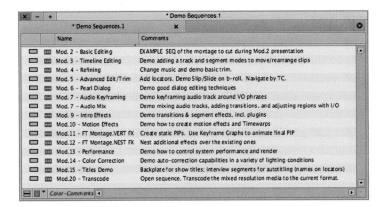

Figure 4.8
A bin in Text view displaying the Comments column.

Comments versus Markers

Clip comments tend not to be as useful as markers for adding notes to specific clips in a sequence because, unlike markers, the timeline does not display comments unless it has been reconfigured. If the online editor does not reconfigure his timeline, he will have no idea the comments are there. Additionally, there is also no central place to view all the comments, unlike the Markers tool, and comments do not move forward to Avid Pro Tools.

Comments are more useful at the bin level, because they will be shown without additional configuration when the bin is in Script view. Table 4-1 summarizes the characteristics of both of these features.

Table 4-1   Comments versus Markers

Markers	Comments
Available in eight colors	Not color coded
Visible on the timeline by default	Not visible on the timeline by default
Readable by Avid Pro Tools	Not readable by Avid Pro Tools
Available from a centralized Markers tool	No centralized tool available

Color-Coding Clips

Color-coding clips can be a very effective way to further organize your clips and expedite your workflow. Colors can be used for a variety of uses. For example, color tags can identify clips that come from the same camera or shoot and will need similar color or audio correction. Colors could be assigned based on the status of usage rights, such as cleared, pending, restricted, and so on.

Colors can be assigned to clips in the bin, and will show on all segments of that clip in the timeline. A color can also be assigned to an individual segment in the timeline, as a way to flag just that one segment, rather than all material from a given clip.

Media Composer 6 makes it easy to incorporate Clip colors into your standard workflow, because the Clip Color column is now enabled in bins by default. The new color picker also has twice as many preset colors as Media Composer 5.

Let's look at the different ways to customize the color of clips in the bin and in the timeline.

Assigning Clip Colors in Bins

You can assign one of the eight presets or any of the 16.7 million custom colors to clips in a bin. This is referred to as setting the "source clip" color. The color assigned to a clip in a bin can also be used to color the clip in the timeline. Swatches are convenient when sorting a bin by clip color, because the clips will sort by one of the 16 colors. Sorting by custom colors is less predictable because it's less likely that an editor will pick the same color every time from the 16.7 million custom colors.

When assigning colors to a clip, you can assign a color to one clip at a time, or to multiple clips at the same time.

To choose a color for one clip in a bin, you can use preset swatches:

1. Right-click the color swatch adjacent to the clip's icon in the bin.

2. Choose one of the eight preset color swatches, as shown in Figure 4.9.

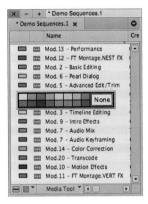

Figure 4.9
Sixteen preset color swatches.

You can use a custom color instead. Use the same technique, but hold the Alt key before right-clicking the color swatch. Media Composer will present the Macintosh or Windows color picker, from which you may choose any of 16.7 million colors, as shown in Figure 4.10.

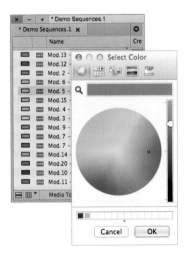

Figure 4.10
Need more colors? Hold Alt when you right-click the color swatch in Text view.

This method works well for assigning colors to multiple selected clips:

1. Select one or more clips to which you want to assign a color.

2. Choose EDIT > SET CLIP COLOR > [SELECT A COLOR].

The clip's icon turns the selected color.

Using Clip Colors in the Timeline

You can use colors to highlight the following types of clips in the timeline:

- Displaying clip colors overrides any track color you assign from the timeline's fast menu.

- For HD and SD projects, DVCPRO HD clips are colored light red. You cannot customize this color, which is an indicator that DVCPRO HD media plays by skipping frames. To avoid skipped frames, use the Transcode command and select a compatible resolution.

- Offline or mixed rates color indicators override any custom local or source colors you assign.

Tip: If you are working in a MultiRez environment, you can also use colors to track available resolutions.

Displaying Clip Colors in the Timeline

Media Composer can be configured to display clip colors in the timeline. Those clip colors can be the source clip colors, which allow the colors you assign to clips in the bin to also be used to color the clips in the timeline. The colors can also indicate if a clip has media offline, which is a useful way to see at a glance if your timeline has offline media before outputting it. You might be doing a conform from SD to HD and want to mark all the clips that don't match your project format with a specific color, which makes it easier to see how much more of the timeline must be conformed to HD.

1. Click the timeline **Fast menu** button, and select **Clip Color**. The **Clip Color** dialog box opens, shown in Figure 4.11.

Figure 4.11

Editors can communicate by setting clips to meaningful colors. Perhaps a green clip means "This is an expensive shot!" Choose the timeline's fast menu > Clip Color.

2. Select one or more of the following options:

Option	Description
Offline	Colors clips that have offline media.
Mixed Rates	Colors clips whose frame rates do not match the sequence frame rate. A different color is available for each frame rate.
SD/HD	Colors clips that do not match the video definition type of the project format—that is, in an HD project this option colors the SD clips, while in an SD project this colors the HD clips.
	You can also display clip text that can help you to identify particular clips by selecting Clip Text > Clip Resolutions from the timeline fast menu.
Timeline Local	Colors clips to which you have assigned a local color in the timeline.
Source	Colors clips to which you have assigned a color in the bin. (Colors assigned to sequences, groups, motion effects, and title clips do not appear as source colors in the timeline.)

Changing the Display Colors

Most people have a favorite color. Maybe you do. Maybe you want to see your favorite color on the timeline when your HD/SD media is mismatched, instead of the default gold color. You can do that. In fact, you can change the display colors for any of the color codes, such as resolution tracking, offline, mixed rates, and SD/HD.

To change the display colors:

1. Click the timeline **Fast Menu** button, and select **Clip Color**. The **Clip Color** dialog box opens, as shown in Figure 4.11.

2. Click the color swatch for the option you want to change. A color picker grid opens.

3. Click a color in the grid.

The color you select becomes the display color for that option.

Resetting the Display Colors

If you've customized the display colors and then change your mind, you can reset them by using the following steps:

1. Click the timeline **Fast Menu** button, and select **Clip Color**. The **Clip Color** dialog box opens.

2. Click **Default Colors**.

The Offline, Mixed Rates, and SD/HD color swatches reset to their default colors.

Local Clip Colors Are Assigned to Clips in the Sequence

You can assign local colors to clips in a sequence, for example, to indicate clips that should be grouped together. You could select entire scenes or acts and give all the clips in the scene the same color. This makes it easier to identify scenes. You can add local clip color to make clips stand out for any other reason while you are working in the timeline window.

Assigning a Local Clip Color

To assign a local clip color, you select multiple segments in the timeline and then specify the color, using the following steps:

1. Click the timeline **FAST MENU** button and choose **CLIP COLOR**. The **CLIP COLOR** dialog box opens, as shown in Figure 4.11.

2. Select **TIMELINE LOCAL** and then click **OK**.

3. Enable at least one of the **SEGMENT MODE** buttons on the **SMART TOOL** and select a clip you want to color.

4. Do one of the following:

   - Right-click on the selected segment(s). Choose **SET LOCAL CLIP COLOR > [COLOR]** to select a standard color.

   - Select **EDIT > SET LOCAL CLIP COLOR > [COLOR]** to select one of the 51 preset local clip colors.

The assigned local color appears in the clip in the timeline.

To Remove a Local Clip Color

You can remove the local clip color(s) that has been assigned to a clip using the following steps:

1. Click one of the **SEGMENT MODE** buttons and select the clip whose color you want to remove.

2. Select **EDIT > SET LOCAL CLIP COLOR > NONE**.

The assigned local color no longer appears in the clip in the timeline.

 Take a moment to complete Exercise 4, Part 3.

Collaborating on *Batman Begins*

A few years ago, I was working for Avid and we got a call from the post-production crew of the film *Batman Begins.* They had a very fast workstation-based Avid Media Composer in their edit suite. The offline editor was preparing a rough cut of a scene and, at the studios, the director was shooting additional shots for the same scene. They wanted to be sure that the additional shots would be the right ones for the sequence, so they called for workflow advice.

We decided they would bring the offline sequence to the set by copying it onto a laptop. On set, they were able to connect their camera to the laptop and record directly into the editing system, after which they would cut the shots into the timeline.

It was a great workflow because it let the editor continue to work on the show, while production crew were able to see how the work they were doing would fit in to the bigger picture. It also saved a lot of time, which saves a lot of money. Without this workflow, they would need to wait for the editor to get the footage and send word that the shots worked. With this workflow, they confirmed that the shots worked immediately and could strike the set (tear it down) immediately after the shots were verified in the edit.

Play Together

In this section, you'll be introduced to workflows that enable you and other editors to work on the same projects and media. Those workflows are driven through media management acrobatics. "Play together" refers not only to editors collaborating, but it also refers to media and clips playing together.

There are three popular collaborative workflows addressed in this section:

- Duplicating media and bins
- Offline with low-resolution media; online with high-resolution media
- Sharing media and bins

You'll also draw upon your skills involving the Relink tool, as well as the Media and Consolidate/Transcode tools.

Avid Slogans

For you historians, "Play Together" was also one of Avid's slogans for a couple years, after "Tools for StoryTellers" and before "Make, Manage, Move Media."

Duplicating Media and Bins

In this scenario, you have a working Avid project with bins and media. You will duplicate the project and media, which another editor will work on. After working independently on your own copies of the project and media, you and the other editor bring your bins into the same editing system and assemble the final show by splicing your sequences together into a new sequence.

Here are some useful scenarios for duplicated media and bins:

■ Another editor will cut some of the scenes of a show. You will incorporate those scenes back into your project.

■ Another editor will recut your existing scenes in order to prepare the show for an alternative market (such as cutting out more risqué bits, to make it suitable for younger audiences).

■ A copy of the project and media are being provided to an advertising agency, which will prepare the trailer and commercial promos.

■ The sound editor wants the original audio media and bins.

■ The Visual Effects or Production units need a copy of the work-in-progress edit to verify the material they are creating follows the right angles and eye-lines as the existing scenes.

If the intent is for the work of both editors to be merged into a final sequence, consider using clip colors on the sequences and then clear the bin names to reduce ambiguity as to who cut which sequences.

Advantages of using duplicated media and bins include:

■ Sharing the work means finishing faster.

■ Editors can be in separate locations with no network connectivity between editing systems.

Disadvantages of using duplicated media and bins include:

■ The two copies of the project will be out of sync once editors begin working independently.

■ There needs to be clear rules about who edits what. If both editors cut the same scene, it will be difficult to reintegrate those two scenes into a single one.

■ If footage is added to one project, it won't appear in the other project.

■ Edits operate as isolated islands: Neither editor can see the work of the other editor until footage is merged, which may result in adjacent scenes having a different sense of timing, look, or feel.

The Plan

You'll use the Consolidate tool to duplicate the media that is required for the other editor, and then you'll copy the project files. You could duplicate all of the media, or just the media that's required for the scenes being cut by the other editor.

Duplicating All the Media

To efficiently duplicate all the media, consider using the Media tool. The Media tool can expose all of the master clips associated with the project, making it a convenient and centralized place to begin the consolidation of media onto a drive that'll be taken by the other editor.

Duplicating Only Needed Media

If the other editor is cutting a select number of scenes, and the master clips for those scenes are easily sifted (or, better yet, located in their own bins), select those master clips in their bins and consolidate just that media.

Tip: Be mindful that an editor might find another clip useful, even if it wasn't a clip originally intended for the scene. The other editor might be able to make a clip work by flipping it, or using it as a cut-away to hide another edit. For that reason, if storage space permits you to give the other editor all the media, go for it.

Duplicating the Project

After consolidating the media to duplicate it, you must remember to copy the project. In Lesson 1, "How Workflow Makes, Manages, and Moves Media," you learned about the Avid project folder and where bins are stored. Refer to "Locating the Project Folder" in Lesson 1 for the technique to locate the project folder.

If the media has been consolidated onto an external drive, you would likely place the project files there, too. Placing the project folder on the external drive is only a matter of convenience for the purpose of delivering the project to the other editor. You would not typically store your project and media on the same drive, as the loss of the drive would result in the loss of both media and sequence. Alternatively, you could compress the project into an archive and email it.

You have now duplicated media and bins. Let's see some workflows that extend from having duplicated media and bins.

Using the Duplicated Project

The Consolidate tool was used to duplicate media. The project folder or some bins were copied to another editing system. Now you and another editor are working on duplicates of the same project. You could be in adjacent edit suites of the same broadcast facility, but to make it more interesting, let's imagine that one editor is in Nova Scotia, and the other editor is in Atlanta.

The drive containing the media was sent by FedEx, and the project was zipped and emailed. Tasks that can be performed by you and the other editor include:

- Incorporate the scenes cut in Atlanta into the sequence in Nova Scotia

- Review and critique each other's edits

- Color-correct in Nova Scotia and send the corrected scenes to Atlanta over instant message chat (such as iChat, AOL IM, or Skype)

Each of the previous scenarios relies on the fact that bins are small and contain only metadata, and that clips link to media files. Once you and another editor have the same media files, you can share bins over email or through instant messaging, and the clips and sequences in those bins will link to the media on either editing system.

Caution: These techniques work because both editors have the same media. Once either editor ingests and incorporates new material, the related sections of a timeline will be displayed as *Media Offline* on the other editor's workstation because the other editor is missing the newer media.

Sharing a Sequence with Another Editor

You share a sequence with another editor by placing the sequence in a bin and giving it to the other editor. You do not simultaneously work on the same sequence at the same time.

To share a sequence with another editor, follow these steps:

1. Place the sequence (or a duplicate of it) into an empty bin, and then save the bin using FILE > SAVE BIN. (If you don't use SAVE BIN, the bin file might be empty when you send it.)

2. RIGHT-CLICK the bin in the project window and select REVEAL FILE.

3. RIGHT-CLICK the revealed Avid bin and choose COMPRESS (OS X Lion) or SEND TO > COMPRESSED FOLDER (Windows).

4. Send the compressed file using the electronic method of your choice.

Sharing a Section of Sequences with Another Editor

As opposed to sharing an entire sequence, you may find it preferable to share a portion of a sequence with another editor. You might be sharing a few scenes of a very long documentary. Although sequences don't take up a lot of space, compared to the media files, they still could be a few megabytes and that's significant when sending emails.

To share a section of a sequence:

1. Create a bin. This bin will be sent to the other editor.

2. Load the sequence in the timeline.

3. Mark **in/outs** around the section of interest.

4. Create a sub-sequence, by **Alt**-dragging anywhere in the **Record** monitor to an empty bin. Save the bin using **File > Save Bin.**

   Sub-sequencing a sequence is similar to making a subclip of it. Only the portion from the IN mark to the OUT mark is saved to a bin.

5. Save the bin and compress it for electronic transfer by continuing from Step 2 of the previous section, "Sharing a Sequence with Another Editor."

When the other editor receives the bin, he can unzip it and either copy it into his project folder, or open the bin from the location of his choosing by using **File > Open Bin,** as shown in Figure 4.12.

Figure 4.12

Choosing File > Open Bin allows you to open bins that are not located in the project folder.

Handling the Media Offline Message

Upon receiving the bin, the other editor will open it in Media Composer and load the sequence. When Media Composer opens the sequence, it will read the clips in the sequence and retrieve the media by searching its media database. If it all works, the sequence's media will be online and everything is great. In some scenarios, particularly after media has been further consolidated from other projects, the media might not automatically link.

There are two quick steps you can do to try to get the media to come online, before using the Relink tool, which is covered in Lesson 13, "Mastering the Media." It is preferable to use these steps first because they are quick and can't hurt, unlike the Relink tool, which could, if used incorrectly, change the media associated with a sequence to one of an undesired resolution (codec) or take the media offline.

In the event that the sequence does not link to the media already on the system, you should try the following steps:

1. Choose FILE > REFRESH MEDIA DIRECTORIES.

   Media Composer will compare the contents of the managed media folders with the items in the media databases and fix any inconsistencies. If files have been moved without Media Composer being aware of it, this command will help Media Composer catch the discrepancies and keep the database accurate.

2. Choose FILE > LOAD MEDIA DATABASE.

   Media Composer's databases can be quite large, so to conserve memory (RAM), Media Composer loads portions of the database on-demand. It knows what is "demanded" based on what bins you have opened. You might open a bin with a sequence, but the bins with the master clips are closed, so Media Composer does not have all the database in memory yet. This command tells Media Composer to load the rest of the database, which often causes offline clips to come online, almost magically.

3. Select the sequence in a bin, and then select CLIP > RELINK.

Relinking is covered in Lesson 13.

Shared Media and Bins with Avid Unity

In the previous section, you learned about duplicating media and a project. This allows two editors to work independently on the same material, and then merge the final results by exchanging bins. It's effective when editors are across the country, but it's a lot of effort when the editors are in the same building, or when there are more than two editors involved. It also doesn't scale well: The more editors who are working on a show, the more time spent dealing with synchronizing the media files between editing suites, often by consolidating to external hard drives, walking them to the other suite, and then further copying media. For some facilities, "media monkey" is a full-time job.

The solution is Avid Unity.

Avid Unity centralizes media storage on a server. Instead of a stack of external hard drives in your edit suite, your computer is connected to the server with a fiber channel or Ethernet cable. The server pools together arrays of hard drives to create a massive pool of shared, redundant, scalable storage.

Curious about Avid Unity? Read more about it on Avid's website:
http://www.avid.com/US/products/family/ISIS-Unity.

On the Web **Avid offers numerous technical training and certification courses for Avid**
Unity. Read more about those at http://www.avid.com/training.

Unity Saves the Day at Danish Broadcaster TV2

One of the Unity sites I worked at with Avid is Danish broadcaster TV2. At their Copenhagen 24-hour news centre, they had an Avid Unity with 384 hard drives. Can you imagine 384 hard drives connected to a single edit suite? Their hard drives were pooled together and the media on those drives was available to over 100 devices within their organization, including journalist's desktops, Avid editing suites, and the facility's Avid AirSpeed playout/ingest servers.

The week before Christmas in 2006, I was in the server room at TV2 and one of the Unity hard drives failed. Unity has an application for monitoring the performance and reliability of the components, as shown in Figure 4.13, which is used to notify staff of little problems before they become big problems. One moment all the drives were green, the next, one was flashing red.

We had already begun broadcasting the evening news, and we played the stories directly from Unity to an Avid AirSpeed playout server (a networked VTR). Editors were also cutting stories for the late-night news using footage on Unity. Other than myself, nobody noticed the drive failure. No footage went offline. No angry broadcast facility types came storming in and throwing their stack of papers in the air. Nothing. The drive failure was a secret between Unity and me.

When that drive failed, nobody noticed because Avid Unity had already duplicated the media onto other drives. When the drive failed, Unity simply switched gears and started providing the backup copy. At the same time, it began a process called "redistribution," whereby it was preparing for the unlikely event that another drive would fail before the first drive was replaced with a spare.

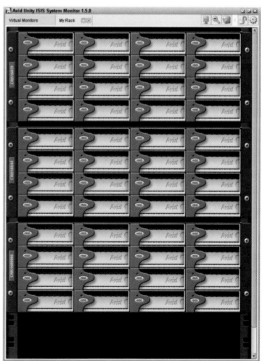

Figure 4.13
96 drives in an Avid Unity ISIS.

The one truth you must know about hard drives is this: Hard drives will fail. They'll all eventually crash. One day a hard disk will begin making a clicking sound. It's called the "click of death." It's not "If my hard drive crashes," it's "When my hard drive crashes." It's not a slight to hard drives, it's that they have moving parts and those parts will wear out.

Note: SSD hard drives are different; they have no spinning disks. Time will tell how they hold up in the long run, but for now they seem quite reliable, although they are more expensive than disk-based drives and therefore tend not to be used for video storage, where you want the most gigabytes for the dollar.

Avid Unity was designed with the knowledge that hard drives fail. It protects media from the eventual failures through a number of techniques, including:

■ Continuously redistributing media over multiple drives to guarantee uptime in the event of a failure

■ Allowing drives to be hot-swapped: Removed and replaced while the system is running

■ Monitoring the health of the drive and reporting this to the site administrator

As you move into cutting features, primetime TV, reality TV, and news, you are more likely to be working with editing systems connected to Unity: An Avid Unity Environment.

Note: There are other shared-storage systems, aside from Avid Unity. Many of them do an admirable job trying to be Avid Unity, but they are not Avid Unity. Media Composer and Unity are made to work together. You might think of it like iPod and iTunes: They are tightly integrated because the iTunes developers and the iPod developers work together, sharing knowledge to ensure an integrated product ecosystem. You could use another MP3 player, but the experience probably won't be as smooth, and when it comes to needing support, good luck—to which company do you turn? The same is true for Media Composer and Unity.

If you've looked at Avid Unity in the past and found it too expensive, check it out again. In 2011, Avid introduced two new models of Unity, including the ISIS 5000, targeting smaller post-production facilities and educational environments.

Avid Unity provides centralized storage, which:

- Is easy to allocate between suites, on an ad-hoc as-needed basis

- Is easy to expand by adding more hard drives to the centralized pool of storage, which then makes it available for all the edit suites

- Saves time because the offline editor, online editor, and sound editors can all access the same footage at the same time

- Opens a significant number of new workflow options

Note: **There are two variations of Avid Unity that you'll likely encounter: Avid Unity MediaNet, now discontinued, and Avid Unity ISIS. From the perspective of an editor, you work on both of them the same way. They differ in how they are implemented by the Avid Certified Support Representative (ACSR), the IT technician trained in supporting Avid solutions at a broadcaster or post-production facility.**

Avid Unity Usage Scenarios

Avid Unity ISIS lets you share bins and projects across the network. When you place your bins and projects on Avid *workspaces* (drive volumes provided by Unity), several users can work on the same project and media at the same time.

For example, you can create sequences in one bin while an assistant recaptures media in another bin. At the same time, the users add audio effects or titles to other bins in the project.

Each editor performs tasks from her own editing system. Media Composer provides a locking mechanism to help you keep track of who is currently working in a bin. The method allows one user to write to a bin; multiple users can read the files in that bin.

Caution: **The lock does not prevent you from deleting the media in a locked bin if you have write access to the workspace. It ensures only that you do not overwrite changes to the bin.**

In an Avid Unity environment, Media Composer creates and stores projects and bins in your Avid projects folder (usually on an internal drive). If you move or save these projects and bins to the workspace, only one editor can change or update the contents of a bin at a time. That doesn't prevent you from opening the clips and playing the clips. You can even cut those clips into a sequence, as long as that sequence is located in a bin that you *can* change.

Unity Rule #1: You can't make changes to a locked bin.

Unity Rule #2: The first person to open a bin wins the right to change/update the contents. The bin will be locked for everyone else.

Unity Rule #3: You forfeit the right to write to a bin when you close the bin. At that point, it's fair game for anyone else to open it and win the right to change/update it.

Sharing Bins and Projects with Avid Unity

Projects, bins, and media are three different kinds of computer files. Projects are actually folders along with a couple files for project settings (containing default sample rate, start timecode, and so on). Bins are saved as .avb files, and media files are .mxf files in a folder on Unity.

The location of the project and bins affects how sharing works in an Avid Unity Environment. This section considers two scenarios—sharing only bins and sharing bins and projects.

Sharing Only Bins

If you share only bins, you store the project on your local system and store bins (.avb files) and media files on the shared workspace. You can have some bins on your local hard drive and some on the Unity workspace. Other Avid Unity users will not see the bins on your internal drive, only those on the workspace.

Media Composer identifies the shared bins in the project window as shown in Figure 4.14. Specifically, Media Composer:

- Stores the bin in a Unity Bins folder in the project window. This folder is similar to the Other Bins folder.

- Displays a second column of information for the bin that identifies the computer that currently has the bin locked.

- Uses bold text to identify bins that are locked by another user.

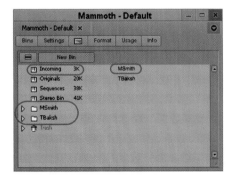

Figure 4.14
Media Composer's project window in an Avid Unity Environment. A bin that is locked for editing (bold text, top left), the name of the computer that currently has the bin locked (top right), and folders for each computer that accesses the project (bottom).

Sharing Bins and Projects

If you share bins and projects, you create and store the project folder and bins on the shared workspace (or copy an existing project, bins, and the related media files). Media Composer identifies information from each suite sharing the workspace as follows:

- Creates a project folder for each computer that accesses the project. Media Composer adds your computer's name to the folder name to create a unique name and stores any project-specific information in the folder. This prevents users from overwriting the project-specific data for other users.

- Displays an extra column in the project window that identifies the computer that has the bin locked, as shown in Figure 4.14.

- Uses bold text to identify bins that are locked by other users.

- Creates a folder at the top level of the shared workspace called Unity *Attic*. This folder contains backup files for each project on the shared volume.

Tip: Depending on the number of users sharing a workspace, you might want to increase the number of files that Media Composer stores in the Unity Attic folder. You do this from the Settings tab of the Project Window > Bin Settings. It is a user setting, so it must be done for each user profile in each suite that is using Media Composer on the same workspace.

Opening a Shared Project

To open an existing project on the shared volume:

1. In the **SELECT PROJECT** dialog box, navigate to the project on Avid shared storage. To do that, click the icon of a folder, which enables you to browse the network and file system.

2. The **PROJECT** window opens.

3. Double-click a bin icon to open one of the bins.

The bin appears with a **BIN LOCK STATUS** button, shown in Figure 4.15. You can click the red (locked) or green (unlocked) **BIN LOCK STATUS** button to view a history file that shows which computers and users have modified the bin and the date and time of the modifications.

When a bin is unlocked, you have permission to make changes. You should not make changes to a locked bin.

Note: The Bin Lock Status button does not appear if the bin is not on genuine Avid shared storage.

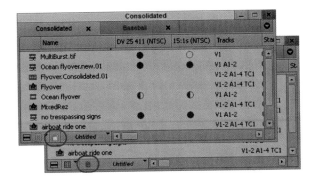

Figure 4.15
The Bin Lock Status button. Green means the bin is unlocked and red means the bin is locked.

Working with Locks and Shared Bins

Media Composer uses a locking mechanism to help you keep track of who is currently working in a shared bin. Only one user can write to the bin, but multiple users can read the files in the bin.

The user who opens the bin first controls the lock and obtains write access to the bin. Bold text in the project window also identifies bins that are locked by another user. When the person who controls the lock closes the bin, it becomes available for another user to open and control the lock.

If one user has the lock and another user has the same bin open, when the first user closes the bin, the second user must close and reopen the bin to control the lock.

You can instruct your Avid editing application to keep a bin locked even after you close it. You can also open a bin without taking control of it.

Opening a Bin Without Changing the Lock

You can open a bin without locking it for other editors. You might know for certain that another editor will be working on a sequence in the bin, and Unity is reporting that the other editor has yet to open the bin. Your interest in the bin is only to read the contents of it.

If you were to open it normally, you would be assigned the lock and only you could modify the bin's contents. To open a bin without changing the lock, you simply Alt/Option-double-click the bin in the project window.

Locking and Unlocking Bins

A bin might contain items that you do not want to be easily changed. Those items may include an opening sequence for a TV show, or reusable items such as your company's logo.

You can lock a bin on Unity, so write privileges are not granted when another editor opens the bin:

1. Select one or more bins in the project window.

2. Right-click the bin icon and select LOCK PROJECT BIN.

An asterisk appears next to the username in the project window. In this case, the bin remains locked even after you close it.

To unlock a bin, you right-click the bin in the project window and select Unlock Project Bin.

Tip: The Lock Project Bin and Unlock Project Bin commands are also available from the Clip menu.

Caution: In the unlikely event that Media Composer crashes while an editor has the lock for one or more bins, the lock might remain until the crashed system is restarted and the bin is opened, then closed to reset the lock. The lock mechanism works in part by placing a lock file (with the .lck extension) in the same folder as the bin. To force a bin to unlock, you can have a Unity Administrator delete that .lck file.

Never delete the .lck file for a bin that is in use by a functioning Media Composer system, as this can lead to bin corruption.

Considerations for Working with Shared Bins and Projects

The following information is provided to improve performance when working with shared bins in an Avid shared storage environment.

■ Do not use the same name for your editing system machine name and your user name. Do not use the same name for security objects such as machine names, user names, group names, and domain names. If any two security objects have the same name, Windows might become confused and sharing might not work properly.

■ Do not use the same prefix for machine names in a shared environment. No full name can be a prefix of another name. If one of the systems has a machine name that is the full name, and others in the environment have the prefix as part of their machine name, problems can occur. For example, if an editing system has a machine name ABC and additional editing systems in the shared environment have machine names ABCnn and ABCxx, the following problems could occur:

- When the system with the machine name ABC is writing to a directory, the systems whose machine names have the same prefix (ABCnn and ABCxx) might not be able to access the directory.

- When the system with the machine name ABC is rendering, systems whose machine names have the same prefix (ABCnn and ABCxx) might be unable to launch.

Caution: Avid recommends that you do not use a common prefix for machine names. If you must use a common prefix, make sure all the names are the same length (ABC01, ABC02, ABC03, and so on).

- Do not use Windows Explorer to examine, copy, or manipulate shared bin files or shared project folders or their contents when you use those files or folders. If you do, when you attempt to access those shared bins or projects you might experience delays accompanied by a progress dialog box that says, "Filesystem busy, retrying (MESSAGE)." If the busy condition persists, a failure message appears. Make sure that you are not using Windows Explorer for the shared bins you are trying to access, and then try the operation again.

- When you have an environment in which more than five users are sharing bins on Avid shared storage, Avid recommends using an Avid Interplay server in the workgroup environment.

- When an Avid Interplay server is available in an Avid workgroup environment, Avid does not recommend sharing bins or projects. Use the Avid Interplay server and the Interplay Window to share media. All editing systems in a workgroup environment that include an Avid Interplay server must have the Avid shared storage client software installed. The Media tool might become unreliable if an editor in the Avid shared storage workgroup environment does not have the Avid shared storage client software installed.

Restrictions and Limitations for Locked Bins

The following restrictions apply to bins that are locked by another user:

- You cannot select a locked bin for operations such as capture, title creation, and import. This helps to minimize the problems of modifying a locked bin.

- You cannot drag an item to a locked bin.

- If you drag an item from a locked bin to a writable bin, the Avid system creates a duplicate (not a copy) of the selection in the writable bin. The original item is not removed from the locked bin. This operation is the equivalent of duplicating a selection and then dragging the duplicate to another bin.

- You cannot move a bin that is locked by another user.

- If you modify a locked bin, your Avid editing application does not let you save the bin to the same name, but it lets you save the bin to another name.

However, this causes duplicate bin IDs and might cause system-level conflicts with the contents of the two bins. Your Avid editing application sees the duplicate contents of these bins and resolves the conflicts by newest modifications. Avoid creating duplicate bins when you modify a locked bin. If you do create a duplicate bin, you should manually merge the changes into the original bin and delete the duplicate bin.

Caution: **The lock does not prevent you from deleting the media in a locked bin if you have write access to the workspace. It ensures only that you don't overwrite changes to the bin.**

Limitation When Using the Shared Bin Lock Icon

Occasionally, when two editors attempt to open a shared bin at the same time, both editors get the green lock icon. However, only one editor really has the lock, and that editor's machine name appears beside the bin name in both project windows.

Both editors can modify their copies of the bin, but only the editor who controls the lock, as indicated in the project window, can save that bin. The other editor is warned that the bin is locked but is allowed to save a copy of the changed bin.

Avid recommends that you use the Save Bin Copy As button and continue working.

Review/Discussion Questions

1. What's the difference between markers and comments with regard to how they function in a bin? (See "Comments versus Markers" on page 173.)

2. What's the difference between markers and comments with regard to how they function in Media Composer's Timeline window? (See "Comments versus Markers" on page 173.)

3. How can markers be used to collaborate with other editors cutting the same sequence? (See "Comments versus Markers" on page 173.)

4. Why are clip comments not the preferable technique to communicate with a Pro Tools editor, in contrast to using markers? (See "Comments versus Markers" on page 173.)

5. How do you assign one of the 16 color swatches to a clip? How do you assign one of the 16.7 million colors to a clip? (See "Assigning Clip Colors in Bins" on page 174.)

6. Why might you want the timeline to visually indicate the clips that do not match the project format? (See "Displaying Clip Colors in the Timeline" on page 176.)

7. How does Local Color differ from Source Color? (See "Assigning Clip Colors in Bins" on page 174.)

8. Give one or two scenarios where you might choose to use Local Clip Color. (See "Local Clip Colors Are Assigned to Clips in the Sequence" on page 178.)

9. You and another editor are sharing the job of editing a large documentary. All the media is on your system, along with the master clips. You are on the West Coast; the other editor is on the East Coast. The final show will be output from your system. What workflow do you propose? How will you review the other editor's edits as she completes scenes? How will she incorporate your work into her sequences for scene-to-scene consistency? (See "Duplicating Media and Bins" on page 180.)

10. What are some differences between local storage (external media drives) and Avid Unity storage? (See "Avid Unity Usage Scenarios" on page 187.)

11. How do you share a portion of a sequence with another editor, after providing that editor with a duplicate of your media? (See "Sharing a Section of Sequences with Another Editor" on page 183.)

12. After another editor sends you a sequence, you open the sequence but the media is reported as being offline. You are certain you have the media. What two things might you try prior to choosing Clip > Relink? (See "Handling the Media Offline Message" on page 183.)

13. How does the project window change when you are working from a project stored on Avid Unity? (See "Sharing Bins and Projects with Avid Unity" on page 188.)

14. You need to use some clips in a Unity shared bin, but you do not want to lock the bin because you know another editor will be cutting a sequence in that bin. How should you approach the situation? (See "Opening a Bin Without Changing the Lock" on page 180).

15. You are cutting a reality TV series with seven additional editors. You each cut a portion of a show, frequently including flashback material from previous episodes. How would your workflows be different if your team used separate, local storage in contrast to if your team used an Avid Unity ISIS? (See "Avid Unity Usage Scenarios" on page 187.)

Using Markers and Comments

In these exercises, you will practice adding markers and comments to sequences in order to practice the collaborative techniques presented in this lesson.

Media Used:
Agent MXZero

Duration:
20 minutes

Exercise 4.1: Adding Markers

The Markers tool can be used as a task list, allowing you to easily jump to different markers, toggle their colors, and assign tasks to other editors. You can also configure the Markers tool to display thumbnail images.

1. Open the **AGENT MXZERO PROJECT > 201 > LESSON 4 > MARKERS AND COMMENTS** bin.

2. Open the **THURSDAY EDIT FROM WEST COAST** sequence.

    This is a sequence sent from another editor. Initially, the media may not be online. Continue with the exercise anyway.

3. Open the **MARKERS** tool (choose **TOOLS > MARKERS**).

    A list of the markers appears in the window, similar to Figure EX4.1.

#		Name	TC	Track	Comment
0001	◊	Woody v6	01:15:15:10	TC1	Commercial Break expected here
0002	◊	Woody v6	01:13:41:14	V1	Shot requires colour correction: Too much magent.
0003	◊	Woody v6	01:14:35:14	A2	Dinner Bell sound effect

Figure EX4.1
The Markers tool showing a list of markers.

4. Enable the image display by using **SHOW IMAGES** from the **FAST MENU** of the **MARKERS** tool, as shown in Figure EX4.2.

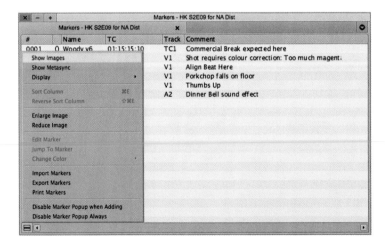

Figure EX4.2
Enable the marker images.

5. Double-click any marker. The timeline's **POSITION INDICATOR** jumps to the marker, and the marker is displayed in the **RECORD** monitor.

6. Edit the marker by clicking the colored dot in the **RECORD** monitor. The **MARKER** window appears, as shown in Figure EX4.3.

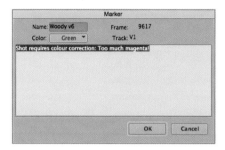

Figure EX4.3
The Marker window.

7. Change the name assigned to this marker from **WOODY V6** to *YOUR NAME*.

Exercise 4.2: Adding Timeline Comments

You can also add comments to individual clips. You do that from the bin containing the source clips, but you can also do it to clips already in a sequence on the timeline.

1. Open the **AGENT MXZERO PROJECT > 201 > LESSON 4 > MARKERS AND COMMENTS** bin.

2. Open the **THURSDAY EDIT FROM WEST COAST** sequence.

3. Position the **CURRENT TIME INDICATOR** (blue line) in the middle of any clip in the timeline.

   Comments are added to the clip under the **CURRENT TIME INDICATOR** for the top-most track.

4. Enable **V1**; disable all other video tracks.

5. From the **CLIP NAME MENU** located in the top-right of the **RECORD** monitor, select **ADD COMMENTS**, as shown in Figure EX4.4.

6. Add a comment, such as "**MUST GET AUTHORIZATION FOR THIS CLIP.**"

7. Click **OK**.

   Do you see your comment on the clip on the timeline? Do you see any indication in Media Composer that the clip has a comment? You don't.

   Media Composer doesn't give you any heads-up that there are comments associated with clips.

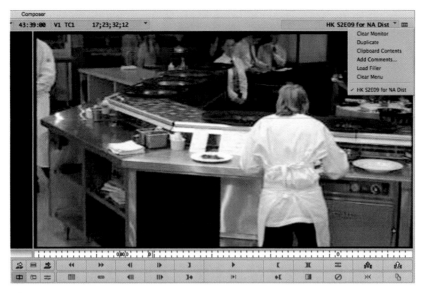

Figure EX4.4
Add comments to a clip using the Clip Name menu above the Record monitor.

8. Select the timeline's **FAST MENU** (lower-right corner), and then choose **CLIP TEXT > COMMENTS**, as shown in Figure EX4.5.

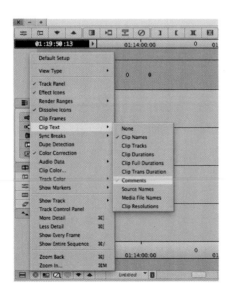

Figure EX4.5
Configure the timeline to show comments.

The timeline should now display comments. You may need to enlarge your track height to make room for the additional text.

In the Avid Learning Series Track enlarging is covered in *Media Composer 6: Part 1—Editing Essentials*, part of this Avid Learning Series, and is covered in MC101 at Avid Learning Partners. There are a few methods covered in that course, one of which is to select Edit > Enlarge Track while the timeline is active.

Exercise 4.3: Adding Bin Comments

The Comments column is always visible from Script view, but it is not available from Text view unless you manually add it, which is the objective of this exercise.

1. Open the **AGENT MXZERO PROJECT > 201 > LESSON 4 > MARKERS AND COMMENTS** bin.

2. Switch to **SCRIPT** view using the **BIN VIEW** menu, as shown in Figure EX4.6.

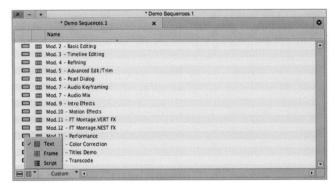

Figure EX4.6
The Bin View menu allows switching between the Frame, Text, and Script views.

3. Enter some comments of your choosing into the Comments boxes, as shown in Figure EX4.7.

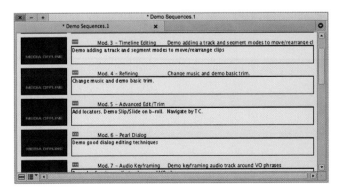

Figure EX4.7
Comments are always visible from Script view.

4. Switch from **SCRIPT** view to **TEXT** view.

5. Click the bin's **Fast menu**. Choose **Columns** and look for a **Comments** column, as shown in Figure EX4.8. You should not see one.

Note: If the column is there, select it and stop the exercise. It has been added since the publication of this book.

6. Cancel the **Show/Hide Columns** window and change the **Bin view** to **Custom**, as shown in Figure EX4.9.

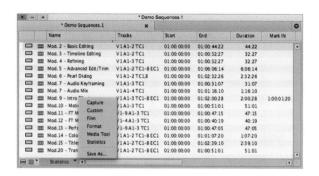

Figure EX4.8
Note that Bin > Fast Menu > Choose Columns is missing the Comments column.

Figure EX4.9
Bin views have preset sets of columns, including Custom, which only has name and clip color.

7. Click to the right of the **Name** column and enter **Comments**.

   Media Composer should update the bin, adding the **Comments** column and populating the new column with the text that you added in Script view, as shown in Figure EX4.10.

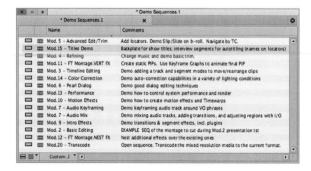

Figure EX4.10
Voilà! Media Composer shows comments in a bin's Text view.

You've now had some practice using some collaborative techniques with Media Composer. In the next lesson, you'll learn how to use the multicam features of Media Composer.

Multicamera Editing

This lesson explains the Multicamera editing feature of Media Composer and how you can use it to quickly edit scenes simultaneously recorded with two or more cameras.

Media Used: Picture and Sound

Duration: 60 minutes

GOALS

- Provide advice to a production on planning for multicamera editing
- Learn the technique and synchronization options for creating group clips
- Differentiate between group and multigroup clips
- Prepare Media Composer for multicamera editing
- Manage MultiCamera mode when editing with three or more camera sources
- Edit a multicamera sequence

Preparing the Production Team

Your production team shoots the footage that you'll edit. If you intend to edit using the MultiCamera feature, you should meet with your production's technical producer (or camera operators) to ensure footage is shot in a way that's optimal for multicamera editing. But what would you ask them to do? What tips might you give? That's the topic of this section, along with a refresher on the multicamera editing workflow.

Multicamera Editing Speeds Production

When a performance is recorded, the production team will obtain multiple angles and takes in order to provide you, the editor, with the raw material from which you select the best performances and create the best story. A production with a single camera will obtain the multiple angles and compositions (such as close-up and wide shots) by having the performers repeat the scene after repositioning the camera. The actors must be consistent in their performances, otherwise continuity discrepancies will hinder your ability to cut between the various takes.

A production will often use a single camera because of budgetary constraints: One camera is often half the price of having two cameras. Having two cameras, however, means it takes half as much time to record the takes because one camera can focus on the main character with a close-up, while the other camera remains in a wide shot. Considering that a production might be renting a soundstage and have a crew of 20 or more people on set, the use of a second camera can offset its cost by shortening production, which reduces wages and facility rental expenses.

A third camera scales nicely to allow a close-up of two people in a dialogue, plus a wide shot to establish their position on the set. Many primetime television sitcoms use a three-camera setup, which is shown in Figure 5.1.

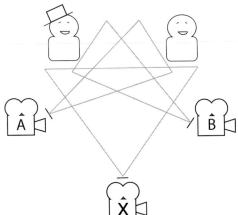

Figure 5.1
Three Camera Setup: Cameras A + B are medium shots, camera X is wide.

Soap operas must produce a significant amount of footage each day and the use of multiple cameras can allow a good performance by the actors sent for editing without requiring further takes. With three cameras, the editor has a shooting ratio of 3:1 and enough material to focus the attention of the audience through the choice of angles.

Shooting a Barbara Walters– or Oprah Winfrey–style interview is practically impossible without at least two cameras: You'd never expect them to run through the interview with the camera facing the respondent, and then run through it again after resetting the camera and positioning it at the interviewer.

Lastly, music videos, sporting events, and concert performances may use 8, 10, or even 20 cameras. A complex concert might have cameras on each performer— three wide shots of the band (from the left, center, and right angles) and multiple cameras recording the audience. Audience camera operators scour the fans looking for those golden moments where a fan is gleefully singing along.

After the recording has completed, the footage is ingested just like any other footage is ingested. Whether it be using Avid Media Access (AMA) or the Capture tool, the footage needs to be in an Avid bin.

Typically, the clips are labeled to identify the scene, take, and the camera angle. For example, "31-8-A" means "Scene 31, Take 8, Camera A." (Someone must have had the giggles on set; that's a lot of takes.)

The Multicamera Experience

Avid's multicamera editing allows you to view and cut among clips presenting different camera angles of a single scene or event, while keeping all of these matching clips synchronized. The ability to maintain synchronization throughout the process saves countless hours compared with loading and matching shots individually.

When you edit using the MultiCamera feature of Avid Media Composer, you collect clips associated with a particular scene into a *grouped* clip. A grouped clip is like an envelope that contains the original related clips. When you put that one grouped clip onto the timeline, you'll have access to the clips it contains. This is a more efficient approach than creating a video track for each angle and trimming the clips on each layer to control which angle is visible, which is how you would edit in the absence of the MultiCamera feature.

Note: If you've ever used a DVD with the "angle" feature, you're already familiar with the approach to multicamera editing in Media Composer. There is a single clip (like a single DVD) and once you play it, you can alternate between the different included angles.

Synchronization Options

When you create a group clip, Media Composer will need to synchronize the individual clips with each other: As you cut from camera A to camera B, you want to see the same moment in camera B's media as you saw on camera A, not a few seconds earlier or later, because that would create sync and continuity errors.

Timecode Sync Overview

A quick and accurate way to synchronize clips is to have all cameras using the same timecode. Media Composer will compare the timecodes and synchronize the clips when you create a group clip.

Figure 5.2 illustrates two clips using common timecode.

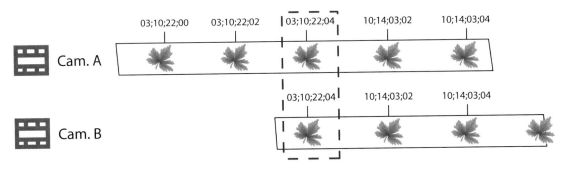

Figure 5.2
Two clips with synchronized timecode.

Camera A was recorded first and Camera B was recorded slightly later, so clip A has a bit more footage at the head. Both clips have common timecode, so Media Composer will align the two clips using that timecode and place them into the grouped clip.

Establishing that sync point is easier when your camera crew follows a few guidelines.

Timecode Sync Guidelines for Camera Crew

Timecode sync requires that the clocks on each camera be synchronized, something like how secret agents synchronize their watches at the beginning of a mission. For that to happen, the cameras have to support an external timecode connector (often labeled "EXT. TC"), which is usually implemented on the camera as a BNC spigot found on prosumer and higher-end cameras. You would not find EXT. TC connectors on cameras purchased at a consumer electronics shop, but you would from many Sony or Panasonic professional resellers.

For cameras that support external timecode, you synchronize their clocks using a method along the lines of the following, being mindful that the specifics might vary by camera model:

1. Choose one camera as the "master" camera.

   The master camera is the authoritative camera. Its clock gives its timecode to the other cameras. The other cameras are referred as "slave" cameras.

2. Use the menu of the master camera to set the timecode generator (TCG) to internal timecode (sometimes written as "INT. TC").

   The timecode generator is the camera's private clock for timecode and is unrelated to the time-of-day clock in the camera. Setting the timecode generator to internal timecode instructs the generator to create its own timecode instead of using an externally generated timecode.

3. Connect a BNC cable from "EXT. TC OUT" of the master camera to "EXT. TC IN" of a slave camera.

   The step in which cameras are connected is sometimes called "jamming the cameras."

   This camera will not generate its own timecode, but instead will synchronize its timecode generator with the timecode coming in on the EXT. TC IN connector.

4. Use the menu of the slave camera to set its timecode generator to use "EXT. TC."

5. Confirm that both cameras now display the same timecode.

   You only need to jam the cameras for a few seconds, just long enough for the slave camera to read the timecode being sent from the timecode generator of the master camera. After that, the cable can be disconnected.

6. Disconnect the BNC cable and repeat from Step 3 for each slave camera.

For the price that might be paid for one camera with external timecode capabilities, you can often buy two or more cameras without them. Productions operating on a constrained budget—in particular independent music videos—will often shoot with multiple cameras, but without jammed timecode.

That's no problem, it's just a slightly modified workflow with one extra step and it's explained in the next section.

Visual or Audio-Based Sync Overview

Timecode syncing works well because timecode allows Media Composer to iden-tify identical instants of time in different clips. Even if your cameras don't have the ability to be synchronized using external timecode, as long as you can identify the instant in different clips, you'll still be able to create a grouped clip.

For Media Composer to use that kind of clip, you need to open each source clip, find a frame that they each have in common, and place a mark IN on that frame. The mark IN will be used when you create a group clip, after which it can be removed. It's not used for editing, only for synchronizing. It doesn't matter if the IN is toward the beginning, middle, or end of the clip, just as long as it identifies a moment in time that's common among all clips, as shown in Figure 5.3.

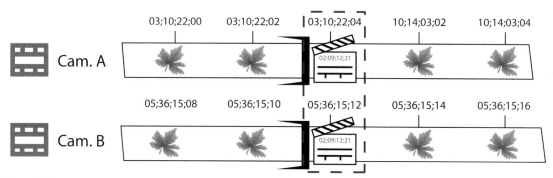

Figure 5.3
Multiple clips that contain the same unique frame can be synchronized by placing an IN mark on the common frame, such as a frame in which a slate slaps closed.

Tips for finding common frames:

- A camera flash. Camera flashes are quick but bright and therefore notice-able.

- A performer's arm movement. If a rock star throws his hand in the air, it's easy to find and mark an IN.

- A drum beat. If all cameras are recording audio, you can find the same drum beat, word, cymbal crash, or any other audio cue.

- A clapper or slate. This is explained in the next section.

Visual or Audio-Based Sync Guidelines for Camera Crew

One of the best tips you can give your camera crew, when using cameras that do not have timecode sync, is this:

1. Use a slate.

   It doesn't have to be a Hollywood slate; it can be two pieces of 2×4" lumber that are clapped together, or even just someone's hands clapping.

2. Have all cameras focus on the slate (or impromptu clapper).

3. Clap the slate, or pieces of wood, or whatever you have.

The clap action creates a visual and audible reference that you can locate in each of your source clips. When you capture the footage from those cameras, you'll place an IN mark at the clap, and Media Composer will use that IN mark to synchronize the content of the various cameras.

Final Tips for Camera Crews (Regardless of Sync Method)

Between the recordings of takes, there are often short gaps and camera operators may instinctively pause the recording to save storage space. When the cameras are paused and resumed, gaps in the recording are created, which means footage after that point will not be synchronized in the group clip. To work with clips recorded with pauses, you need to subclip and individually group the subclips into a new group clip.

One way to avoid the problem of gaps in the recording is to have the camera operators not stop recording. If they do stop recording, ask that they reestablish a sync point for you by rerecording the clap of the slate.

Finally, many cameras can be set to record in one of two modes: Free Run or Record Run. The setting controls whether or not the clock stops when the recording stops. Free Run sets the camera to continuously roll the clock (increment the timecode), even when the camera is paused. Record Run means the timecode incrementing when the recording stops. You may want to advise your camera operators to set their cameras to Free Run, so even if they do pause the recording (or change tapes), the clock will continue to increment and all cameras will maintain timecode sync. This means your camera operators can pause the recording and when they resume, the timecode will continue to be consistent across all recordings.

Avid's Multicamera Editing Workflows

You use multicamera editing to complete your rough-cut in less time with fewer sync and continuity errors than you would have if you created the rough-cut using traditional methods. After the rough-cut has been created, you deactivate MultiCamera mode and refine your edit using the full suite of trim functions available in Media Composer.

The steps of the multicamera workflow are:

1. Create a group clip, syncing the camera angles based on timecode, IN point, or INK number. (INK is used instead of timecode with some film formats.)

2. Load the group clip into the SOURCE monitor, and splice the entire group into a sequence.

3. Enter MULTICAMERA mode, which gives you a QUAD (OR NINE) SPLIT display, so you can view multiple camera angles.

4. Play back the material, and cut on-the-fly by using the MULTICAMERA keys to select different camera angles.

   The camera angles you select with the MULTICAMERA keys are recorded as cuts in the timeline and are displayed in the Record monitor.

5. Use the arrow keys to select edit points and switch to different angles throughout the master scene in the sequence.

6. Leave MULTICAMERA mode to trim and make additional adjustments.

The details of those steps are discussed in the following sections.

Creating Group Clips

Grouping creates a separate group clip out of a single set of master clips, from the start (or IN) point to the end (or OUT) point of the longest clip. The Group function allows you to sync clips based on common source timecode, auxiliary timecode, or marks placed in the footage.

Note: You can create grouped clips using captured or AMA-linked clips. Previous releases of Media Composer did not allow AMA clips to be used when creating a group clip, but that limitation no longer exists. If you find that performance of MultiCamera mode is poor, however, you may find an improvement in performance by consolidating or transcoding the clips onto your managed media drives.

To create a group clip:

1. If you are using an IN or OUT mark for the sync point, load the clips and mark an IN point at the sync point at the start of each clip, or mark an OUT point at the sync point at the end of each clip.

   Ideally, during production, a slate was recorded at the head (or tail) of each tape, which you use for marking IN (or OUT) points. (At the shoot, all cameras record a common slate at the beginning of each tape.)

If the shoot didn't use a slate, use any single, discrete visual or aural event recorded by all cameras simultaneously. For example, if six cameras tape a concert, you can use a distinct sound to mark the IN point.

2. In the bin, select the clips you want to group together, as shown in Figure 5.4.

Name	Camera1	Start	Drive	Video	Offline
▭ 0209A02 DIN SVC RED.new.01	A	17;50;24;00	MediaDrive E – HK	15:1s (NTSC)	
▭ 0209B02 DIN SVC RED.new.01	B	17;50;24;00	MediaDrive E – HK	15:1s (NTSC)	
▭ 0209C02 DINNER SERVICE BLUE.new.01	C	17;50;24;00	MediaDrive E – HK	15:1s (NTSC)	
▭ 0209D09 DIN SVC SABRINA SERVES.new.01	D	17;50;24;00	MediaDrive E – HK	15:1s (NTSC)	
▭ 0209E02 DIN SVC BLUE.new.01	E	17;50;24;01	MediaDrive E – HK	15:1s (NTSC)	
▭ 0209F08 DINNER SERVICE.new.01	F	17;50;24;00	MediaDrive E – HK	15:1s (NTSC)	
▭ 0209J02 DIN SVC RED.new.01	J	17;50;24;00	MediaDrive E – HK	15:1s (NTSC)	
▭ 0209T11 DIN SVC RED.new.01	T	17;50;24;00	MediaDrive E – HK	15:1s (NTSC)	
▭ 0209U02 DIN SVC RED.new.01	U	17;50;24;00	MediaDrive E – HK	15:1s (NTSC)	
▭ 0209V12 DINNER SVC RED.new.01	V	17;50;24;00	MediaDrive E – HK	15:1s (NTSC)	
▭ 0209W11 DINNER SERVICE.new.01	W	17;50;23;29	MediaDrive E – HK	15:1s (NTSC)	
▭ 0209X10 BLUE KITCHEN DINNER SERVCE.new.01	X	17;50;24;00	MediaDrive E – HK	15:1s (NTSC)	
▭ 0209Y12 DIN SVC BLUE.new.01	Y	17;50;24;00	MediaDrive E – HK	15:1s (NTSC)	
▭ 0209Z12 DIN SVC BOTH.new.01	Z	17;50;24;00	MediaDrive E – HK	15:1s (NTSC)	

Figure 5.4
All of these clips are from separate cameras that recorded the scene simultaneously.

Note: A grouped clip in Media Composer can contain over 400 clips, of which up to nine will be displayed at a time when in MultiCamera mode, and you can then swap the bank of nine cameras that are displayed at a time. This allows you an almost limitless number of cameras in Media Composer's MultiCamera mode.

3. (Optional) Sort the clips.

The order of clips in the bin determines the order in which the clips are displayed when grouped together and displayed in the Source monitor. Thus it is a good idea to develop a good, consistent clip-naming scheme.

4. Choose **BIN > GROUP CLIPS**, or press **SHIFT+CTRL/CMD+G**.

5. The **GROUP CLIPS** dialog box appears, as shown in Figure 5.5.

Figure 5.5
The Group Clips dialog box.

6. Select an option, based on the following:

- *IN points or OUT points*—To sync according to IN or OUT points set in each clip.
- *Source Timecode*—To sync based on matching timecode.
- *Auxiliary TC1–TC5*—To sync based on Auxiliary TC.
- *Film TC/Sound TC, INK Number, or Auxiliary Ink*—These three options apply only to 24p and 25p projects. With *Film TC/Sound TC*, sync is based on matching film and sound timecode recorded in the field.

NOTE: Source Timecode and Auxiliary options require that the clips must have matching timecode in the same column.

7. Click **OK**.

A group clip appears in the bin, with the name of the first clip in the group, followed by the file name extension Grp.n, as shown in Figure 5.6.

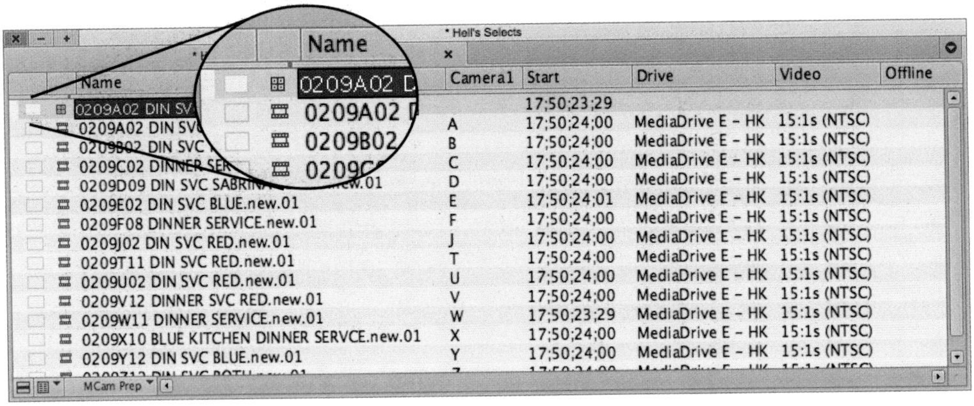

Figure 5.6
Group clip in a bin.

8. (Optional) Rename the group clip.

Creating Multigroup Clips

Multigrouping is used in large multicamera productions, such as situation comedies, in which all synchronous camera shots are recorded sequentially with the same timecode.

Multigrouping takes the Group function one step further, literally stringing numerous sequential groups into a rough sequence. For this reason, multigroups are also known as *sequence clips*.

For example, let's say you're about to cut a four-camera sitcom project, represented by the clips in Table 5-1. The cameras are named A, B, C, and X, which is a traditional camera naming scheme.

For example, Scene 5 in Table 5-1 consists of four takes. Multigrouping strings these takes together into a sequence. You can edit one take as you would any group clip, and you also have easy access to all of the scene's footage.

Table 5-1   Scene 5 Breakdown

Scene/Take	Cameras	Start Timecode	Comments
5/1	ABCX	1:00:00:00	Entire scene
5/2	ABCX	1:04:00:00	Entire scene, second time
5/3	ABCX	1:10:00:00	Entire scene, second half only
5/4	AX	3:00:00:00	Needed to retake part of the scene at the end of the day, but needed only two cameras

You can also use multigrouping in other situations. For example, let's say six cameras are used in a music concert, and each shooter is independent of the others, stopping and starting the camera at will. The camera's timecode generators are using Free Run mode and all cameras have been jammed for timecode synchronization at the beginning of the day, as described in "Timecode Sync Guidelines for Camera Crew" on page 204.)

To use multigrouping to piece together the shots:

1. (Optional) Sort the clips by name in the bin.

2. Select all of the clips you want to combine in the multigroup.

3. Choose BIN > MULTIGROUP.

4. Select an option in the SYNC SELECTION dialog box.

5. Click OK.

Media Composer creates a group clip for each take in the bin, and then creates a multigroup clip by stringing together these group clips. The multigroup clip has the same icon as the group clips, but the icon is preceded by a tiny plus sign as shown in Figure 5.7.

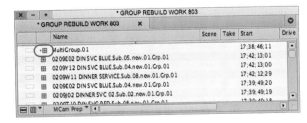

Figure 5.7
Multigroup clips are differentiated from a group clip by the presence of a plus symbol.

Exploring Additional Grouping Methods

In this section, several methods to create matched clips in preparation for multicam editing are presented. This assumes that your source material was not optimally prepared for multicam editing and/or that time is an important factor.

Fast Workflow for Footage Synced with Slave Timecode from Tape

Scenario: The material was shot on tape with slave timecode, but during capture, the entire clip from slate to the end of the take is not captured, but simply from start to end of the action. This might be done, for example, if the camera ran for minutes after the slate and before action began. There was no need seen to capture all of the "dead time." Thus, you have no slates.

1. Give each bin into which you will capture clips the name you gave the physical tape.

   Tape names should match everywhere—on the physical tape, the tape name in the Capture tool, and bin name.

   In these scenarios, assume a tape naming convention where several cameras are recorded for each tape—for a six-camera shoot you might have Tape 1/Camera A = 001A, Tape 1/Camera B= 001B... Tape 1/Camera F= 001F. Then Tape 2/Camera A = 002A, and so on.

   If your tape-naming scheme simply uses numeric increments—001, 002, and so on—follow this naming convention.

2. Capture each complete action for each take, with handle, on tape 001A.

3. If speed is of the essence, don't take the time to name the clips. Each clip will be named the bin name (which is also the tape name) followed by a number, such as 001A 01, 001A 02, and so on.

4. To facilitate sorting later, add a one-character prefix to each clip name. For this first tape (and bin), add an A to the beginning of each clip.

After capturing Tape 001A, you obtain the clips for the other cameras by exporting an Avid Log Exchange (ALE) file. This process unlinks the media and creates new clips upon import, which you can then use to recapture the same content from the other camera's tapes.

The next steps take you through the process of exporting to ALE:

1. Display the following headings in the tape bin and save this bin view as **ALE**:

    Start

    End

    Tracks

    Tape

2. Select all clips in the bin.

3. Choose **FILE > EXPORT**.

4. Open the **EXPORT** settings, and choose **AVID LOG EXCHANGE** from the pop-up menu, as shown in Figure 5.8.

Figure 5.8
Exporting an Avid log exchange (ALE) file.

5. Click **SAVE AS** and name the export setting **ALE EXPORT**.

6. Save the exported file to your drive and close the bin.

7. Create a new bin, called **001B**, or whatever the tape name is.

8. Select the **ALE** bin view.

9. Choose **FILE > IMPORT**.

10. Select the **ALE** file you just created and press **OK** to import the file and create new clips.

    Notice that the **NAME, START, END, TRACKS**, and **TAPE** column data has not changed.

11. Manually change the first character of each clip in the 001B bin from A to B. This will facilitate sorting and sifting.

12. Change the tape name to match the **TAPE 001B** clips.

13. Use **CLIP > MODIFY** to the **SET SOURCE** option to give these clips the tape ID 001B.

14. Repeat this process for the rest of the tape 1 cameras, as well as the remaining tapes.

Note: When you import an ALE, the project association of the clips is set to the current project. This can be desirable in some scenarios and undesirable in others. It can have a huge impact on media management in scenarios where you have a lot of projects, and where the project name is the main criterion for sorting or sifting.

Fast Workflow for Footage Synced Without Slave Timecode

Scenario: You're working on a reality show or low-budget documentary. Several cameras were used in the shoot, and no slave timecode was recorded.

In this scenario, the production used dual-system audio (audio recorded separately on a digital audio recording device). If you're lucky, the cameras will also have recorded sync audio.

How do you prepare to group clips? Use a method sometimes referred to as "sync-stacking."

To use sync-stacking:

1. You'll be loading different tapes on different video tracks, and you'll want to switch easily between monitoring multiple video tracks.

2. Load the audio, recorded separately, for tape 001 into the timeline on tracks A1 and A2.

3. Display waveforms so you can match the audio tracks from multiple cameras as well as the separate recording device.

4. Load the video and audio for Tape 001, Camera A into the Source monitor and edit it into the sequence on tracks V1, A1, and A2. (If audio was also recorded separately, edit that audio onto two audio tracks.)

5. Use **LIFT/OVERWRITE** segment mode editing to line up the tracks, using the waveforms as a guide.

   If you have standard dual-system audio—the picture has no associated audio as part of the same clip, and audio recorded separately without video—use Sync Point Editing (SPE).

6. Repeat for additional Tape 1 Camera B, C, and so on, stacking each camera on a higher video track, and always syncing to the video on track V1.

You'll probably have one track of video and two tracks of audio for each tape. In that case, edit the three tracks onto incrementally higher tracks (first: V1, A1, and A2, second: V2, A3, and A4, and so on).

7. Repeat this procedure for Tape 2, 3, and so on.

8. Use Match Frame from a sync point in the timeline to locate a common Mark IN on the master clips in the Source monitor.

9. Create a group clip as normal. Each master clip now has an IN mark that can be used as a reference for syncing.

Real-World Story of Network TV Documentary Edit

Productions record audio both on dual system (using digital disc recorders, solid state chip recorders, and DAT) and for each camera. I've worked on numerous shows where that was done. Sometimes the sound recordist sends a reference or confidence mix back to the cameras.

I recently worked on a pilot where we shot multicam, using up to four cameras. Sometimes we had six talent, all individually miked with wireless lavs. The recording engineer used a state-of-the-art box called the Cantar, by Aaton, a combined digital disc recorder/mixer. He recorded all six lavs isolated as well as creating a stereo mix of those six tracks—so we were dealing with eight tracks altogether, with timecode smart slated. The cameras ran "free run" time of day; we only had approximate sync, not slave code. The engineer sent wireless reference audio—the stereo mix—back to the cameras.

When I brought in the video for the edit, due to technical difficulties beyond our control, I lost all the original timecode. My solution was to build sync stacks and the waveforms were very helpful in lining things up. So, sometimes I would have the eight tracks from the digital recorder and maybe six more tracks (three cameras/stereo reference audio), with the fourth camera MOS locked off a lipstick camera.

Grouping Together Fewer Than Ten Clips

Scenario: You just have a few clips to group together. Here's another way to create the matched clips, prior to grouping.

Tip: **If you're not comfortable unlinking clips from their media, do not use this method. Instead, export an ALE.**

1. Duplicate clip 1 by pressing **Ctrl/Cmd+D**.

2. To unlink the duplicate clip:

   a) Select the clip in the bin.

   b) Press the **Ctrl/Cmd+Shift** keys and choose **Clip > Unlink Bin Selection**.

   The **Relink** command has changed to **Unlink** because of the key press, and the clip is unlinked from the media.

3. Use **Clip > Modify**, and the **Set Source** option to give these clips the Tape ID 001B.

4. Repeat Steps 1–3 for all clips to be grouped.

5. Capture the media for all clips.

Ganging Footage in Monitors

Scenario: You don't want to take the time to group clips, or you just need to review one or two alternate camera angles next to a shot in the sequence. Instead, you'll use ganging to sync multiple cameras with pop-up monitors.

The Gang function locks monitors in sync so that you can move through footage in two or more monitors simultaneously.

Gangs

Gang simply means that when one item is moved, another item is moved. In this case, when the Current Time indicator of one monitor is moved, the other one is moved too. The icon shows two control knobs with a rubber band between them, indicating one will cause the other to move.

The same word is used for street gangs: When the leader of the gang moves, the other members move too.

In addition, you can use ganging as an alternative to MultiCamera mode to have your group clip stay in sync with the sequence.

Finally, it's a way to match two sequences when you need to check shots from one cut to another.

To gang the Source and Record monitors:

1. Load several clips and sequences into their own pop-up monitors by
   Alt/Opt+double-clicking one of the selected items. You can also load a
   clip into the Source monitor, and a sequence into the Record monitor.

2. Place the position indicators so that they are in sync.

3. Click the **Gang** button for each monitor that you want to synchronize, as
   shown in Figure 5.9.

4. When you select the Source monitor **Gang** button, the Record monitor
   Gang button automatically becomes active.

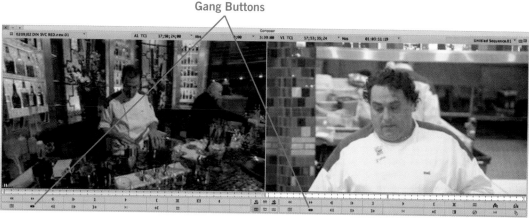

Figure 5.9
Gang buttons are located in each monitor; a green status indicator appears below the Source and Record
monitors when Gang is enabled.

5. As you move through footage in one monitor, the footage in all other
   monitors freezes. The footage is updated when the play stops. Simultaneous
   full-motion playback is not possible, although sync is maintained at all
   times.

EXERCISE   *Take a moment to complete Exercise 5, Part 1.*

Setting Up Multicamera Editing

You learned to prepare group clips in the previous sections. In this section, you
reap the benefits of group clips by using them for multicamera editing. This is
where the fun begins. You edit a group clip into the timeline, enable MultiCamera
mode, and play back as you cut between cameras in real-time.

Note: The process from this point forward will somewhat resemble a live master control room, into which multiple *iso*lated camera feeds (ISO cams) are sent. There is a person whose job role is "switcher" and a director who watches all the feeds and calls the shots by using terminology such as "Ready 2. 2!" That means "Prepare to switch to ISO Camera 2" and the second "2" means "Go!"

Although there are multiple isolated cameras feeding into the switcher, only one video is coming out at a time. That output is called the "linecut."

Editing the Group Clip into the Timeline

After you create a group or multigroup clip, you need to put it into the timeline. Treat it like any other clip because there is nothing special about putting a group clip into the timeline.

The timeline adds a unique identifier to indicate the presence of a group—the first clip's name (as selected in the bin), followed by the letter G, as shown in Figure 5.10.

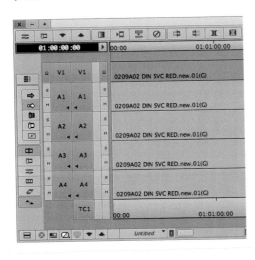

Figure 5.10
Group clip in a sequence, indicated by the (G).

Activating MultiCamera Mode

MultiCamera mode gangs all clips in the group clip displayed in the Source monitor with the sequence displayed in the Record monitor. All clips are synchronized and continually updated during playback and editing.

The Source and Record monitors are ganged under one set of controls, specifically, the Record monitor controls. The controls under the Source monitor are removed when you are in MultiCamera mode.

With a new sequence loaded in the timeline, you choose Special > MultiCamera Mode, or press Shift+Ctrl/Cmd+M, to activate MultiCamera mode.

All camera angles are displayed in the Source monitor and have been synchronized by the Avid system.

To deactivate MultiCamera mode and return to Source-oriented editing, do one of the following:

■ Deselect Special > MultiCamera Mode, or press Shift+Ctrl/Cmd+M.

■ Load a clip into the Source monitor.

■ Enter another mode such as Trim mode.

Displaying Quad Split or Nine Split Mode

Once in MultiCamera mode, the Source monitor displays the clips, by default, in Quad Split Source mode, in which up to four clips of your group/multigroup clip are displayed in four quadrants.

Note: When you use Quad Split or Nine Split buttons, you should be in MultiCamera mode.

To change between Quad Split and Nine Split modes:

1. Activate the **Source** monitor.

2. Choose **Tools > Command Palette**, and click the **MCam** tab as shown in Figure 5.11.

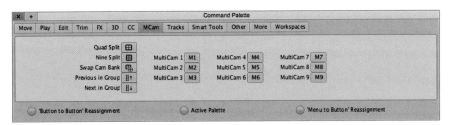

Figure 5.11
MultiCamera tab (MCam) of the Command palette.

3. Click the **Active Palette** button.

You can also map the buttons you need to keys or buttons on the interface.

In the Avid Learning Series

For information on remapping buttons and using the Command palette, check out *Media Composer 6, Part 1: Editing Essentials*, part of the Avid Learning Series, or consider taking Media Composer 101 at an Avid Learning Partner.

4. Click the **QUAD SPLIT OR NINE SPLIT** button, depending on the number of panes you want to display in the Source monitor.

Note: The Quad Split button is also in the Source/Record monitor fast menu.

5. To switch to the next bank of four or nine camera angles, click the **SWAP CAM BANK** button.

You can swap banks on-the-fly while playing in **QUAD SPLIT** mode, but not in **NINE SPLIT** mode.

6. To return to full screen display, deselect the **QUAD OR NINE SPLIT** button.

Displaying the Clip's Name in a Quadrant

The Source monitor can be configured to temporarily display the names of the individual clips while in MultiCamera mode.

To display clip names in their quadrants, click the Source monitor and then hold down the Ctrl/Cmd key. The clip names appear below the quadrants as shown in Figure 5.12.

Clip DIN SVR SABRINA SERVES in the Lower-Left Quadrant

Figure 5.12
Clip names in the quadrants of MultiCamera mode.

Assigning Another Clip to a Quadrant

By default the clips are displayed in quadrants in their order in the group clip (which was determined by the clip order in the bin). You can assign a different clip to a quadrant, if you like. **To do so:**

1. CTRL+ALT/CMD+CLICK a quadrant and choose a different camera angle (or choose **SEQUENCE**) from the menu that appears, as shown in Figure 5.13.

Figure 5.13
Changing the position of clips in the 4-up or 9-up display.

2. Choose **RESTORE DEFAULTS** from the menu to return to default angles, which is based on the sort order of the clips in the bin at the time the group clip was made.

Editing Audio

There are two basic methods for setting up audio in a multicamera sequence.

■ Scenario 1: There is one audio source for multiple video sources. This scenario is typical for situation comedies and high-end music videos.

■ Scenario 2: In production, each camera recorded both audio and video, and you want to access all of the audio tracks when you cut the program. This scenario uses the Audio Follow Video option.

Using the Audio Follow Video Option

The Audio Follow Video option instructs the system to switch both audio and video for each camera angle. (Use this option with Scenario 2 in the previous section.)

Audio Follow Video overrides the timeline track selectors and switches audio in track A1 only. Audio Follow Video edits appear in the timeline as match frames (the transitions contain an equals sign).

To set up Audio Follow Video:

1. In the Composer settings, activate the **SECOND ROW OF INFO** option.

2. Click the **GROUP MENU** icon, which is in the second row of information above the Source monitor. The **GROUP** menu appears, as shown in Figure 5.14.

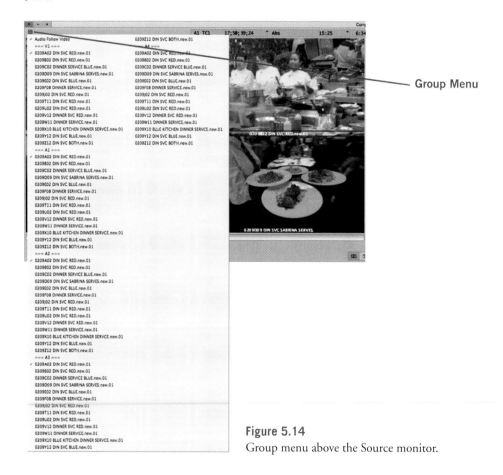

Group Menu

Figure 5.14
Group menu above the Source monitor.

Note: The Group menu may not appear above the Source monitor if your Composer window has been resized to be small, or if you haven't allowed Media Composer to display the second row of data. You can enable the second row of data from the Composer settings. Choose Window > Data Display at Top.

You can select and patch group clip video and audio tracks, which are listed in the Group menu.

3. Select video or audio channels from any clip in the group to patch the video or audio channels to the tracks available in the sequence.

4. Choose the **AUDIO FOLLOW VIDEO** option to switch both audio and video for each camera angle when you cut.

The Group Menu icon turns green to indicate Audio Follow Video is enabled.

Multicamera Performance

To play back a group clip in a 4-up or 9-up split screen, you must be in MultiCamera mode.

When Media Composer is playing a clip in 4-up or 9-up mode, it must read four or nine media files from the hard disk, decode them, and composite them into the Source monitor, as well as display the linecut in the Record monitor. That puts a significant demand on your storage subsystem as well as your computer's processor.

The following section provides tips concerning playback performance for MultiCamera mode.

Tip: **If you notice frames are dropping during playback, decrease the size of the Composer window until playback becomes smooth.**

Storage subsystems have to move the media files from the disks to the processor. If your media files are large, that can cause a strain on your system. The more compressed your media files are, the faster they can be read from the disk. You will find 15:1s standard definition media is very small and will stress your storage subsystem the least. If your media was captured at the 2:1 Avid resolution (codec), your media files would be 30x larger and your computer may not be able to read all nine video media files plus the audio media files quickly enough to allow for real-time multicamera editing.

HD clips are even larger. If you're trying to perform real-time multicamera editing using HD source material, you could transcode it to SD 15:1s and afterward relink your sequence back to the HD media.

If your storage subsystem is very fast, your bottleneck could be your processor. Perhaps your computer's processor is too slow. In that scenario, you might find that Media Composer is able to present real-time multicamera editing using 1:1

SD uncompressed footage, particularly if MultiCamera mode is using a 4-up display in the Source monitor. The 1:1 resolution will usually perform better than 2:1 or 3:1, despite its larger file size, because the video frames don't need to be decompressed first, which reduces the load on your processor and results in improved performance. (Again, this is only the case when your storage system is fast enough that reading four streams of 1:1 SD media is not a problem.)

Additional Multicamera performance tips:

- MultiCamera editing works best with 8-bit resolutions. If you use 10-bit media, Media Composer will treat it as 8-bit media while MultiCamera mode is running, which may result in a slight degrading of image quality temporarily, only while MultiCamera mode is enabled.

- You can change the playback quality to Best Performance (yellow/yellow) mode when editing SD projects, and it's automatically set to that for HD projects.

- Four streams are easier to play than nine streams, so if your system can't perform well with a 9-up display, switch to the 4-up display.

Note: Older Avid editing systems used to require that multicamera clips be encoded using one of the "m" resolutions, like 4:1m or 2:1m. This is no longer the case, and there is no requirement to use the m resolutions.

Use the Quad Split (or Nine Split) button to switch the Source monitor between Full-Monitor display and Quad/Nine Split Source viewing and editing modes.

Editing a Multicamera Sequence

To cut multicamera material, you use the MultiCamera keys to select different camera angles. These changes in camera angle are recorded as cuts in the sequence.

1. Play the multicamera material in the timeline.

   The Quad Split display and Record monitor display update automatically during playback.

2. When you want to cut to a different camera angle, press one of the MultiCamera function keys. The default keys are:

   - For Quad Split view, press function keys F9–F12.
   - For Nine Split view, press function keys F9–F12 and Shift+F9–F12.

Aside from using the keyboard's function keys, you can also press a number key on the numeric keypad. The arrangement of the numbers on the numeric keypad correlates to the angles in the split display as follows:

- 7 key switches to upper left
- 8 or 9 switch to upper right
- 4 or 1 switch to lower left
- 2, 3, 5, or 6 switch to lower right

You can also cut to a different camera angle by clicking a camera angle in the split display.

A cut is made starting at the position indicator and ending at the end of the current segment (which may, of course, be the end of the sequence).

The sequence updates in the Quad Split display and in the Record monitor display during playback, which means that you typically make your cuts on-the-fly as you play through the sequence. The timeline updates when you stop playback.

Use of Function Keys with Macintosh Computers

The function keys of a Macintosh computer are used to provide OS X features such as changing the song in iTunes, raising or lowering the volume, or activating one of the many Exposé/Mission Control features.

For Media Composer to recognize the keyboard's function keys, you need to hold the Fn key while pressing the function key. The Fn key is located either in the lower-left corner of the keyboard for portables, or under F13 on a full-size external keyboard. As keyboard combinations vary, it may be elsewhere on your Mac's keyboard.

Alternatively, you can configure OS X to always use the function keys as genuine function keys. In that scenario, you need to hold Fn to activate the system feature, such as changing the volume.

To configure a Macintosh keyboard so the function keys are interpreted as function keys:

1. Open the Apple Menu > System Preferences > Keyboard.
2. Select Use all F1, F2, and so on, as standard function keys.

Playing a Linecut on the Source and Client Monitors

You can play the edited sequence, called a *linecut*, on the Source monitor while in Quad Split Source view and Nine Split Source view. The Client monitor also plays the linecut.

Note: The Client monitor displays only SD multicam sequences. You can view playback of HD multicam sequences in the Source monitor only.

To play a linecut on the Source and Client monitors:

1. Open the **COMPOSER** settings, as shown in Figure 5.15.

Figure 5.15
Control playback of multicamera clips and sequences in the Composer and Client monitors.

2. Click the **MULTICAMERA** tab.

3. Click the **SPLIT MODE PLAY** pop-up menu, and select **QUAD OR NINE SPLIT**.

4. Click the **MULTICAMERA MODE CLIENT MONITOR** pop-up menu, and select **LINECUT**.

5. Click **OK**.

Editing On-the-Fly

You can add edits on-the-fly by pressing a single MultiCamera key. Of course, you can also use the Add Edit button if you map it to the keyboard. After the edits are added, you use one of the switching techniques from the previous section to switch the clip from edit to edit.

This method is especially useful when editing to music because it allows you to cut to the music without pausing.

To add edits:

1. Load the group or multigroup clip into the Source monitor and edit it into a sequence.

2. Play the sequence, and each time you want to make an edit, press a **MultiCamera** key (it doesn't matter which one).

3. To remove your edits, do one of the following:

   - Lasso the edit(s) to enter **Trim** mode, and press the **Delete** key.
   - Mark an **IN** and **OUT** around the area with edits you want to remove, and choose **Clip > Remove Match Frame Edits**.

4. After adding the edits, place the position indicator within each segment and use the **Up** and **Down Arrow** keys to switch camera angles.

Refining the Edit

When you have finished your rough-cut of the sequence, you can refine the sequence in all the usual ways. For example, use trimming, slipping, and sliding to adjust edit points and shot content.

Switching Clips with the Arrow Keys

After you have edited the multicamera sequence, you can change any segment in the sequence to a different camera angle. This process does not add a cut point.

To switch camera angles:

1. With the **Record** monitor active, place the position indicator within a segment you want to change.

2. Press the **Up Arrow** (**Previous In Group**) key and **Down Arrow** (**Next In Group)** key to switch the clip for that segment.

Tip: You can also right-click (Windows) or Shift+Control+click (Macintosh) on the segment and choose a camera angle from the menu that appears.

The system cycles through all of the clips in the group clip, even if all camera angles are not displayed in the Source monitor. (The Record monitor displays all camera angles as you scroll through them.)

If the number of camera angles exceeds the number of panes, you can also press the Swap Cam Bank button to display the next bank of cameras.

 Take a moment to complete Exercise 5, Parts 2 and 3.

Committing Multicamera Edits

You can remove the grouped clips in a sequence and replace each of them with its selected clip. This might be useful if you experience poor performance with a very complex multicamera sequence on a slower system; for example, on a sequence that uses many multicamera clips and many effects or color corrections.

To commit multicamera edits:

1. Select the sequence you want to affect.

2. Right-click the sequence and select COMMIT MULTICAM EDITS.

Your Avid editing application duplicates the sequence, and then replaces each grouped clip in the duplicate sequence with its selected clip. The original sequence is unaffected and still contains the grouped clips.

   Take a moment to complete Exercise 5, Part 4.

Review/Discussion Questions

1. What kind of productions are suitable for a multicamera editing work-flow? (See "Multicamera Editing Speeds Production" on page 202.)

2. Are there any kinds of productions that would not benefit from a multi-camera workflow? If so, what are they? (See "Multicamera Editing Speeds Production" on page 202.)

3. During hiatus after a season of very high ratings, your production's techni-cal director has decided to switch the sitcom from shooting single camera to shooting multicamera for the next season. What advice might you offer to the director and the camera operators? (See "Synchronization Options" on page 204.)

4. How does your multicamera workflow (or work load) change when your production shoots using cameras that are not capable of synchronizing exter-nal timecode? (See "Visual or Audio-Based Sync Overview" on page 206.)

5. What is external timecode (EXT. TC) and how does it improve a multi-camera workflow? (See "Timecode Sync Overview" on page 204.)

6. How can using a slate or clapper during production assist you in grouping clips during post-production? (See "Visual or Audio-Based Sync Overview" on page 206.)

7. List the steps involved in the multicamera editing workflow. (See "Avid's Multicamera Editing Workflows" on page 207.)

8. Why is it recommended that you sort the clips in the bin before grouping? (See "Creating Group Clips" on page 208.)

9. What is the difference between a group clip and a multigroup clip? (See "Creating Multigroup Clips" on page 210.)

10. Where is the Gang button located for each monitor? (See "Exploring Additional Grouping Methods" on page 212.)

11. What shortcut keys do you use to activate MultiCamera mode? (See "Activating MultiCamera Mode" on page 218.)

12. How do you display the clip name in a MultiCamera quadrant? (See "Displaying the Clip's Name in a Quadrant" on page 220.)

13. When would you use the Audio Follow Video option? (See "Using the Audio Follow Video Option" on page 221.)

14. What are the steps involved in adding edits on-the-fly in a multicamera sequence? (See "Editing On-the-Fly" on page 226.)

Editing a Scene from Hell's Kitchen

In this exercise, you'll edit a scene from *Hell's Kitchen,* a reality TV show featuring Gordon Ramsay. If profanity and hot tempers stress you, you might consider skipping this particular exercise. Then again, if profanity and hot tempers stress you, you're possibly in the wrong industry.

You'll create the rough-cut using multicamera mode, and you'll need to configure Media Composer to optimally handle a group clip having 14 source clips.

The *Hell's Kitchen* production has contestants divided into two teams, identified as the red and blue teams, and they must work in the kitchen of a restaurant under their chief, Chef Gordon Ramsay. *Hell's Kitchen* has no opportunities to stop and reshoot a scene, so 10 or more cameras are used to record all the action.

All cameras record four channels of audio. The audio consists of the natural ambient sound, as well as sound provided by wireless microphones. Some cameras are in the dining area and at the serving bar, whereas the others are in the kitchen. As a result, during editing you may hear sound that is unrelated to the picture. You will have to adjust audio separately, as needed.

Media Used:
Picture and Sound, (Optional) Hell's Kitchen from Cengage

Duration:
45 minutes

GOALS

- Prepare group clips for a reality TV show
- Perform manual multicam editing
- Add edits on-the-fly
- Perform "live switching"-style multicamera editing

Exercise 5.1: Preparing to Use the Media

The project files that come with this lesson include two versions of the same Hell's Selects bin, as shown in Figure EX5.1.

Figure EX5.1
A DVD and web versions of the Hell's Selects bin are provided.

The DVD that ships with this book includes media files that are each just one minute. Those media files are linked to the clips in *Hell's Selects (DVD Media)*.

Optionally, you can download companion media files for this book from www.courseptr.com/downloads. The companion media files include six-minute-long versions of the same clips, which are linked to the *Hell's Selects (Web Media)* clips. You may find it more real world to download the longer clips, which will prove to be more challenging to edit than to use the shorter versions on the DVD.

Throughout these exercises, use whichever *Hell's Selects* bin corresponds to the media you have available.

In a classroom environment at an Avid Learning Partner, consult with your instructor or just try the Web Media clips to see if they're online. Otherwise, use the DVD media.

Exercise 5.2: Editing Multicam Material with Sync Timecode

In this exercise, you'll group together a clip from each of the 14 cameras for *Hell's Kitchen,* Episode 2, Season 9.

The clips have matching timecode.

To prepare the *Hell's Kitchen* material:

1. Open PICTURE AND SOUND > LESSON 5 > HELL'S SELECTS.

2. Sort the bin based on the contents of the CAMERA1 column.

3. Create a group clip from all clips in the Hell's Selects bin. Use matching timecode.

4. Create a new sequence in the LESSON 5 SEQUENCES bin.

5. Edit the group clip into the timeline.

6. Activate MULTICAMERA mode by choosing SPECIAL > MULTICAMERA MODE (or pressing SHIFT+CTRL/CMD+M).

All camera angles are displayed in the Source monitor and are synchronized. A green line appears below the selected camera angle.

Exercise 5.3:
Editing the Hell's Kitchen Material

After you've prepared for multicam editing by grouping your clips and creating a sequence, the fun can begin. Your mission is to jump in with the multicam features and start cutting. In this exercise, you'll create cuts by using the mouse to click on the angle while the sequence plays. In the next exercise, you'll focus on the keyboard technique.

1. Play the sequence created in the previous exercise.

2. While playing, click on the angle you want to see in the sequence.

   The sequence updates to perform the cut during playback.

3. When you're finished, review the scene.

4. Refine the sequence by trimming, slipping, and sliding to adjust edit points and shot content.

5. Try using the ripple trim (yellow roller) to tighten the scene by removing frames from the beginning and end of each shot.

When you enter Trim mode, you automatically leave MultiCamera mode.

Exercise 5.4: Exploring Multicam Editing Keyboard Techniques

Aside from using the mouse to perform edits on-the-fly, you can also use keyboard shortcuts, such as F9–F12 (with and without Shift) and the keys of the numeric keypad. In this exercise, you'll practice using the keyboard shortcuts to perform a live edit.

Note: Computers that lack the numeric keypad, including many laptops, will not be able to switch on-the-fly using the numeric keypad for hopefully obvious reasons.

OS X users may need to enable the function keys as described in "Use of Function Keys with Macintosh Computers" on page 225.

Adding edits on-the-fly using the keyboard:

1. Play the sequence.

2. Each time you want to make an edit, press one of the MULTICAMERA function keys (F9–12 and SHIFT+F9–12) or one of the numeric keypad buttons.

3. After adding the edits, stop the playback and place the position indicator within each segment and use the UP and DOWN ARROW keys to switch camera angles.

4. Right-click a segment in the timeline to choose another angle.

5. Refine the sequence by trimming to adjust edit points and shot content.

Script Integration and ScriptSync

Editors are storytellers. Be it dramatic stories, feature films, or interview-laden documentaries, the story underlines your picture and sound choices. So Media Composer supports that by allowing you to shift your project management from isolated bins to the script itself.

All the clips that would normally be placed into a bin are now placed into a script. Instead of opening bins to find clips, you open a script. You advance to the scene you're editing, and your shots are available in the context of the story. It's a wonderful way to remain story-focused and it's the topic of this lesson.

Media Used: Agent MXZero

Duration: 60 minutes

GOALS

- Using script integration
- Marking with ScriptSync
- Editing with the Script window

What Is a Lined Script?

A lined script is exactly what it says: A script with lines through it. The lined script is typically the responsibility of the Script Supervisor on set. After the scenes have been recorded, the editor will be provided with the lined script, who uses it as a tool.

The lined script can provide an editor with answers to such questions as:

- Do I have coverage for these lines of dialogue?

- How many takes do I have of this character's lines?

- What's the name of the clip that's used for this wide shot?

Slates Capture Production Metadata

A slate, or "clapper," is that symbol of the production industry: a handheld sign with information about the shot that's about to be recorded. The name itself extends from traditional slates, such as those used in one-room school houses that were essentially small chalkboards.

A slate was used in front of the camera to record the scene number and take number of the shot that was about to be filmed. An editor can then search through the film looking for the slates to identify the footage that came after it. A slate might also be recorded while being held upside down, which indicates it is a "tail slate" and identifies the material that preceded it: It's at the tail of the footage.

Slates can also record timecode, the director and production names, and other such information about the footage. In this way, a slate provides a traditional means for adding metadata video or film footage.

The arm on the slate provides an audible cue, the sharp "clap," as well as a visual cue, which is the moment the arm hits the base. Those visual and audible events can be used to synchronize the picture and sound at a later time, which was often necessary for film recordings, which recorded only picture and not sound. Many productions still use separate audio and video recordings because of the flexibility in allowing the camera and the audio recording equipment to be placed in different positions on set.

Role of the Script Supervisor

The Script Supervisor works on the set of a production, ensuring that lines from the script are available to the cast as needed, and ensuring that information from the slates is annotated back onto the script. The script annotations usually document the scene number and take number.

The action begins with, well, "action!," but the recording starts a few moments earlier when the slate is revised for the upcoming scene and take. It's placed in front of the camera and in that way the contents are recorded to the film. At the same time, the Script Supervisor records the same information onto the script.

Each time a scene (or a part of a scene) is recorded, the Script Supervisor notes the scene and take numbers, and draws a line vertically through the portion of the script that corresponds to the performance. These hand-written lines indicate that "These words were spoken during this take." In any scene, there will often be some lines spoken by an off-camera actor. To indicate an off-camera line, the script supervisor squiggles the line.

Lined Script Support in Media Composer

The lined script is traditionally used as a tool for managing scene and take information during post-production on a dramatic feature film or television production. With Avid Media Composer, script integration allows you to adapt the lined script to the digital realm for use in any type of production.

Media Composer has script integration, and an optional add-on component called ScriptSync. Script integration requires you to import the script as a text file and re-apply the lines. ScriptSync extends the capabilities of script integration by automating the synchronizing of footage to the words in the script, which saves you time by helping you accurately and quickly locate the footage that corresponds to the script.

Using Script Integration

Script integration creates a digital version of the traditional lined script and attaches clips to it. When clips are attached to a script, they are called slates and show the clip's representative frame. Information from the Take column in the bin is added to the virtual slate, and you can see the scene and script page numbers.

When you use script integration, you create a Script object in the Project window that essentially functions as a special kind of bin that contains all of your source material related to the script.

Some scenarios for using script integration include:

■ Scripted television documentaries with a team of dedicated writers, where you might have a detailed script with specific suggested sound bites to drive the story along.

■ Scripted, story-driven content including sitcoms.

■ Documentaries and interview-intensive shows, where you have had the interviews transcribed and want to associate the transcription with the clip for rapid searching and finding of audio queues.

Note that even if you don't have a detailed script, you are still probably working with scores of transcribed interviews. In this case, you can still easily use script integration to map these transcribed interviews for easy access to specific sound bites. This will greatly reduce time spent hunting and pecking for "the perfect bite," because with Media Composer's text finding capabilities, you can easily search for a keyword within the script to locate bites quickly and efficiently.

Tip: Many cities have companies that offer transcription services. You give them the audio files; they give you a text file. If you're working with interviews, you might consider sending your audio for transcription in this form, as opposed to assigning one of the production's staffers to perform the transcribing.

Script Integration Workflow

There is a bit of work involved in setting up script integration, but the time and effort you put in at the beginning is repaid in productivity at the end. ScriptSync can significantly reduce the time required to finish the setup of script integration, but regardless of whether you have ScriptSync, the workflow begins with the same tasks.

This is the overall workflow for using script integration:

1. The script supervisor creates a lined script during production, or a transcript is created after the interview.

2. Source footage is ingested into Media Composer.

3. The script is imported into Media Composer.

4. Clips are turned into slates by dragging them from a bin into the Script window.

5. Specific lines in the script are associated with audio cues in the slates using specialized script integration tools or the optional Avid ScriptSync.

6. The editor uses the fully prepared Script window to edit the program.

The end result is a populated Script window, complete with slates and lines, as shown in Figure 6.1.

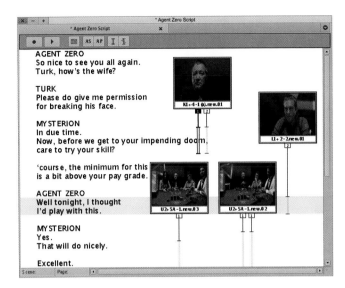

Figure 6.1
The Script Integration window.

Preparing a Script for Script Integration

Before you can use script integration, you need to prepare the script correctly. You can write the script in any program you like, from Notepad to Final Draft, and you can write it on any device that you like, from an iPad to a 1980s IBM electronic typewriter. Okay, maybe not the typewriter, but the point is that you don't need anything special to create the script for use with Media Composer. In fact, the only thing Media Composer requires is that you save the script as a plain-text file.

A plain-text file does not have multiple fonts, or font styles like bold or italic. It doesn't have forced page breaks, or different colors. It's plain, that's why it's called a "plain text" file. Your mission is to get whatever application you used to create the script to save (or export) it as a plain-text file.

You normally will have two files for your script:

- The original file, with rich text formatting, which is used by whatever application you used to write the script.

- The Avid-ready file, as a plain-text file, which you created by saving your regular script in the plain-text format.

For specific instructions on how to save your script in plain-text format, you'll need to consult the application's user's guide.

The following table lists some formats that work well and don't work so well as plain-text files for Media Composer:

Works Well	Don't Use
Plain text	Word (.doc or .docx)
ASCII text	Rich text (.rtf)
UTF-8 text	PDF
Unicode text	

When saving your script file, you must use a filename of 32 characters or less. (This rule also applies to bin names.) If you use more than 32 characters, Media Composer won't import the script.

Note: Although Word is listed in the *Don't Use* column, note that it's specifically the .doc or .docx formats that you can't use. You can certainly write your script in Microsoft Word and then save a copy of the script as a plain text file for use with Media Composer.

When saving the file for Media Composer, you may be given the option to pre-serve or save line breaks (LRs). Select that option; otherwise, you may find that when you import the script into Media Composer, all the words are on a single line instead of spaced out on the virtual pages.

Importing the Script into Media Composer

You import the script into Media Composer by selecting the Project window and choosing File > New Script. The script is imported into the Script window, as was shown in Figure 6.1.

 Take a moment to complete Exercise 6, Part 1.

Additional Tips for Creating Plain-Text Files

There are some additional tips that may assist you in creating plain-text files using popular applications that ship with Windows and OS X Lion. These may change with updates to the operating system, but generally the concepts are the same as software is revised:

- WordPad (Windows): Choose Text Document when saving.

- TextEdit (OS X Lion): Choose Format > Make Plain Text. Then choose File > Save and select UTF-8 Encoding as the file type.

- Microsoft Word (Windows and OS X Lion): Choose File > Save As..., and then set the format to Plain Text.

Tip: If the entire toolbar at the top of the Script window is not visible, drag the right edge of the window to the right to expand the window.

Media Composer copies the script from its original location and places it in your Project folder along with your bins. The script also appears in the Project window, as is shown in Figure 6.2.

Figure 6.2
Scripts appear in the Project window.

You can have as many scripts as you like in your project, the same way you can have as many bins as you like. You might choose to have separate scripts per dramatic act, or separate scripts per interview for a documentary.

Tip: If you're working with multiple scripts in a project, keep things organized by placing them into a folder in the Project window.

Linking Clips to Scripts

When a clip is associated with a script, it is presented as a slate in the Script window. There is no practical limit to the number of slates that can be represented in a script.

When you associate a clip with a script, you can associate either subclips or master clips. If one clip has multiple takes, you should use the subclip feature to divide that clip into individual subclips. You then separately associate each subclip with the script.

To link clips to the lines of a script, perform the following steps:

1. Select a clip. Play it if you need to determine the lines that it covers.

2. Highlight the covered lines within the **SCRIPT** window using one of the following two techniques:

    ● Drag through the lines.

    ● Click the first line and **SHIFT+CLICK** the last line.

3. Drag the clip that has those lines from the bin onto the highlighted text within the Script window.

The slates appear in the Script window, as shown in Figure 6.3.

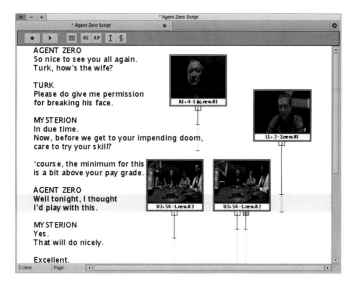

Figure 6.3
Slates in the Script window.

Figure 6.3 shows four slates, but one of them is unlike the others. Can you find the one with the difference?

Adding Takes to Existing Slates

The slate in the lower-right corner of Figure 6.3 has two takes associated with it. Each take is represented by a tab under the slate, with the number on the tab representing the take number. That slate has takes 1 and 2, and take 2 is the selected take as indicated by the dark background.

To associate a take with an existing slate:

1. Select the region of the script that the take covers.

2. Drag the associated clip from the bin onto the existing slate. (Or if you haven't yet added the slate, select multiple takes in the bin and drag them to the highlighted section of the script.)

3. There is a correspondence between the **TAKE** column of the clip's source bin and the **TAKE** number in the slate. If the **TAKE** numbers aren't displayed, you can add the take numbers manually in the bin's **TAKE** column, as shown in Figure 6.4.

The new take appears in the slate and is applied to the same region of the script as the existing take.

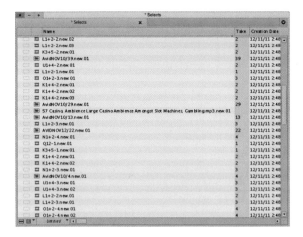

Figure 6.4
Take numbers are derived from the bin's Take column.

Working with Slates

When a clip is associated with lines of a script, it's called a *slate*. Slates in a script can be manipulated in the following ways (making sure to first click the slate):

■ To select a slate with multiple takes, Shift+click the takes you want to select or drag the mouse cursor across the takes you want to select.

■ To select the entire script and all slates and takes, press Ctrl/Cmd+A. Then if you double-click one take, all takes of all slates are loaded into the Source monitor.

■ Reduce the slate size by pressing Ctrl/Cmd+K; increase their size by pressing Ctrl/Cmd+L.

■ Change the representative frame (thumbnail) displayed in a slate by using the Jog buttons (1, 2, 3, and 4) on the keyboard.

■ Hide slates (the slate number remains) by choosing Script > Show Frames.

■ Move a slate by Ctrl/Cmd+dragging it.

■ Delete a slate by clicking a take number, and pressing the Delete key. To delete more than one take, Shift+click the take numbers or drag the cursor across the take numbers and then press Delete. (Caution: You cannot undo the deletion of a slate or take.)

Loading and Playing Takes in the Source Monitor

After the Script window has been configured by linking clips/slates to lines of dialogue, the Script window can generally be used instead of bins for editing. The slates in the Script window can be loaded into the Source monitor.

There is a shortcut for playing clips without loading them in the Source monitor:

- Click a slate (or take) and click the Play button in the Script window's toolbar.

The slate turns green, and the associated clip is loaded into the Source monitor and begins playing. The clip plays back in a continuous loop until you press the spacebar. If you selected more than one take, each take plays in sequence.

There are also several ways to load slates:

- Double-click a slate (or take) to load the associated clip into the Source monitor.

- Select multiple takes (Shift+select additional takes), and then double-click any take you selected. Media Composer loads the selected takes into the Source monitor, and you can select them by using the Clip Name menu.

When loading slates, the Current Time indicator of the Source monitor will be located at the last known position within the clip. A little computing magic can take loading of clips from ordinary to extraordinary: It's a feature called Interpolate Position.

Interpolate Position

Interpolation works like this: You have one take that covers six lines of dialogue, and the take (source clip) is one minute long. How many seconds from the beginning of the clip might you expect to find the third line of dialogue?

Half-way: 30 seconds

That's the calculation that Media Composer does when you double-click the intersection of a take and a line of dialogue, provided that you have first enabled Interpolate Position.

To enable Interpolate Position:

- Select Script > Interpolate Position

Interpolate Position works best when the actors deliver their lines at an even pace, and there is a minimal amount of dead air in the clip. "Dead air" refers to non-spoken content at the beginning or end of the clip, such as dramatic pans or establishing shots, which result in the interpolation calculation being inaccurate.

To increase the accuracy of the interpolation, you can add script marks manually, or use ScriptSync to have Media Composer add them automatically. The next section covers script marks.

Adding Script Marks

You use script marks to associate particular lines in the script with the corresponding points in your clips. With script marks, Media Composer can better interpolate the clip's position.

Script marks appear as black triangles, as indicated in Figure 6.5.

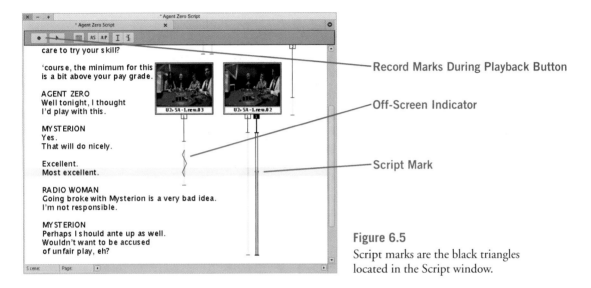

Record Marks During Playback Button

Off-Screen Indicator

Script Mark

Figure 6.5
Script marks are the black triangles located in the Script window.

Adding Script Marks Manually

You can manually add script marks by finding spoken words in the clip and associating them with words in the script using the Add Script Mark button. The Add Script Mark button needs to be mapped from the Command palette because it is not normally under the Source monitor.

To place script marks manually:

1. Map the **ADD SCRIPT MARK** button (choose the **COMMAND PALETTE >
   OTHER** tab) to a button or to the keyboard.

2. Double-click in the **SCRIPT** window at the intersection of a take and the line of dialogue that you want to mark, as shown in Figure 6.6.

   The take is selected in the slate, the selected line of the dialogue is highlighted, and the clip loads into the Source monitor.

3. Play or jog through the take in the **SOURCE** monitor, or place the **CURRENT TIME INDICATOR** on the exact frame.

4. When playback reaches the selected line of dialogue, click the **ADD SCRIPT MARK** button or press the **ADD SCRIPT MARK** key.

The line is marked in the **SCRIPT** window with a small horizontal bar, as was shown in Figure 6.5. Playback also stops.

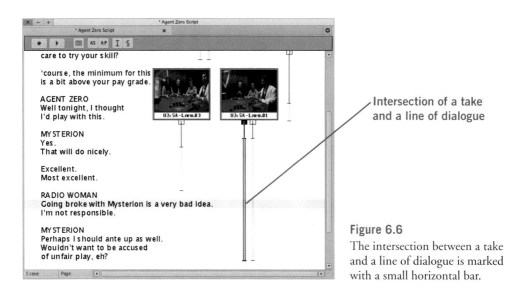

Intersection of a take and a line of dialogue

Figure 6.6
The intersection between a take and a line of dialogue is marked with a small horizontal bar.

5. Repeat Steps 1–4 to add more script marks.

Automated Screening and Marking

You can combine the screening process with the marking process. This is a more efficient approach to both review your footage and create your script marks. The Script Integration window contains a record button that's vital to this technique. When you use the record button, Media Composer plays a take and your job is to click on the corresponding line of dialogue when you hear it. Each time you hear a line in the clip, click in the script.

To use automated screening and marking:

1. Select one or more takes in the **SCRIPT** window.

If you select multiple takes, you will mark each take consecutively. The one you are currently marking has the green line.

2. Click on the line in the script where you want to start recording.

3. Click the **RECORD** button, located in the **SCRIPT** window's toolbar.

The first selected take turns green in the Script window, the clip or subclip is loaded into the Source monitor, and the clip or subclip begins playing.

4. As you hear a line of dialogue, click on the matching line in the **Script** window.

   A script mark is created for each line of associated dialogue, as shown in Figure 6.7.

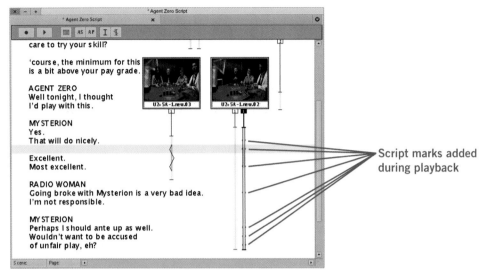

Figure 6.7
Script marks recorded automatically during playback.

5. Continue to mark additional sync points while recording using any of the following methods:

   - Click a line that already contains a mark to replace the previous mark and update the sync point in the clip.
   - Click a line in the script before or after the range of the existing take line, and the mark is added while the take line is extended to include the new line.
   - Use variable-speed play controls (**J-K-L** keys on the keyboard) to shuttle, step, or pause during playback.
   - Press the **Tab** or **Shift+Tab** keys on the keyboard to begin playback of the next or the previous take.

Tip: You can scroll through the Script window without affecting playback.

   As each take reaches its end, the system automatically loads and plays the next take.

6. Continue to place marks until all your takes have been screened.

You have now added script marks and significantly improved the accuracy of the Script window's Interpolate Position.

Editing Script Marks

You can delete and move script marks after you have added them using the following methods:

■ To move a script mark manually, Ctrl/Cmd+drag the mark.

■ To delete a script mark, click on it and press the Delete key. Respond to the prompt.

■ Choose Script > Hold Slates Onscreen to scroll a script in the Script window while keeping the slate on-screen for as long as the take lines remain on-screen.

Tip: To make Hold Slates Onscreen the default behavior, go to the Script settings before opening the Script window.

Loading and Playing Marked Segments

Once you have placed marks syncing lines in your script to points in the source clips, you can quickly load and cue takes for selected lines of dialogue. You can load a single take, or you can load all the coverage for a range of lines.

To load the marked segment of a take:

■ Double-click the script mark at the line of dialogue that you want to cue.

The take is loaded into the Source monitor and is cued to the synced line of dialogue. An IN point is placed at the sync location.

To load all the coverage for a range of lines:

1. Select the lines in the SCRIPT window, dragging through all intersecting takes (and through one or more script marks).

   The script lines and takes are highlighted.

2. Click the PLAY button in the SCRIPT window to screen the takes for those lines, or click the RECORD button to add script marks.

The takes load and play back one after another. You can use the Tab key or J-K-L keys to jump between takes and to control playback.

 Take a moment to complete Exercise 6, Part 2.

Additional ScriptSync Options

There are additional options in the toolbar and in the footer of the Script window.

Toolbar Items

The buttons in the toolbar help manage the script marks, playback, and marking the digital script to match the original paper script. The buttons are shown in Figure 6.8.

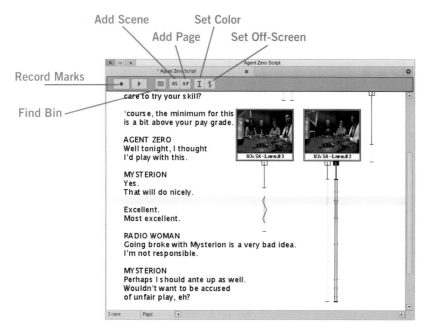

Figure 6.8
Script window toolbar.

The Record Marks and Play buttons in the toolbar were covered earlier in this lesson.

If you want to locate a bin that a slate is in, click the take and then the Find Bin button. The bin appears, with the clip selected in it.

The Add Scene and Add Page buttons let you enter information that is in the printed script into the Script window.

1. Click the line on which you want to add a scene or page number.

2. Click either the **ADD SCENE** or **ADD PAGE** button.

3. Enter the scene or page number into the dialog box.

4. Click **OK**.

You can now advance to a particular scene or page by clicking in the Scene or Page box at the bottom of the window, which displays a dialog box, as shown in Figure 6.9.

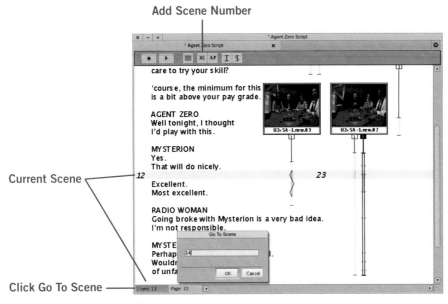

Figure 6.9
Scene and page management features of the Script window.

The Set Off-Screen button lets you mark a slate or part of a slate as dialogue coming from off-screen. A squiggly line running through the dialogue conventionally indicates off-screen dialogue, and this button adds it to the online script.

To set off-screen lines:

1. Select the slate (or take), or portion of it, that you want to mark as off-screen. (If you select a portion of the text, you must also select the slate or take.)

2. Click the **SET OFF-SCREEN** button, and a squiggly line is added.

The Set Color button lets you create a colored slate, which could be useful to assist in organizing and quickly identifying related slates.

To set the slate color:

1. Select the lines of text for which you want a red slate.

2. Click the **SET COLOR** button, and a colored slate appears. (Click it again to remove the color.)

Bin-Like Functionality

The Script window behaves in many ways like a bin. You place clips inside of it, which displays them as slates. You can reposition those slates, change the size of them, and load them into the Source monitor.

The text in a Script window can be cut, copied, and pasted and you can search the text of the script using Edit > Find. The Find feature, in combination with script interpolation, is a quick way to locate key phrases or words in transcribed interviews.

Note: Media Composer has an optional paid feature called PhraseFind. PhraseFind is a faster and more accurate way to find particular phrases, using speech pattern recognition technology. The same underlying technology is used in ScriptSync.

About Nexidia's Technology

The following is an overview on how Nexidia technology, which powers ScriptSync, works. It is an except from their website:

Nexidia's technology is unique because it analyzes the 30-40 individual sounds of a given language (phonemes) rather than trying to recognize the half-million or so words that make up that language. In other words, we convert text to sounds, then look for that string of easily recognized sounds in your media.

This approach is far more accurate than speech-to-text applications. Nexidia's dialogue analysis easily handles slang and proper names, is highly tolerant of spelling errors and poor audio quality, and doesn't require frequent dictionary updates. It also supports multiple languages and dialects.

Nexidia's dialogue analysis technology is extremely fast. With current applications indexing audio at approximately 200x real-time per CPU core, a standard 12-core workstation can index 20 hours of media in less than a minute. Once analyzed, 100,000 hours of media can be searched in less than a second.

Results are consistently more accurate than speech-to-text transcriptions. Because Nexidia's technology analyzes the individual sounds of words, it is not dependent on text-based dictionaries. The benefits are many. There is no need to constantly update dictionaries to search for new terms. Proper names, slang, and new terms such as "Facebook" or "Blogosphere" are easily recognized. It's also forgiving of spelling variations such as "Gadhafi" or "Qaddafi," and highly tolerant of individual accents and poorly recorded audio.

Source: http://www.nexidia.com/media/technology, retrieved Jan-01-2012.

Using Avid ScriptSync

ScriptSync uses award-winning, patented phonetic-indexing technology to analyze the audio portion of a clip and match it to lines of the script text. ScriptSync works much faster than real-time, so long interviews can be synced to source footage within seconds. ScriptSync even works wonderfully with accents and ad-libs.

Marking with ScriptSync

To add script marks automatically with Avid ScriptSync:

1. Select one or more takes that include audio.

2. Double-click any line in the take to select the take and load it into a monitor.

3. Select Script > ScriptSync.

   The ScriptSync dialog box opens, as shown in Figure 6.10.

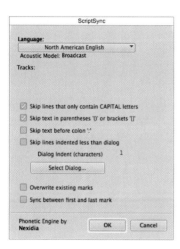

Figure 6.10
Preparing to recognize speech and script text.

4. Select options as described in Table 6-1, which has been provided by the Avid TechPubs team as part of the Media Composer 6 User's Guide.

5. Click OK. The syncing process starts.

6. Optional: Press Ctrl+. (period) to cancel the process after it has started. When ScriptSync finishes, your take includes a script mark for every line of text the application found in the audio.

7. Check through the marks. If ScriptSync missed any, add them manually as described earlier in the lesson.

Table 6-1   ScriptSync Options

Option	Description
Language	Select the language version (this setting is for both the audio and the text).
Tracks	Select the audio tracks you want as input to ScriptSync.
Skip lines that only contain CAPITAL letters	Dramatic scripts often use all-capital letters to identify the speaker or for scene descriptions.
Skip text in parentheses "()" or brackets "[]"	For parenthetical expressions in your script that are not spoken.
Skip text before colon ":"	Select this option if your script places a character's name before a colon.
Skip lines indented less than dialog	Select this option if action is indented less than dialogue in your script. Type the number of characters that the dialogue is indented or click the Select Dialog button, select one line of dialogue from the Script and spaces are calculated automatically.
Overwrite existing marks	Select this option if the take you are syncing already contains script marks and you want ScriptSync to update those marks.
Sync between first and last mark	Select this option to restrict ScriptSync to analyze only the script between the lines of text and the media specified by the first and last script marks in a take.
	If there is only one mark in the take, ScriptSync goes from the first mark to the end of the take and media. This is useful if there is non-dialogue talking that you don't want to be marked.
	ScriptSync operates only until the last mark in the text.

Purchasing ScriptSync

ScriptSync is an optional add-on technology for Avid Media Composer. Upon purchasing the add-on, you are given a license code that you enter into Media Composer and it activates the feature.

There is a related technology called Avid PhraseFind, which allows searching the audio of clips in bins. It is not related to script integration and cannot be used to automate the creation of a script's marks.

Tip: For information on purchasing Avid ScriptSync powered by Nexidia, visit the ScriptSync section of Avid's website: http://www.avid.com/US/products/scriptsync.

Take a moment to complete Exercise 6, Part 3.

Editing with the Script Window

To use the Script window most effectively during a session, make sure you have added your preferred takes, alternative takes (indicated with colors), and script marks. It might take some extra time to set up the Script window, but you are now ready to compensate for that extra time at the beginning with a whole new way of editing.

Rough Cutting: The Traditional Way

You can quickly assemble a rough-cut from the Script window much as you would from a bin.

1. Open the **SCRIPT** window for the current cut.

2. Double-click the script mark of the first preferred take to load it into the Source monitor. The IN point is already marked and cued.

3. In the **SOURCE** monitor, mark an **OUT** at the appropriate point.

4. Enable the appropriate source and record tracks.

5. Splice in or overwrite the shot.

6. Repeat these steps until you have moved through Page 1 of the script.

7. Fine-tune the edits by using normal trimming and editing procedures. Continue to use the **SCRIPT** window to quickly load and cue alternative takes as necessary.

Rough Cutting: Using Single Mark Editing

Using the Script window in combination with the Single Mark Editing feature (also called mark-and-park editing), you can edit in a highly streamlined manner. Single mark editing allows you to establish a single mark, and then use the location of the Current Time indicator to determine the second mark when making the edit.

Tip: The Single Mark Editing option is selected from the Edit tab of the Composer Settings dialog box. This option allows you to skip several steps by performing edits on-the-fly while playing back clips without marking OUT points.

To assemble a rough-cut using Single Mark Editing:

1. Select the SINGLE MARK EDITING option (Choose the COMPOSER SETTINGS > EDIT TAB).

2. Play or shuttle through the clip and mark an **IN** point using the keyboard shortcut.

3. Continue to play and use the SPLICE-IN (**V** KEY), OVERWRITE (**B** KEY), or REPLACE EDIT (MAP TO A KEY) keyboard shortcut when you have reached the appropriate OUT point.

   The edit is performed on-the-fly without adding the second mark.

4. Repeat these steps for the remaining clips.

Rough Cutting: Splicing a Script Range

You can also instantly splice clips linked to ranges of script directly from the Script window into the sequence. To use this feature, you should first carefully mark with script marks the ranges in the script.

During editing, you can use the Ctrl and Alt keys (Windows) or the Ctrl key (OS X Lion) to instantly splice clips linked to ranges of script directly from the Script window into the sequence. To use this feature with accuracy; you should carefully mark with script marks the ranges of script during the screening and marking phase.

To splice a range:

1. Lasso the script marks for the lines (and optionally, takes) you want. (Select multiple takes if you want to view multiple readings in the sequence.)

2. Mark an **IN** point or place the position indicator in the sequence where you want to splice in the segment.

3. Hold down CTRL/ALT (Windows) or CMD/OPTION keys (OS X Lion). A splice-in arrow appears when you point to a take.

4. Double-click the first script mark of the first take you selected.

The shots for the lassoed section of the script are spliced into the sequence.

EXERCISE *Take a moment to complete Exercise 6, Part 4.*

Enriching Scripts

Media Composer's Script Integration tool allows you to add metadata to the script. You can make a script more useful by adding page numbers and scene numbers, which makes it easier for you to collaborate with someone who has the printed version of the script.

You can also make the digital script more closely match the printed script by adding off-screen indicators, which appear as squiggly lines on the script and make it easier for you to determine the lines that are spoken on-camera instead of off-camera.

 Learn more about enriching script by completing Exercise 6, Part 5, and then continue and cut a scene entirely from the script in the final exercise of this lesson—Exercise 6, Part 6.

Review/Discussion Questions

1. What's the difference between script integration and ScriptSync? (See "Using Script Integration" on page 237.)

2. How do you prepare a script for importing into Media Composer? (See "Preparing a Script for Script Integration" on page 239.)

3. How do you re-open the Script Integration window after you've closed it? (See "Using Script Integration" on page 237.)

4. Describe one way you can add multiple takes to a slate. (See "Adding Takes to Existing Slates" on page 242.)

5. How do you add a script mark manually to the script? (See "Adding Script Marks" on page 245.)

6. How can you play through, one after the other, all the takes of a line of dialogue? (See "Loading and Playing Marked Segments" on page 248.)

7. How can you move an existing mark in the script? (See "Additional ScriptSync Options" on page 249.)

8. Describe the process of marking with ScriptSync. (See "Marking with ScriptSync" on page 252.)

9. How do you obtain ScriptSync? (See "Purchasing ScriptSync" on page 253.)

10. How does single-mark editing assist in editing with the Script window? (See "Rough Cutting: Using Single-Mark Editing" on page 254.)

11. In what ways are bins and the Script window similar? (See "Bin-Like Functionality" on page 251.)

Using Script Integration and ScriptSync

In this exercise you'll begin to build a sequence using script integration. If your system is equipped with ScriptSync, you will also have an opportunity to establish script marks using it, otherwise you will add the script marks using a manual method.

Media Used:
Agent MXZero

Duration:
40 minutes

GOALS

- Prepare and perform for script integration
- Familiarize yourself with the selected footage
- Add script marks manually to the script
- Add script marks automatically to the script
- Use Avid ScriptSync
- Add pages and scene metadata
- Use the Find feature
- Mark off-screen text

Exercise 6.1: Preparing the Script

Script-based editing requires that the script be saved as a plain-text file. The script has been provided with this lesson in Microsoft Word format, which is not compatible with Avid script integration. Your first step is to prepare the script by opening it and saving it as a plain-text file.

Both Microsoft Windows and OS X Lion have the ability to open Microsoft Word files and save them as plain-text files using applications included with each operating system. Windows includes WordPad and OS X Lion includes TextEdit.

1. Open AGENT ZERO.DOC by double-clicking it from the LESSON 6 STUDENT MATERIALS folder.

   The lesson files are included with this book's companion DVD. In an academic environment, the materials may be located elsewhere. Consult your instructor for assistance, if needed.

   Depending on your operating system and installed applications, the script will likely open in Microsoft Word, WordPad, TextEdit, or Pages.

   Notice that the script contains bold, italic, and normal font styles, and also includes page numbers in the footer and the script name in the header.

2. Save the script to your desktop as AGENTZERO.TXT.

   Use the information in "Preparing a Script for Script Integration" on page 239 to save the script as a plain-text file. Do not use a filename with more than 32 characters, because Media Composer will reject the file.

Exercise 6.2: Familiarizing Yourself with the Project

Metadata from the Take column of the bin is useful when working with the Script window. You'll now familiarize yourself with the footage that has been provided for the exercise. You'll also ensure the Take column has been properly prepared (hint: it hasn't been) and you'll set the correct Project format to match the source material used in this lesson.

1. Open the AGENT MXZERO > 201 > LESSON 6 - MULTICAM.

   Two bins are provided for you. LESSON 6 SELECTS contains the source clips, whereas LESSON 6 SEQUENCES is where you are to create the sequence you will create in this exercise.

The clips in **LESSON 6 SELECTS** begin with a letter that reveals the angle:

K: Mysterion

U: Wide shot of the card table, Lady Chopsticks, Turk, and Agent Zero

L: Medium shots of Agent Zero

2. View the bin in **TEXT** view and add the **TAKE** column.

    Each clip has the take number indicated in brackets. For this particular show, the takes are identified using letters as opposed to numbers. Ensure that every clip has the correct value for the Take. Any clips that have a hyphen instead of a letter must be corrected.

3. Optional: Switch back to **FRAME** view.

4. Set the **PROJECT WINDOW > FORMAT > PROJECT TYPE** to 23.976.

    The clips for this lesson have been transcoded to standard definition with the 35:1 codec to allow the lesson material to fit on the disc(s). There is no particular benefit to transcoding media for use with script integration.

5. Choose **FILE > NEW SCRIPT**.

6. Locate and import the **AGENT ZERO.TXT** script.

The Script window appears and the Agent Zero script has been imported. This procedure copies the script to the Project folder, giving it an .avc file extension, and places it in the Project window, along with the existing bins and folders. Media Composer will treat the script like a bin and will back it up to the Avid Attic.

The original Agent Zero.txt is no longer referenced. Changes to the original Agent Zero.txt file are not reflected by the Script Integration window. If you need to revise the script, you should either do so in the Script window, or reimport the script as another script.

Exercise 6.3: Associating Takes with the Script

Begin by focusing on dialogue for your rough-cut. Create slates with associated takes for the L-series of shots, such as L1+2-1(a), L1+2-2(a), and so on:

1. Scrub through the clips and determine which lines of dialogue they cover.

2. Highlight the covered lines within the **SCRIPT** window by dragging the cursor through those lines.

3. Drag the clip from the bin onto the highlighted text within the SCRIPT window.

   The slate appears in the SCRIPT window.

4. Associate the remaining takes with this slate by dragging other takes from the bin and dropping them onto the existing slate.

5. Repeat for additional series of takes.

Try a faster process:

1. Play through U1+4-1(A) and determine which lines of dialogue it covers.

2. Highlight the covered lines within the SCRIPT window by dragging the cursor through those lines.

3. Select U1+4-1(A) and U1+4-1(B) and drag them from the bin onto the highlighted text within the SCRIPT window.

   The slate appears in the SCRIPT window, with takes attached to the slate.

4. Add the remaining clips (all of the K-series, as well as U1+4-2(A) and U1+4-3(B)) using the method you choose. After this step, slates should exist for all clips in the LESSON 6 SELECTS bin.

Exercise 6.4: Adding Script Marks Automatically

Let's use automated screening and marking to mark two clips from the K-series.

1. Select all of the takes in one of the L-series slates in the SCRIPT window. Be sure to select the individual takes by clicking the tabs underneath the slate as opposed to the slate itself.

2. Click the RECORD MARKS button in the SCRIPT window toolbar.

   The slate for the first selected take turns green in the SCRIPT window, the clip is loaded into the Source monitor, and the clip begins playing.

3. As you hear a line of dialogue, click on the matching line in the SCRIPT window.

   A script mark is created for each line of associated dialogue.

4. When the first clip is finished, the next one turns green. Repeat the marking procedure for the remaining takes in the L-series.

Using Avid ScriptSync (Optional)

If you have ScriptSync or the ScriptSync trial installed on your Media Composer system, use ScriptSync to mark the next series of clips. Otherwise, continue adding script marks using the Record button as described previously.

1. Continue in the same script as you were preparing in the previous section: **AGENT ZERO**.

2. Select the takes that do not yet have line script marks.

3. Select **SCRIPT > SCRIPTSYNC**.

   The **SCRIPTSYNC** dialog box opens. The default settings are OK.

4. Click **OK**.

The syncing process starts. Upon completion, double-click the intersection of a take and a line of dialogue and confirm that ScriptSync has accurately and rapidly added script marks to the take.

Exercise 6.5: Enriching Scripts with Metadata

When the script was saved in plain-text format, the contents of the header and footer might not have been integrated into the plain-text file. This is because headers and footers contain information that's usually specific to the printed, layed out page, whereas plain-text formats have no layout and therefore the placement of the header and footer information would interrupt the body content.

Regardless, you may notice that there are page numbers in your text file. If they are there, you might see "53" at the bottom of the text file, and your mileage may vary as for page numbers elsewhere in the text file.

With lengthy scripts, it's often useful to incorporate the page numbers back into the Avid Script window. This allows you to quickly make correlations between the printed script and the Avid script. Likewise, it's also desirable sometimes to have the scene numbers associated with the Avid script.

Once the page numbers and scene numbers are associated with the script, you can use the Go To Page and Go To Scene features of the Script window to quickly "flip" through the digital script. This can be particularly useful if your director tends to arrive script-in-hand and refer to scenes and pages from his or her printed copy.

To add page and scene numbers:

1. Scroll to the top of the script.

2. Click the **AP (ADD PAGE)** button at the top of the **SCRIPTSYNC** window.

3. In the **ADD PAGE** dialog box that appears, type **53** and press **ENTER**.

   A 53 is added to the line, and the Page box at the bottom of the window contains a 53.

4. Click the **AS (ADD SCENE)** button at the top of the **SCRIPTSYNC** window.

5. In the **ADD SCENE** dialog box, type **4** and press **ENTER**.

   A 4 is added to the Scene box at the bottom of the window.

6. Scroll to the end of the script.

7. Click the **PAGE** box at the bottom of the **SCRIPT** window. Type **53** and press **ENTER**.

The Script window will scroll to the beginning of page 53.

Finding Lines

You can also search the Script window by pressing Ctrl/Cmd+F. The F shortcut is for the Find command, which is also available by choosing Edit > Find.

1. Press **CTRL/CMD+F**.

2. Find **PAY GRADE**.

   The script should scroll to this dialogue, spoken by Mysterion.

3. Double-click the intersection of the **PAY GRADE** line and one of Mysterion's takes. Confirm that the script mark is accurate and Mysterion does, indeed, say "pay grade" at that point.

This technique is exceptionally useful in long-form interviews, where the interview has been transcribed and script marks have been added. Your director might say, "Find the section where she talks about cats," so you press Cmd/Ctrl+F, type "Cats," and press Enter. You then double-click the intersection point to load and cue the clip. Ta'da. You'll be one of the fastest editors your director has ever worked with.

Squigglies 101: Indicating Off-Screen Text

Add a squiggly line to some off-screen dialogue for one of the close-up shots of your choice:

1. In the **SCRIPTSYNC** window, double-click a take to load it into the Source monitor.

2. Identify which section or sections of the script have off-screen dialogue.

3. Select the first off-screen section of the script. Make sure that the take remains selected.

4. Click the **Set Off-Screen** button to add the squiggly line to this take for the selected portion of the dialogue.

5. If there are any other off-screen sections in this take, mark them as well. Continue to mark off-screen sections in additional takes as time allows.

Exercise 6.6: Editing with the Script Window

Now that you have created script marks and done a few other things, it's time to edit.

To begin to assemble a rough-cut:

1. Select the lines in the **Script** window, dragging through all intersecting takes.

2. Click the **Play** button in the **Script** window to screen the takes for those lines.

   The takes load and play back one after another. You can use the **Tab** key or **J-K-L** keys to jump between takes and to control playback.

3. Decide which clip you want to use for the first dialogue portion of the scene.

4. Double-click the script mark of the first preferred take to load it into the **Source** monitor. The IN point is already marked and cued.

5. Place marks and perform the edit.

6. Repeat these steps until you have used the available material. If you like, use single mark editing to quickly add shots to the sequence.

   • Select the **Single Mark Editing** option (choose the **Composer settings > Edit tab**).

   • When you double-click on a script mark, the IN point is marked automatically. The Current Time indicator will be interpreted as the OUT mark as opposed to normal behavior in which the last frame of the clip would used as the OUT mark in this scenario.

   • Continue to play and use the **splice-in (V** key), **overwrite (B** key), or **replace edit** (map to a key) keyboard shortcut when you have reached the appropriate OUT point.

7. If necessary, fine-tune the edits by using normal trimming and editing procedures.

Time permitting; continue practicing by creating a rough-cut of the Agent Zero scene.

Advanced Dialogue Editing

In the process of clay sculpting, you shape a mound of clay by adding raw material until the general shape emerges. Then you use specialized tools, like fine wires and picks, to whittle away the excess clay until your finished sculpture emerges. Editing is not dissimilar: You build a rough cut by throwing clips onto the timeline, but it's not until you cut away the excess that a polished story emerges. To create the precise, fine edits that are needed in the craft of video editing, Media Composer has specialized trim tools.

This lesson delves deep into the Media Composer Trim tool in the context of editing a dialogue scene, although the tools and techniques are applicable no matter what kind of content you're cutting.

Media Used: None

Duration: 45 minutes

GOALS

- Learn to edit by using a Radio Edit
- Understand why dynamic trimming often creates more natural edits
- Be able to isolate a problematic frame or audio glitch to the outgoing or incoming clips
- Use the keyboard to perform precise trims
- Create and remove split edits
- Understand why clips go out of sync and learn techniques to restore sync
- Learn how and when to trim in two directions simultaneously
- Understand asynchronous trimming, which involves trimming two heads or two tails

How Trimming Works

Trimming works on the basis that the length of a clip in the timeline is not necessarily proportionate to the length of a clip's media file. When you trim, you adjust the clips in the timeline to show more or less of the original media.

Trimming is an expected part of the editing process. If you always set perfect IN and OUT marks, you would not need to trim. During your rough cut, let yourself go wild—throw those clips into the timeline. When it's time to refine, the Trim mode will be ready.

Note: Some functions of the Trim tool expect that your clips have handles. That means the clip is shorter than the media file to which it points. Handles are the frames before the IN mark and after the OUT mark. If you don't use IN and OUT marks, or if you set them to the very beginning and end of the clip, you will be able to trim to remove frames, but not to lengthen clips. You can't lengthen a clip if there's no more media.

Trim Tool: Reloaded

Normally, for general-purpose editing, Media Composer operates in the Source/ Record editing mode. In Trim mode, things work and behave a little differently. Refer to Figure 7.1 as you review the following items that change as a result of working in Trim mode.

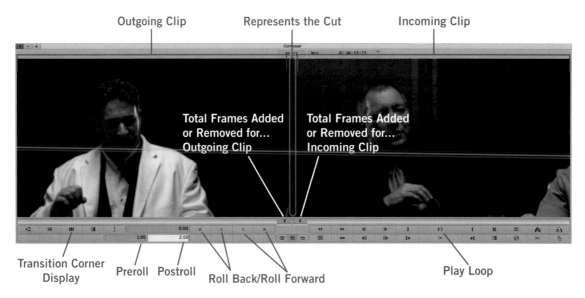

Figure 7.1
Media Composer's Trim mode.

Incoming and Outgoing Frames

The Source and Record monitors are replaced with Outgoing (left) and Incoming (right) frames, respectively. The Outgoing (left) monitor shows the last frame you'll see before the cut, whereas the Incoming (right) monitor shows the first frame you'll see after the cut.

The line that divides the Outgoing and Incoming shots represents the edit (the cut) in the timeline.

Playback Function Changes

The Play button is replaced with a Play Loop button, which responds to the keyboard shortcut of spacebar. In Trim mode, the default method of playing is playing in a loop, which means Media Composer begins playing back before the edit, and then plays to a certain point after the edit, at which time it repeats. (The fact that an editor can listen to the looped playback again, and again, and again, and again, and again, and again...without becoming, herself, loopy lends credence to the notion that editors are a different caliber of person.)

The amount of time that Media Composer plays before and after an edit is referred to as preroll and postroll, respectively, and you can set your own times in the boxes shown in Figure 7.1. In Figure 7.1, playback includes one second of media before the edit, followed by two seconds of media after the edit.

You might want to change the pre- and postroll settings in scenarios where there is a short shot and you don't want the playhead to roll over into the adjacent shot (second-previous or second-next shot from the edit). You want to focus the playback to include just the two shots that are related to the cut you are trimming.

Tip: To permanently change the default preroll/postroll settings, adjust them using Project Window > Settings > Trim.

Trim Counters

You'll either add or remove frames to one or both sides of the edit as you trim. To help you keep track of the number of frames changed since you entered Trim mode, Media Composer displays A and B side trim counters, shown with purple backgrounds in Figure 7.1.

The numbers are cumulative, so if you add ten frames but remove six, the number will be four. If you then exit Trim mode and re-enter Trim mode, the number is back to zero, because Media Composer only tracks the changes while you are in Trim mode and then clears the changes when you exit and re-enter. If you hold Alt/Option while going back into trim mode, Media Composer will retain the previous values of the Trim counters.

The actual meaning of the Trim counters is as follows:

- The A-Side counter (outgoing clip) indicates the change in the position of the clip's OUT mark. A positive number means the OUT mark was moved later in time, thus making the clip longer. A negative number means the OUT mark of the outgoing clip was moved earlier, which shortens the clip.

- The B-Side counter (incoming clip) indicates the change in the position of the clip's IN mark. A positive number means the IN mark was moved forward in time, which shortens the clip, whereas a negative number indicates the IN mark was moved earlier in time, which lengthens the clip.

By using a combination of single roller trims, in which only one side of the edit is affected, you can easily have numbers that are not the same, because you've removed or added more frames from one side than the other. If you use only a double-roller trim, both shots are changed simultaneously and in the same direction, and the numbers will match, as is the case in Figure 7.1

Trim Buttons

Trim mode displays four buttons under the outgoing (left) monitor, which are also mapped to keys on your keyboard, shown in Figure 7.2. The buttons are used to perform the following functions when editing at 30 frames per second (fps):

- << Trim Left 10 Frames: Keyboard Shortcut: M
- < Trim Left 1 Frame: Keyboard Shortcut: ,
- > Trim Right 1 Frame: Keyboard Shortcut: .
- >> Trim Right Ten Frames: Keyboard Shortcut: /

The actual number of frames moved varies depending on your frame rate. For example, instead of moving 10 frames, they only move eight frames when editing at 24fps.

Figure 7.2
The trim keys on the keyboard correlate to the trim keys in Trim mode (as shown in Figure 7.1).

Tip: You can't change the number of frames that are trimmed when using the buttons or shortcut keys. You can, however, use the numeric keypad to enter precise edits, as described in the following section.

You can use those buttons or keyboard shortcuts instead of dragging the trim rollers in the timeline. The keys are not the same as 1–4 on the keyboard, although they do move the Current Time indicator by the same number of frames. The difference is that the 1–4 keys will move the Current Time indicator, and exit Trim mode instead of performing a trim, whereas the Trim Left/Right buttons (and their corresponding keyboard shortcuts) will perform a trim and not exit Trim mode.

There is one substantial difference between the Trim Left/Right buttons on the screen in contrast to the corresponding keys on the keyboard: The keyboard keys will not cause Play Loop to be interrupted, whereas the onscreen keys will cause playback to be stopped. This becomes important when you're trimming on-the-fly using Play Loop.

Tip: Generally, in Media Composer, pressing any onscreen button will cause playback to be interrupted, while key presses are fine and do not interrupt playback.

Specifying the Clips Affected by a Trim

Trim mode can affect either the outgoing or incoming footage, or both. The kind of trim you are performing—single roller versus dual roller—is controlled by the position of the rollers on the clips in the timeline.

Note: If rollers are not on a clip, the clip is not participating in the trim.

You can switch to a single or double roller trim by clicking on the Outgoing frame, Incoming frame, or on the line that divides both of them, as shown in Figure 7.3.

You can also use the keyboard shortcuts P, [, and] to toggle the rollers to the outgoing, both, or incoming shots, respectively. Again, the benefit to using the keyboard to toggle the rollers is that Media Composer will not stop playback if you use the keyboard shortcut. This allows you to play in a loop, and while playing, change the rollers and then use the M,./ keys to move the rollers. Each time the loop restarts, Media Composer updates the timeline based on your key presses and you can see the change.

Figure 7.3
Toggle the Trim mode by clicking on the clip(s) to be adjusted in the Composer window.

Edits, Including Trims, Are Applied Immediately

In Media Composer, you'll rarely find an Apply button. As you press buttons and keys, the action is performed immediately. When you play in a loop as part of Trim mode and you press the keyboard shortcuts to reposition the rollers, the trim is applied immediately and when the loop is restarted, the Media Composer time-line is redrawn to reflect the edit you performed.

If you don't like the edit, you can press Edit > Undo. There are 99 levels of Undo in Media Composer 6. That means you can make 99 trim adjustments and back out of all of them, but if you made 100 mistakes, you're a bit out of luck when it comes to Undo.

Jumping Between Edits in Trim Mode

The keyboard shortcuts A and S are used to jump to the previous and next edits, respectively, while staying in Trim mode. If you are not already in Trim mode, these keys will put you in it. They are different from the Fast Forward/Rewind buttons in that fast forward/rewind will not cause you to enter Trim mode.

Using Relative Timecode Offset for Trimming

You can use the numeric keypad, located on the left side of a full-size (extended) keyboard, to move the rollers while in Trim mode.

To move rollers earlier:

■   Enter the negative symbol followed by the number of frames, and then perform the edit by pressing the Enter key.

Checking for Handles

Sometimes it's useful to know how many handles you have in a clip. *Handles* are the frames before the IN mark or after the OUT mark for a particular clip. Final Cut Pro 7 editors are accustomed to double-clicking a clip in the timeline in order to determine the number of handles in the viewer. In Media Composer, the same functionality can be achieved by using Match Frame, covered in Lesson 3, "Advanced Picture Editing."

To determine the number of handles:

1. Position the Current Time indicator at an edit.

2. Perform a Match Frame.

The original clip will be opened and an IN mark will be added at the frame that corresponds to the edit in the timeline. Any frames before or after that are the available handles.

Note: Use the Enter key associated with the numeric keypad, as opposed to the Return key associated with the alphanumeric portion of the keyboard.

For example, you could enter Trim mode and type **-35** (and then press Enter). That will move the rollers back 35 frames. If the Trim mode is set up for a single roller trim, this will either move the OUT mark back 35 frames, which shortens a clip, or it will move the IN mark back, which will lengthen a clip. If the Trim mode is configured for a dual-roller trim, this will move both edits back 35 frames, shortening the outgoing clip and lengthening the incoming clip, by adding frames to the head of the incoming clip.

99 Is Greater Than 100

Media Composer examines whether you enter two or three digits as you type on the numeric keypad. Entering two or fewer digits indicates that you are entering a frame count—from 0 to 99 frames—whereas entering three or more digits indicates you are entering timecode, from 1 second (1:00) onward. By Media Composer's way of doing math, 100 is less than a third of 99, because 100 is interpreted as one second (1:00) whilst 99 is interpreted as three seconds, nine frames (3:09) based on a project at 30fps. If you genuinely want to enter a frame count larger than 99, type it in as normal and then press the lowercase f before pressing Enter. The lowercase f causes Media Composer to re-interpret the entry as a frame count in excess of 99. For example, 99f will change the display from "99" to "3:09".

Tip: You can also use this technique for moving the Current Time indicator when not in Trim mode.

If you're using a keyboard that doesn't have a numeric keypad, such as a laptop computer, you'll find it almost impossible to enter timecodes. The numeric keys along the top of the alphabetical keys are used for functions like Play and Play Loop and for enabling the video and audio tracks. If you want those number keys to be interpreted as though they are the numeric keypad, tap the Control key twice. Those keys will temporarily be interpreted as being the same as the numeric keypad, instead of performing their normal functions.

Digital Audio Scrubbing

When trimming, it may be helpful to hear the audio samples so you can locate particular audio cues. Audio Scrubbing is the feature in Media Composer where snippets of audio are played each time the blue Current Time indicator is moved. Activate audio scrubbing temporarily by pressing and holding the Shift key while moving the Current Time indicator, or activate it indefinitely by enabling Caps Lock.

Unobstructed Waveforms

Sometimes the rollers will obstruct the waveforms. You can't see small audio ticks because Media Composer is putting the roller directly on top of the audio waveform, as shown by comparing Figures 7.4 and 7.5. In Figure 7.4, there is a small waveform near the edit but you can't see it because of the roller. In Figure 7.5, it's revealed because transparent arrows are used instead of opaque rollers.

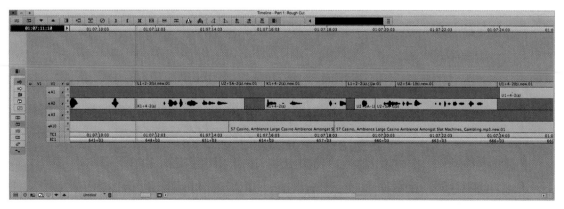

Figure 7.4
The trim rollers are obstructing the waveform on the incoming clip.

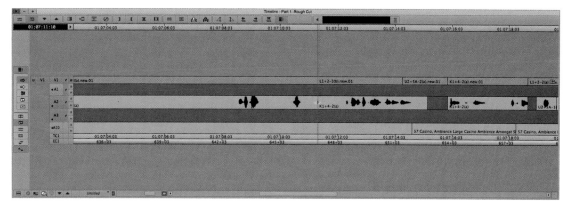

Figure 7.5
The waveform is easier to see when transparent arrows are displayed instead of solid rollers.

You can configure Trim mode to display small semi-transparent arrows instead of the relatively large opaque rollers by selecting Arrows at Selected Transitions in Trim settings, as shown in Figure 7.6.

Figure 7.6
It's easy to replace the opaque rollers with transparent arrows using Trim settings.

Tip: A quick way to access Trim settings from within Trim mode is to right-click in the Composer window and select Trim Settings, or press Ctrl/Cmd+=.

Creating a Radio Edit

Long before television, radio dominated the mass entertainment market. Radio programs like *War of the Worlds*, voiced by actors and enriched with sound effects and music, were broadcast as hundreds of thousands listened weekly to their favorite programs. There is something to be said for being able to create a compelling story from the sound and dialogue alone, without any pictures.

In fact, Gene Roddenberry, creator of *Star Trek,* once commented that when he was learning to be a storyteller, he would sit with his back toward his television and listen. In this exercise, he developed skills in timing, pacing, and dialogue editing.

The technique of editing a show while disregarding the visual content is referred to as *performing a radio edit.* Your goal in a radio edit is to ensure that the pacing and delivery of the lines is natural and appropriate for the genre. You want to ensure comedies are funny and dramas are dramatic by ensuring the lines are delivered at the right pace. You're as interested in the timing of when the lines are delivered as when they are not. Sometimes the most poignant note in a symphony is a rest, and in a film, the extra beat (pause) you add after a line can be more effective than any close up or additional line of dialogue.

Disabling the Video Monitoring

Media Composer tracks can be enabled for monitoring and enabled for editing, and those two enablements are independent of each other. When a track is enabled for monitoring, it can be seen or heard. When it is enabled for editing, clips on the track can be trimmed, lifted, extracted, and edited.

Figure 7.7 shows where to click to toggle the editing or monitoring of tracks.

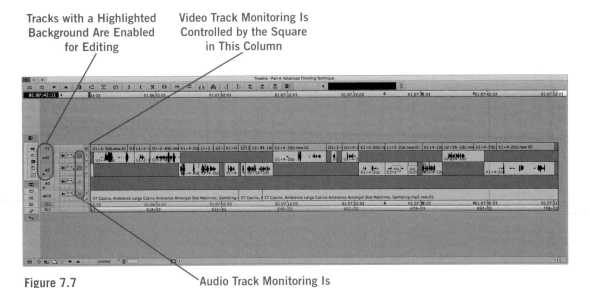

Tracks with a Highlighted Background Are Enabled for Editing

Video Track Monitoring Is Controlled by the Square in This Column

Figure 7.7
Enabling tracks for editing and monitoring.

Audio Track Monitoring Is Controlled by the Power Button

Note: Final Cut Pro 7 editors can think of enabling tracks as similar to the Auto-Select, whereas monitoring tracks in Media Composer is similar to enabling a track in Final Cut Pro 7.

When performing a radio edit, you might prefer to totally disable the video monitoring by clicking the video monitor. If you do that, remember to leave the video tracks enabled for editing. While your focus on a radio edit is the audio, by leaving the video tracks enabled, they will also be trimmed and you will not likely put your clips out of sync.

Tip: Editing video and audio tracks together reduces the risk of breaking sync. You can also enable sync locks, covered in the following section, to further reduce the risk of breaking sync.

Sync Locks

Media Composer includes sync locks, which prevent two or more tracks from falling out of sync. When enabled, Media Composer either prevents an edit from happening, or adds filler, as is required to prevent the loss of sync.

When Sync Locks are enabled, shown in Figure 7.8, Media Composer will play a *bonk* sound when the feature activates. Enabling sync lock when doing your radio edit is a surefire way to ensure you do not accidentally forget to trim the video while focusing on the audio.

Figure 7.8
Sync locks enabled for V1, A1, and A2.

Add Edit

Aside from Sync Locks, another way to maintain sync while trimming across multiple tracks is to add edits to filler. Rather than taking the time to carefully deselect the tracks with video, you can add edit points to filler only by adding the Alt/Opt modifier key.

To add edits to all filler tracks, regardless of track selection:

1. Position the CURRENT TIME INDICATOR at the desired location.

2. ALT/OPTION+CLICK the ADD EDIT button.

 Take a moment to complete Exercise 7, Part 1.

Using Dynamic Trimming

The previous section covered a kind of trimming that could be called *static trimming*. It's a very functional, although basic, way to trim using the Trim tool. But the Trim tool has many more secrets lurking under the surface and they emerge when the Trim tool is playing back in a loop. They are referred to as dynamic trimming (or trimming on-the-fly) and the goal is for you to perform your trim during playback.

Good trimming can evoke an emotional response. The act of speaking is based on a sense of timing and rhythm, and to trim naturally, you need to hear the audio and see the video in real-time as opposed to adjusting a trim, playing it back, stopping, and then repeating the process.

You may have had the (mis)fortune of working with a producer who asks you to play the timeline and then he snaps his fingers and blurts out "THERE!," at the moment where he wants an edit to occur. Although it might seem a bit rude, he's essentially doing dynamic trimming—while the piece is playing, you fall into the rhythm of the performance and the existing cuts, and from those you derive the natural place for the next edit.

There is no toggle switch, nor any button that must be pressed to instruct Media Composer to allow dynamic trimming. It's always on. That's convenient but it could be a bit dangerous because some features—like Mark IN and the J-K-L keys—take on alternative behaviors when used from within Trim mode, as you will soon read.

Tip: Remember: If it isn't in motion, it's not dynamic.

Shortcuts While Playing in a Loop

While Media Composer is playing in a loop, you can use the keyboard shortcuts of M ,. / to move the rollers forward or backward, as discussed in a previous section and shown in Figure 7.2. Because the sequence is playing while you use these keys, this is a form of dynamic trimming.

Isolating the Incoming or Outgoing Side

When playing in a loop as part of Trim mode (and only when playing in a loop), the Go to IN (Q) and Go to OUT (W) keys on the keyboard take on new behaviors. They affect the playback of the loop by isolating it to one side of the cut or the other.

- Q: Play the outgoing clip, from the preroll position through to the edit, and then repeat.

- W: Play from the cut forward to the postroll position, and then repeat.

Media Composer provides two visual cues in the Composer window to indicate that you have isolated one side of the edit, as shown in Figure 7.9.

Figure 7.9
Visual cues that the outgoing or incoming sides have been isolated.

1. The **PLAY LOOP** icon updates with an arrow, indicating that the playback occurs up to the edit or from the edit. In Figure 7.9, the Q key was used and the playback occurs up to the edit and then repeats.

2. The corresponding preroll or postroll box is highlighted in green.

To cancel the isolation and return to the normal behavior of playing through the edit, press the same key that was previously pressed. For example, if you are playing up to the edit and then repeating, the Q key was used. Pressing the Q key a second time cancels the feature and restores Play Loop to its normal behavior.

Using Mark IN to Adjust an Edit

While playing in a loop from within Trim mode, pressing the Mark IN key on the keyboard (not the button on the interface) causes the trim rollers to jump to wherever the blue line was at the moment you pressed the Mark IN key.

This feature is useful for aligning edits to a beat in a music clip, or for getting an edit at a precise moment based on feeling. If you can loop through an edit and say "THERE!" at the precise place where you want the edit to occur, this feature could very well become one of your favorites.

To adjust an edit using Mark IN:

1. Enter **TRIM** mode.

2. Place rollers at the appropriate points.

3. Begin playing in a loop (keyboard shortcut: 6).

4. Press **MARK IN** (keyboard shortcut: I) when you hear the place where you want the edit to be located.

J-K-L Trimming

You should be familiar with the shuttle controls of J-K-L, where J plays backward, L plays forward, and the more times you press them, the faster the playback. K means stop, and K+L or K+J results in slow-motion playback with a kind of analog audio scrub that sounds like a traditional reel-to-reel tape deck or someone slowing down a record player.

Using the J-K-L controls in Trim mode allows you to actually perform the trim while you watch the footage. Instead of moving only the playhead, J-K-L in Trim mode will move the actual rollers, provided you stop playback using the K key instead of the spacebar.

This method is powerful because it plays your incoming and/or outgoing material beyond the edit point, allowing you to see your source material. You can use this technique to trim long sections of clips quickly, for example, trimming in additional interview material while you watch it in real-time, or faster than real-time.

To use J-K-L trim:

1. Enter **TRIM** mode.

2. Place rollers at the appropriate points.

3. If you want to trim back from the edit, press the **J KEY** alone or **J-K** combination. At the desired frame, release the keys to stop playback and perform the trim.

4. If you want to trim forward from the current edit, press the **L KEY** alone or **K-L** combination. At the desired frame, release the keys to stop playback and perform the trim. The system tracks the overall number of frames you have trimmed from either side in the outgoing and incoming trim boxes.

5. If you are not sure which way you want to trim, press the **J KEY** to back up a little, and then press the **L KEY** to take you forward again. Press the **K KEY** to choose your new edit.

Note: **J-K-L trim will never completely trim away a shot. It will stop when one frame of the clip remains. If you trim away too much material, just reverse your direction to add more of the shot back in.**

Trimming with J-K-L keys also allows you to scrub audio as you trim. Especially in slow-motion, or ¼ speed, J-K-L trim can allow you to hear the precise point a sound begins or ends, even if it is not clearly visible in the waveforms.

Note: Audio scrubbing with J-K-L sounds quite different than audio scrubbing with Caps Lock enabled. When scrubbing using the J-K-L keys, the audio sounds like a traditional reel-to-reel tape player, with high pitch smooth sounds at fast speeds and low pitch smooth sounds at slow speeds. Scrubbing with the Caps Lock enabled, called digital audio scrubbing, sounds very choppy and computerized.

EXERCISE   *Take a moment to complete Exercise 7, Part 2.*

Using Split Edits

A *split edit* occurs when the video and audio do not cut at the same time. Figure 7.10 shows an edit before it's split, and Figure 7.11 shows the same edit after the split. Notice that despite the split, the clip still finishes at the same time.

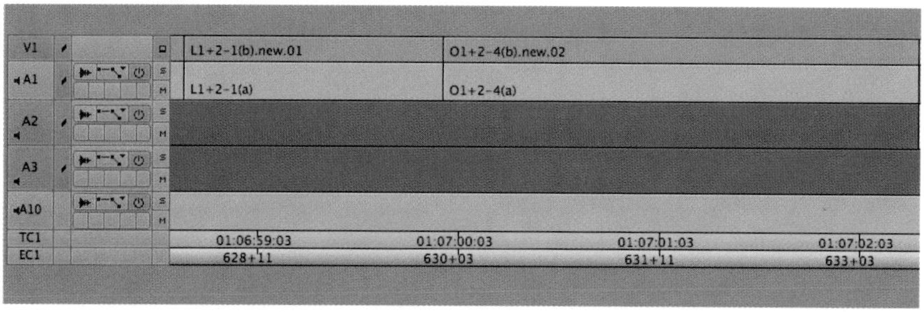

Figure 7.10
An edit before being split.

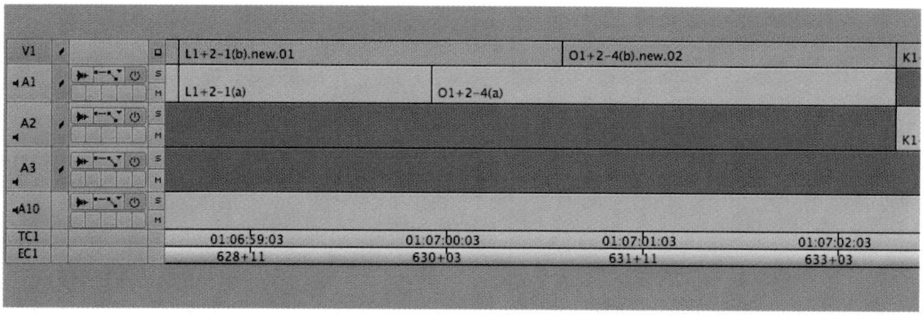

Figure 7.11
An edit after being split.

Split edits are created in a way that affects only one edit. Usually, that's done using a dual roller trim on the video track only. By the time you begin adding split edits, you've probably already completed the radio edit and your audio edits are fine, so you would not want to change it further.

The reason you use split edits, sometimes called L-edits or L-cuts, is because they allow you to model the real world. People will change what they're looking in at in response to sound. In other words: Sound motivates a visual change.

For example, picture a classroom with students and a teacher. One student is looking out the window. The teacher snaps her fingers and the student looks in the direction of a snap. A more vivid scenario is the sound of a car crash while you're walking down the street. You hear the sound, so you turn your head. You don't turn your head first, nor do you turn it at the exact same moment as the sound occurs, because you have no reason to. It takes a beat to recognize the sound, so when you create a split edit, you often allow the audio to lead the video so it gives a reason for the cut. In this way, the cut becomes a bit less obvious and a bit more transparent.

Most primetime TV shows and most movies are almost entirely split cut. Although sound often follows video, there are also times when you might want a visual cue to provoke an audio cue, although that scenario is less common.

Creating Split Edits

There are two ways to create a split edit easily in Media Composer. The first way is to use Trim mode to perform a double-roller trim. The other way is to use the Extend feature.

Creating split edits using dual-roller trim:

1. Start by editing a sequence using straight cuts.

2. Enter TRIM mode at the transition where you want the split edit to occur.

3. Turn off the TRACK button(s) for either audio or video, depending on whether you want to extend the video over the audio or the audio under the video.

4. Ensure you're in dual-roller TRIM mode where both sides of the cut have the trim rollers visible, and then use your mouse and drag the edit point to the left or the right in the timeline. Notice how the edit point changes as you drag. You can also use any other trim method to adjust the edit point.

5. Play your edit while still in TRIM mode by pressing any of the PLAY buttons on the keyboard (apart from J and L unless you want to J-K-L trim), or clicking the PLAY button on the interface, which has now automatically become the PLAY LOOP button, since you are in TRIM mode.

6. Exit TRIM mode by clicking on the TRIM button on the screen or by clicking on the TRIM key on the keyboard.

Using Extend Edit

The Extend function allows you to adjust transition points without going into Trim mode. With this feature, you roll an edit point left or right in the timeline, thus trimming frames from one side of the transition and adding them to the other. The Extend function prevents you from losing sync, and also enables you to mark the edit point on-the-fly.

1. Start by editing several straight cuts together.

2. Play the edit that you want to adjust and decide where you want the edit to begin or end.

3. If you want the edit to start earlier than it does, mark an IN at that point. If you want it to end later than it does, mark an OUT at that point. In Figure 7.12, the edit point will be extended to the mark OUT.

4. (Optional) To create a split edit, turn off the **Track** button(s) for either audio or video, depending on whether you want to extend the video over the audio, or the audio under the video.

5. Click the **Extend** button to trim the edit back to the IN or forward to the OUT.

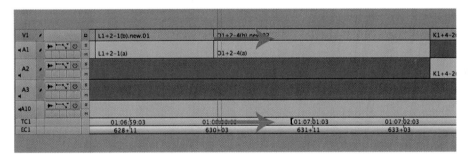

Figure 7.12
Extending an edit to the OUT mark.

Tip: To create a split edit on-the-fly, map the Extend button (choose Tools >
Command Palette > Trim tab) to a keyboard shortcut. You can navigate with
J-K-L, Mark IN or OUT, and use Extend all without moving your hand position
on the keyboard.

Using Trim versus Extend Edit to Create Split Edits

You can create split edits using either Trim mode or Extend edit. The choice of which one to use is largely a matter of personal preference. Here are some points to consider:

- You can use Extend edit to create split edits on-the-fly (see the previous tip) while doing your final run-through.

- You can't break sync using the Extend function.

- Use Trim mode if you are fine-tuning your program in Trim mode.

Removing Split Edits

There are various reasons why you would want to remove a split edit. For example, you may want to segment drag a split edit in the timeline, but can't without breaking sync. In this case you might want to quickly remove the split first, segment drag the clip, and then add the split back.

Removing a split edit is easy if you remember this simple rule: *That which giveth the split edit, taketh away the split edit.*

In other words, to remove a split edit simply use either the Trim mode or Extend edit techniques you've learned already, in reverse.

   Take a moment to complete Exercise 7, Part 3.

Advanced Trim Techniques

When you start trimming in Media Composer, you typically select a single or double-roller trim, and then move the trim rollers in either a forward or backward direction. A secret of professional editors is that it's possible to move an edit in both a forward and backward direction simultaneously, which is the focus of this section.

Bidirectional Trimming

You don't have to orient all of the trim rollers in the same direction. You can trim the head on some tracks while trimming the tail on others. This is especially useful when overlapping dialogue in narrative editing, or dialogue and natural sound from cutaway material.

To trim in two directions simultaneously:

1. Enter Trim mode at the transition you want to adjust.

Using the **Focus** command or **zoom** slider will make it much easier to set the trim rollers accurately.

2. **Shift-click** to place trim rollers on the desired side of the edits on each track in the sequence, as shown in Figure 7.13.

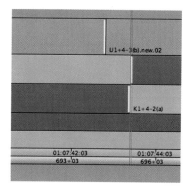

Figure 7.13
Rollers on opposing sides of the edit.

3. Click the **trim** roller on the track you want to use as the watch point.

    This roller indicates the type of trimming that J-K-L trimming will perform. For example, if you click on a head trim roller, pressing the J key will add material to all selected tracks and pressing the L key will remove material from all selected tracks. If you click on a tail trim roller, pressing the J key will remove material from all selected tracks and pressing the L key will add material to all selected tracks.

4. Trim using any of the trim methods you would normally use.

Tip: When getting started with this technique, you may find it easiest to start by dragging the trim rollers. Media Composer will display ghosted edit points allowing you to see the direction each roller is moving.

Asynchronous Trimming

Media Composer enables you to select two A-sides (tails) or two B-sides (heads) anywhere in the timeline and perform an asynchronous trim on those two edits.

Here's just one scenario illustrating this feature's usefulness. You are well into the edit and need to shorten clip 1 in a sequence. Unfortunately, the duration of the scene is already locked. What are your options? Well, you could use a dual roller trim at the edit point between Clip 1 and the next clip, Clip 2, but that would change the head frame edit on Clip 1, which you don't want. Alternatively you could slide Clip 2, but that would change the head frame edit on the following shot, Clip 3, which you also don't want.

Since neither single trim approach really works, you'll likely do an A-side trim on the tail of Clip 1, write the number of frames trimmed on a piece of paper, and then find the tail of another shot in the scene that you could extend. It works, but hopefully you won't get distracted while you're searching for that other clip.

The solution? Asynchronous trimming.

In this scenario you'll trim the tail of two shots, as seen in Figure 7.14. You can just as easily trim the heads of two clips.

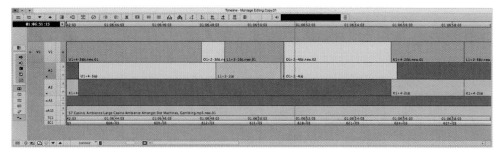

Figure 7.14
The green shots' tails will be trimmed.

1. Lasso the edit between the clip you want to trim and the next clip.

2. Switch to an **A-SIDE** trim.

3. **SHIFT+CLICK** on the other two rollers.

    The timeline is shown in Figure 7.15.

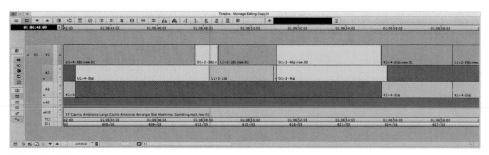

Figure 7.15
Notice that the trim rollers, unlike in Slide mode, point in the same direction.

Tip: To use J-K-L or on-the-fly trim, place the Position Indicator on the trim handle you want to control from. Then if you trim backward, for example, with J+K, the other roller trims forward.

4. Use any trim technique you desire (drag rollers, J-K-L, on-the-fly, and so on).

During the trim, notice that the trim rollers move in opposite directions—frames are added to one clip and the same number of frames is removed from the other clip. The duration of the sequence has not changed.

After making the trim, the timeline looks like Figure 7.16.

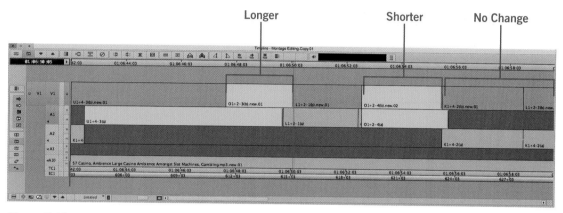

Figure 7.16
After: one shot is longer, one is shorter and the downstream shots are unchanged.

Tip: Alt/Option+U will re-enter Trim with your previous trim-roller setup enabled. This is a big time saver if you are working with complex trim setups.

EXERCISE   *Take a moment to complete Exercise 7, Part 4.*

Review/Discussion Questions

1. Identify six or more ways that the Composer window changes when you are in Trim mode. (See "Trim Tool: Reloaded" on page 268.)

2. In Trim mode, you perform a single-roller trim on the incoming clip by entering +10, -5, and then press the comma key twice. What numbers are in the Trim Counter boxes and in what way have you modified the outgoing and incoming clips? (See "Trim Counters" and "Using Relative Timecode Offset for Trimming" on pages 269 and 272, respectively.)

3. What's the significant difference between pressing the Trim Left/Right buttons on the Composer window in contrast to pressing them on the keyboard? (See "Trim Buttons" on page 270.)

4. What are two ways to toggle between trimming the Incoming or Outgoing clip, using the mouse? (See "Specifying the Clips Affected by a Trim" on page 271.)

5. How do you specify the clips affected by a trim using only the keyboard? (See "Specifying the Clips Affected by a Trim" on page 271.)

6. Upon entering Trim mode, the trim rollers are obscuring the audio waveform. How can you fix this? (See "Unobstructed Waveforms" on page 274.)

7. What's the difference between using the numeric keypad to enter –100 as opposed to –30 when cutting in a sequence having a frame rate of 24fps? (See "Using Relative Timecode Offset for Trimming" on page 272.)

8. What is a radio edit? (See "Creating a Radio Edit" on page 275.)

9. Describe two ways to perform dynamic trimming in Media Composer. (See "Using Dynamic Trimming" on page 278.)

10. When playing in a loop, how do you isolate playback to just the incoming clip? (See "Isolating the Incoming or Outgoing Side" on page 278.)

11. You're in Trim mode and you use the K+L keys to perform an analog audio scrub. What happens when you let go of the keys? How does this differ from performing the same function in Source/Record mode? (See "J-K-L Trimming" on page 280.)

12. What is an Extend edit? (See "Using Extend Edit" on page 283.)

13. How does your choice of an IN mark or OUT mark influence the behavior of the Extend Edit feature? (See "Using Extend Edit" on page 283.)

14. When might you use bidirectional trimming? (See "Bidirectional Trimming" on page 284.)

15. When might you use asynchronous trimming? (See "Asynchronous Trimming" on page 285.)

16. Compare and contrast bidirectional trimming and asynchronous trimming. (See "Advanced Trim Techniques" on page 284.)

Performing Advanced Editing

In these exercises, you'll practice the advanced editing techniques you've learned in this chapter.

Duration:

75 minutes

GOALS

- Minimize the amount of times that you exit and re-enter Trim mode. Try to perform the entire exercise by only entering Trim mode once.

- Use the A and S keys to move between edits

- Select the kind of trim (single roller/double roller) using the P, [, and] keys

- Move the rollers using the buttons in Trim mode

- Move the rollers using the keyboard shortcuts for left/right ten/one frames (keys: m ,. /)

- Move the rollers by entering an offset using the numeric keypad

- Avoid using the mouse to move the rollers

- Practice using J-K-L trim to align edits to the beat

- Practice using Mark IN to align an edit with a beat

- Practice asynchronous trimming

- Practice trimming in two directions (bidirectional)

Exercise 7.1: Performing a Radio Edit

In this exercise, a rough cut of the Agent Zero scene has been created. The editor is no longer on the project and you have been hired to finish the edit. The purpose of this exercise is to allow you an opportunity to practice using Trim mode with its keyboard shortcuts. You are not to use Lift or Extract, nor are you to use the Smart Tool.

To perform a radio edit:

1. Open the AGENT MXZERO PROJECT > 201 > LESSON 7 DLG. EDITING > LESSON 7 SEQUENCES > PART 1: ROUGH CUT.

2. Disable V1's VIDEO MONITORING.

3. Perform a radio edit using the goals outlined at the beginning of this exercise.

You may edit nonlinearly, in any order, starting wherever in the sequence you like.

Exercise 7.2: Using Dynamic Trimming

In this exercise, you are going to edit a montage of shots from Agent MXZero to music, using two dynamic trim methods—J-K-L and Mark IN.

To practice using dynamic trimming:

1. Open the AGENT MXZERO PROJECT > 201 > LESSON 7 DLG. EDITING > LESSON 7 SEQUENCES > PART 2: DYNAMIC TRIMMING.

2. Shuffle the clips by repositioning them using the SPLICE/OVERWRITE SMART TOOL (yellow arrow). Avoid having adjacent shots of the same characters.

3. Enter TRIM mode and use the dynamic trimming techniques to align each edit to a beat.

The video track contains more material than the audio track, so you will need to remove some footage from the video track. Do not remove any clips entirely; only trim away at the head or tail of some shots.

Exercise 7.3: Creating Split Edits

In this exercise, you practice creating split edits using dual-roller trim as well as the using the Extend function.

Duplicate the sequence from Exercise 7.1 and name the duplicate Part 3: Split Edits. Then go through each edit and add split edits using Trim mode as well as Extend.

Exercise 7.4:
Using Advanced Trimming Techniques

In this exercise, you will use asynchronous and bidirectional trimming to perform some complex trim operations on the Agent Zero sequence. During this module, practice reentering trim using the Alt/Opt key. It is especially useful when doing complicated trims, such as those in this exercise.

1. Open the AGENT MXZERO project and choose 201 > LESSON 7 DLG. EDITING > LESSON 7 SEQUENCES > PART 4: ADVANCED TRIMMING TECHNIQUES.

2. Go to 01:07:30:00 (approximately). The clip is surrounded by blue markers.

   The producer wants to see more of the agent before cutting to the villain.

3. Before you trim, take a moment to recognize the inherent limitations on this trim:

   ● The action of the villain's shot begins at the cut. Extend or dual-roller trim or sliding would affect that. In this scenario, you do not want to affect that.

   ● You can't change the incoming frame of this shot because the producer likes it. (No slipping.)

   ● You do not want to change the overall length of the timeline, as the sequence has already been cut to time.

   The solution is to trim two tails—an asynchronous trim—as shown in Figure EX7.1.

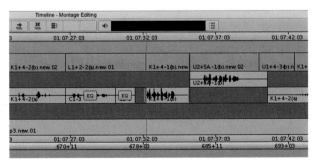

Figure EX7.1
Asynchronous trim: two tails being trimmed.

4. Set up the trim as shown in Figure EX7.1.

   You need to select one edit point normally, and then use the Shift modifier key to add the other roller.

5. Trim the tail by moving forward, to the right, approximately half a second.

The clip of the agent will be longer, and the tail of the villain will be shorter, but the head of the villain clip will be unaffected, although it will occur a half-second later in the timeline than it originally did.

Now you'll practice bidirectional trim.

6. Go to the **Pink** marker.

This section needs to be tightened. There are too many beats between the wide shot of the villain and the reverse shot of the agent receiving poker chips.

7. Use **Trim** mode to select the edits as shown in Figure EX7.2.

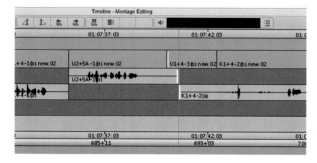

Figure EX7.2
Preparing for a bidirectional trim.

8. Drag any of the rollers according to the arrows in Figure EX7.3.

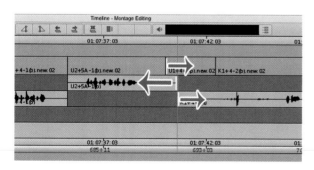

Figure EX7.3
Rollers move in opposing directions during a bidirectional trim.

Working with Multichannel Audio

In this lesson, you learn to work with multichannel audio. You learn how to create stereo and surround sound pans and you'll learn how to import, capture, and create multichannel clips.

Media Used: Agent MXZero

Duration: 45 minutes

GOALS

- Learn how multichannel editing differs from single-channel editing
- Understand the usage scenarios for stereo, 5.1, and 7.1 audio tracks
- Create multichannel audio clips through importing, capturing, and modifying existing clips
- Use the Track control panel for soloing and muting audio tracks
- Automate the pan of audio clips in both a stereo and surround sequence
- Differentiate between sequence format and the mix mode
- Use the Advanced Panner feature of the Audio Mixer

Understanding Tracks, Channels, and Voices

Media Composer's support of multichannel audio allows you create surround sound audio mixes directly within the editing system, using standard tools like the Audio Mixer. Multichannel support is relatively new in Media Composer, with stereo support being added in Media Composer 5 and surround sound being added in Media Composer 6.

There are a few terms—tracks, channels, and voices—that are helpful to understand when dealing with multichannel audio. These terms are also used throughout the Avid documentation.

Tracks Contain Clips of the Same Type

A *track* is the traditional track in the sense of a sequence. It's where you place a clip. Tracks are specific to the kind of clip they can contain.

For example, a video track contains a video clip, whereas an audio track contains an audio clip. New in Media Composer 6 is support for 7.1 and 5.1 surround sound audio clips, while Media Composer 5 added support for stereo tracks. Just as a video track contains a video clip, a 5.1 surround audio track contains a 5.1 surround audio clip.

A Channel Is a Physical Connection

A *channel* is a hardware input or output. In the sense of Media Composer, channels will correspond to something physical with your computer or video/audio I/O hardware. For example, an Avid Nitris DX has four analog audio channel inputs and outputs. A laptop often has two channels for output (to the left and right of the stereo headphone jack).

Channel also refers to a component of a multichannel clip, hence the name multichannel. For example, a stereo audio clip has two channels of audio. The clip itself goes on one stereo track.

A Voice Is a Distinct Sound

A *voice* refers to an individual stream of audio played back by Media Composer. A voice corresponds to a media file. Media Composer separates audio on the media drive—one file per channel—and each one that is being played simultaneously is referred to as a *voice*.

If all the audio media files are a choir, the members who are actively singing are the ones who have a voice. Media Composer is capable of playing back 16 voices at once and not a single voice more. It's important for you to consider how many voices individual clips require so you don't accidentally have a scenario whereby a clip's voice is unheard because it's the 17th voice.

For example, a 7.1 surround sound clip will use eight voices during playback. That means you can play only two 7.1 surround sound clips simultaneously because their total voice count is 16. This is covered in more detail later in this lesson in "Using Audio Scrub" on page 306.

Multichannel Enhancements in Media Composer

It's helpful for understanding the power of multichannel editing to compare it to the older, non-multichannel workflow.

In the traditional workflow, Media Composer only supported what are now referred to as *mono audio tracks*. If you imported a stereo MP3 music file, the resulting clip in your bin would have two mono audio channels—one representing the voice intended for the left speaker, and the other representing the voice for the right speaker. When the clip is placed in a sequence, it uses two tracks. The left channel appears on one track and the right channel appears on another, as shown in Figure 8.1.

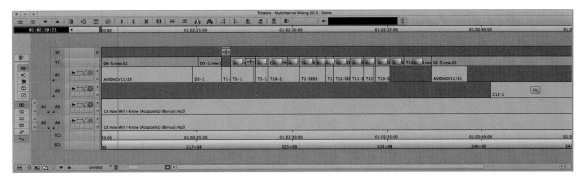

Figure 8.1
Traditionally, an imported stereo MP3 results in two mono tracks: A1 and A2.

As the audio is spread over two separate tracks, the Audio Mixer allows separate adjustments to the left and the right side, shown in Figure 8.2. Separate adjustments for the left and right channels of a stereo music file originally created in stereo isn't the natural way to adjust the levels of stereo audio. On your portable music player, when listening to your favorite artist, you adjust the volume and both speakers adjust. You do not have separate volume controls for left and right speakers.

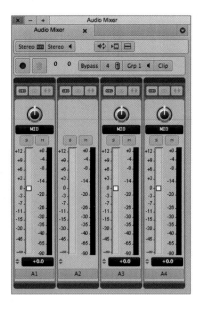

Figure 8.2
Mono tracks are adjusted
separately using the Audio Mixer.

By tapping into the multichannel capabilities of Media Composer, you can specify that the clip is genuinely stereo and it will appear on the timeline using a single track, as shown in Figure 8.3. The track is called a *stereo audio track* and the double-speaker icon on the track selector indicates that the clips it contains actually consist of two separate voices.

Mono Audio Track Indicator (Single Speaker Means Single Channel)

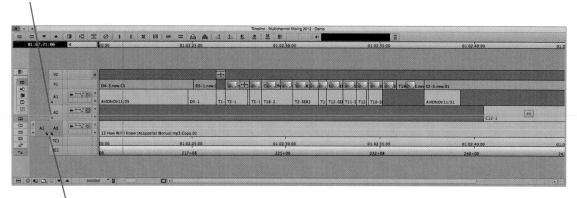

Stereo Audio Track Indicator (Two Speakers Mean Two Channels)

Figure 8.3
A sequence having two mono tracks (A1-2) and a single stereo track (A3) is represented by the double-speaker icon.

Mono tracks can only represent one channel of the stereo pair, whereas a stereo track will represent both channels. When the Audio Mixer is used with a stereo track, a single slider is available to adjust the volume, just like a portable music player, as shown in Figure 8.4. When the slider is adjusted, the levels of both the left and right channels are affected uniformly.

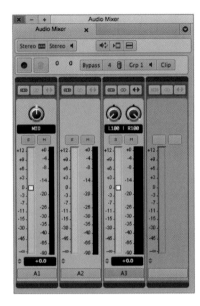

Figure 8.4
The Audio Mixer handles stereo audio tracks by presenting a single slider.

You can also explicitly specify that clips contain stereo audio, and those clips will now take a single track on the timeline instead of two separate tracks. Likewise, you can specify that clips contain 5.1 or 7.1 surround sound mixes, and those will take a single track on the timeline instead of 6 or 7 tracks, respectively.

Tip: Like pairs with like. If you have a clip with a 7.1 surround track format, you must put that clip on a 7.1 surround audio track. Mono audio only goes on mono tracks.

Even if you don't create surround sound mixes, you can benefit from using the multichannel capabilities of Media Composer.

Creating Multichannel Sequence Tracks

You create multichannel audio tracks the same way you create traditional (mono) audio tracks. Choose the Clip menu as shown in Figure 8.5, or right-click in the timeline.

Figure 8.5

Create multichannel audio tracks by choosing Clip > New Audio Track.

The kind of track is indicated on the track selector in the timeline, as shown in Figure 8.6.

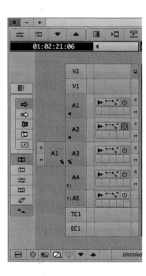

Figure 8.6

A sequence having multiple types of audio tracks.

In Figure 8.6:

- Track A1 and A2 are mono tracks

- Track A3 is a stereo track

- Track A4 is a 5.1 surround track

- Track A5 is a 7.1 surround track

Media Composer supports 24 audio tracks per sequence, in any combination, but that doesn't mean you'll hear all 24 tracks. Media Composer is limited to just 16 voices, as previously discussed in "A Voice Is a Distinct Sound" on page 294.

Note: Lesson 11, "Real-Time AudioSuite (RTAS)," introduces the topic of mixing down audio. Through an audio mixdown, you can combine the 16 tracks and multiple voices into a reduced number of voices that Media Composer is able to play back concurrently. Refer to Lesson 11 for more information on audio mixdowns.

Creating Multichannel Source Clips

In the previous sections, you've learned that a stereo sequence track can only receive a stereo clip, and a 7.1 surround track can only receive a 7.1 surround track. This is the *like receives like* principle. But where do those multichannel source clips come from? They come from the same places mono source clips come from—you import them, capture them, or modify an existing mono source clip to make one.

One of the beautiful things about editing multichannel audio in Media Composer is that in the timeline, you don't treat it any differently than traditional mono tracks.

The techniques for creating multichannel clips are discussed in the following sections.

Importing Multichannel Clips

Audio files that you import may contain multiple embedded channels. That should come as no surprise: An imported MP3 song will almost certainly come with at least a left and right channel. You can also have audio files (or video + audio files) with 16 audio tracks.

While importing an audio file, you can tell Media Composer that the individual channels in the file should be grouped together into stereo or surround sound clips. Specify the multichannel configuration of a file by opening the Import options, selecting the Audio tab and selecting Multichannel.

Figure 8.7 shows the multichannel import options.

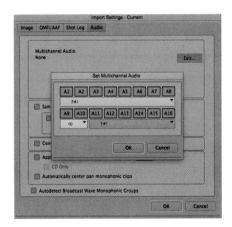

Figure 8.7
Import options allow you to specify the multichannel configuration of the source file.

In this example, channels 1-8 in the file will be grouped together as a 7.1 surround clip (the blue bar), whereas channels 9-10 are a stereo pair (green bar), and the remaining channels are a 5.1 surround clip. It's unlikely you would actually receive an audio file embedding these separate channel configurations into a single file, but it's possible and Media Composer can handle it.

If you were just importing a stereo music clip, you'd indicate that A1 and A2 are a stereo pair, after which they would have a green bar beneath them, as A9 and A10 do in Figure 8.7.

Capturing Multichannel Clips

Capturing from tape involves patching the Audio Out channels of your deck to the Audio In channels of your I/O hardware, which may be Avid's Nitris DX, Mojo DX, or a third-party hardware device supported through Avid Open I/O.

The Capture tool can be configured to automatically group related channels together during the capture, as shown at the top of Figure 8.8.

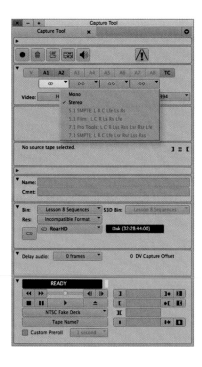

Figure 8.8
Creating multichannel clips during capture.

Modifying a Clip's Track Format

When you create a clip, either through importing or capturing, and you specify that the audio is multichannel, you're just setting the metadata. You're not actually changing how the media is written to the media drive. It's just a switch that's being flipped, a switch that Media Composer uses to determine what can and can't be done with the audio file.

Even if a clip has already been captured, you can flip the switch at any point by modifying the clip's track format, which converts a clip from discrete mono channels to a stereo or surround multichannel clip.

To modify a clip's track format:

1. Select the master clip or subclip in the bin.

2. Choose CLIP > MODIFY... > SET MULTICHANNEL AUDIO.

3. Set the format as shown in Figure 8.9.

Figure 8.9
Modifying a track for multichannel audio.

Using the example in Figure 8.9 as a reference, a clip that had two mono tracks has been configured to use the stereo track format. It can now be placed on stereo tracks in the sequence.

Tip: If you want a clip to be used both on stereo tracks and on mono tracks, duplicate the clip in the bin first. You can modify one while leaving the other, allowing you to use the same media on either kind of track. This does not duplicate the media, and doesn't affect sound quality.

Displaying Track Formats in Bins

A clip that has audio will be set to use any of the four track formats: mono, stereo, 5.1, or 7.1. It's useful to know the track format of a clip so you can properly prepare your sequence to receive the clip. But how can you tell a clip's track format? Although you could open each clip and inspect its track selector panels in the timeline, there's an easier way to do it all from the bin.

You simply add the Track Formats column to the bin as shown in Figure 8.10.

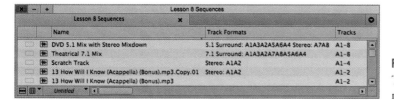

Figure 8.10
The Track Formats column displays multichannel track configuration.

The Track Formats column can be added to the bin the same way any other columns are added—by choosing the bin's Fast menu and then selecting Choose Columns.

Referring to Figure 8.10:

■ The first clip has eight tracks, as shown by A1-8 in the Tracks column. The first six audio tracks are used for the 5.1 surround mix and the final two are used for a stereo mix, as referenced in the Track Formats column.

■ The second clip also has eight tracks, all of which are used for a 7.1 surround mix.

■ The third clip, Scratch Track, has four tracks, as referenced in the Tracks column. The first two tracks are used for stereo mix, which implies the final two tracks are mono tracks.

■ The fourth clip is a two-channel stereo clip, having just two tracks, A1-2.

■ The final clip in the bin has nothing in the Track Formats column, yet the Tracks column indicates that it does have A1-2, which means the audio tracks must be mono.

Tip: When a clip has audio but displays nothing in the Track Formats column, the audio tracks are mono.

EXERCISE   *Take a moment to complete Exercise 8, Part 1.*

Using the Track Control Panel

The Track control panel is used to configure the playback of audio tracks, and to adjust the display of audio features on the timeline on a track-by-track basis. Audio features include the waveform display, or overlays that indicate the volume and pan of individual clips.

Prior to the addition of the Track control panel in Media Composer 5, you had to enable these features using the timeline's fast menu, and they would be enabled for all tracks. The Track control panel is also used to apply RTAS effects, which is covered in Lesson 11.

Expand or collapse the Track control panel using the arrow indicated in Figure 8.11.

Toggle Track Control Panel

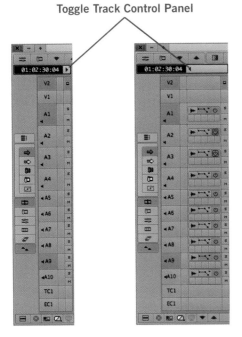

Figure 8.11
Toggle the display of the Track control panel.

Mute and Solo

The playback of audio tracks can be soloed or muted using the buttons shown in Figure 8.12.

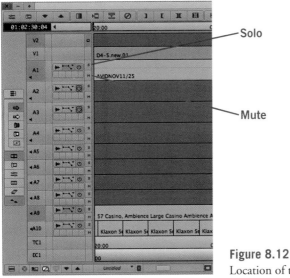

Solo

Mute

Figure 8.12
Location of the solo (S) and mute (M) buttons.

You may solo one or more tracks, which causes the other tracks to be implicitly muted. It's similar to a choir: When someone is performing a solo, the other members don't sing—they are implicitly mute. Implicitly muted tracks have a faded orange color on their mute buttons.

You can explicitly mute a track by clicking its mute button. That's like telling someone in the choir, "Please don't sing." Explicitly muted tracks have a strong orange color on their mute buttons, as shown in Figure 8.13.

Figure 8.13

A soloed track in green (A1), two explicitly muted tracks in a strong orange (A6-7), and the remaining audio tracks are implicitly muted (faded orange).

Tip: Toggle the Solo or Mute status for all tracks by Alt/Option+clicking the solo or mute buttons. If multiple tracks are being soloed, this can be a quick way to deactivate the solo for all tracks simultaneously.

When a track is muted, you don't hear it but Media Composer still processes the audio. It still performs real-time level adjustments and still processes any audio effects applied to the muted track. You simply don't hear it: The output of the sound is suppressed.

If you want Media Composer to totally ignore the track and not process anything on it, muting is not the feature you're looking for. You want to make the track *inactive*.

Making a Track Inactive

When a track is inactive, effects and automation are not applied, the audio media is not even read from the media drive, and no CPU power is used for the inactive audio track. That's in contrast to mute.

Making an audio track inactive is like cutting the power to the track. In fact, Avid uses a power button icon to toggle the inactive status of a track, as shown in Figure 8.14.

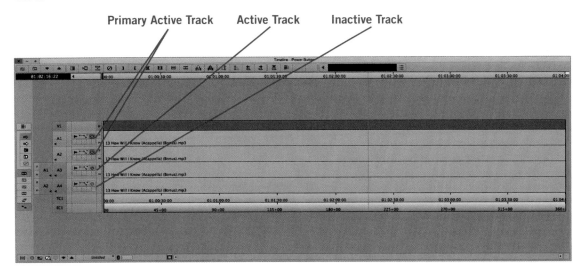

Figure 8.14
A power button is used to make a track active or inactive.

An active track can also be a *primary active track* or just an *active track* (non-primary). Media Composer supports two primary tracks. A primary track is indicated with a square around the power button, shown on tracks A1 and A2 in Figure 8.14.

A *primary active track* is guaranteed to play back regardless of the playback speed, whereas non-primary tracks may not be able to play back at faster than real-time speeds. Audio information in the *primary active tracks* is not dropped when the play speed increases during scrubbing. You'd typically make sure your dialogue tracks are the primary active tracks, whereas background music is more likely to be a non-primary active track.

An active track has the power button enabled but does not have a rectangle around it, shown in Figure 8.14 on track A3.

An inactive track does not have the power button enabled, shown in Figure 8.14 as A4.

To set the primary active tracks:

Alt/Option+click on the active (power) button.

Note: In Lesson 11, you will learn the audio mixdown workflow, which involves making tracks inactive after they have been mixed down, so you still have a record of their original arrangement in your timeline.

Although Media Composer supports 18 tracks, which could each be 7.1 surround tracks and theoretically support up to 192 voices, Media Composer supports 16 voices. The voices are allocated based on which tracks are active when playback begins. They are not dynamically distributed based on where clips are located on the timeline, so give consideration to which tracks of the 18 are going to use the 16 available voices.

Using Audio Scrub

Audio scrubbing allows you to hear the audio as you move through the footage at times other than when Media Composer is playing back footage normally. *Scrubbing* means moving back and forth in the same spot (like scrubbing burnt eggs out of a frying pan). Usually, you scrub the timeline with the Current Position indicator until you find a particular audio cue. There are two kinds of audio scrubbing: digital and analog.

Media Composer's Digital Audio Scrub feature is enabled whenever the keyboard is set to *uppercase* mode. How do you make the letters uppercase? Press Shift or press Caps Lock. That's how you engage Digital Audio Scrub.

With Digital Audio Scrub enabled, moving the Current Position indicator (blue line) plays back one frame's worth of audio. It sounds very computerized, hence the "digital" part of the name.

You can also use Analog Audio Scrub when using J-K-L to play back at speeds faster or slower than real-time, normal video speed. The more times you press L, the faster Media Composer plays back forward. Likewise, the more times you press J, the faster it plays backward.

The playback rates are 1x, 2x, 3x, 5x, and 8x the normal frame rate. As Media Composer plays back faster and faster, it's less able to keep up with processing all of the audio tracks and some will not be played. The tracks that won't be dropped, however, are the *primary active* audio tracks.

Table 8-1 summarizes the number of voices that are supported at specific play rates.

   Take a moment to complete Exercise 8, Part 2.

Table 8-1 Supported Voices at Scrubbing Speeds

Speed	Number of Supported Voices
Normal speed	16 voices
Two times normal speed	16 voices
Three times normal speed	2 voices
Greater than three times normal speed	0 voices

Working with Surround Sound

You don't need a stereo, 5.1, or 7.1 timeline track in order to create surround sound mixes. You can create a delightful 7.1 surround sound mix from a sequence having only mono tracks. It's not what kind of tracks or source clips you have; it's how the clips on those tracks are played out of the various speakers. That's what gives you a surround sound mix.

Media Composer supports surround sound environments having six or eight speakers, in which one of them is a LFE (subwoofer), designated by *.1*, and the other five or seven speakers are positioned around the listener. Put together, you get 5.1 and 7.1 surround, meaning five main speakers plus one LFE, shown in Figure 8.15, or seven main speakers plus one LFE, shown in Figure 8.16 from the Media Composer 6 User's Guide.

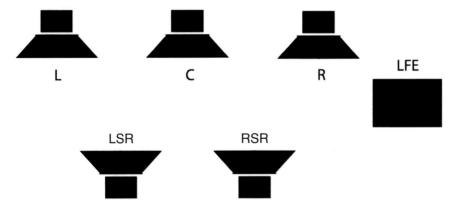

Figure 8.15
5.1 SMPTE Surround Sound Configuration: left (L), center (C), right (R), left surround rear (LSR), right surround rear (RSR), and low frequency effects (LFE) speakers.

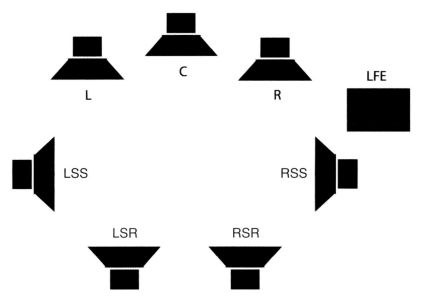

Figure 8.16
7.1 SMPTE Surround Sound Speakers: left (L), center (C), right (R), left surround side (LSS), right surround side (RSS), left surround rear (LSR), right surround rear (RSR), and low frequency effects (LFE) speakers.

Editing in surround sound and monitoring surround sound are different things. Monitoring requires specific hardware: you need the speakers. Editing doesn't require specific hardware, although it can be challenging to paint when you're blindfolded. Likewise it's challenging to edit a surround sound mix when you can't hear it in surround.

Nonetheless, Media Composer differentiates between surround sound editing and surround sound monitoring. You can edit in multiple formats (stereo, surround 5.1, and surround 7.1) and have Media Composer remap the output channels to a different format. For example, you could edit in surround, and then perform three separate outputs: surround, stereo, and mono.

Sequence Audio Format

Your sequence has a picture format, specified in the Project window. It also has an audio format, specified in the Audio Mixer. You indicate your sequence's audio format from the Sequence Mix Format button shown in Figure 8.17, and your hardware output using the Mix Mode Selection button, also shown in Figure 8.17.

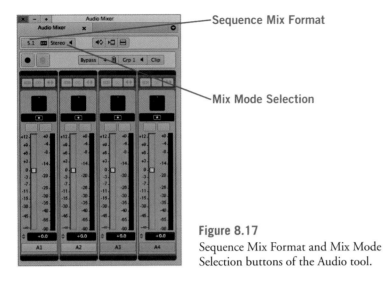

Sequence Mix Format

Mix Mode Selection

Figure 8.17
Sequence Mix Format and Mix Mode
Selection buttons of the Audio tool.

Sequence formats may be any of the following:

■ Stereo sequence

■ 5.1 surround

■ 7.1 surround

Changes to the sequence format result in changes to how the Audio Mixer processes pan. In a surround sound sequence, Media Composer allows you to pan the sound among the front, back, and sides of the room. In the Stereo sequence format, Media Composer allows you to pan the sound only between the left and the right sides of the room.

Audio Mix Mode and Monitoring Options

In order to hear a surround sound mix, you need surround sound hardware. That hardware connects to the speakers through which your surround sound mix will play. The software-based version of Media Composer can use a third-party card such as a SoundBlaster card, or you can use the Avid Nitris DX or Mojo DX hardware, which has an HDMI connector capable of transmitting surround sound to a receiver. You can also use the digital and analog connectors on the Avid Nitris DX hardware.

The mix mode sets your speaker layout, so Media Composer sends the correct signals to the associated outputs on your hardware. The mix mode addresses the following questions:

■ Do you have two, six, or eight speakers?

■ How are your surround sound speakers connected to your hardware?

- How does a stereo sequence play back when you have 7.1 surround speakers?

- How does a 5.1 sequence play back when you only have two speakers?

The mix mode is separate from your sequence format. The mix mode formats may be among any of the following:

- Stereo

- Mono

- 5.1 Film: L C R Ls Rs Lfe

- 5.1 SMPTE: L R C Lfe Ls Rs

- 7.1 Pro Tools: L C R Lss Rss Lsr Rsr Lfe

- 7.1 SMPTE: L R C Lfe Lsr Rsr Lss Rss

You'll notice there are two kinds of 5.1 surround and two kinds of 7.1 surround. That's because there are different standards for how the output channels on the hardware are mapped to specific speakers in the room. The list of speaker positions that follows corresponds to the audio outputs for that mix mode format.

Table 8-2 compares the two 5.1 formats. Notice that if you selected the 5.1 format for your particular hardware setup, you'd be sending the subwoofer (low frequency effects) sound to one of your rear monitoring speakers. If you don't know how your audio monitors are configured in your room, ask your site engineer.

Table 8-2   Comparison of 5.1 Film and 5.1 SMPTE Mix Modes

Output	5.1 Film	5.1 SMPTE
A1	Left Front	Left Front
A2	Center Front	Right Front
A3	Right Front	Center Front
A4	Left Surround	Low Frequency Effects (subwoofer)
A5	Right Rear Surround	Left Rear Surround
A6	Low Frequency Effects (subwoofer)	Right Rear Surround

If your sequence format is surround, but your mix mode is *stereo*, Media Composer will route the sound intended for the surround speakers to one of the two stereo speakers. It knows to do this because of the combination of sequence format and mix mode settings. Figure 8.18 has an Audio Mixer set to edit in surround but creates a stereo mix on playback.

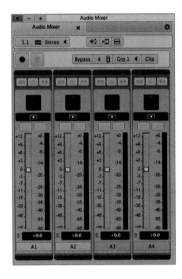

Figure 8.18
The Audio Mixer using a 5.1 surround sequence format and a Stereo mix mode.

The settings of Figure 8.18 result in audio being remapped as shown in Figure 8.19.

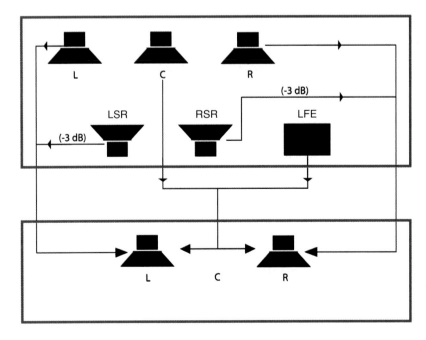

Figure 8.19
The sequence format of 5.1 is mapped to a Stereo mix mode during playback.

Note: For the exact mappings between the sequence format and mix mode, check the *Avid Media Composer User's Guide* section called "Surround Monitoring." It presents a table that shows how the matching is performed for a number of format and mix mode combinations.

Note: Avid Nitrix, Mojo DX support analog and digital audio surround sound monitoring. You can also use third-party hardware. See the *Media Composer Editing Guide* for instructions on how to configure your audio hardware for surround sound monitoring. It's available within Media Composer from Help > Documentation (PDF).

Using the Audio Mixer for Multichannel Mixing

You can use the Audio Mixer to adjust the extent to which individual speakers play a clip through any of the speakers. The Audio Mixer tool updates its interface with controls or buttons that are appropriate for mixing in the specified sequence format. For example, you mix differently for a stereo sequence format than a surround sequence format because they have a different number of speakers. The Audio Mixer reflects the sequence format, as shown in Figure 8.20.

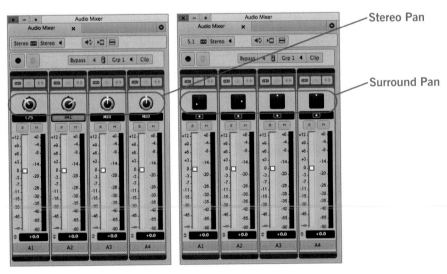

Figure 8.20
Audio Mixer for Stereo (left) and Surround Sound (right) mixing.

This section focuses on using the Audio Mixer for adjusting pan, whereas Lesson 9, "Fundamentals of Audio Mixing," focuses on adjusting audio levels.

Stereo Panning

When your sequence is set to a stereo sequence format, the Audio Mixer displays the pan value and knobs as shown in Figure 8.20. The sequence being mixed in Figure 8.20 has mono tracks in the timeline. If the sequence has stereo tracks, two pan knobs will be present for each strip in the mixer, as shown in Figure 8.21.

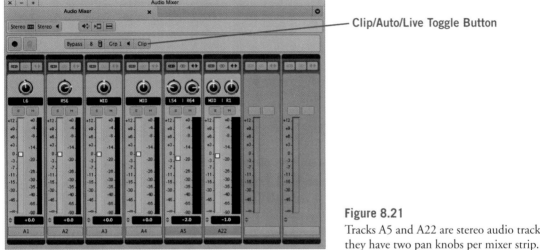

Clip/Auto/Live Toggle Button

Figure 8.21
Tracks A5 and A22 are stereo audio tracks; they have two pan knobs per mixer strip.

When your sequence format is set to *stereo*, the pan knobs specify how much of the clip's sound is coming out of the left or right speakers. You can pan the sound of a train moving from left to right by setting the Audio Mixer to *auto* and then making adjustments to the pan values. This is referred to as automating the pan.

To automate a sound's pan from left speaker to right speaker:

1. Place the **CURRENT POSITION INDICATOR** toward the beginning of the clip.

2. Set the **AUDIO MIXER** to **AUTO MODE** by clicking the **CLIP/AUTO/LIVE TOGGLE BUTTON**, shown in Figure 8.21.

3. Rotate the **PAN KNOB** to the left.

4. Reposition the **CURRENT POSITION INDICATOR** to a later point in the same clip.

5. Rotate the **PAN KNOB** to the right.

6. Play through the clip to hear the pan.

You can use the Track control panel to enable the display of pan information on a clip in the timeline, as shown in Figure 8.22.

Enable Pan Display on A3   Right 100%   Left 100%

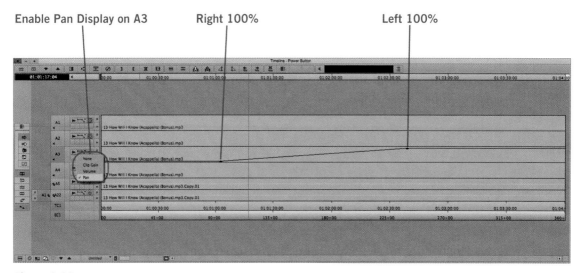

Figure 8.22
An audio track in the timeline displaying pan keyframes.

Displaying pan information in the timeline is helpful in confirming the presence of automated pans and also helpful in adjusting the pans. Once the pan information is shown on the timeline, you can also drag the keyframes on the clip in the timeline to further adjust the pan.

EXERCISE *Take a moment to complete Exercise 8, Part 3.*

Surround Panning

You perform basic surround sound mixing using techniques similar to those used when mixing stereo. Instead of a pan knob that adjusts from left to right, you're presented with a *surround panner*, which represents a view from the ceiling of the listening environment. Refer to Figure 8.23 and note the surround panners (green grids) at the top of each track.

The presence of the surround panners has nothing to do with the kind of tracks you have on the timeline. It has everything to do with the sequence format. Surround panners are available when your sequence format is set to 5.1 or 7.1 surround.

The surround sound panner contains a yellow dot, which represents the current pan location within the surround environment. As you drag the dot within the box, you are panning the sound. Media Composer then adjusts how much of the sound is sent to each speaker in order to position the sound in the room.

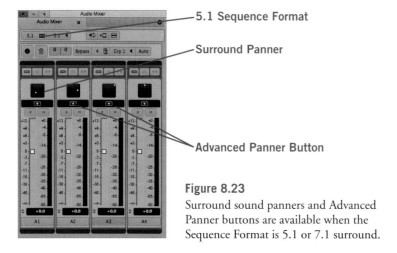

5.1 Sequence Format

Surround Panner

Advanced Panner Button

Figure 8.23
Surround sound panners and Advanced Panner buttons are available when the Sequence Format is 5.1 or 7.1 surround.

Referring once again to the surround panners in Figure 8.23:

- The clip on track A1 will be played mostly from the left surround (rear) speaker.

- The clip on track A2 will be played equally from the left front and left surround speakers, because this is a 5.1 sequence format playing to a 5.1 mix format.

    If the mix format was 7.1, the majority of the sound would be played by the left center surround speaker, because 7.1 surround systems have that speaker, unlike 5.1 surround systems.

- The clip on A3 will play using the front left speaker.

- The clip on A4 will play through the center speaker.

The center speaker is often used for character dialogue, particularly during medium and wide shots, which suggests A4 is a dialogue track, and the other tracks are ambience and effects or possibly music.

You pan a sound within the 5.1 or 7.1 surround sound environment as easily as you do in a stereo environment. The only difference is that you are repositioning the yellow dot in the panner, instead of rotating the pan knob. Refer to the previous section, called "Stereo Panning," for the technique.

Advanced Surround Panning

Media Composer 6 has a fantastic new addition to the Audio Mixer tool, which makes surround panning a breeze. It's called the *advanced panner*, and it's activated by clicking the Advanced Panner button located under the standard panner, as was shown in Figure 8.23.

The advanced panner, shown in Figure 8.24, takes over the Audio Mixer window in order to provide a detailed room with added controls for the LFE (subwoofer) and center speaker, which are not adjustable using the standard surround panner.

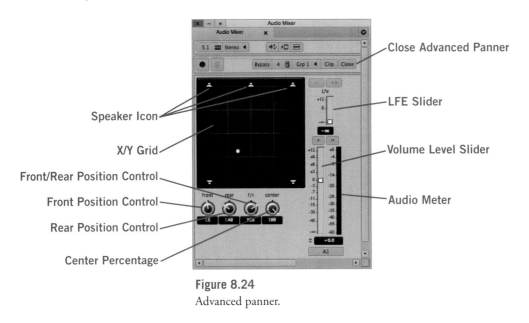

Figure 8.24
Advanced panner.

The advanced panner's larger interface for the X/Y grid makes it easier to position the yellow dot, which represents where the sound will be positioned in the sound field of the listening environment. In Figure 8.24, the sound for this clip will be positioned toward the rear of the audience's left side.

Aside from dragging the yellow dot, you can also adjust the control knobs for more accurate placement. For example, the f/r (front/rear) control will position the dot toward the top (front) or bottom (rear) of the X/Y grid (listening environment) without the possibility of it moving to the left or the right.

You can also direct sound to the low-frequency effects (LFE/subwoofer) using the LFE slider. On its scale of 0–100, you could direct 80% of the sound of rumbling thunder to the LFE, which, when played on a well equipped home entertainment system, is sure to be felt as well as heard.

Sometimes you want sound to come from a specific speaker, as opposed to a region of the room, such as when a character is off-screen left and is yelling to someone on screen right. The quickest way to pan a clip to a specific speaker is to simply click the speaker. The yellow dot will snap to the speaker icon in the X/Y grid.

To close the advanced panner and return to the standard Audio Mixer, click the *close* button, indicated in Figure 8.24.

Tip: If you frequently use the advanced panner and find yourself closing the advanced panner then opening it for another track, there is an easier way! You can Alt/Option+click the track number in the lower-right corner of the advanced panner. A menu will appear containing the names of the other audio tracks. Use that menu to work on another track.

With an understanding of the techniques for working with multichannel mixing, you are now ready to move onto Lesson 9, in which you'll continue your learning of the Audio Mixer by adjusting audio levels to achieve balance.

 If you have surround sound hardware, take a moment to complete Exercise 8, Part 4.

Review/Discussion Questions

1. What's the difference between a track and a channel? (See "Understanding Tracks, Channels, and Voices" on page 294.)

2. What's a *voice*? (See "Understanding Tracks, Channels, and Voices" on page 294.)

3. Why is it important for a Media Composer editor to understand how many voices are used by a specific kind of audio track? (See "Using Audio Scrub" on page 306.)

4. In Figure 8.6, how many voices are required to play the timeline? (Assume there is a clip on each track.) (See "Understanding Tracks, Channels, and Voices" on page 294.)

5. Under what circumstance would you want to create a stereo track instead of one or more mono tracks in a sequence? (See "Creating Multichannel Sequence Tracks" on page 297.)

6. When would you want to create a 5.1 or 7.1 surround sound track in a sequence? (See "Creating Multichannel Sequence Tracks" on page 297.)

7. What are two ways to create a 5.1 surround sound clip? (See "Creating Multichannel Source Clips" on page 299.)

8. You've imported a music file and it has two mono audio tracks. You delete the original file, then realize that it would be better if it had a single stereo track. What can you do? (See "Creating Multichannel Source Clips" on page 299.)

9. You're about to import an audio clip. It has six tracks and was provided to you by an audio effects engineer, who informs you that the tracks conform to the 5.1 SMPTE surround format. How do you properly import this file? (See "Importing Multichannel Clips" on page 299.)

10. An HDCAM SR tape has been delivered to your suite. The audio on the tape's eight tracks conforms to the 7.1 Pro Tools format. The deck is connected using dual link HD SDI cables, which is the correct way to connect this deck in this scenario. How do you configure the Capture tool to properly ingest the audio in the 7.1 format? (See "Capturing Multichannel Clips" on page 300.)

11. You notice a track in the timeline has a letter "m" with a faded orange background. What does this tell you about one or more other tracks in the timeline? (See "Mute and Solo" on page 303.)

12. When playing back your sequence faster than real-time, the tracks containing dialogue drop out—you can't hear them. How can you fix this? (See "Using Audio Scrub" on page 306.)

13. How many 7.1 surround tracks can be active simultaneously in a sequence? (See "Making a Track Inactive" on page 304 and "A Voice Is a Distinct Sound" on page 294.)

14. What's the difference between sequence format and mix mode? (See "Working with Surround Sound" on page 307.)

15. You are unable to set your audio mix mode to any of the surround sound options. Why is that? (See "Audio Mix Mode and Monitoring Options" on page 309.)

16. You've mixed a 5.1 surround sequence and now must create a stereo output. How do you configure the Audio Mixer? (See "Audio Mix Mode and Monitoring Options" on page 309.)

17. A producer has dropped in to your edit suite, concerned about the stereo output that you are creating from a sequence originally mixed in 5.1 surround. (This is the scenario from Question 16.) He's worried that the stereo mix will not include any of the sound originally intended for the surround (rear) or center speaker. How do you alleviate his concern? (See "Audio Mix Mode and Monitoring Options" on page 309.)

18. Why would you choose to use the advanced panner as opposed to the standard panner? (See "Using the Audio Mixer for Multichannel Mixing" on page 312.)

19. You want your audience to feel, as well as hear, the deep rumbling of an avalanche. The theatre that is screening the film has an excellent sound system. How can you make this happen? (See "Advanced Surround Panning" on page 315.)

20. You have a mono sound effect of an airplane flying overhead. How do you add life to this sound effect after placing it in the timeline? (See "Using the Audio Mixer for Multichannel Mixing" on page 312.)

Working with Multichannel Audio

These exercises allow you to practice the multichannel features discussed in this lesson. You will import and modify multichannel clips, use multichannel sequence tracks, and practice automated panning.

Media Used:
Agent MXZero

Duration:
20 minutes

GOALS

- Be able to import multichannel audio

- Use the Clip > Modify feature to change the Track Formats of an existing clip

- Understand how primary active tracks affect voices during playback

- Use Pan controls in the Audio Mixer and the timeline

- Understand the differences between sequence audio format and mix mode

Exercise 8.1: Modifying Clips and Experimenting with Voices

In this exercise you will modify some mono audio clips to create a surround sound clip. You will then place the clips in a timeline and observe how the track and clip types must match. You will configure your bin to display the audio track format so you can monitor the column as you work through the exercise. Then, you will import an existing music file as a stereo clip and place it on a stereo track in a sequence.

1. Open **Agent MXZero > Lesson 8 > Lesson 8 Sequences**.

2. Open the **Test Tone** clip into the **Source** monitor.

   It has eight tracks of tone media, which use eight voices. The Track selector panel lists tracks A1-8.

3. Select the **Test Tone** clip in the **Lesson 8 Sequences** bin.

4. Choose **Clip > Modify > Set Multichannel Audio**.

5. Select the drop-down under **A1** and **A2** and choose **7.1 Pro Tools**. Click **OK**.

   The clip has been updated with the new clip format. The Track selector panel now lists A1 with a small "7.1" symbol, indicating the clip's audio is in the 7.1 audio format.

6. Add the **Track Formats** column to the bin by choosing the bin's fast menu and then select **Choose Headings > Track Formats**.

   The Track Formats column confirms that the Test Tone clip is a multi-channel 7.1 clip. Next, you will insert this test tone into the beginning of the Remix sequence.

7. Open the **Remix** sequence in the **Record** monitor.

8. Enable **Sync Lock** for all tracks.

   The Remix sequence consists of only mono audio tracks. The audio format of source clips must match the track format in the sequence, and there are no 7.1 tracks in the sequence. The A1 track of the Source monitor is unable to pair with any of the existing tracks in the timeline.

9. Select **Clip menu > New Audio Track > 7.1 Surround**.

   Now the source clip has a 7.1 sequence track and can receive source clips having the 7.1 track format.

10. Splice the clip into the sequence using the **SPLICE-IN** button.

    In the final section of this exercise, you will import a music clip while setting it to stereo at the time of import. By setting clips to their proper track format during import, you won't have to modify them after the fact.

11. **RIGHT-CLICK** in the bin and select **IMPORT**.

12. Navigate to the **MATERIALS FOR IMPORT** folder that accompanies this book.

13. Select **LESSON 8 STUDENT MATERIALS > ZERO THEME A.WAV**.

14. Click the **OPTIONS** button.

15. Select the **AUDIO** tab of the **IMPORT OPTIONS** dialog box, as shown in Figure EX8.1.

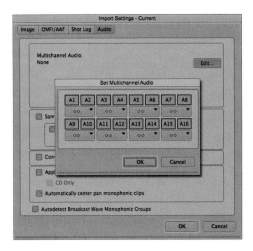

Figure EX8.1
Audio Import Options allow you to configure multichannel track formats.

16. Click **EDIT** from the **IMPORT OPTIONS** dialog box.

17. Configure A1 and A2 as stereo tracks.

18. Press **OK** twice to accept the dialog boxes.

19. Import the file.

20. Confirm that the music was imported as a stereo clip by consulting the **TRACK FORMATS** column of the bin.

21. Create a new stereo track, called **A11**, in the **REMIX** sequence.

22. Add the **ZERO THEME A** to the beginning of the sequence.

    ZERO THEME A will be the backing music and will play under the sound effects and dialogue.

Exercise 8.2: Understanding Active and Inactive Tracks

In this exercise, you will perform a set of experiments to better understand how the different kinds of sequence audio tracks affect Media Composer's ability to play audio. By understanding how Media Composer plays up to 16 voices, you will be better able to predict the performance of your editing system.

Open or continue editing the Remix sequence from Exercise 8, Part 1. There are now 10 mono tracks, 1 stereo audio track, and a 7.1 surround audio track.

The 7.1 surround clip originally had eight tracks, and even though it is now occupying a single track on the timeline, it still will result in eight voices being played. Likewise, the stereo clip originally had two tracks (left channel and right channel), and it now also takes one track in the timeline.

Even though the multichannel clips occupy single tracks, Media Composer still uses the same number of internal resources to play them: The stereo clip is like playing two mono tracks, and the 7.1 surround clip is like playing eight mono tracks. In other words, the stereo clip requires two voices, and the 7.1 clip requires eight. The total voice count for the sequence is 20, but Media Composer is capable of playing back only 16 voices.

When the 7.1 track and the stereo track were added to the sequence, Media Composer deactivated some of the audio tracks to ensure that no more than 16 voices would be played back concurrently.

1. Determine which track or tracks are inactive in your timeline. Try to make them active. You will not be able to make all the tracks active because of the 16-voice limit.

2. Add another 7.1 audio track.

3. Activate both of the 7.1 tracks and play the sequence.

   Of the tracks that can be active, only two of them will be active when playing back at 3x real-time. The other ones will not be played at the 3x real-time speed.

4. Use **J-K-L** playback to play back the sequence at 3x real-time. Achieve this by selecting the sequence and pressing **L** three times.

5. Check the Track control panel to determine which tracks are the primary active tracks by checking for the square around the **ACTIVE** (**POWER**) button. During playback, confirm that those are the only tracks you hear when playing back at 3x real-time.

6. Try **Alt/Option+clicking** on the 7.1 surround track to make it the primary active track.

   The 7.1 surround track uses eight voices, but only two can be active, so no tracks will be indicated as the primary track.

7. Try **Alt/Option+clicking** on the stereo track. The stereo track, which uses just two voices, indicates that it is the primary track.

Media Composer is capable of allowing only two voices to play back at the 3x speed. When dealing with mono tracks, which use a single voice each, you can have two mono tracks both set as the primary active tracks. A 7.1 surround track uses eight voices, so it cannot be made the primary active track. Media Composer will use the first two channels of the surround clip but that is not reflected by the Track Active button.

Exercise 8.3: Stereo Panning

In this exercise, you will automate the pan of one or more audio clips using the Audio Mixer and observe the resulting changes on the timeline overlay. You will then automate the pan of another clip using just the timeline's pan overlay.

1. Configure your **Audio Mixer** to use the stereo sequence format and a stereo mix format.

2. Open **Lesson 8 Sequences > Remix sequence**, or continue with it from the previous lesson.

   The Remix sequence contains a series of sound effects for gunshots.

3. Use the techniques presented in "Stereo Panning" on page 313 of this lesson to automate the pan of the gunfire, panning the sound of the bullets from one side of the screen to the other.

4. Enable the pan display using the Track control panel (see Figure 8.22 of this lesson). Your pan animations should be visible on the timeline clips.

5. Adjust the pan of the gunfire shots by manipulating the keyframes on the clips. Try adjusting the rate of the pan by **Alt/Option-dragging** the keyframes left or right to change the slope of the curve, which alters the speed of the pan.

You have now added life to your clips by automating their pans.

Exercise 8.4: Using Surround Panning (Optional)

This exercise requires surround sound monitoring hardware. It's similar to the previous exercise, except you will be automating the pan around all of the speakers instead of just left or right stereo speakers/headphones.

1. Configure the **Audio Mixer** to use a 7.1 surround sequence format and a 7.1 Pro Tools or SMPTE mix mode. If you do not have surround sound monitoring capabilities, select a stereo mix mode.

2. Perform the same steps as in Exercise 8.3, but create pan automation in the surround sound field using the advanced panner.

Once of the great things about editing multichannel clips in Media Composer is that they are not treated any differently than the traditional mono clips. The Audio Mixer updates to give you the best interface for the kind of sequence format you are using, but the approach to adjusting the pan, automating the pan, and working the clips in the timeline is consistent regardless of track type.

Fundamentals of Audio Mixing

When you're working as a picture editor, don't forget about the sound. "I'm sending it to an audio editor" isn't an excuse for not finessing your soundtrack because Media Composer has many audio tools that are easy to use and can help you and your producer visualize the finish piece. There's little worse than having a beautiful image only to be distracted by unmixed audio or an unwanted background sound. This chapter covers the fundamentals of audio mixing so you can avoid such a pitfall.

Media Used: Agent MXZero

Duration: 60 minutes

GOALS

- Understand why picture editors should have basic sound editing expertise
- Learn how to use the Audio tool and Mixer for achieving balance in an audio mix
- Understand dynamic range as it applies to audio
- Be able to use the decibels full scale (dBFS) readings to determine how an audio mix needs to be adjusted
- Differentiate among attenuation, gain, and decibels
- Learn how to adjust the audio levels of source clips
- Understand the Media Composer mixing workflow
- Be able to mix a sequence in Media Composer and export it for further mixing in Avid Pro Tools

Sound Mixing Is Important

Great picture deserves great sound. Silent movies were not so silent, thanks to the addition of piano accompaniment. In 2012, significant attention was paid to *The Artist*, which had no dialogue but definitely wasn't a silent film owing to an emotive score.

When it comes to creating your soundtrack, take your visual element as a reference but think beyond the frame. Gene Roddenberry once said that everything that's visible and moves on the bridge of the *(Star Trek) Enterprise* needs to have a sound effect—each blinking light, each door that opens. If it's on the screen and moving, give it a sound. Even the appearance of a title fading and moving into position can be backed with a subtle whoosh or flutter, as appropriate.

In contrast, Walter Murch has said in interviews and in *In the Blink of an Eye* that it's sometimes the sounds that are not represented by things in the frame that end up contributing to the scene, such as the sound of the train in *The Godfather* as Michael kills someone for the first time.

In short, your sound complements, augments, and enhances your picture. When there are multiple sounds playing back, it takes some skill to make the individual sounds work together. That's the skill of sound mixing, which is the topic of this lesson.

Goals of Sound Mixing

Your goal as a sound mixer is to do more than to make it "sound good." There's little worse than having a beautiful image only to be distracted by unmixed audio or an unwanted background sound.

You have artistic and technical responsibilities, some of which are summarized in the following sections.

Achieving Balance

You need to control which sound is dominant to the audience, much like how you control which picture is dominant through your shot selection. With 4, 8, or even 24 audio tracks, you need to ensure that the voiceover is dominant in comparison to the background music, and when the voiceover is silent, the music or other sound compensates by becoming louder so the overall level is consistent throughout the piece.

You must ensure that important audio is not buried under sounds that contribute less to the storytelling.

Broadcast Delivery Requirements

Your audio will have a "normal" audio level, referred to as the reference tone. When you add tone at the beginning of the video, you are defining the reference tone, which says, "This is the volume that most of the sound will be at. Some sounds might be louder, and some might be quieter, but this is the normal level."

Your broadcaster will usually specify that the sound not exceed reference by more than a specific amount, such as eight decibels (dB).

Broadcasters usually have their videos on a server and the server connects to a transmitter. Between the server and the transmitter are some devices that regulate the picture and sound levels, ensuring that sound levels aren't too loud. It's better to reduce the levels yourself to bring your sequence into conformance with the broadcaster's requirements, so you're in control, as opposed to leaving it for the broadcaster's automatic sound limiter machinery.

Tip: Always check with your broadcasters to ensure you know their expectations. Don't assume the upper limit is 8dB over reference—it may be more or less. When selling to international markets, check the requirements of the new broadcaster. Many broadcasters will clip, limit, or compress audio levels that exceed the expected thresholds. You are better off being in control of fixing the audio as opposed to leaving it to the broadcaster's audio limiter.

What Is Dynamic Range?

Dynamic range refers to the difference between the quietest and loudest sounds. Too much dynamic range can be annoying for your audience: some people will likely keep their finger on the volume and adjust it to try to make the audio levels consistent, others will just change the channel! On the other hand, the absence of dynamic range can also be detrimental. Imagine a symphonic concert without crescendos; it would be boring and not very *dynamic*.

Note: Dynamic range is also a term that's used for the picture. When it's used for picture, it refers to the variation between the darkest and lightest pixels. That's also referred to as *contrast*.

dBFS: Decibels Full Scale

Digital Audio is measured using the *decibels full scale* (dBFS). The dBFS measurement scale, shown in Figure 9.1, sets 0 as a maximum value, representing the loudest possible value. Anything louder than 0 is clipped, resulting in digital distortion. Anything quieter than 0dBFS has a negative value. For example, –20dBFS is quieter than –10dBFS.

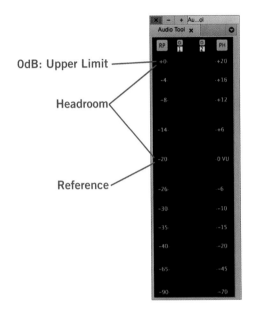

Figure 9.1

The dBFS scale; distortion occurs at 0dB. North American reference tone is usually –20. Louder sounds are –20dB to 0dB; quieter sounds are –20 and lower.

In many North American post-production facilities, –20dBFS is the reference level, whereas the number varies in other countries. Regardless of how many tracks are playing, the mixer will aim to have the output average at –20 most of the time. Setting –20dBFS as a reference level allows 20dB of *headroom*. The headroom is used when the soundtrack requires a loud bang or someone is shouting. In a scene with an explosion, the levels might, for example, reach –10dBFS.

If the reference level was –4, the headroom would be only 4dB and the difference between an explosion and someone speaking would neither be realistic nor as noticeable.

One of your roles as mixer is to keep an eye on the dynamic range and ensure that, overall, your audio levels register at the reference level. If the levels are constantly above or below reference, you'll need to make an adjustment to the levels to bring them into alignment.

The best way for you to monitor audio levels within Media Composer is to use the Audio tool.

The Audio Tool

The Audio tool (choose Tools > Audio Tool) provides accurate monitoring of audio levels. Depending on the number of output channels available on your audio hardware, it will display two, four, eight, or more meters representing the output of each channel.

The left side of the tool features the digital scale, whereas the right side is an analog scale, as shown in Figure 9.2. This lesson focuses exclusively on the digital scale.

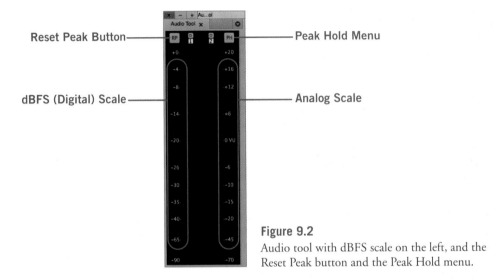

Reset Peak Button

Peak Hold Menu

dBFS (Digital) Scale

Analog Scale

Figure 9.2
Audio tool with dBFS scale on the left, and the Reset Peak button and the Peak Hold menu.

The Audio tool can be resized to be taller, which allows the meters to display more detail.

Tip: The audio meters located in the timeline are useful as a general point of reference, but aren't good for accurate measurements because they are not labeled. Instead, use the Audio tool.

Using the Console Window to Check Audio Levels

As you play material in the Source or Record monitors, Media Composer tracks the peak values that are processed through the Audio tool. You can use the Console to access this precise information about audio peaks in a sequence.

1. Load the sequence into the **RECORD** monitor.

2. Open the **AUDIO** tool and press the **RESET PEAK (RP)** button, shown previously in Figure 9.2.
   This clears the peaks of any previously played material from memory.

3. Play the sequence or the suspect portion of the sequence.

4. Open the CONSOLE window by choosing TOOLS > CONSOLE.

5. Click in the lower area of the CONSOLE window and type the following command:

    dumpmaxpeaks

6. Press ENTER.

A list of peak values is displayed in the Console window, as shown in Figure 9.3.

Figure 9.3
Peak values displayed in the Console window.

Using Figure 9.3 for reference, if your reference was set to –20dB and the broadcast specification allowed up to 8dB above reference, the program would be significantly over broadcast spec. Allowable values would be up to –12, and in Figure 9.3, the values reached –3.0, which is 9dB louder than the maximum allowable –12.

The **dumpmaxpeaks** command does not indicate where the peak occurs in the sequence, only the maximum gain processed since the memory was last cleared.

Once you find the illegal levels, correct them using the Audio Mixer tool.

During the finishing process, review sessions are common. Leverage the time spent in a review session to also check audio levels. If illegal levels are found, you'll probably also have a good idea of where in the program to start looking.

Using the Audio Tool to Generate Test Tone Media

The Audio tool can also be used to generate tone media. The tone media will be saved to a bin, which you can then load into the Source monitor and place into the timeline.

To generate test tone media:

1. Select the AUDIO tool and then choose PH MENU > CREATE TONE MEDIA.

2. Specify the number of tracks and the reference tone level, as shown in Figure 9.4.

3. Select the bin. You might want to create a special bin for the test tone, slates, and imported color bars.

Figure 9.4
The Create Tone Media dialog box shows that a clip with eight tracks of tone at 1,000Hz will be generated.

4. Click **OK**.

The tone media now exists in the bin, as shown in Figure 9.5. You may add it to a sequence by treating it like any other source clip. Adding reference tones to the beginning of your sequence lets the receiver of the sequence (or tape) know your reference level and calibrate their audio monitors the same way.

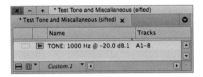

Figure 9.5
Audio clip generated with eight tracks.

Sound Mixing Vernacular

There are some terms that are frequently used in audio mixing and editing. It's useful for you to be familiar with these terms so you can "talk the talk," so to speak.

Decibel

A *decibel* is a unit of measurement used to describe how loud a sound is relative to the threshold of hearing (the softest sound the human ear can perceive). Abbreviated as dB, it represents the smallest possible increase or decrease in volume that a human can perceive.

Gain

Gain is an amplification of the audio signal. The amount of gain is measured in decibels. To apply gain is to turn up the volume. (To apply a lot of gain a lot is to do like Mars in the 1980s: *Pump Up the Volume!*)

Attenuate

This is the opposite of gain—*attenuate* means to make the volume quieter. Attenuating the background music means to reduce the levels. (If your child is screaming, you could say to him "Attenuate your voice immediately!")

Tip: When mixing, remember that sound levels are relative. If something is too quiet, you can either apply gain, or you can attenuate everything else.

 Take a moment to complete Exercise 9, Part 1.

Creating a Mix

When you mix, or add, two audio signals you combine the sound waves from each signal. The process of combining audio signals is called *summing*. This brings up the most fundamental principle in audio mix theory:

When you double the power output of a sound, the overall loudness of the sound increases by 3dB for each source.

Tip: The summarized version of the rule is this: The more sound waves, the louder the total output.

You would never want to solo (isolate) a track, and then adjust the audio to be perfect for that one track. That's a poor workflow because, once you enable all the tracks, you'll find the final level will be louder than the individual tracks and you'll need to adjust them all again. When adjusting your audio mix, do it in the context of the entire mix and leave all your tracks on.

Also note that an audio mix perfected in a stereo audio environment will sound significantly different when it is delivered according to mono standards and vice versa. Your audio mix may sound too weak or quiet or too strong and over-modulated. Always be sure to create your audio mix using the final delivery standard of the project.

Consider Your Environment

Prior to beginning your audio mix, consider your environment by listening to it. Turn off ambient background sound, such as air conditioners and fans. Be aware of the sound that's naturally in your environment and consider that it won't be there for your audience. Ideally, make the room as audio-neutral as possible.

You should also calibrate your audio monitors. *Audio monitors* are higher-end speakers with better fidelity than regular desktop multimedia speakers. Calibrating your audio monitors consists of playing a sound at your reference level and adjusting the levels on the monitors to a point that feels comfortable. Once you've set your audio monitors, don't change them. If something is too loud in your sequence, attenuate it through an adjustment with Media Composer's Audio Mixer tool.

On the Web For detailed information on calibrating your audio monitors (speakers), try http://audiodesignlabs.com/wordpress/2008/05/ professional-monitoring-system-calibration/.

Tip: To play a reference tone, select Tools > Audio Tool > PH > Play Calibration Tone.

Using the Audio Mixer

The Audio Mixer tool is the general tool that you use to create a mix, as was introduced in Lesson 8, "Working with Multichannel Audio." Aside from adjusting pan, it's also used to perform attenuation or gain on clips relative to the level at which they were ingested into the Media Composer system.

The sliders for each clip can be adjusted on a scale from +12 to negative infinity dB. The adjustments are *relative*, not absolute. When setting a slider to +12, you are applying a gain of 12dB to the original level. An adjustment of –10dB means the level has been attenuated by 10dB. You are not setting the audio level of the clip to –10. That would be an absolute adjustment and it isn't possible to absolutely set a clip's level to a specific dB using the Audio Mixer.

Tip: The Audio Mixer only allows you to apply a gain of 12dB. The AudioSuite tool, however, allows you to apply a gain of up to 96dB. AudioSuite is covered in Lesson 11, "Real-Time AudioSuite (RTAS)."

Source-Side versus Record-Side Audio Mixer

The Audio Mixer behaves subtly different depending on whether the Source monitor or the Record monitor is active.

■ When the Record monitor is active, the Audio Mixer is adjusting the clip(s) under the Current Position indicator (blue line) in the timeline.

■ When the Source monitor is active, the Audio mixer is adjusting the source clip and that adjustment is saved with the clip in the bin.

Source-side adjustments are very handy: If you have a clip that is too quiet or too loud, open it into the Source monitor and make an adjustment using the Audio Mixer. Thereafter, each time you re-open the clip, the level is set.

A typical example of when this is particularly useful involves importing audio from a compact disc. Audio from a compact disc is often imported *hot* (too loud). Media Composer does allow you to apply gain/attenuation on import of audio files (using Import Options), but if you forgot to make that setting, you can make the adjustment afterward using the Source monitor and the Audio Mixer.

Changes you make to a clip in the Source monitor have no effect on existing instances of that clip in the sequence.

Understanding the Mixing Workflow

Performing an audio mix consists of:

1. Separating your audio clips onto related tracks.

2. Setting an overall level for a track or region of a track.

3. Performing attenuation or gain adjustments to individual clips in a track or region.

4. Performing attenuation or gain adjustments to sections within an individual clip (fading something up or down).

5. Applying specialized effects to further enhance the dynamics and balance of the audio mix.

Steps 3 and 4 are particularly noteworthy as they indicate that each clip in Media Composer can have an overall adjustment that is consistent for the entire clip, and each clip can have variable levels within it. The two adjustments are cumulative.

The first adjustment, called a *clip gain*, lets you set a clip to approximately the correct level, whereas the later adjustment, a *volume adjustment* (previously called "auto gain") allows you to ride the levels within a clip, making the audio quieter in some parts of the clip and louder in others.

Volume adjustments are ideal for music tracks that back a voiceover, and for quick adjustments like diminishing the effect of quarter-second lip-smack by the voice-over talent prior to beginning a sentence, or for ducking music under voiceover, as shown in Figure 9.6.

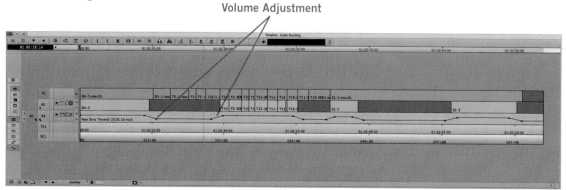

Figure 9.6
Volume adjustment is used to reduce audio levels on A5 when audio also exists on A1.

Separate the Audio Tracks

Separating the audio tracks, sometimes called creating a *checkerboard* layout and shown in Figure 9.7, makes it easier to apply adjustments to an entire set of related clips. You use the Lift/Overwrite tool (red arrow) to vertically move the clips such that related clips are on the same track. For example, the voiceover is on A1, male character lead is on A2, female character lead is on A3, room tone is on A4, music is on A5 and A6, and sound effects are on A7-12, or some variation on that theme.

You make it easier to work with music clips if, instead of having them on two tracks such as A5 and A6, you convert the music clip to a stereo clip and use a stereo track instead. Stereo tracks allow you to use one track on the timeline to represent the left and right channels of an audio clip. Creating stereo tracks and modifying clips for stereo is covered in Lesson 8.

Tip: For consistency in placing your audio clips on specific tracks, consider renaming your audio tracks as discussed in Lesson 3, "Advanced Picture Editing."

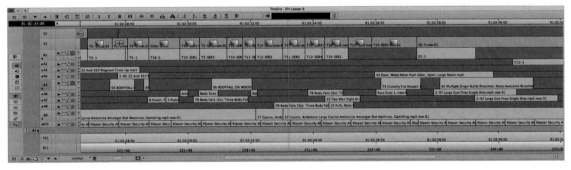

Figure 9.7
Checkerboarding places related clips on the same tracks.

Adjusting Clip Gain

When adjusting clip gain, the overall level for a particular clip, ensure the Audio Mixer is set to Clip mode as shown in Figure 9.8. Clicking the button toggles the mixer among the Clip, Live, and Auto modes.

The Clip Gain adjustments can be reflected on the timeline, as shown in Figure 9.9, if the Clip Gain option is selected in the Track control panel.

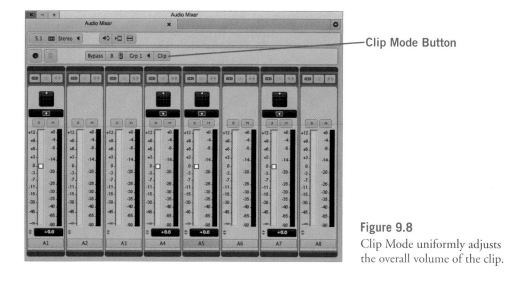

Clip Mode Button

Figure 9.8
Clip Mode uniformly adjusts
the overall volume of the clip.

Clip Gain Enabled for A1   Clip Gain Shown on Segments

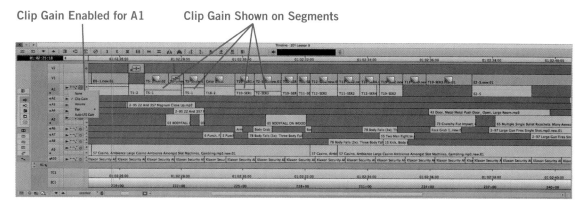

Figure 9.9
Clip gain on the audio clips and selected in the Track control panel.

The Audio Mixer's fast menu is aware of IN and OUT marks in the timeline. By removing the IN and OUT marks, the fast menu commands affect all clips on all enabled tracks, as shown in Figure 9.10. If an IN and OUT mark are present on the timeline, the Audio Mixer's fast menu updates to apply the adjustments only to the clips that fall from IN to OUT, as shown in Figure 9.11. The IN and OUT marks do not have to encompass the entire clip, because clip adjustments are applied to the entire clip, not to a portion of it.

Note: For information on adjusting clip pan, see Lesson 8.

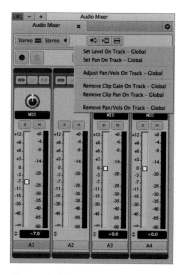

Figure 9.10
Audio Mixer's fast menu: commands will be applied to all clips on the selected tracks.

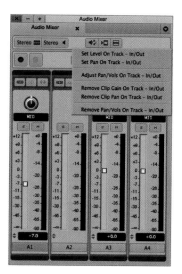

Figure 9.11
Audio Mixer's fast menu: commands will be applied from IN to OUT.

Set Level on Track Global/IN - OUT

Start your audio mix by setting the clips on a track to an appropriate level. Since you have previously separated the clips onto related tracks, this step can quickly be performed by:

1. Removing the **IN** and **OUT** marks from the timeline.

2. Enabling all tracks that you intend to adjust.

3. Parking the **CURRENT POSITION INDICATOR** over a section of the timeline where there are clips present on each track that you want to adjust (without a clip under the Position indicator, the sliders do not appear in the Audio Mixer).

4. Using the **AUDIO MIXER** to set the level for each clip to a proper reference level.

5. Choosing **AUDIO MIXER > FAST MENU > APPLY TO TRACK GLOBAL**.

After this step has been performed, background sound should be quieter than voiceover and foreground sounds. If needed, you can perform this step on a per-scene or per-section basis by using IN and OUT marks to define the beginning and end of the section you want to set.

Set Levels for Specific Clips

The next step is to play the sequence and make individual clip adjustments on a per-clip basis. Two adjacent clips may have different audio levels even if they are from the same performer. The different audio levels are often the result of reconstructing the narrative by re-ordering the shots or editing out words and phrases.

Figure 9.12 shows audio clips with individual adjustments. Although the adjustments were made using the Audio Mixer, they are visible in the timeline because the tracks are set to display Clip Gain.

Figure 9.12
Audio clips with individually adjusted clip levels.

Adjust Levels on Track

After you've adjusted the levels in the series of shots, attenuating some, applying gain to others, in order to have a consistent level, you may find that the overall scene is too loud or too quiet.

Media Composer allows you to perform an adjustment on all clips on a track, or just from IN to OUT. The Audio Mixer > Fast Menu > Adjust Pan/Vols on Track/Global command adds or subtracts the current clip level of each clip. The key feature of Adjust Pan/Vols is that it allows you to preserve the relative differences to each clip that you made in the previous two sections.

After selecting Adjust Pan/Vols on Track, the dialog box shown in Figure 9.13 appears.

Figure 9.13
An adjustment of +3dB will be applied to all clips affected by this adjustment.

You may not always need to use adjust levels, but it's handy to know that it's there when you do.

Adjusting Clip Volume by Adding Keyframes

Clip volume adjustments affect the levels within a clip over time. Sometimes called *rubberbanding*, you can add keyframes and set the levels at particular points. When you adjust clip volume on a music track, in order to keep levels low during the voiceover, and to increase the levels when the voiceover has finished, you perform *audio ducking*. The volume levels are ducking below the voiceover and coming up after.

When adjusting clip volume, you should consider making your audio tracks large enough that you can see the relative dB overlay that appears after the first keyframe has been applied to the clip, as shown in Figure 9.14.

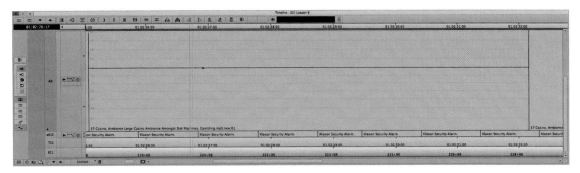

Figure 9.14
Audio volume with relative dB adjustment overlay.

To enable the overlay in the timeline, choose Volume from the Track Panel.

Creating an Audio Mixing Workspace

To take your audio mixing to the next level of efficiency, consider creating one or more audio mixing workspaces, using Media Composer 6's flexible and new Workspace feature. You can remove the Source monitor and make the Record monitor smaller, which gives you room to open the Audio Mixer with all 16 strips visible.

To further maximize screen real estate for audio, you could merge other tools into the Audio Mixer's window. For example, you could drag the Project window's tab into the Audio Mixer window, which merges the two windows. When you do audio mixing, you're unlikely to need the Project window, so condensing it into the Audio Mixer's window makes sense. You could also add the EQ tool, although it doesn't stretch to fit the width of the wider Audio Mixer window, so it may look odd. However, it's conserving space to give the maximum amount of room to the timeline and the Audio Mixer.

Once your Audio Mixer is open, you could make the timeline larger.

You may want to save a Timeline View preset with enlarged audio tracks and reduced video track heights. You can then associate that preset with your new workspace, and map your new mixing workspace to a keyboard shortcut.

A Timeline View preset stores all the settings found in the Timeline window's fast menu. Aside from clip frames (thumbnails), track heights, and clip text, the timeline's fast menu also includes a group of Audio Data settings. The Audio Data settings include Waveform, Clip Gain, and Volume, and a toggle called Allow Per Track Settings. The Audio Data items are global settings that affect all tracks in the timeline, which is contrary to options in the Track control panel, which allow you to toggle the display of waveform, clip gain, and volume on a track-by-track basis, provided Allow Per Track Settings is enabled. If you disable Allow Per Track Settings, the Track Control Panel options don't affect the display of the timeline tracks.

When configuring a Timeline View for an Audio Mixer workspace, you might consider disabling Allow Per Track Settings, and turning on the waveform display, so all tracks will have waveforms displayed.

Media Composer 6 introduces the ability to add volume keyframes by using the sliders of the Audio Mixer, provided that the Audio Mixer is in Auto mode, shown in Figure 9.15. Auto Mode is the default mode of the Audio Mixer. The Add Keyframe command is mapped to the apostrophe key (') by default. Until you add a keyframe, you will not see the overlay nor the black line that represents the audio adjustment.

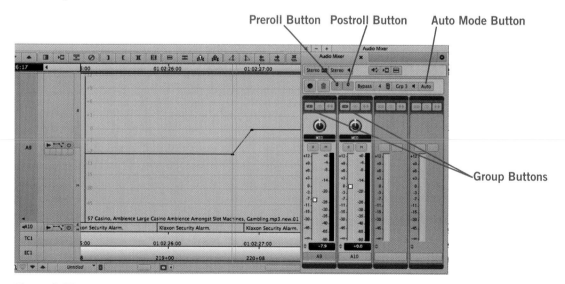

Figure 9.15
Audio Mixer set to Auto: adjusting the sliders will add volume keyframes for variable level adjustments within a clip.

Adjusting Clip Volume Dynamically

You may also make adjustments during playback by pressing the Record button in the Audio Mixer when it is set to Auto mode. In that situation, you are recording the changes you make to the sliders. You are not recording sound through a microphone or any of the audio inputs on the system. After the recording, keyframes are added to the clips in the timeline.

To adjust clip volume dynamically:

1. Set the AUDIO MIXER to AUTO mode.

2. (Optional) Mark a region of the timeline using IN and OUT marks.

   If you don't specify IN and OUT marks, Media Composer will begin recording from the location of the Current Position indicator.

3. (Optional) Specify a preroll amount, in frames, as shown in Figure 9.15.

   A preroll amount instructs Media Composer to begin playing prior to recording your changes to the audio sliders. You might set this to 48 (two seconds in a 24fps project) to give yourself a couple seconds to get ready after you press RECORD.

4. Click the RECORD button.

5. Drag the sliders to attenuate or apply gain to the clips on the timeline.

Adjusting volume dynamically is often used for music beds. You'll watch the video and look at the clips coming up on the timeline, lowering the slider when narration occurs, and raising it when there is no narration. Using a mouse, you can only drag one slider at a time. That makes it hard to ride the sliders for music, if the music is stereo and spread onto two separate mono tracks. All the more reason to set the audio track format to stereo for the clip: You get a single slider that's easy to adjust and only takes the space of one strip in the audio mixer.

Alternatively, if there are a few tracks that must be adjusted together, you can group them together using the Group button, as shown in Figure 9.15. For a group to be effective, there has to be more than one member (otherwise it's just kind of sad, a group of one!), so be sure to enable the Group button for all tracks that should be adjusted together.

Tip: Having problems moving that one mouse around for 16 sliders? It's a rather tough job to move all the sliders independently with one mouse. Avid has a solution for that: *control surfaces*. There are a variety of control surfaces manufactured by Avid that have physical mixing control strips, just like in a recording booth.

Tip: As Media Composer plays, you can ride the sliders with 10 fingers instead of one mouse. Avid's Artist Control series allows you to mix and match control surfaces. You can have 16 sliders, a set of color correction trackballs, and a transport mechanism for a physical shuttle/jog control. Each control surface has buttons that you can remap using the same technique you use to remap the buttons on your keyboard.

Some third-party external mixers from companies such as Yamaha and JL Cooper are also supported by Media Composer. Check Avid.com/support for a list of supported third-party external mixers.

After recording dynamic volume adjustments, you may find that there are a lot of keyframes in the timeline. In fact, while making an adjustment to the slider, you could have one keyframe per video frame, such as 24 or 30 per second. If you then try to adjust the curve by manipulating the automatically recorded volume keyframes, you'll find it very tough. You have two choices:

- You can group the keyframes within IN and OUT marks, which will adjust all of them while keeping their relative differences.

- You can select the Audio Mixer > Fast Menu > Filter Automation Gain on Track/Global. This reduces the number of keyframes while preserving the overall shape of the curve. You may have to run it a couple times to reduce the number of keyframes sufficiently.

Add Audio Dissolves (Crossfades)

Adding audio crossfades is as simple as adding a quick transition. Regardless of which transition you select, Media Composer will apply a dissolve to the audio transitions, which will either crossfade one audio clip into another, or fade a clip in or out, depending if the transition is at the beginning or end of the clip, respectively.

Note: You can also use keyframes and a volume adjustment to fade a clip in or out, but you can't use keyframes to crossfade two clips on the same track.

You might find that in some scenarios when you create a DVD, the audio at a cut has a "pop" sound or a slight tick. You can eliminate those pops by introducing a short two- or four-frame audio dissolve onto the problematic cut.

 Take a moment to complete Exercise 9, Part 2.

Understanding Avid Pro Tools Interoperability

It's a rare person who can master both the video and the audio realms. Often the role of picture editor is separated from the role of sound editor, and the extent of your job as a video editor is to get the audio to a good place before sending it to a sound editor, who will make it fantastic.

Media Composer excels at picture editing and has a robust set of audio editing tools, but Avid Pro Tools has a more powerful, focused set of audio tools. This part of the lesson is about how the two applications work together.

Note: Avid changed the names of some features of Media Composer in order to make them align with the names of similar features in Pro Tools. This common vocabulary makes it easier for editors of both systems to communicate, and just makes sense since Avid is one company. Examples are "volume automation" and "markers" instead of the term "automation gain" and "locators," respectively, from Media Composer 5.

Metadata Goes to Pro Tools

The most basic way to send audio from Media Composer to Pro Tools is to export a mixed-down WAV or AIFF file and import that into Pro Tools. But then the Pro Tools editor would have a couple tracks of waveform with no metadata.

A better way is to export in a format like AAF that includes the rich metadata that you've already created within Media Composer.

Some of the metadata that goes from Media Composer 6 to Pro Tools 10 includes:

■ Clip definitions, including track layout

■ Clip names

■ Broadcast WAV metadata

■ Markers, including marker colors

Using an AAF file, you can begin an audio edit in Media Composer and work with Media Composer's audio tools, while being assured that the mix you've created will carry over to Pro Tools, where the sound editor can use it as a starting point.

The following audio features can be adjusted in Media Composer and then can be further adjusted in Pro Tools:

■ Clip gain

■ Volume and pan automation

- Avid EQ
- Clip pan
- Crossfades (including location and duration)
- AudioSuite plug-ins and RTAS effects

The important thing to note in this list is that those items are no longer pre-rendered in Media Composer during an export, forcing the audio editor to accept them or discard the rendered version. The metadata that is included in the AAF and is sent to Pro Tools allows them to be re-created in Pro Tools as they were in Media Composer.

Sending Sound from Media Composer to Pro Tools

The best way to send your sequence to Pro Tools is to perform an AAF export. You can choose a range by setting IN and OUT marks, or export the entire sequence. You can include links to the media files or you can embed them. In the end, you have an AAF that contains all the metadata described in "Metadata Goes to Pro Tools" and either embedded media or linked media.

It's also possible to perform a copy or consolidation of the media to a separate folder, and have the AAF link to the media in that folder.

To send to Pro Tools:

1. Choose FILE > EXPORT. The EXPORT AS dialog box appears.

2. Click OPTIONS, which is part of the EXPORT AS dialog box

   By clicking OPTIONS, you can configure an EXPORT SETTING, which determines how Media Composer will export the sound's metadata and media files.

3. Choose to export as an AAF, as shown in Figure 9.16.

4. Select EXPORT METHOD > CONSOLIDATE TO FOLDER.

5. Select RENDER VIDEO EFFECTS (Remember: Pro Tools can't render video effects so they would not show up in the guide track otherwise).

6. Select a MEDIA DESTINATION folder.

7. Select SAVE to save the export setting and return to the EXPORT AS dialog box.

8. Select SAVE again, this time from the EXPORT AS dialog box, to begin exporting the sound using the export setting.

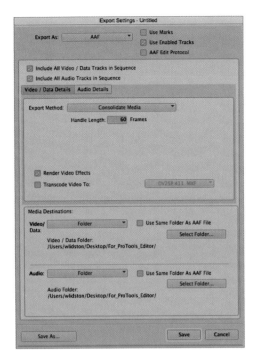

Figure 9.16
AAF export from Media Composer.

The Pro Tools editor will then import the AAF. When that occurs, Pro Tools might alter some of the original audio if bit rates or sample rates were mixed in the Media Composer sequence.

Sample Rates and Bit Depths Don't Mix

Pro Tools 10 supports mixed bit depths in the same session; however, mixed sample rates are still *not* supported. For best results, you'll need to convert a Media Composer sequence containing mixed sample rate audio to a single sample rate in MC *before* you export to Pro Tools. Sample rates of 44.1kHz or greater are required. The 32kHz sample rate is not supported in Pro Tools.

Sending Finished Sound from Pro Tools to Media Composer

After the Pro Tools editor has finished the sound mix, the audio must come back to Media Composer for insertion into the sequence.

Two common techniques for sending audio from Pro Tools to Media Composer are AAF and Bouncing.

Export Tracks as AAF/OMF

The audio can be either linked (associated) or embedded into the AAF/OMF.

Upon import, Media Composer will create an audio sequence (no video) with the associated clips in the bin. You can then integrate that audio sequence into your sequence with the finished video.

Tip: If you're using an Avid Unity or centralized file server, linking will create a smaller file that references the original media, but it requires that both the Pro Tools workstation and the Media Composer workstation have access to the same file share using the same UNC (Universal Naming Convention) paths. If you're running Media Composer and Pro Tools on the same system, this is an ideal choice.

Bounce to Disk

Pro Tools can export the session (audio sequence) to a WAV file, which is referred to as *bouncing* the session to disk.

Media Composer will import the WAV and you edit it back into the sequence.

Tip: When you overwrite the WAV file back into the sequence, consider either using a duplicate of the original sequence, or overwriting the bounced WAV audio into new tracks. Then disabling monitoring of the original tracks. This lets you see the positioning of the original clips and lets you easily export the audio again from Media Composer, if required, while also allowing the bounced audio from Pro Tools to be in the same sequence.

Co-Installation with Avid Pro Tools

Media Composer 6 and Pro Tools 10 can be installed on the same computer at the same time. Not only does co-installation make it easier to flip between the two applications, but it also allows Media Composer and Pro Tools to use each other's hardware.

Note: It's imperative that you check the README file that ships with Media Composer to ensure that your specific system and software releases are compatible for co-existence. Media Composer and Pro Tools both have specific version numbers, like 6.0.2 and 10.0.1. The README file will indicate which versions are compatible and you should never assume that you can upgrade one application without possibly having to upgrade the other to a compatible version.

Failure to confirm the compatibility of the specific versions of the applications could result in metadata not moving correctly between them. Or worse, it could impede one application's (Media Composer or Pro Tools) ability to launch or operate correctly.

Pro Tools HD Native and Pro Tools HDX hardware is supported for Media Composer audio playback. Pro Tools HD (TDM) cards are not. Pro Tools software can only use the original analog Mojo or Mojo SDI for video playback. Adrenaline, Nitris, Mojo DX, and Nitris DX hardware are *not* supported in any version of Pro Tools software.

 Take a moment to complete Exercise 9, Part 3.

Review/Discussion Questions

1. Why should video editors care about sound mixing? (See "Sound Mixing Is Important" on page 328.)

2. What are some of the goals of sound mixing? (See "Goals of Sound Mixing" on page 328.)

3. What does it mean to "achieve balance" in a sound mix? (See "Achieving Balance" on page 328.)

4. How do you know what to use as the reference level? (See "Broadcast Delivery Requirements" on page 329.)

5. With –20dBFS as a reference level, give an example of a quiet sound, a loud sound, and an excessively loud sound. (See "dBFS: Decibels Full Scale" on page 330.)

6. What's the difference between the audio meters in the Audio tool and the auto meters on the timeline? (See "The Audio Tool" on page 331.)

7. How do you generate test tone using the Audio tool? (See "The Audio Tool" on page 331.)

8. How do you determine the peak value after playing a sequence? (See "Using the Console Window to Check Audio Levels" on page 331.)

9. What's the difference in the behavior of the Audio Mixer when the Source monitor is active in contrast to when the Record monitor is active? (See "Source-Side versus Record-Side Audio Mixer" on page 335.)

10. Describe the mixing workflow. (See "Understanding the Mixing Workflow" on page 336.)

11. What metadata will move from Media Composer to Pro Tools when a WAV file is exported from Media Composer? (See "Metadata Goes to Pro Tools" on page 345.)

12. What metadata will move from Media Composer to Pro Tools when an AAF file is exported from Media Composer? (See "Metadata Goes to Pro Tools" on page 345.)

13. How does Pro Tools handle AAF files with mixed sample rates or bit depths? (See "Sample Rates and Bit Depths Don't Mix" on page 347.)

14. How does Media Composer benefit from being installed on a Pro Tools HD system? (See "Co-Installation with Avid Pro Tools" on page 348.)

15. How can a Pro Tools editor send the revised audio back to Media Composer? (See "Sending Finished Sound from Pro Tools to Media Composer." on page 347.)

Working with Sound

These exercises allow you to practice the audio and sound-related features discussed in this lesson. You will review and fix some sound issues, organize your sound effects, and learn to export a mix to Pro Tools.

Media Used:
Agent MXZero

Duration:
55 minutes

GOALS

- Learn how to develop an ear for proper audio
- Review and fix a sequence that has some issues with its audio
- Add music, sound effects, and ambience to a scene from Agent MXZero
- Organize sound effects on the timeline
- Export a mix to Pro Tools

Exercise 9.1: Analyzing Audio

In this exercise, you will review a sequence that has some issues with its audio. After reviewing it, you'll learn how to describe the problems and how you might fix them. Be sure to use proper terms and reference the Audio tool when describing the problem.

If this lesson is part of classroom-based training, your instructor may facilitate a class discussion regarding the sequence's audio.

To begin developing your ear for audio:

1. Open AGENT MXZERO > LESSON 9 - MIXING > LESSON 9 SEQUENCES > PART 1 – ANALYZE.

2. Open the AUDIO tool (choose TOOLS > AUDIO TOOL).

3. Play the sequence and critique the audio mix.

When reviewing the sequence, consider the following questions:

- Is the audio clear?

- Has balance been achieved?

- Which sounds are too loud? Too quiet?

In the next exercise, you will create your own mix for this video sequence.

Exercise 9.2: Creating a Mix

In this exercise, you will add music, sound effects, and ambience to a scene from Agent MXZero. It has music and it has a combination of clips with audio and MOS clips. You'll add multiple audio tracks in order to organize your timeline, with sound effects on their own tracks and ambience and music on others.

To practice audio mixing:

1. Open AGENT MXZERO > LESSON 9 - MIXING > SOUNDS.

   This folder contains four bins that contain the clips that you will use in this exercise.

2. Open AGENT MXZERO > LESSON 9 - MIXING > SEQUENCES > PART 2 - BUILDING A SOUND MIX.

3. Add sound effects, music, and ambience, adjusting levels as required to ensure a proper balance is achieved.

While practicing this exercise, please avoid referring to the earlier sequence and duplicating the other editor's work. Make it your own by considering the environment that the character is in, and creating his opponents by adding sound effects that represent them. The audience doesn't have to see the source of the sound effect to know that a big bad villain caused it.

Exercise 9.3: Sending Sound to Pro Tools

In this exercise, you will export the mix you created in Exercise 9.2. The Pro Tools editor is at a different location, so you will need to ensure that the media and metadata are both included.

Use these steps to export an AAF with linked, consolidated media to a folder on your desktop:

1. Right-click AGENT MXZERO > LESSON 9 - MIXING > SEQUENCES > PART 2 - BUILDING A SOUND MIX and select EXPORT. The EXPORT AS dialog box appears.

2. Click OPTIONS, which is part of the EXPORT AS dialog box.

3. Choose to export as an AAF.

4. Select EXPORT METHOD > CONSOLIDATE TO FOLDER.

5. Select RENDER VIDEO EFFECTS.

6. Select a folder on your desktop as the MEDIA DESTINATION folder. (Create a folder on your desktop if necessary.)

7. Select SAVE to save the export setting and return to the EXPORT AS dialog box.

8. Select SAVE again, this time from the EXPORT AS dialog box, to begin exporting the sound using the export setting.

Media Composer consolidates the media used by your sequence, places it in your selected Media Destination folder, and exports an AAF file containing your sequence metadata. The clips in the AAF point to the consolidated media in the Media Destination folder.

If this was an actual post-production scenario, you would then deliver that AAF file and the consolidated media to the Pro Tools editor, by using an external hard disk or copying it to a network folder.

Adjusting Audio EQ

This lesson covers audio equalization (EQ) principles and techniques. You'll learn how to perform EQ adjustments in order to enhance sound by emphasizing some frequencies while de-emphasizing others.

Media Used: Agent MXZero

Duration: 60 minutes

GOALS

- Understand EQ terminology, including frequency and Q
- Be familiar with four general-purpose EQ filters and understand when and how to use them
- Realize that common sounds often fall into predicable frequency ranges
- Learn the frequency ranges for human speech
- Be able to use the Audio EQ tool, including use of the sliders and presets
- Understand the curve in the Audio EQ tool's graph
- Use the EQ III AudioSuite plug-in for advanced EQ
- Understand when it's best to use the Audio EQ Tool in comparison to EQ III

Understanding Audio Equalization (EQ)

Sometimes simply adjusting volume for clips within a sequence, as covered in the previous lesson, is not enough to perfect the quality of the sound in your show. Despite your best efforts to record clean audio in the field, your audio may contain unwanted sounds, or it might sound muddy or flat. Sometimes the project might require you to alter the sound to create a specific mood or effect. Audio equalization (EQ) allows you to correct audio and create effects that might be required in the final mix.

An EQ adjustment allows you to boost or cut audio based on a particular frequency or range of frequencies. You can raise or lower the volume of a particular audio frequency to make it more or less audible.

EQ adjustments are powerful but they cannot make something out of nothing; they can only adjust sound frequencies that are present in the sound.

When adjusting EQ, you usually try to make as small of a change as possible. Any time you make an EQ adjustment, you are changing the original audio because you are changing the waveform. For example, you should try to isolate the smallest bandwidth to adjust, and make the smallest dB adjustments you can.

In many ways, EQ is to audio what color correction is to video. A shot may be in focus and well framed, but the colors might seem off, or the image might look flat or dull. It's also possible that the shot just doesn't evoke the kind of emotion it should. A colorist would color-correct the shot to make the colors accurate and then use some artistic license to make the colors inspire emotion from the viewer. Likewise, you can make similar adjustments to audio, remove the dullness and make it vibrant, by applying an audio EQ adjustment.

Common Uses for EQ

The audio of your soundtrack lives in a soundscape. In that soundscape, there is room for bass, midtones, and treble sound. A soundtrack that sounds *full* and *complete* has diverse sounds that are spread out in the soundscape. Some sounds have bass, some have treble, and others have midtones.

An audio clip that you consider to be a midtone, such as someone speaking, might actually include frequencies that overlap into the bass space and possibly other frequencies that overlap into the treble space. A music track will likely fill the soundscape by having its own range of sounds from bass to treble.

If you have too many clips in the same part of the soundscape, they will compete and overlap and your audience may not be able to easily distinguish the sounds.

The speech of your characters may not be intelligible because other clips have frequencies that compete.

One of your primary reasons for using EQ, therefore, is to whittle away unwanted frequencies from clips in order to make room in the soundscape for other clips with similar frequencies to the ones you are removing. For example, if you have speech on A1 and music on A2, you could use an EQ on A2 to reduce the frequencies that are usually used by speech. It's like cutting a hole in the music to make room for the speech.

The most common uses for EQ are:

- To correct audio that sounds dull, thin, or muddy.

  For example, if a lavalier mic was placed under an interviewee's tie or jacket, the voice may be muffled. You can often correct the voice by boosting the midrange (3–4kHz) by +3dB.

- To eliminate unwanted noise in the lower frequencies (mic handling, low-frequency hum, or low-frequency wind noise) by dropping out frequencies below 100Hz.

  This step often eliminates noise that you won't notice with small speakers but would be a problem when playing back on big speakers. Also, dropping out low bass frequencies may improve listener comprehension.

- To make dialogue more intelligible.

  The midpoint of the human voice lies around 1kHz. (Sibilant S's lie at the top of the range. A voice over the telephone occupies a quite narrow range at around 1kHz.)

  For the human voice, you generally can adjust low frequencies to affect tone, and adjust high frequencies to affect presence. The midrange, around 1kHz, is where you adjust for intelligibility.

- To contain audio, which allows the listener to hear only specific sounds.

- When adjusting the recording of an instrumental band, you might put a high-pass filter on everything except bass instruments: bass drum, bass guitar, and string bass. High-pass filters allow the higher frequencies to pass. This removes the incidental low frequencies from those instruments, leaving room in the soundscape for the real bass instruments to shine.

- Create audio effects. You might create an audio effect to simulate someone talking on a speakerphone or a mobile telephone, or on a science fiction show you might distort the audio so it sounds like it's coming from a far away space station.

EQ Terminology

Understanding how EQ works depends on your knowledge of a few specific terms. These terms will be used repeatedly when discussing EQ and are a fundamental part of the sound engineer's vernacular.

Frequency

Consider the phrase "I frequently take trips down south" or "The mail delivery is not very frequent." In those two sentences, the speaker is describing how often something occurs or repeats, perhaps per year or per week. The term *frequency* is a measurement of how often something happens in a particular time period, whereas *hertz* is how often something happens in one second.

Sound is created by sending vibrations through the air, which ultimately vibrate your eardrum. Frequency describes how many vibrations are being caused per second. Once you know the frequency of a sound, you can affect it using EQ.

Sound frequency is a measurement of the number of cycles of a sound wave per second, usually referred to as hertz, abbreviated Hz (1,000Hz = 1kHz.) Frequency causes pitch. The higher pitched a sound, the more frequent the vibrations that create the sound.

Putting this in practical context, consider the human voice. To create sound, air passes through the vocal cords, vibrating them. Males typically have larger vocal cords (so large they are encompassed by the Adam's apple and project through the neck) than females. The larger vocal cords vibrate more slowly and produce a deeper sound than the smaller, tighter female vocal cords, which produce a higher-pitched sound.

The vocal cords vibrate at approximately 1,000 times per second, which is the same as saying they vibrate at approximately 1,000Hz. Males, slightly less; females, slightly more. With that in mind, you can say the human voice is at a frequency of about 1,000Hz, or 1kHz. If you wanted to emphasize the human voice, you would start by emphasizing the 1kHz frequency, and frequencies slightly above and below it.

Note: Human speech occurs at around 1kHz.

Octave

An *octave* is a doubling or halving of a particular sound frequency. If you have a given sound and you double the number of vibrations per second, the frequency, you have a new frequency one octave above the original.

For example, if you're a singer and you're singing a particular note, and then you sing the note one octave higher, your vocal cords are vibrating twice as fast as they were before. If you sing a note one octave lower, your vocal cords are vibrating at half the rate. The three frequencies create the same musical note, just higher or lower than the original.

In terms of EQ effects, octaves are used to specify the *width* of the adjustment. For example, you have the human voice at 1,000Hz and you want to emphasize it. You can't make the 1,000Hz frequency louder while leaving the 999Hz and 1,001Hz frequencies. (Not unless the person is genuinely monotone!) You're more likely to make the 1,000Hz frequency louder, plus a quarter-octave on either side, which will adjust frequencies ranging from 875Hz to 1,250Hz.

Q

Q is the term that means the range of frequencies that are affected by an EQ adjustment. Q refers to the width of the adjustment (from one frequency to another) and is usually expressed in terms octaves or fractions of an octave.

In the previous definition, octave, the example given has a *Q* of ¼ octave.

Boost/Cut

This is an increase (boost) or decrease (cut) in the volume of a particular frequency. The difference between the original level and the new level is measured in decibels.

■ An audio frequency increased by 10dB is written as +10dB and is considered to have been boosted by 10dB. An example is boosting the 1kHz frequency by +5dB to bring a human voice more forward.

■ An audio frequency reduced by 10dB is written as −10dB and is considered to have been cut by 10dB. An example is cutting the 100Hz frequency to reduce the bass in a clip.

Tip: **The more you work with sound while thinking about it as frequencies, the more you'll be able to sweeten, fix, improve, and otherwise use audio effectively.**

Audio EQ Filters

An Audio EQ *filter* is a collection of three parameters: A frequency, along with a value for Q, and an action to boost (increase) or cut (decrease) those frequencies.

Some editing systems use the term *filter* like Media Composer uses the term *effect*. In those other editing systems, there is a menu of all the filters and you apply that specific filter to an effect. When working with Audio EQ, the *filter* does not have the same meaning. There is no menu of all the EQ filters. In Media Composer, you use an EQ effect, and based on how you configure the Q and cut or boost values, you are creating an EQ filter within the EQ effect.

Tip: When you use the Audio EQ tool (choose Tools > Audio EQ), Media Composer automatically applies the Audio EQ effect to the affected clip in the timeline. Unlike video effects in the Effects palette, you do not apply the EQ effect first and then modify it in the Effect Editor. Just open the Audio EQ tool, change the sliders, which defines a filter, and an Audio EQ effect will be added to the clip automatically.

There are five common types of EQ filters: parametric, shelving, high-pass, low-pass, and notch filters. These are discussed in more detail in the following sections.

Parametric Filter

A parametric filter boosts or cuts a specific frequency and a range of adjacent frequencies based on the Q, as shown in the graph of Figure 10.1.

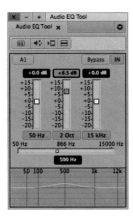

Figure 10.1
The Audio EQ tool configured as a parametric filter.

Referring to Figure 10.1, the frequency that is the focal point of the parametric filter is 500Hz, which resides in the exact middle of the Q. The Q itself is specified by the middle slider, which indicates the Q is two octaves wide. Frequencies contained within the Q on either side of this focal point are boosted or cut by the filter along a bell curve, gradually leading up to and down from the focal point, which is represented by the graph in Figure 10.1.

Note: Parametric filters can have very wide Qs or relatively narrow ones. Support for various Q widths varies between EQ effects. The EQ effect that's used by the EQ tool allows only two octave or ¼ octave Qs, whereas the EQ III effect allows you to custom set the Q. The Audio EQ effect (added by the Audio EQ tool) and the EQ III effect (added by the AudioSuite tool) are discussed later in this lesson.

Notch Filter

Notch filters are similar to parametric filters, but have a very narrow Q. In some instances the Q may be only as wide as 1Hz. These filters are primarily used for "surgical" operations, such as to isolate a specific frequency and boost it or remove it entirely.

For example, an audio recording may have a hum at 50Hz as a result of an ungrounded mic cable. Using a notch filter, you can isolate the 50Hz frequency and cut it while leaving the other frequencies unaffected, as shown in Figure 10.2.

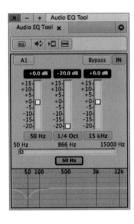

Figure 10.2
The Audio EQ tool configured as a notch filter.

Notice in Figure 10.2 that the Q on the middle slider has been set to ¼ octave, and the frequency has been set to 50Hz. Also notice that the curve shown in the graph is encompassing frequencies on either side of 50Hz. A Q of ¼ octave for a frequency of 50Hz means a range of 44Hz to 62.5Hz, which is pretty wide for a notch. Well, it might not even be considered a real notch because of that width. The Audio EQ tool's user interface doesn't allow you to set a tight enough Q for many notching scenarios.

Avid's engineers were aware of the common problem of hum on an audio recording resulting from an ungrounded cable, so they built the Audio EQ tool with some preset filters to solve common problems, including one specifically for notching out 50Hz, shown in Figure 10.3.

You can see the tight notches in the graph of Figure 10.3. The notches remove 50Hz as well as the three octaves of 50Hz, 100Hz, 200Hz, and 400Hz, which are harmonics of 50Hz. The harmonics are notched because sometimes a hum will exist at harmonic intervals too. (If you're familiar with a music keyboard, you can think of 50Hz as a low C, 100Hz is the next C note, 200Hz might be Middle C, and 400Hz is the C note above Middle C.)

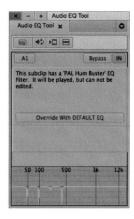

Figure 10.3
The Audio EQ tool using the PAL Hum Buster preset.

Tip: If you want to create tight notch filters, consider using the EQ III effect that's part of AudioSuite, instead of using the Audio EQ tool. The AudioSuite EQ III effect allows custom values for Q, so you can create a very targeted, specific notch filter.

High-Shelf and Low-Shelf Filters

A shelf filter boosts or cuts frequencies above or below a particular frequency. Figure 10.4 shows a high-shelf filter that cuts all frequencies above 6kHz by –20dB.

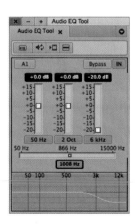

Figure 10.4
The Audio EQ tool configured with a high-shelf filter.

In Figure 10.4, the amount of the cut is set with the third slider, appropriately named the high-shelf slider, while the starting frequency for the high-shelf is defined directly underneath the slider: 6kHz.

Here's just one of many scenarios where you might use a high-shelf filter: You're cutting a scene featuring a teenage house party. In the living room, everyone's partying and dancing to music. Then you cut to a scene of a bedroom where two characters are talking. To maintain consistency that they are at the same party, and in the same house, you want the music to continue under their dialogue.

Low-frequency sounds travel through walls better than high-frequency sounds, as anyone who's lived in an apartment with neighbors who own a home theatre system is well aware. (Boom, Thump. Thump.) To simulate the effect of music from another room coming through a wall, you can apply a high-shelf filter to the music to diminish the high-frequency sounds. The intelligibility and detail of the sound will be reduced, but the presence and power will remain. You could then attenuate the track using the Audio Mixer to reduce the power, so it's not as loud in the bedroom as it is in the living room.

High-Pass and Low-Pass Filters

Similar to high- and low-shelf filters, these filters affect all frequencies higher or lower than a given value, but instead of reducing the levels by a given amount, they gradually eliminate it. A high-pass filter allows the high frequencies to pass while eliminating low frequencies. A low-pass filter does the opposite: low frequencies pass and high frequencies are eliminated.

Sometimes it helps to have an image to remember what a high-pass or low-pass filter does. There's a fancy nightclub with a bouncer who lets in the pretty people and rejects people who don't meet the dress code: No ball caps allowed. The bouncer is a kind of filter—anyone who dresses well may pass, anyone who doesn't dress well is rejected. Likewise, a high-pass filter will allow any high-frequency sounds to pass, while any frequencies that are not high are not allowed.

High-pass and low-pass filters gradually *roll* the level to −∞dB (negative infinity), which is an audio engineer's way of saying the volume gets turned all the way down.

Figure 10.5 illustrates a low-pass filter, which allows the low notes to pass. The high notes are rolled to −∞, which eliminates them.

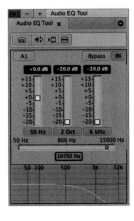

Figure 10.5
The Audio EQ tool configured as a low-pass filter; the high frequencies are eliminated.

Note: The difference between a shelf and a pass is that a shelf alters the frequencies to a particular level, leaving the sounds there, just boosting or cutting
them, whereas a pass actually removes frequencies so they are no longer
part of the sound.

Using Average Frequencies
for Common Sounds

The previous section began by defining an EQ filter as consisting of a range of
frequencies and an action to perform on those frequencies, like boosting or cutting
them. But how do you know which frequencies to use? Well, treat Table 10-1 as
a kind of cheat sheet. It lists frequencies and the sounds that are normally found
at those frequencies. Table 10-2 lists frequencies that are often reduced.

Table 10-1   Frequency Ranges of Common Sounds

Frequency Ranges	Example
20Hz to ~14kHz, acoustic	Normal range of adult human hearing (Most teens and children can hear frequencies beyond this range—from 14kHz up to ~16kHz.)
16Hz to 32Hz	The human threshold of feeling, and the lowest pedal notes of a pipe organ.
32Hz to 512Hz	Rhythm frequencies, where the lower and upper bass notes lie.
512Hz to 2.048kHz	Defines human speech intelligibility, gives a horn-like or tinny quality to sound.
2.048kHz to 8.192kHz	Gives presence to speech, where labial and fricative sounds lie.
8.192kHz to 16.384kHz	Brilliance, the sounds of bells and the ringing of cymbals. In speech, the sound of the letter "S."

These tables are only a starting point, not die-hard commandments. Once you
create a filter using the frequencies in the tables, you'll likely have to tweak them
along with the Q to hone in on the frequencies you want to adjust. When creating EQ filters, one of your goals is to adjust the frequency and Q specifically
enough to only change the frequencies you intend to change, while leaving the
others as they were originally recorded.

Table 10-2 Common Frequencies for EQ Elimination/Reduction

Frequency	Description
10Hz	10Hz, cyclic rate of a typical automobile engine at idle (equivalent to 600 rpm).
50Hz	Electromagnetic—standard AC mains power (European AC, Tokyo AC).
60Hz	Electromagnetic—standard AC mains power (American AC, Osaka AC).
100Hz	Cyclic rate of a typical automobile engine at redline (equivalent to 6,000 rpm).
16.7kHz	Approximately the tone that a CRT television emits while running.

*This information is licensed under the GNU Free Documentation License. It uses material from the Wikipedia article "Orders of magnitude (frequency)."

Exploring Audio EQ Tools and Plug-Ins

Media Composer provides three tools to manipulate audio EQ:

- The Audio Equalization (EQ) tool, which adds the Audio EQ effect
- The AudioSuite tool, which adds the EQ 3 7-Band effect
- The RTAS tool, which adds the EQ 3 Insert on an entire audio track

The EQ tool (Tools > EQ Tool) and AudioSuite plug-in (Tools > AudioSuite > EQ 3) support real-time EQ on individual clips. The RTAS version of the EQ III plug-in is applied to an entire track using RTAS inserts, which are the topic of the next lesson.

Each of these tools allows you to adjust the high, low, and midrange frequency ranges of an audio clip. The AudioSuite EQ III effect allows significantly more control by allowing the adjustment of seven bands instead of the three available in the Audio tool's EQ effect.

As with any other Media Composer effect, you can save audio EQ effects to a bin and reuse them in different circumstances.

Using the Audio EQ Tool

The Audio EQ Tool (Tools > Audio EQ) allows adjustments on three bands—low-frequency (LF), mid-frequency (MF), and high-frequency (HF)—which correspond to bass, midtones, and treble, respectively. The bands are represented by sliders, shown in Figure 10.6.

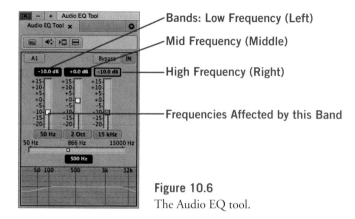

Bands: Low Frequency (Left)

Mid Frequency (Middle)

High Frequency (Right)

Frequencies Affected by this Band

Figure 10.6
The Audio EQ tool.

Each band controls the levels of its respective frequencies. In Figure 10.6, the low-frequency band is affecting frequencies less than 50Hz, whereas the high-frequency band is affecting frequencies greater than 15kHz. Those values are indicated under the bands.

By adjusting the three sliders and their associated controls, you can use the EQ tool to create a parametric, high-shelf, or low-shelf filter. The techniques for creating those three filters are discussed in the following sections.

Parametric Filter

The center slider in the Audio EQ tool controls the parametric filter.

With the parametric filter, you can:

- Select a frequency between 80Hz and 12kHz
- Boost or cut the frequencies by +15dB or –20dB
- Select the Q used by the parametric filter

The parametric EQ filter allows Q values of either ¼ octaves or two octaves. The frequency range will be either an eighth of an octave or one full octave on either side of the focal frequency.

A menu under the middle slider allows selecting of the Q value, as shown in Figure 10.7.

Note: The AudioSuite and RTAS EQ III effects allow custom Q settings other than ¼ and two octaves.

For example, a parametric filter focused on 800Hz (the midpoint of the parametric curve) with a two-octave Q will affect frequencies ranging from 400Hz to 1.6kHz with the peak difference in gain occurring at 800Hz.

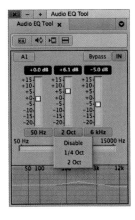

Figure 10.7
The Octave menu under the mid-frequency band allows selection of a ¼ or two-octave Q.

High-Shelf and Low-Shelf Filters

The left slider controls the low-shelf of the EQ tool's filters. It has a menu that allows frequencies below 50Hz, 80Hz, 120Hz, or 240Hz to be boosted or cut, as shown in Figure 10.8.

The right slider controls the high-shelf filter. It allows frequencies above 6kHz, 8kHz, 12kHz, or 15kHz to be boosted or cut. The high shelf affects all frequencies from the high shelf's selected value to 20kHz.

Figure 10.9 shows the high shelf's menu, displaying the available frequencies at which the shelf will begin.

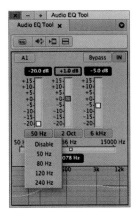

Figure 10.8
The low-shelf filter affects all frequencies from 20Hz to the value specified in the low-shelf filter menu.

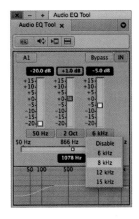

Figure 10.9
The high-shelf filter is being set to affect all frequencies from 8kHz to 20kHz.

You can think of the shelf filters like the treble and bass in your car stereo. If you increase the high-shelf filter, the sound gets brighter; decrease it and the sound gets flat and dull. If you increase the low-shelf filter, the sound gets more "boomy" and if you decrease it, the bass drops out.

Tip: You can't enter a custom value for the high- or low-shelf filters; you can only choose one of the preset values on the menus. If you need a value that's not on the menu, consider using the AudioSuite or RTAS EQ3 effects, which do allow for custom values.

Graphical Representation

In addition to the three band sliders, a graphical representation of the EQ adjustment is shown at the bottom of the Audio EQ tool. The graph represents the changes in decibels caused by the low-shelf, parametric, and high-shelf bands of the EQ tool.

Tip: Here are two tips for you:

1. You can hide the graph from view by turning up the triangular icon in the top-right side of the Audio EQ tool.

2. You really shouldn't hide the graph from view. It provides useful information!

The horizontal centerline of the graph is 0 (zero), which is the natural level for the clip. As you adjust the sliders downward, the curve moves below the zero line and the corresponding frequencies are de-emphasized. Likewise, as you adjust the sliders upward, the curve also moves upward and the corresponding frequencies are emphasized.

The parametric midrange allows a smooth transition from de-emphasized frequencies to emphasized frequencies.

The graph is only provided for informational purposes. It's not interactive: you can't drag in it. The EQ III effects, however, do have a graph with which you can interact to define the filters. The EQ III effects are discussed later in this lesson.

Adjusting Audio with the Audio EQ Tool

You can use the Audio EQ tool to apply an Audio EQ effect to one or more clips at the same time.

To adjust audio EQ using the Audio EQ tool:

1. Load the sequence containing the audio track.

2. (Optional) Isolate a portion of an audio segment by placing add edits.

3. (Optional) Mark a range of audio segments by adding **IN** to **OUT** points in the track.

4. Select **Tools > Audio EQ**.

5. Select the tracks to be adjusted in the timeline or in the Audio EQ tool's **Track Selection menu**.

   If multiple tracks are enabled in the timeline, plus signs (+) appear next to the enabled tracks in the Audio EQ tool.

6. (Optional) Click the **Play Loop** button, located in the Audio EQ tool.

   Media Composer will select the clip to which the EQ has been applied, and loop it. While it's looping, you can interact with the Audio EQ tool without interrupting playback, which is contrary to normal Media Composer behavior, in which clicking buttons stops playback.

7. Change a value in the Audio EQ tool using any of the methods you use in the Audio Mixer tool.

8. Select **Audio EQ Tool Fast menu > Set EQ - In / Out** to apply the adjustments to the range of selected clips (if applicable), as shown in Figure 10.10.

Figure 10.10
The Audio EQ tool's fast menu can be used to apply an EQ effect to all clips from IN to OUT, and can also be used to apply preset EQ effects.

If the sequence does not have an IN or OUT mark, the fast menu will allow the EQ effect to be applied to all clips on the track.

Using Looped Playback

You can use the Audio Loop Play button to create or change an EQ effect while a clip is playing.

If there is no existing EQ effect on the clip before you start, you do not hear any changes until you click the Audio Loop Play button to stop and replay the effect.

As you adjust the EQ values on an existing EQ effect, you might not hear the results immediately. It takes a few seconds for the changes to be applied to the clip.

If you adjust EQ while using the Audio Loop Play button, here are ways to improve the response time:

■ Monitor as few audio tracks as possible.

■ Deselect the video track, if practical.

■ Use IN and OUT points to narrow your interval to adjust.

EXERCISE   *Take a moment to complete Exercise 10, Part 1.*

Using the AudioSuite EQ III Plug-In

AudioSuite digital audio effects are audio plug-ins that expand Media Composer's audio capabilities. AudioSuite plug-ins are applied to individual clip segments in the timeline, and many can be played in real-time. Even if the AudioSuite effect is not real-time, rendering of audio is almost real-time.

Another category of effects, called real-time AudioSuite (RTAS) plug-ins, are track-based, and are the topic of the next lesson.

Note: Media Composer uses "EQ III" as well as "EQ 3" when referring to these AudioSuite effects. The AudioSuite menu lists "EQ 3," but when the effect's interface is displayed, it shows "EQ III." In this lesson, as in Media Composer, "EQ 3" and "EQ III" refer to the same thing.

You apply an AudioSuite EQ III effect by opening the AudioSuite tool (Tools > AudioSuite) and selecting a plug-in, which results in the AudioSuite effect being applied to the clips under the Current Position indicator for the selected tracks in the timeline. The AudioSuite effects do not exist in the Effect palette. The audio effects that appear in the Effect palette are RTAS effects, which are different than segment-based AudioSuite effects.

AudioSuite's EQ III Plug-Ins

There are two varieties of the AudioSuite EQ III effects—a 1-band version and a 7-band version—both shown in Figure 10.11.

The EQ III plug-ins (1-Band EQ III and 7-Band EQ III) have similar parameters and purposes as the Audio EQ tool, but they come with a few more bells and whistles. As effects originally designed for use with Avid Pro Tools, they have a rich, interactive, and realistic interface that's different from the normal Media Composer interface.

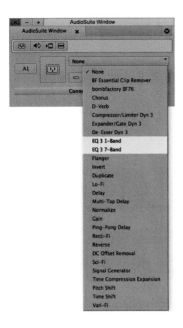

Figure 10.11
The AudioSuite menu of effects (plug-ins): there are two
EQ 3 effects, which differ in the number of bands available.

One of the most notable changes is that these plug-ins have an interactive graph
that you can manipulate to build your EQ filters.

EQ III 1-Band Effect

The EQ III 1-Band effect, shown in Figure 10.12, features a Type control that allows
you to choose the kind of filter you want. Setting the type results in the curve
graph being configured to match that type.

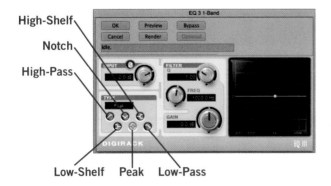

Figure 10.12
The AudioSuite EQ III 1-band effect.

You can further manipulate the curve by dragging the circular control nodes in the
graph, or you can manipulate the dials. The dials can be rotated by dragging them.
By adjusting the Q and Freq dials, the curve becomes wider or narrower (Q), or
the entire curve shifts left or right (Freq). The Audio EQ tool had preset values

for Q, but the EQ III has a dial so you can use any Q value. It's easiest to see how it works by doing it, so feel free to experiment with the dials and observe the effect on the graph. The Gain dial is used to specify if you're cutting or boosting the levels of the frequencies selected by the graph.

Note: If the High-Shelf and Low-Shelf options look more like tuning forks than shelves, it's because the icon is showing that the shelf can both attenuate or apply gain to the signals, hence the curve going up or down and the icon showing both scenarios.

The filter types are shown in Figure 10.13.

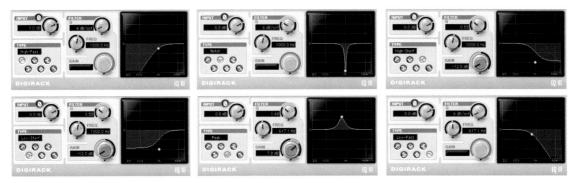

Figure 10.13
The six EQ filters available in the EQ III effect.

Did you notice the Peak filter? The EQ III plug-ins use the term *peak* instead of *parametric*. They're the same thing.

In comparison to the Audio EQ tool, the EQ III 1-band effect has more control over Q and also has a notch filter that can be narrowed down to a very specific frequency. The Audio EQ tool, however, has three bands that can be adjusted independently, whereas the EQ III 1-band has, as the name suggests, just one band.

Its big brother, the EQ III 7-band effect, however, offers the best of both worlds—lots of granularity for selecting specific frequencies, and seven bands.

EQ III 7-Band Effect

The EQ III 7-band effect, shown in Figure 10.14, gives you the ability to manipulate seven different bands of frequency. This means that you can hone in on very specific parts of the frequency curve to boost or cut different parts of the signal.

IN buttons enable or disable the curve. You must click on these to enable the last two bands.

Low frequencies have been rolled off via a Low-Shelf filter.

The frequency range of the human voice has been boosted.

The frequency of the sibilant "s" has been cut via a Notch filter.

Both of the filters on the left and right parts of the curve can be toggled from a Peak to a Shelf filter, depending on how you want to shape the signal.

Each of the central bands is a "Peak and Notch" band. You can control the width of the EQ band by widening or narrowing the bandwidth with the Q dial.

Figure 10.14
The AudioSuite EQ III 7-band effect features seven filters, plus direct dragging of the graph.

In Figure 10.14, the design of the curve is meant to boost qualities of the human voice while decreasing sssssibilant s's, which occur at the upper range of the human voice's frequencies, as referenced in Table 10-1. The effect also removes low-frequency rumbles that might have been picked up by the microphone due to wind.

A brief tour of the seven bands follows:

■ A high-pass filter (HPF) and low-pass filter (LPF) exist on the extreme ends of the frequency spectrum.

■ Moving inward from both ends are a low-frequency (LF) and a high-frequency (HF) filter. The effect interface allows you to choose between having them be peak filters (parametric) or shelf filters.

■ The three central bands are identified as low-mid, mid, and high-mid frequencies—LMF, MF, and HMF, respectively. They can be peak (parametric) or notch filters. The only difference between a peak and a notch filter is the width of the Q. Notch filters are very specific because they affect only a few frequencies, whereas peak filters affect a wider range of filters using a curve.

■ Each of the seven bands has an IN button that's used to enable the band. By default, the high-pass and low-pass filters are not enabled, but you can enable them by clicking their IN buttons.

Applying the AudioSuite EQ III Effects

AudioSuite effects can be applied to a segment in a sequence or to a master clip in a bin. If applied to a master clip, a new master clip will be created.

To apply an AudioSuite EQ III effect to a segment in a sequence:

1. Park on an audio segment in the sequence.

2. Select the track containing the segment and deselect all other audio tracks.

   AudioSuite effects are applied to all segments at the current position on all selected tracks.

3. (Optional) Isolate a portion of an audio segment by placing add edits.

4. (Optional) Mark a range of audio segments by adding **IN** to **OUT** points in the track. This applies the EQ effect to full clips from the IN point to the OUT point.

5. Choose **TOOLS > AUDIOSUITE**. The **AUDIOSUITE TOOL** opens, as shown in Figure 10.15.

Figure 10.15
The AudioSuite tool.

6. Select one of the EQ III plug-ins from the effect selection menu, as shown in Figure 10.16.

Figure 10.16
The AudioSuite tool's effect selection menu.

7. Choose the drive where you want to render the effect.

8. Click the purple plug-in icon to open the effect's interface.

9. Adjust the EQ filters as desired.

10. Click **OK** to save the filter and return to the AudioSuite window.

11. Render the effect by clicking the **RENDER EFFECT** button.

AudioSuite effects can also be rendered using any of the standard rendering commands.

Caution: **Always check the mix after applying an AudioSuite effect. Many plug-ins affect a clip's volume.**

Audio clips in the timeline do not support nesting of AudioSuite effects. You can't apply more than one AudioSuite effect to a clip; however, you can apply the Audio EQ and one AudioSuite effect to the same clip.

If you want to apply multiple AudioSuite effects to the same clip, you have to apply the effect to a master clip in a bin, and then render the clip using the AudioSuite tool. AudioSuite will then create a new audio clip in the bin, to which you can apply another AudioSuite effect and render out a new audio clip. You can repeat that procedure indefinitely, each time applying another AudioSuite effect.

To apply an AudioSuite effect to a master clip:

1. Choose **TOOLS > AUDIOSUITE**. The **AUDIOSUITE WINDOW** opens.

2. Drag a master clip into the AudioSuite window. The AudioSuite window expands to display the master clip options, as shown in Figure 10.17.

Figure 10.17
The AudioSuite window configured for working with master clips.

The interface updates to reference the selected clip and the **MASTER CLIP** button is highlighted to indicate that the effect will be applied to a master clip.

Tip: **Disable the Master Clip button if you want to affect a clip in a sequence.**

3. Select the desired effect from the **Plug-In Selection** pop-up menu.

4. Select the drive where you want to render the effect.

5. Choose the bin where you want to save the processed clip.

6. Click the large, purple plug-in button to open the effect's interface.

7. Adjust the effect as desired.

8. Click **OK** to return to the **AudioSuite window**.

9. Render the effect by clicking the **Render Effect** button.

The processed clip and an effect template containing the effect configuration are saved to the selected bin. If you need to recreate the effect on another clip at a later time, you can drag the effect template to the AudioSuite tool to load effect settings.

Attacking an Unwanted Noise

It is not uncommon to find that you can hear that you have a problem in the audio, but you're not sure at what frequency or frequencies the problem is audible. The first step is to isolate the frequency or range of frequencies where the problem occurs.

You can use the "search and destroy" method to locate the area:

1. Select a narrow (also referred to as a "high") Q. In the Audio EQ tool, a good starting point is the ¼ octave in a parametric filter. With the AudioSuite EQ III plug-in, a good starting point is a Q of 10 or greater.

   Although you might be tempted to lower the level in the parametric filter to eliminate the problem, remember, you haven't yet isolated the frequency for the offending sound.

2. Increase the EQ band's gain by approximately +10dB.

   By applying gain to the unwanted sound, it will be much more noticeable —you want to be able to exaggerate the unwanted sound. Once you find the sound, you can bring down the slider.

Caution: Use caution in regards to your personal monitor volume when increasing the band's gain. As a rough rule of thumb, people generally *perceive* a difference of +10dB to be roughly two times louder. Thus, if the frequency you seek to eliminate is particularly harsh or pronounced and you're searching for it with the maximum boost of +18dB, you're going to give your ears a rather unpleasant taste of that harsh frequency almost four times louder than it was originally!

3. Keep the other EQ bands set to **0.0dB Gain**.

4. If you're not dealing with a short clip, mark an **IN** and **OUT** to isolate a small area to loop-play.

5. If you're using the Audio EQ tool, loop-play the section. If you're using the AudioSuite EQ III, click the **Preview** button. While playing, adjust the frequency for the EQ band. With the Audio EQ tool, this is accomplished by adjusting the **EQ Range** slider. With the AudioSuite EQ III plug-in, this is accomplished by adjusting the **FREQ** knob. Start with a best guess as to which frequency has the unwanted sound.

6. While still loop-playing, if the unwanted sound is not at this frequency, adjust the frequency a little farther along the frequency range, and then wait for the system to catch up and play the new frequency.

7. Repeat the previous step until you can hear the offending sound. This is the frequency you want to adjust.

8. To fix the problem, do one of the following:

   - If you want to eliminate the sound (such as a 60-cycle hum), drag the gain control all the way down.

   - If you want to simply reduce the sound, drag the gain control down as little as possible to get the improvement you want. Don't forget—when you work with EQ, you want to retain as much of the sound as you can.

   - If you want to affect a larger range of frequencies, decrease the Q.

   - Of course, instead of diminishing or eliminating a sound, you might want to augment it by increasing the gain so the sound is more pronounced.

Audio EQ Examples

The following examples show two different ways to use EQ to remove excess bass from an audio track. In these examples, assume that a low-frequency rumble in the sound track is very pronounced and EQ is used to de-emphasize it. Also assume that there are voices on the same track. The human voice covers a wide range of frequencies, and the challenge is to preserve the bass frequencies of the voices while de-emphasizing the rumbling sound.

Consider that the goal of the adjustments is the final sound. You should use small adjustments to preserve as much of the original sound track as possible. Do not be overly concerned about specific parameter values.

Low-Shelf Example

This example adjusts the bass by first applying a low-shelf filter. It's illustrated in Figure 10.18.

To de-emphasize the bass, you simply drop the low shelf to –20dB. However, there are voices on this track, and simply dropping the low shelf also removes some bass from the voices.

To compensate for the loss of bass:

1. Use a wide Q midrange setting to create a wide midrange.

2. Move the midpoint of the mid band curve to around **88-90Hz**.

3. Boost the midrange of the mid band to **+7.7dB**.

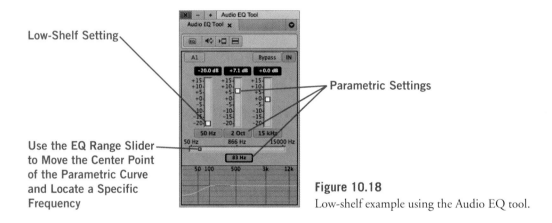

Figure 10.18
Low-shelf example using the Audio EQ tool.

Small Octave Range Example

This example, shown in Figure 10.19, uses the parametric midrange to isolate the particular frequency you want to de-emphasize.

To isolate the frequency:

1. Use a moderate Q setting range.

2. Set the midrange **EQ GAIN** to **+15dB**.

3. Use the **EQ FREQUENCY** control to move the midpoint of the mid band until it isolates the bass frequency.

In this case, the bass frequency that you want to de-emphasize is approximately 80Hz. Once you locate the frequency you want, you can adjust it as needed.

Use the EQ Range Slider to Move the Center Point of the Parametric Curve and Locate a Specific Frequency

Figure 10.19
Small-octave example using the Audio EQ tool.

Using EQ Tool's Preset Filters

Media Composer provides a set of preset EQ tool filters. The preset filters make it easy to perform some quick and common effects, including assisting you to:

■ Reduce the hum on a line

■ Make two people sound like they're having a conversation over a phone

■ Remove hiss

■ Boost or cut the bass

Some of the preset filters can use a kind of internal voodoo magic to configure the EQ tool in a way you could never configure it. For example, refer back to Figure 10.3. It shows four notch filters. The EQ tool doesn't allow for a narrow-enough Q to do a proper notch, nor does it allow for four bands. But when you use the hum-buster preset filters, it can do the job quite well. When you're using one of those preset filters that goes above and beyond the ability of the EQ tool's sliders, the EQ tool will hide the sliders since you can't further customize or tweak those presets.

In addition to the 12 presets that ship with Media Composer, you can also add your own custom EQ effect templates to the fast menu of the EQ tool.

Note: Although the Audio EQ tool offers preset filters, the AudioSuite EQ III effects do not. This section applies only to the Audio EQ tool.

To apply an audio EQ preset:

1. Place the **CURRENT POSITION INDICATOR** over the clip in the sequence where you want to apply an effect.

2. Enable the clip's audio track, disabling the other audio tracks,

3. Choose an **EQ EFFECT** from the **EQ TOOL FAST MENU**, as shown in Figure 10.20. The effect is applied to the clip where you are parked.

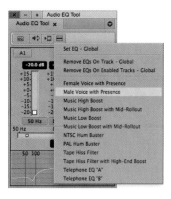

Figure 10.20
The EQ tool's fast menu contains
12 preset EQ filter templates.

4. To see the parameter values of one of the EQ templates that cannot be edited, view the **CONSOLE WINDOW** after you apply the effect.

One of the most useful ways to implement the preset EQ effects is to give yourself a starting point for an EQ adjustment by looking to see how the preset handles a given problem. Although you cannot edit existing EQ presets, you can at least use the basic principles to start off in creating your own effects.

E X ERCISE   *Take a moment to complete Exercise 10, Part 3.*

Saving Your EQ Filters as Effect Templates

As with Avid video effects, you can create effect templates to save the parameters of an effect to the bin. You can reuse the effect by dragging it back into the AudioSuite or EQ tools.

To save an EQ effect to a bin:

1. Drag the **SAVE EFFECT TEMPLATE** icon from the Audio EQ tool or plug-in window to a bin. The **SAVE EFFECT TEMPLATE** icon is indicated in Figure 10.21.

2. Rename the effect, which appears in a bin, to indicate the type of EQ saved.

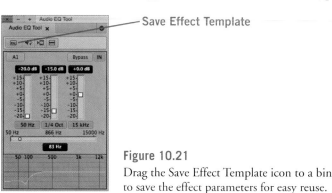

Figure 10.21
Drag the Save Effect Template icon to a bin
to save the effect parameters for easy reuse.

Applying Multiple EQ Effects

Unlike with video effects, you cannot directly apply multiple EQ effects to segments in the timeline. However, there will be circumstances where you need to manipulate the audio using more than one effect. This can be accomplished using an audio mixdown, which is discussed in Lesson 11, "Real-Time AudioSuite (RTAS)."

Adding an EQ Template to the AudioSuite EQ Tool Fast Menu

Your Avid editing application stores predefined EQ templates in a special bin named Site_EQs_Bin.avb. You can add your own EQ templates to the Audio EQ tool fast menu by storing your EQ templates in the same bin as the predefined templates.

To add an EQ template to Site_EQs_Bin:

1. Open the bin containing your EQ templates.

2. Select FILE > OPEN BIN. A dialog box opens.

3. Navigate to the bin named SITE_EQs_BIN.AVB in one of the following locations:

   (Windows) *drive*:\Program Files\Avid*Avid editing application*\SupportingFiles\Site_Effects

   (Macintosh) Macintosh HD/Applications/*Avid editing application*/SupportingFiles/Site_Effects

4. Double-click the SITE_EQs_BIN.AVB file. The SITE_EQs_BIN window opens.

5. Drag one of your EQ templates into the SITE_EQs_BIN window.

6. Name the template by clicking the text and typing a name.

7. Close the bin. Your Avid editing application does not save the effect to the bin until you close the bin.

8. Click the AUDIO EQ TOOL FAST MENU button, and look for your new template.

Adding an EQ Template to the AudioSuite EQ Fast Menu

Although Media Composer does not ship with any AudioSuite EQ templates, you can add your own to the AudioSuite fast menu. Your Avid editing application stores predefined AudioSuite templates in a special bin named Site_AudioSuite_Bin.avb. You can add your own templates to the AudioSuite fast menu by storing your templates in the same bin as the predefined templates.

To add an EQ template to the Site_EQs_Bin:

1. Open the bin containing your AudioSuite templates.

2. Select **FILE > OPEN BIN**. A dialog box opens.

3. Navigate to the **AUDIOSUITE SITE** bin file in the following location:

    (Windows) *drive*:\Program Files\Avid*Avid editing application*\SupportingFiles\Site_Effects\Site_AudioSuite_Bin.avb

    (OS X Lion) Macintosh HD/Applications/*Avid editing application*/SupportingFiles/Site_Effects/Site_AudioSuite_Bin

4. Double-click the **SITE_AUDIOSUITE_BIN** file. The **SITE_AUDIOSUITE_BIN** window opens.

5. Drag one of your AudioSuite templates to the **SITE_AUDIOSUITE_BIN** window.

6. If you have not already done so, name the template by clicking the text and typing a name.

7. Close the bin. Your Avid editing application does not save the effect to the bin until you close it.

8. Click the **AUDIOSUITE FAST MENU** button to locate your new template.

 Take a moment to complete Exercise 10, Part 2.

Review/Discussion Questions

1. What's the difference between the EQ tool and AudioSuite's EQ III effects? (See "Using the Audio EQ Tool" on page 365 and "Using the AudioSuite EQ III Plug-in" on page 364.)

2. What is frequency? (See "Frequency" on page 358.)

3. How do octaves relate to frequencies? (See "Octave" on page 358.)

4. When creating an EQ filter, what information are you providing to the filter by setting a value for Q? (See "Q" on page 359.)

5. How are a parametric and a notch filter similar? (See "Audio EQ Filters" on page 359.)

6. How are a parametric and a peak filter different? (See "AudioSuite's EQ III Plug-Ins" on page 370.)

7. What does a high-pass filter do? Give two examples of when you might use it. (See "Audio EQ Filters" on page 359.)

8. A microphone has picked up a lot of rumbling wind. How might you remove it using the Audio EQ tool? (See "Using the Audio EQ Tool" and "Using Average Frequencies for Common Sounds" on page 365.)

9. What is the purpose of the leftmost slider in the Audio EQ tool? Which filters might require you to use it? (See "Using the Audio EQ Tool" on page 365 and "Audio EQ Filters" on page 359.)

10. Suggest an approach for attacking an unwanted noise. (See "Attacking an Unwanted Noise" on page 376.)

11. What's the process for applying an Audio EQ III effect? (See "Applying the AudioSuite EQ III Effects" on page 374.)

12. How are the seven bands of the Audio EQ III 7-band effect different? (See "EQ III 7-Band Effect" on page 372.)

13. How does the graph of the Audio EQ tool differ from the graph of the AudioSuite EQ III effects? (See "Graphical Representation" on page 368.)

Equalizing Audio

In these three exercises, you'll practice using the Audio EQ tool and the AudioSuite EQ III 7-band effects to reduce hum caused by electrical interference. You'll also apply Audio EQ Tool preset filters and create your own telephone-style filter.

Media Used:
Agent MXZero

Duration:
25 minutes

GOALS

- Add and adjust Audio EQ effects
- Use Audio EQ with other audio tools and techniques to mix audio

Exercise 10.1: Removing a Hum with the Audio EQ Tool

In this exercise, a clip has a noticeable 60Hz hum. An ungrounded XLR microphone cable often causes 60Hz hums. XLR microphone cables have three conductors, one of which is a grounding wire that's used to carry away unwanted electromagnetic interference. Electrical power in North America usually operates at a frequency of 60Hz, so laying an extension cable adjacent to an ungrounded microphone cable often introduces a tone to the signal at 60Hz.

You'll use the Audio EQ tool's preset to remove the hum.

Note: Electrical power in Europe tends to be at 50Hz, so the hum created by power mains and ungrounded microphone cables is at the 50Hz frequency.

To remove the hum using the EQ filter presets:

1. Open the AGENT MXZERO > 201 > LESSON 10 > LESSON 10 SEQUENCES > PART 1: HUM BUSTING EQ TOOL.

2. Open the AUDIO tool.

3. Play the sequence, paying attention to Turk's clip on A3.

   Turk's clip starts at 06:51:05, although it's the only one on A3 so it will be easy to locate. You can hear a humming sound in the background of the clips that resembles a ground fault hum. This particular hum is a simulated 60Hz hum, with partials (harmonics) at 120Hz, 240Hz, and 480Hz.

4. Open the AUDIO EQ tool, and apply the preset NTSC HUM BUSTER filter from the Audio EQ tool's fast menu.

Caution: Always monitor the audio levels with the Audio tool to ensure that your adjustments do not overdrive the signal.

Use the remaining time in the exercise to increase the presence of the character's vocals. Try using the Male Voice with Presence preset and notice the parametric curve displayed in the EQ tool's graphical display. Then remove the preset and try to create a similar curve yourself.

When working on the Turk character (large man, white jacket), you'll need to place the midpoint of the parametric curve slightly lower than when dealing with the other characters, owing to his naturally deeper voice.

Exercise 10.2: Removing a Hum with the AudioSuite Tool

Now you're going to remove the hum again, this time using the 7-Band EQ 3 and the "search and destroy" technique, not the Audio EQ tool and its preset Hum Buster filter.

To remove a hum using the AudioSuite tool:

1. Open AGENT MXZERO > 201 > LESSON 10 > LESSON 10 SEQUENCES > PART 2: HUM BUSTING AUDIOSUITE.

2. Solo **A3** to isolate the clip.

3. Mark an **IN** and **OUT** to isolate a few seconds of the clip.

4. Select TOOLS > AUDIOSUITE.

5. Select the **7-BAND EQ 3** plug-in, and click the socket to open the plug-in interface.

6. Set the **LF BAND TYPE** to **PEAK**.

7. Set the **LF Q CONTROL** to **10**.

   A narrow Q is ideal because 60Hz hum does not affect surrounding frequencies. Always change as few frequencies as possible to preserve the original integrity of the sound.

8. Set the **LF GAIN CONTROL** to **+18DB**.

   Remember, exaggerating a sound is a good way to precisely locate its frequency or frequencies. Then you can easily eliminate the sound. You'll use the low-frequency (LF) band to isolate and eliminate the fundamental frequency of the hum.

9. Press the **PREVIEW** button to loop-play the section.

10. While the section is playing, choose a frequency using the **LF** control. Start at approximately 200Hz.

11. While still loop-playing, drag the **EQ** control a little farther down the frequency range, and then wait for the system to catch up so you can play the clip at the new frequency. Repeat until the hum is very pronounced. (This should occur at around 60Hz.) 60Hz is the frequency you want to adjust.

12. To eliminate the sound, set the **LF GAIN** to −18dB or lower. Now adjust the **Q** control and determine the best setting.

13. Click the **BYPASS** toggle button to compare the altered version with the original audio. (You can also add an **ADD EDIT** within the audio clip, adjust one side, and compare to the unaltered side.)

To truly eliminate 60Hz hum, you'll need to remove the first few harmonics of 60Hz too. Use the LMF, MF, and HMF bands of the 7-band EQ 3 to eliminate overtones at 120Hz, 240Hz, and 480Hz. Once you've finished, you can save the effect to combat 60Hz hum in future projects.

Exercise 10.3: EQ for Creative Storytelling

In the previous exercises, you performed EQ adjustments for technical corrections. But EQ isn't just about fixing poorly recorded audio. You can also use it for creative storytelling, because sound can also communicate information about the space in which someone is located.

Sound can reverb in a grand hall, like a church, or echo like in a canyon. Sound can also be tinny and thin, like when it's coming through the tiny speaker of a phone or earpiece.

In this final exercise of the EQ lesson, you'll use pre-built Audio EQ tool filters to affect sound so that it sounds like it's coming from a phone. You'll then remove the pre-built filter and create the same effect on your own.

1. Open AGENT MXZERO > 201 > LESSON 10 > LESSON 10 SEQUENCES > PART 3: TELEPHONE.

2. Locate the two clips containing a blue marker.

    The two clips with the blue markers, located at the end of A2, contain the voice of the agent's assistant back at headquarters. She's monitoring the agent's move and communicates to him through an earpiece. You'll make the sound resemble an earpiece by applying an Audio EQ Filter preset.

3. Apply the AUDIO EQ TOOL > FAST MENU > TELEPHONE A preset to the audio clip at 01:07:26:19.

4. Play back the audio and then replace the filter with the TELEPHONE B preset.

    Compare the two telephone effects, paying as much attention to how they sound as to how they look in the graphical display at the bottom of the Audio EQ tool. It's now time to create your own, using that graphical display for your inspiration.

5. Remove the Audio EQ filter preset, which restores the Audio EQ tool's sliders. Use the sliders to create a similar EQ filter by trying to recreate the shape of the curve from the preset TELEPHONE filters.

You've now learned to create Audio EQ filters for individual clips in your timeline. In the next lesson, you'll learn to create more sophisticated high-pass, low-pass, and parametric audio EQ filters that affect the entire audio track and don't require rendering.

Real-Time AudioSuite (RTAS)

In this lesson, you will learn the workflow for using real-time AudioSuite (RTAS) effects. RTAS effects are applied to an entire track, so they affect every clip on the track. You will continue to learn to perform EQ adjustments and will be introduced to another RTAS effect, the Compressor/Limiter.

Media Used: Agent MXZero

Duration: 30 minutes

GOALS

- Work with real-time AudioSuite plug-ins
- Explore common applications of RTAS effects
- Learn how and when to use the Compressor/Limiter effects
- Understand how an audio mixdown lets you use 24 tracks with 16 voices

Introduction to AudioSuite Plug-Ins

There are a wide variety of AudioSuite plug-ins that extend the audio editing capabilities of Media Composer. Where did they come from?

Once upon a time there was a company called DigiDesign, which excelled at creating audio editing systems. There was also a company called Avid, which excelled at video editing systems. The two companies merged, creating a company with excellence in both video and audio editing systems.

Avid's audio editing system, Pro Tools, uses an audio plug-in architecture called AudioSuite. The AudioSuite plug-ins extend the capabilities of Pro Tools, allowing it to perform more complex audio manipulations. The engineers on the Media Composer team found AudioSuite so impressive and so powerful that they met with the Pro Tools engineers and integrated AudioSuite plug-in capabilities in Media Composer.

In the previous lesson, you learned the AudioSuite EQ III effects as well as the basics of using the AudioSuite tool.

Media Composer 5 team then implemented the RTAS functionality that had been available in Pro Tools for years. RTAS allows Media Composer to process up to five AudioSuite effects per track in real time, provided that your computer has ample processing power.

Note: RTAS effects are applied on a per-track basis, whereas AudioSuite effects (which are non-real-time) are applied on a per-clip basis. The AudioSuite tool was covered in the previous lesson; this chapter focuses on RTAS effects.

In Lesson 9, "Fundamentals of Audio Mixing," you learned that it's advantageous to separate your audio clips onto related tracks. That workflow lends itself well to working with RTAS, because it's easy to apply one or more real-time AudioSuite effects to a particular track, which will affect all clips on the track, possibly fixing hundreds of clips by applying a single effect.

AudioSuite Plug-Ins Extend Media Composer

RTAS plug-ins are audio effects that you apply to (or insert on) tracks, rather than on segments within your sequence. These inserts let you process audio material on a track in real time so that you can apply the effects to a sequence and play them back or output them without rendering them first. This lets you add a type of audio track effect that Avid Pro Tools also supports.

When using AudioSuite plug-ins, keep the following in mind:

■ Some plug-ins can only be used on a clip-by-clip basis but cannot be applied to entire tracks using the RTAS.

■ Some plug-ins are compatible with both clips and RTAS.

■ RTAS compatible plug-ins must be designed to work with the kind of multi-channel track you are using. There are more RTAS plug-ins available for mono tracks than there are for 7.1 surround tracks.

Working with Multichannel Tracks

You'll find there are very few RTAS effects that can be used with multichannel tracks. Unless the effect was designed for 5.1 or 7.1 surround processing, you can't use it on a 5.1 or 7.1 track.

You can ask Media Composer to split multichannel tracks into individual mono tracks. This also affects stereo tracks. To do this, you choose Clip > Split All Tracks to Mono. After your multichannel tracks have been split into mono tracks, you can use any of the RTAS mono effects, which are the most abundant kind of RTAS effect in Media Composer 6.

RTAS Compared with AudioSuite Effects

RTAS effects will affect all clips on the track. Therefore, it's important to have your track contents separated. If you want to affect only a few clips on one track, instead of the entire track, you should apply an AudioSuite effect instead. AudioSuite is intended to be applied on a clip-by-clip basis.

Another difference between RTAS effects and AudioSuite effects is that RTAS allows five effects to be applied at a time, whereas clips on the timeline can support only one AudioSuite effect at a time. If you need multiple AudioSuite effects, put the related clips on their own track and apply RTAS effects.

RTAS Considerations When Collaborating

The real-time AudioSuite functionality is provided using plug-ins. Media Composer 6 ships with plug-ins that Media Composer 5 didn't have, and Media Composer 5 ships with plug-ins that Media Composer 4 didn't have. Further, it's possible to buy additional RTAS plug-ins to extend the audio capabilities of the RTAS and AudioSuite tools.

When collaborating with other editors on different Media Composer systems, you should ensure the other editing systems have the same plug-ins that you used.

Inserting RTAS Effects

When you apply an RTAS effect to an audio track, you are *inserting* the effect into the processing pipeline of the track. It's more common for someone to say they've created or added an *insert* to the track. The term stems originally from audio editing equipment.

Media Composer supports five concurrent RTAS effects per track, which means Media Composer supports five inserts per track. You might think of an insert as a "slot" and you can plug an RTAS effect into the slot. The inserts are labeled *a, b, d, c, e,* and *f.*

RTAS effects are processed in order of insert *a* through to insert *f.* The order is significant and shouldn't be used haphazardly, because the output of the first insert is then used as the input of the next insert. The processing order is like an assembly line, with insert *a* being the first stop on the line, and then the affected audio is sent along to the next insert.

You can see the five available inserts, as well as whether there is an effect applied, by expanding the Track control panel on the timeline as shown in Figure 11.1.

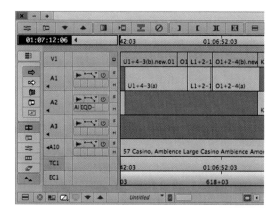

Figure 11.1

The Track control panel displays five audio inserts per track; A2 has three effects on inserts *a, b* and *c,* whereas inserts *d* and *f* are empty.

There are three ways to insert RTAS effects into a track: dragging, right-clicking, and using the Insert buttons.

Drag from Effect Palette

Media Composer's effects palette features more than 80 RTAS effects spread over 23 categories. The categories are grouped by track type (such as mono, stereo, 5.1, and 7.1 surround) and then by effect type, as shown in Figure 11.2.

Figure 11.2
RTAS effects in the Effect palette.

You can apply an RTAS effect to a track by dragging it from the Effect palette to one of the Insert buttons (in the Track control panel), or directly into the middle of the track. If you drag the RTAS effect to the middle of the track, Media Composer will ask which of the five inserts to use for the effect.

Note: When selecting an effect to drag from the Effect palette, be mindful that you can only drag stereo effects to stereo tracks, mono effects to mono tracks, and so on.

Right-Click from the Track Control Panel

You can also add RTAS effects to a track by right-clicking in the Track control panel and using the pop-up menus, as shown in Figure 11.3.

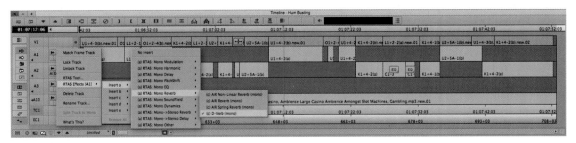

Figure 11.3
Add RTAS effects by right-clicking the Track control panel.

Other Methods for Adding RTAS Effects

Each track has five Insert buttons as part of the Track control panel. Aside from dragging an effect to those buttons, you can also click one of the buttons. Media Composer will display the RTAS tool, shown in Figure 11.4.

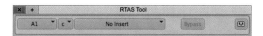

Figure 11.4
The RTAS tool with no effect on track A1, insert *c*.

The RTAS tool is also available from Tools > RTAS. You then select the track, insert, and effect using the drop-down menus of the RTAS tool.

Copying an RTAS Effect

With the Track control panel open, you can copy RTAS effects from one track to another by holding Alt/Option and dragging the Insert button from one track to another. This is useful when you've customized an effect and want to apply it to other tracks.

You can also use this technique when you're about to change an effect and want to easily revert back to the original version if you don't like the changes. Create a new track that has no clips on it, and which you never expect to place clips. Consider that a kind of temporary "scratch track."

Copy the original RTAS effect that you like to the scratch track. Then make changes to the original RTAS effect. If you don't like the changes and want to revert to the original effect, you simply copy it back from the temporary track to the original Insert button.

Editing an RTAS Plug-In

After you insert an RTAS plug-in on an audio track, you can access the plug-in controls by using the Track control panel or the RTAS tool. When you click on an RTAS Insert button in the Track control panel or an effect in the RTAS tool, the controls for the plug-in appear in the RTAS tool window, as shown in Figure 11.5.

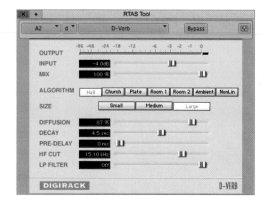

Figure 11.5
The RTAS tool with a D-verb effect on track A2, insert *d*.

You can modify the parameters of the effect as you play your sequence so you can hear how your modifications affect the sound of your audio.

To edit an RTAS effect:

1. If the Track control panel is not visible, click the TRACK CONTROL PANEL button or click the TIMELINE'S FAST MENU and select TRACK CONTROL PANEL.

2. Click the **RTAS INSERT** button for the RTAS effect you want to edit.

If a plug-in is inserted on the track, the Select Effect button displays the name of the plug-in and the RTAS tool opens a window associated with the plug-in, as was shown in Figure 11.5.

EXERCISE   *Take a moment to complete Exercise 11, Part 1.*

Selecting Inserts

If you have multiple inserts on a track, do one of the following to change the plug-in controls that display in the RTAS tool:

■ Click the Select Track or the Select Insert button and select a different insert.

■ Press the arrow keys to cycle through the available inserts. The Up and Down Arrow keys change the selected track. The Right and Left Arrow keys change the selected insert.

Bypassing Inserts

Sometimes you'll apply an insert and then want to hear what audio sounded like prior to the addition of the inserts. To easily compare the before and after, use the Bypass button located at the top of the RTAS, as shown in Figure 11.6.

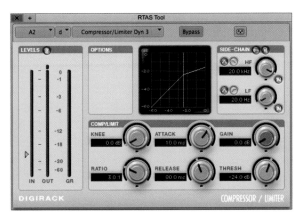

Figure 11.6
RTAS tool with the Compressor/Limiter bypassed.

When highlighted, the insert won't be processed. You can toggle it on and off while playing in real time.

Tip: If you click Ctrl+Bypass (Windows) or Cmd+Bypass (Macintosh), you can disable RTAS effects on all tracks in the timeline.

Ordering RTAS Inserts on a Track

When you combine RTAS plug-ins on an audio track, the order in which you insert them affects how your Avid editing application applies the effects. This can produce different results for your sequence. Your Avid editing application processes RTAS effects in order from left to right as they appear in the Track control panel (insert *a* through insert *e*). For example, if you insert a compressor plug-in to the right of an EQ plug-in, your Avid editing application applies the EQ effect first and then applies the Compressor effect to the result.

Within the world of audio mixing, there is a fair amount of debate over the correct order for effects. In practice, it usually comes down to personal preference and the demands of the particular audio you are working with. Broadly speaking, the following order is generally accepted:

1. Dynamic and EQ effects

2. Harmonic and Modulation effects

3. Delay and Reverb effects

To modify the order of RTAS inserts on a track, click the RTAS filter in the Track control panel and drag it to an empty Insert button.

Note: If you drop an insert on an existing insert, you will replace it, not swap their order. You must have one empty insert on your audio track so you do not replace an existing insert when you reorder the inserts.

 Take a moment to complete Exercise 11, Part 2.

Understanding RTAS Mixdown Workflows

Media Composer is limited to 16 voices, but it features 24 tracks of audio. If each of those 24 tracks of audio was a 7.1 surround track, then 216 voices could be represented (24 tracks * 8 voices) but you couldn't hear them all. How do you make use of all these tracks? Why are they there?

The secret is to use audio mixdowns.

An *audio mixdown* renders the sound from selected tracks into a new clip, which it then places onto another track. The new clip contains the summation of all the sounds from the selected tracks, but now they are pre-processed into a single track. To your ears, there should be no difference in sound between the mixed-down clip and the original tracks, but to Media Composer there is a big difference: Fewer resources are used during playback.

It's helpful to consider mixdowns in context, so consider the following scenario.

You have a sequence with dialogue spread over four tracks, as shown in Figure 11.7. Each of the four tracks has been isolated to a different character. You insert RTAS EQ III effects to each track, customizing the effect per track to give each character's voice presence.

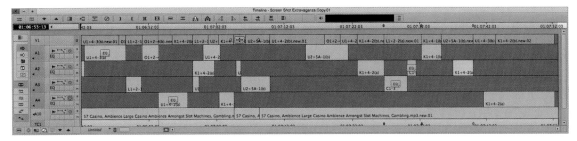

Figure 11.7
Four audio tracks, each with RTAS inserts.

You've even applied non-RTAS AudioSuite effects to a couple of the clips to perform some localized audio adjustments, also shown in Figure 11.7.

The four tracks presently require four voices, leaving 12 voices for other tracks. By performing a mixdown, the content of the four tracks will be merged onto a new clip on a new track, and it'll take only one voice.

To perform an audio mixdown:

1. Enable only the tracks you want to include in the mixdown.

2. Choose SPECIAL > AUDIO MIXDOWN.

   The window in Figure 11.8 appears.

3. Select the destination track type (such as mono, stereo, and so on).

4. Select the destination track number.

5. (Optional) Check the SAVE PREMIX SEQUENCE box.

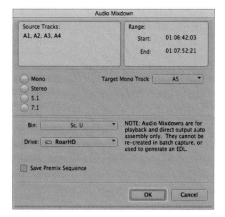

Figure 11.8
The Audio Mixdown window.

A *premix* sequence is a sequence that contains the selected tracks prior to the mixdown. If you intend to delete the original tracks from the timeline after performing a mixdown, it's important to keep a premix sequence in case you need to reassemble the sequence.

6. Click **OK**.

Media Composer combines the selected tracks together into a new clip, creates the new track, and adds the clip to that track, as shown in Figure 11.9.

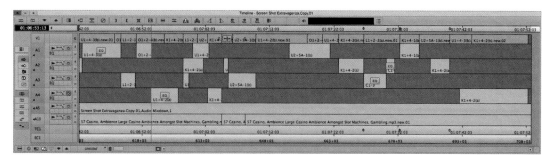

Figure 11.9
A sequence after a mixdown of tracks A1-4.

7. Deactivate the original tracks.

There is no need to keep both the original tracks active or the track containing the result of the mixdown. When you deactivate the original tracks, Media Composer will not process their contents and the voices originally allocated to those tracks can now be used for other tracks.

By keeping the original tracks in a deactivated state, instead of deleting the tracks, it's easy for you to make revisions later. If you needed to make changes, you would reactivate the original tracks, modify the contents, and perform the mixdown again.

E⟨ERCISE   *Take a moment to complete Exercise 11, Part 3.*

Limiting and Compressing Peak Values

In Lesson 9, you learned that audio should not exceed a particular peak limit. By using the Audio tool, you watched the audio meters for peak audio that exceeded a particular threshold and then used the Audio Mix tool to lower the level for the clip.

You were manually limiting the dynamic range of the clip by lowering the overall level. You also learned how to apply keyframes so you could lower a particular range within a clip.

There are a few AudioSuite and RTAS effects that are capable of automating the process. They alter the dynamic range of a clip, so it makes sense that they're found in the Dynamics category of the Effect palette, as shown in Figure 11.10.

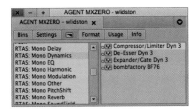

Figure 11.10
The RTAS Dynamics category of the Effect palette.

This lesson focuses on the Compressor/Limiter Dyn 3 effect, shown in Figure 11.11, which performs the role of compressing the audio peaks or limiting them, depending on how you configure the effect.

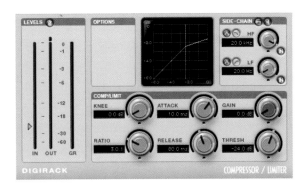

Figure 11.11
The Compressor/Limiter Dyn 3 effect open in the RTAS tool.

Compressors Reduce the Peaks

A *compressor* is one of the most commonly used AudioSuite and RTAS effects. It works by reducing the distance between the highest and lowest volume in an audio track. Compressors are often thought to make things louder, but they actually work by reducing the volume of the loudest parts (peaks) of an audio track.

A compressor basically monitors the volume of the audio stream, and when the volume exceeds a fixed threshold, the compressor reduces the volume by a certain ratio. That ratio is set by you, and it's called the *compression ratio*.

A common use is to apply a compressor to narration or dialogue to keep the voice balanced with the music bed. That prevents the voice track from becoming overpowering, or being buried by the music.

It is important to understand how the compressor acts when approaching this threshold. There are several parameters that define this activity, which can be seen in Figure 11.12.

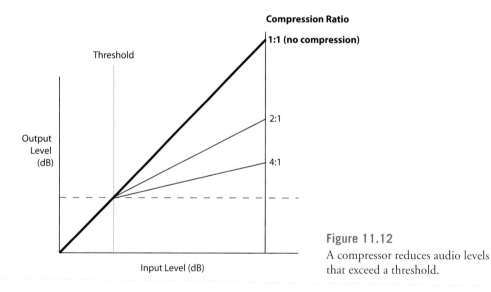

Figure 11.12
A compressor reduces audio levels that exceed a threshold.

Referring to Figure 11.12, consider a scenario where your reference level (average sound level) is −20dB. The allowable peak could be 6dB over reference, which means −14dB. You could then set the compression threshold to −14dB. The dotted line in Figure 11.12 is that −14dB.

If a loud bit of audio were to hit −10dB, it would be 4dB over the threshold. The part that happens next is up to you. It depends on the compression ratio you chose. If you chose a compression ratio of 2:1, the output signal level is cut in half.

But half of what? It's half of however much over the threshold it was. In this example, the audio coming into the compressor was 4dB over the threshold, so it will be compressed to half that—2dB over the threshold. The output level will now be −12dB.

If you set the compression to 4:1, then the compressor reduces the level to 25% of 4dB, which is 1dB, so the output audio is now −13dB.

A compression ratio of 1:1 does nothing at all.

Figure 11.13 shows the same graph with this example scenario illustrated.

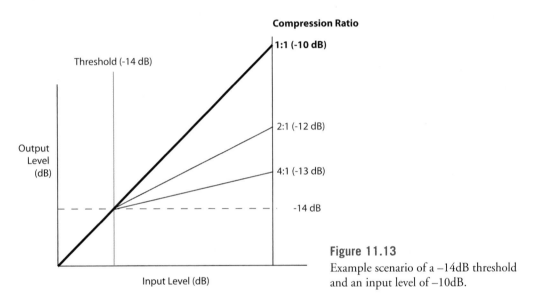

Figure 11.13
Example scenario of a −14dB threshold and an input level of −10dB.

To use Compressor/Limiter Dyn 3 as a compressor:

1. Set the attack time so that the signals exceed the threshold level long enough to cause an increase in the average level. This helps to ensure that gain reduction doesn't decrease the overall volume.

2. Set release times long enough so that if signal levels repeatedly rise above the threshold, they cause gain reduction only once. If the release time is too long, a loud section of material could cause gain reduction that persists through a soft section.

3. Use the built-in metering that allows you to monitor the amount of gain reduction taking place. The Gain Reduction (GR) meter will remain at the 0dB level when the input signal is below the threshold, and fall to the bottom to show the amount of gain reduction in decibels when the input signal exceeds the threshold.

A summary of the parameters found in the Compressor/Limiter Dyn 3 effect is listed in Table 11-1.

Table 11-1 Compressor/Limiter Dyn 3 Parameters

Parameter	Description
In	Indicates the level of the unprocessed input signal to the Compressor/Limiter. You can drag the orange triangle adjacent to this to adjust the threshold.
Out	Indicates the output level of the Compressor/Limiter.
GR	Indicates the amount of *gain reduction* in dB. It remains at the 0dB level when the input signal is below the threshold.
Knee	Allows you to set the rate at which the compressor reaches full compression once the threshold has been exceeded. This parameter ranges from 0 (hardest response) to 30 (softest response).
Ratio	Allows you to set the compression ratio. The range is based on decibels above the threshold. If this parameter is set to 2:1, for example, it compresses changes in signals above the threshold by one half.
Attack	Allows you to set the Compressor's attack time. (The *attack time* is the amount of time the compressor takes to act once the threshold is exceeded.)
	The smaller the value, the faster the attack. The faster the attack, the faster the Compressor applies attenuation to the signal. If you use fast attack times and heavy limiting, you should use a proportionally longer release time, particularly with material that contains many frequent peaks.
Release	Allows you to set the release time. (The *release time* is the amount of time a compressor takes to let up once the audio falls back below the threshold.) If you use heavy compression, you should use proportionally longer release times. This smoothes the change in level and prevents "pumping," which might occur when the Compressor jumps back and forth between compressed and uncompressed signal levels.
Gain	Provides master output gain adjustment. (This allows you to compensate for heavily compressed signals.)
Thresh	Allows you to set the threshold level. Signals that exceed this level are compressed. Signals that are below it are unaffected.
Graph	Allows you to see the effect of your settings by displaying the response curve set by the Compressor/Limiter's Threshold, Ratio, and Range settings.

Limiters Clip the Peaks

A *limiter* prevents signal peaks from exceeding a specific threshold so amplifiers or recording devices are not overloaded.

A limiter is similar to a compressor in theory, but it differs in its degree and ultimate effect. Basically, a limiter is a compressor with a higher ratio, such as at least 10:1 or even 100:1 (100%) and a very fast attack time, as shown in Figure 11.14.

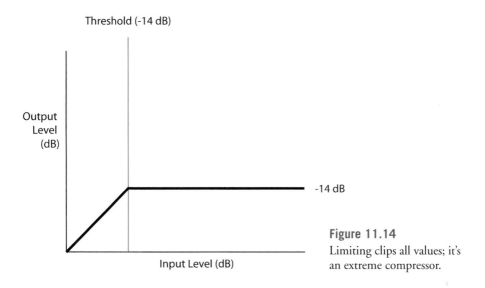

Figure 11.14
Limiting clips all values; it's an extreme compressor.

Brick wall limiting, which is often useful to clip audio levels to ensure a safe program output by not allowing the audio levels to exceed the threshold, has a very high ratio and a very fast attack time. Usually, brick wall limiting constitutes ratios of 20:1 all the way up to 100:1. Because it reduces all audio peaks (thereby eliminating some audio information at the high end), brick wall limiting is usually seen as a safety device in live broadcast situations, rather than as a tool to design the soundtrack.

It is important to understand how the limiter acts when approaching the threshold level set in the Limiter/Compressor effect.

To use Compressor/Limiter Dyn 3 as a limiter:

1. Set the **ATTACK** time to a very small value to ensure that peaks do not happen too quickly for the Limiter to react.

2. Set the **THRESHOLD** to the maximum acceptable output level.

3. Set the **RATIO** to a very high value (> 20:1) to establish the "brick wall" which no peaks can exceed.

A limiter is usually the last thing you do to your audio before sending it out of your editing system. An effective workflow is to mixdown all your tracks to your output format (such as stereo or 5.1 surround) and apply a limiter to that track. Media Composer allows you to mixdown mixdowns, so even if you've already mixed down dialogue tracks and separately mixed down music tracks, you can use those tracks as inputs to the mixdown feature (choose Special > Mixdown) and then apply the Compressor/Limiter Dyn 3 effect to the result.

Compressors Compared to Limiters

Examining the dynamic range of clips that exceed the threshold reveals the key difference between a compressor and a limiter. A compressor simply reduces the extent of the peaks, but the values are still above the threshold. A limiter snips the peaks like a barber's scissors, ensuring that all the levels that were previously above the threshold are now set to the threshold's level.

It's desirable to use a compressor to reduce the variation between the average level (reference level) and the extremes. Using a compressor will help avoid a scenario in which your audience keeps the remote control near by, riding the volume buttons to try to maintain a more moderate sound.

It's desirable to use a limiter when you know for certain that you must never exceed a certain level. Dance clubs often have limiters on their sound systems. Their limiters are set to a threshold value set by the municipalities. That ensures their sound system never plays music louder than what's allowed, and it reduces their chances of getting a ticket for violating noise bylaws. Broadcasters also use limiters on their output signals.

Review/Discussion Questions

1. How would the RTAS EQ III 7-band effects differ from the AudioSuite EQ III 7-band effect? (See "RTAS Compared with AudioSuite Effects" on page 391.)

2. When would you use an RTAS effect instead of an AudioSuite effect? (See "RTAS Compared with AudioSuite Effects" on page 391.)

3. Your sequence consists only of 5.1 surround audio tracks. How will this affect your ability to work with RTAS effects? (See "RTAS Compared with AudioSuite Effects" on page 391.)

4. List three ways to add an RTAS effect to a track. (See "Inserting RTAS Effects" on page 392.)

5. What is an *insert*? (See "Inserting RTAS Effects" on page 392.)

6. Why might you choose to bypass an RTAS effect? (See "Bypassing Inserts Effects" on page 395.)

7. What is an audio mixdown? (See "Understanding RTAS Mixdown Workflows" on page 396.)

8. What's a limiter? (See "Limiters Clip the Peaks" on page 403.)

9. How does a compressor compare to a limiter? (See "Compressors Compared to Limiters" on page 404.)

Working with Real-Time AudioSuite Effects

The sequence in this exercise contains a lot of audio problems, from hums to muffled voices, to hisses and rumbles. It has the making of a perfect audio mixing storm, and your goal is to make it ready for primetime.

You'll fix many of the audio problems using the RTAS EQIII 7-Band effect. You'll also practice the audio mixdown workflow, which allows you to manage the 16 voices available within Avid Media Composer.

Media Used:
Agent MXZero

Duration:
30 minutes

GOALS

- Use RTAS filters effectively
- Improve the tonal balance of an actor's voice
- Create a low-pass EQ filter to remove hiss
- Create a high-pass EQ filter to remove rumble
- Mixdown the tracks into a new mono track
- Apply a Normalize RTAS effect to a mixed down track

Exercise 11.1: Removing Interference and Restoring Vocal Presence

In this exercise, you'll fix a problem with Agent MXZero's voice: It's muffled! There's also some interference. All it takes is one RTAS and your skills to fix all the problematic clips.

1. Open AGENT MXZERO > 201 > LESSON 11 > LESSON 11 SEQUENCES > PART 1: RTAS EQ.

2. Listen to the sequence.

   The audio for the sequence is entirely on track A1. This is typical for dialogue scenes supplied by offline editors. RTAS effects are applied on a track-by-track basis, and must be applied to the entire track, so it's important to separate the audio of each performer onto separate tracks.

3. Create two new mono tracks: **A2** and **A3**.

4. Use the LIFT/OVERWRITE SEGMENT tool (red arrow) while holding CMD/CTRL+SHIFT to move the audio clips to the following tracks:

   A1: Agent MXZero

   A2: Mysterion

   A3: Turk

5. Solo **A1 - AGENT MXZERO** and play the sequence.

   Agent MXZero's audio has interference at 4200Hz, possibly caused by cheap circuitry inside the microphone preamps used during recording, or possibly some sort of wireless interference, such as microwave ovens, neon signs, and so on. To eliminate the problem, you first have to locate the exact frequency that is causing the problem, and then attenuate that frequency with a very sharp (narrow) Q.

6. Apply a **RTAS EQIII 7-BAND EQ** EFFECT TO TRACK **A1**, INSERT A.

   Three ways to apply RTAS effects include: right-clicking an insert and using the contextual menu; clicking on an insert and adding the effect from the RTAS window that opens; or dragging an effect from the Effect palette to the track.

7. Open the **EQIII 7-BAND EQ** effect.

   To locate the frequency of the interference, do the following:

8. Choose one band on the EQ, such as **MF**.

9. Set the Q as narrow as possible, and boost its frequency by **+12DB**.

10. Slowly sweep the frequency across the spectrum from the lowest to the highest point.

    The problem frequency(ies) will jump out of the speakers when the boost crosses it. When the problem is at its loudest and clearest, you've located its fundamental frequency, which can now be attenuated.

11. Attenuate the problem frequency once it has been identified.

12. (Optional) If some of the tone remains, the Q can be widened a touch. Make small, refined adjustments to the Q so as not to remove any of the non-problem frequencies.

You can repeat Steps 9–10 if there are overtones remaining, such as in removing a 60Hz hum. You can use the other bands in the EQIII 7-Band EQ effect, or you can apply a new EQIII 1-Band or 7-Band effect to one of the remaining inserts, *b, c, d, e* or *f.*

Now the interference is gone, but the sound isn't quite right—there's a lack of clarity and it sounds muffled. Although your first thought might be to begin by brightening the high frequencies, it might be better to start by attenuating the low frequencies. A low-cut (high-pass) filter would work, but will also remove the richness from the voice, leaving it thin.

1. Within the **EQ III 7-BAND** effect, create a low shelf at about 120Hz and attenuate until the low parts of the voice sound even again—between 6 and 8dB.

2. Now that you have removed all the excess and unwanted frequencies, you can boost some of the lacking ones. Create a high-shelf filter to boost the high frequencies from about 5kHz by approximately +5dB.

You have now performed a multi-band EQ correction to fix multiple problems. Thanks to real-time AudioSuite, the adjustment is applied to all clips on track A1, and no rendering is required.

In the next exercise, you continue working with this sequence by moving your attention to track A2.

Exercise 11.2: The Royal Rumblessssssssssss

Your sequence continues to be plagued by problems on tracks A2 and A3. In this exercise, the audio on A2 is suffering from a problem of the extremities: hiss in the high-end and rumble in the low-end. These extra sounds inject extra frequencies into the soundscape and detract from the clarity and intelligibility of the speech. Your mission, should you choose to accept it (and hopefully you will), is to eliminate the hiss and rumble.

You'll begin with the hiss:

1. Continue with the sequence from Exercise 11.1: AGENT MXZERO > 201 > LESSON 11 > LESSON 11 SEQUENCES > PART 1: RTAS EQ.

2. Solo **A2**, which contains Mysterion's audio, and play the sequence.

   Mysterion's audio has a consistent hiss in the high frequency range. You'll eliminate it by using a low-pass (high-cut) EQ filter, which allows low frequencies to pass and eliminates the high frequencies. (Remember: In a high-cut filter, the low frequencies are allowed to stay, but the high frequencies don't make the cut. Out they go.)

3. Apply a **RTAS EQIII 7-BAND EQ** effect to TRACK **A2**, INSERT A.

   You're now ready to apply the low-pass (high-cut) filter. The EQ III 7-Band effect does not enable the low-pass filter nor the high-pass filter when the effect is applied. You must enable those by clicking the **IN** button. The IN button is shown as part of the previous lesson in Figure 10.14.

4. Enable the **LOW-PASS FILTER (LPF)** by clicking its **IN** button, as shown in Figure 10.14 of the previous lesson.

   A low-pass filter removes the high frequencies above a certain frequency that you specify using the LPF FREQ dial in the EQ III 7-Band EQ effect. But high- and low-pass filters don't usually harshly cut all frequencies above that level. That would sound odd for any frequencies that move above and below the cutoff point.

   Instead, the high- and low-pass filters apply attenuation to their affected frequencies according to a slope: The frequencies closest to the cutoff are attenuated less than those farther away. The value of Q is used to specify the slope of the cutoff curve. When Q is used with the high- and low-pass filters, its value isn't just octaves, it's decibels per octave, such as 6dB/Oct or 12db/Oct.

   Setting Q to 12dB/Oct will create a steeper curve than a 6dB/Oct. A steeper curve means the reduction happens quicker, so fewer frequencies remain above the cutoff value. Turning the LPF Q dial fully clockwise will create a very sharp dropoff.

5. Adjust the **LPF FREQ** and **Q** values to attain maximum hiss removal while retaining the most of the original high signals from Mysterion's dialogue.

The hiss has been reduced, and Mysterion is now easier to hear, but there's still a rumble in the background. When audio is recorded outside of a sound booth, background sounds from fans and air conditioners or wind are often picked up. Your brain filters them out, but the microphone does not. You need to filter them from Mysterion's dialogue.

6. Use the same technique from Steps 4 and 5, but this time, work with the HIGH-PASS FILTER, HPF, which cuts the low frequencies.

Exercise 11.3: Creating a Mixdown

In this exercise, you'll continue with the previous exercise and use a mixdown to reduce the voice-count requirement for the sequence.

1. Using the techniques from the previous exercise, improve the audio for the other characters by applying EQ effects to their tracks.

2. Follow the techniques in the section entitled "Understanding RTAS Mixdown Workflows" to mixdown the tracks into a new mono track.

3. After mixing down your clips, apply a NORMALIZE RTAS effect to the mixed down track.

This is also a good opportunity to explore some of the other RTAS effects beyond EQ.

Next, perform a common audio finishing task—limiting. The purpose of a limiter is to reduce the dynamic range, allowing you to maintain a strong audio signal throughout the program without exceeding broadcast specifications.

There are several limiters in the RTAS Dynamics category. Try using the Compressor/Limiter Dyn 3 after mixing down all of your audio tracks to a stereo track.

Wrapping Up a Project

This lesson introduces online editing and archival workflows you can use when a project has wrapped up.

Media Used: Picture and Sound

Duration: 30 minutes

GOALS

- Learn techniques for an offline/online workflow
- Prepare to conform an online edit
- Learn video and audio encoding/compression techniques
- Choose the appropriate media resolution and type for the project requirements
- Estimate the media storage requirements using the Avid storage calculator
- Pull a source list from the offline workflow
- Learn to smooth the transition from offline to online
- Decide when it's appropriate to consider creating an online project

Preparing for Online Editing

You can use several finishing tools to conform programs created on other Avid editing systems or those that are provided as an EDL. This section continues the exploration of the online finishing process by discussing some of the decisions and configurations you should make before beginning the conform using each of these tools.

Choosing the Online Editing System

Avid offers three nonlinear editing systems, all of which are considered top of the line: Avid Media Composer, Avid Symphony, and Avid DS (see Figure 12.1).

Each system is capable of real-time, high-definition uncompressed editing, compositing and color correction. Why choose one over the other?

Figure 12.1
Avid Symphony (left) and Avid DS (right).

Media Composer is your general purpose, prime-time editing system for everything from offline to online. Its effects and color-correction capabilities will handle the needs of most productions.

Avid Symphony looks and works just like Media Composer, so it will be easy for you to pick up and be comfortable with. The color-correction toolset, however, is much more elaborate and powerful, and is suitable for the needs of a professional colorist.

Until Symphony 10, released in November 2012 alongside Media Composer 6, Symphony required proprietary Avid hardware. Buying Symphony meant buying Avid Nitris hardware, and that's a significant yet worthwhile investment for a post-production facility. Symphony 10, however, is more like Media Composer: It can run with a variety of hardware or you can run it in a software-only mode.

Avid DS looks and operates similar to, but not exactly like, Media Composer and Symphony. It features the same color-correction capabilities of Symphony, but features enhanced effects capabilities. It's suitable for online editing of effects-intensive TV programming like science fiction shows and graphics/effects intensive prime-time commercials.

Setting the Project's Format

Before beginning your conform, you should select an appropriate resolution for the media you will be capturing by configuring the Project Format settings, as shown in Figure 12.2. Although sometimes the resolution is predetermined by the production or workflow requirements, the following guidelines will help you determine the best resolution to use for your online conform.

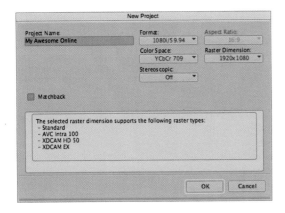

Figure 12.2
Media Composer projects have a Format and a Raster setting.

Project Types

All Avid projects have a format that is specified when you create the project. After they are created, all standard-definition projects can be switched to a 1080-line high-definition format and back again.

To switch a project's format after it has been created:

1. Open the **PROJECT** window and select the **FORMAT** tab, as shown in Figure 12.3.

2. Choose the desired format from the **PROJECT TYPE** pop-up menu.

Table A-1 in Appendix A lists the high-definition project formats that are available for each standard-definition project format. Unless otherwise noted, the project switch is bidirectional.

Figure 12.3
The Format tab of the Project window.

Mixing HD and SD Footage

Projects with similar frame or field rates are considered to be compatible with each other. A 25fps project is compatible with a 50fps project, but not with a 29.976fps project. Basically, projects with a frame rate that is a multiple of another project's frame rate are generally compatible. Notice that in Table A-1 in Appendix A, the compatible projects have the same frame (or field) *rate*.

The older Avid Symphony Nitris, unlike the Symphony Nitris DX, requires not only the same frame (or field) rate, but also the same frame type (interlaced or progressive). Sequences and clips also have formats and share the same compatibility as projects. When you create a new sequence or clip (by import, log, capture, decompose, or some other method) it inherits the project format.

If the SD and HD formats are compatible, sequences and clips of the same two formats are also compatible. This means that you can open a 30i sequence in a 1080i/59.94 project and that a 1080i/50 sequence can contain both 25i PAL clips and 1080i/50 clips.

In NTSC, film-rate projects are recorded to tape with a 2:3 pulldown and a .1% reduction in speed. In PAL, film-rate projects are either recorded to tape with a 4% increase in speed or a 12:1 pulldown. During capture the pulldown is removed and any speed adjustment is compensated for.

Likewise, film-rate projects (24 or 23.976 fps) can also mix SD and HD material even though neither NTSC nor PAL were originally progressive. Because the original SD material has been converted internally to progressive clips, they can be mixed with the HD progressive clips.

If the frame rate of a clip or sequence is not compatible with the current project format, the clip or sequence cannot be loaded into the Source or Record monitor.

In this case, Media Composer will prompt you to convert the sequence to the project's format, as shown in Figure 12.4.

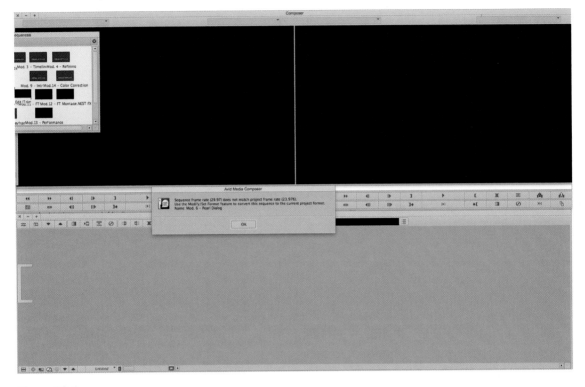

Figure 12.4
Media Composer will prompt to convert sequences to the Project format.

This is a particular issue with 720-line projects on Avid Symphony Nitris as they have the same frame rate as an NTSC or PAL SD project, but not the same frame type. (Remember that 720-line projects are always progressive. There is no such format as 720i.)

Note: Although you can mix SD and HD clips in the same timeline, there are additional steps you should take to ensure the aspect ratio of the clips is correct. See "Integrating Mixed Media" in Lesson 3, "Advanced Picture Editing," for more information.

Understanding Project Format Options

The Format tab in the Project window (refer back to Figure 12.3) lets you change the format of the project to another format that shares the same frame rate.

Changing formats is especially useful if you are working with down-converted HD material in an offline-to-online workflow. In this workflow, HD material is ingested as SD material. This converts the large HD frame to a smaller SD frame, which naturally takes up less space. The SD footage is then further compressed, for even more storage savings.

Each HD format has an equivalent SD format that you can use for offline editing, as shown in Table A-2 in Appendix A.

When it's time to conform the offline sequence to online, you can flip the switch to set your project format to a compatible HD format and recapture. Or, you can be more meticulous and create an HD project from scratch and bring a copy of your SD sequence into it, as you'll do in the exercise at the end of this lesson.

Another use for this feature is if you are working in an HD project and need to capture SD material. For example, when editing a documentary, you may have recent footage in an HD format, but older archival footage might be only available in standard definition because HD video did not exist commonly until the mid 1990s.

In an HD project, you can capture only HD material, and in an SD project, you can capture only SD material. Temporarily changing from an HD project to an SD project gives you access to the SD compressions. You can capture the material you need, and then change back to the HD project and work with both SD and HD clips.

The flip side is also true: You may be working in an SD project and want to import a finished high-definition graphic, logo, or QuickTime movie. If you left your project format in standard definition, the imported item would be resampled to SD. Since you know the item is finished, you can switch to HD, import it, and switch back. Now the media will be genuinely HD, but you can intercut it with the SD material in your edit. When you later conform, you won't need to re-ingest that item because it's already in high definition.

Understanding Raster

Raster refers to the number of columns and rows of pixels, in a given video format. For example, 1920×1080 represents the raster for some HD formats. Provided that both rows and columns are specified, you can consider similar numbers to also be rasters: 1440×720 or 720×480.

Consider the following table. Notice that AVC-Intra and XDCAM HD both support the two rasters. Depending how the footage was recorded, you'll either be editing images with dimensions of 1920×1080, or 1440×1080.

1080 Format	Rasters
Standard, AVC-Intra, XDCAM HD 50, XDCAM EX	1920×1080
DVCPro HD, XDCAM HD, HDV, AVC Intra 50	1440×1080

A "sub-rastered" format doesn't record all of the pixels. The second row of the table, with HD formats using a 1440×1080 raster, are sub-rastered formats. Using a sub-raster instead of a full-raster is another way to reduce the amount of space required for storage, so you may consider it to be a kind of compression that's introduced when the image is recorded in-camera. AVC-Intra cameras will have a toggle that effectively changes the raster between full- and sub-rastered formats. The sub-rastered format will be advertised as allowing more footage on the same P2 card, whereas the full-raster format will be advertised as better quality.

Raster is important for you as an editor, because you want Media Composer to create media that is the best looking without wasting space. If you set the raster to 1920×1080 when your source footage is 1440×1080, all the material that you render will be rendered at 1920×1080. It'll waste space and take more time to render than if you picked 1440×1080. Playback might also be affected, as it requires more work for your computer to process the 25% more pixels.

On the contrary, if you select a raster of 1440×1080 when your material is full-raster HD, your media will be rendered with 25% fewer pixels than it could have, which will cause a reduction in image quality.

Choosing a sub-rastered format when your source material is full-raster will introduce a video distortion called *aliasing*. Most high-definition TVs display 1920×1080 rasters. That means any sequence you cut that's using a sub-rastered format must be restored from 1440 columns of pixels to 1920 columns. That task is accomplished by duplicating 25% of the columns. When adjacent columns of pixels are identical, aliasing is introduced. Aliasing makes diagonal lines look like steps on a staircase.

Figure 12.5 illustrates the effect of aliasing when 1920×1080 content is incorrectly set to a 1440×1080 raster and then restored to 1920×1080. Compare the diagonal lines of letter "A": The image on the right had the wrong raster settings.

Table A-3 in Appendix A lists the format options available. For most HD projects, Media Composer will allow you to select a raster after you have chosen a compatible HD project size.

Tip: If you want to get the best playback performance when mixing resolutions, lower the raster dimensions to the smallest size compatible with your formats, because it is easier to scale down than scale up. When you are ready to output, pick the raster dimension appropriate for your output resolution.

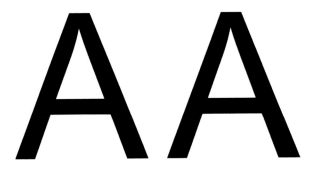

Figure 12.5
Incorrect raster settings can create aliasing, a stair-step effect on diagonal lines visible on the right image.

In summary, you have to consider rasters during online editing because camera manufacturers use various raster types when recording media during acquisition. If you choose a raster that matches your media, your editing system will perform well and there will be no reduction of video quality. If you pick the wrong one, you might cause Media Composer to take longer to render, use more storage space, not perform as well as it could during playback, and introduce aliasing into your video.

As the saying goes: choose wisely. Just remember that Media Composer tells you which acquisition formats are best suited for a given raster. It's in the New Project dialog box, shown in Figure EX12.1.

Estimating Storage Requirements

Although a more accurate estimate can be done once the sequence has been prepared for capturing, you can make a rough estimate of storage requirements before moving to the online system. The amount of space required will always be greater than the length of the program for the following reasons:

- Additional space is required for the handles on each captured clip. Programs edited with many short segments require even more handle space.

- Effects-heavy shows require additional space for both the individual effect elements and the rendered media.

A good estimate is that the total duration of captured media will be between 1.5 and 3 times the duration of the sequence.

To determine approximate storage requirements, refer to Table A-5 in Appendix A.

Managing Sources

A *source* is a tape, drive, memory stick, or other storage device containing raw, original source material. Depending on the complexity of your project, you may have a few sources or as many as several hundred. If these sources are not managed properly, even a small project with just a few sources can become a challenge to complete. A large project of a hundred sources or more can be almost impossible to finish.

If you are not the offline editor, make sure to discuss the following issues with the offline editor.

Tape Naming Conventions

You know the rule: Every source tape that you capture material from must have a unique tape name. Make sure the offline editor knows it too. This is especially true if clips were borrowed from other projects. In these cases it is possible for two sources to have the same name, potentially causing a nightmare during recapturing.

Folder Naming Conventions

Tapes are being replaced by cameras that record files onto one of a variety of storage formats: memory sticks, SxS cards, P2 cards, optical media, and so on. Those storage devices are reused, which means the content must be moved from the memory stick onto more permanent storage, like a hard disk. When the contents of a memory stick are copied onto a hard disk, be sure they are copied into a folder with a unique name, just like you ensure that tapes have unique names. This makes it significantly easier to locate the media for relinking or re-importing.

Source Timecode Issues

There are a wide variety of timecode issues that can cause problems in the online (drop versus non-drop timecode, timecode breaks, multiple identical timecodes on DV tapes, and so on).

Generating a Source List

A *source list* is what its name implies: A list of all the sources (imported files and captured tapes) that were used for a particular sequence. It's useful to generate a source list if you are delivering material to another editor: Treat it as a checklist to ensure you've included all the tapes and files.

You generate a source list with a bin containing the final sequence:

1. Open the bin containing the final sequence or sequences that will be sent to the online.

   The bin should contain only the final sequence(s) and no other sequences or clips.

2. Choose BIN > SET BIN DISPLAY.

   The Set Bin Display dialog box opens, as shown in Figure 12.6.

Figure 12.6
Choose Bin > Set Bin Display
to access this dialog box.

3. Deselect **SHOW CLIPS CREATED BY USER**.

4. Select **SOURCES** from the upper section of the dialog box.

5. Click **OK** to close the dialog box and return to the bin.

   The bin now displays only the sources used by the sequence in the project
   (see Figure 12.7). Two different types of sources are displayed:

Figure 12.7
Bin displaying sources only.

- **Tape-based sources:** Those sources that were captured from tape via a
  deck. These sources are displayed with a "tape" icon. The tape name originally assigned to the captured clips is displayed. Each unique tape name
  is displayed once.

- **File-based sources:** Those sources that were imported or AMA-linked
  from a file. These sources are displayed with a "file" icon. The name of the
  original imported file is displayed. Imported multichannel audio files will
  display the source filename once for each track in the source file (twice for
  imported stereo clips). Imported graphics with alpha will display the source
  filename three times (one for the RGB fill and two for the alpha channel).

6. Select the ICON and NAME columns in the bin.

7. Press CTRL/CMD+E to sort the bin by source type and then by name.

8. Choose FILE > PRINT to print a list of sources to a connected printer.

This bin printout should be used to assemble the tapes to be delivered to the online editor. It can also be used as a list of source files to deliver to the online editor.

Note: The disk location of those files is not displayed in this view but can be accessed by selecting the clip or sequence and selecting Clip > Batch Import command.

Online Editing Delivery Requirements

Just as you have delivery requirements that the final program tape must meet, you should have a set of delivery requirements for all elements delivered to the online editor. If all the elements are not delivered, you may not be able to complete the online edit, or additional costs will be incurred by either sending couriers for missing elements, or fixing elements that weren't delivered properly.

Delivery Requirements for Offline and Import Elements

To ensure that the online editing process goes smoothly, all graphics and animations should meet an online delivery specification. This spec should be given to the offline editor and all graphic artists, animators, and compositors who are providing elements for the project.

Tables A-6 through A-10 (in Appendix A) list typical delivery requirements for graphics and animations.

EXERCISE   *Take a moment to complete Exercise 12, Part 1.*

Creating an Online Project

Although a sequence could certainly be recaptured in the original offline project, there are significant advantages to using a clean project for the online. By creating an online project you can easily configure the project settings and eliminate any possible errors or problems created by the project settings created in the offline edit.

You should create a new online project for each job you are conforming. This ensures that the project format is properly selected and any unique configurations of a specific project do not carry over to the next one.

When preparing an online project, pay special attention to the Project format and the Render settings. If you don't pick the right Project format or Render settings at the beginning, you might have to redo a lot of work later.

The following sections explore the Project format and Render settings in greater detail.

Project Format

You choose the project's format when you create the project. Once the project is created, the format can only be changed to a limited set of other formats. For example, you can change a 30i project to 60i, but you can't change a 30i project to a 24p project. Table 12-1 lists the compatible project formats. All formats in the same table row of Table 12-1 are compatible with each other, and you may toggle between them as needed by using the Format tab of the Project window.

Table 12-1   Compatible Project Formats

SD	HD 1080-Line	HD 720-Line
30i NTSC	1080i/59.94,1080p/59.94	720p/29.97
23.976p NTSC	1080p/23.976	720p/23.976
24p NTSC	1080p/24	
25i PAL	1080i/50, 1080p/25	720p/25
25p PAL	1080p/25, 1080i/25	720p/25
24p PAL	1080p/24	

Despite that rule, Media Composer allows you to change a sequence format. By changing the sequence format, you can convert an HD/24p sequence to HD/60i or any other sequence type. Changing the sequence format was covered at the end of Lesson 2, "Professional Acquisition."

 Take a moment to complete Exercise 12, Part 2.

Ensuring High-Quality Rendering

Part of the online editing process involves rendering media. Despite all the achievements and advances in real-time effects processing, the best way that you can confidently play material without dropping frames is to render it. It can be very frustrating to leave Media Composer rendering a two-hour sequence only to return and find that half of the vertical detail has been removed from effect shots because your system was rendering using the Duplicated Field render method.

In the Avid Learning Series

Even though rendering is covered in the Effects Essentials book, part of the Avid Learning Series, it's important that you configure it correctly for your online edit so it's also mentioned here. For more information, see the book *Media Composer 6 Effects Essentials*, or take MC110 at an Avid Learning Partner.

Media Composer allows you to configure the method of rendering used for motion effects, and timewarps. You can also specify the Image Interpolation method, as shown in Figure 12.8.

Figure 12.8
You can set default settings for rendering using the Render Settings dialog box (choose Project Window > Settings > Render).

Offline editors often choose the most expedient rendering method (for example, Duplicated Field) instead of the appropriate method for the online, which would typically require more time to process in order to achieve great looking results.

If you get a sequence from an offline editor, the effects will be set to whatever setting the offline editor chose, which usually is *Duplicated Field*. Duplicated Field is a render method that's only suitable for rough offline work, because it discards every other horizontal row of pixels (known as a field) and then fills in the blank rows by duplicating the remaining row. Images rendered with duplicated field lose one half of their vertical resolution, which is not something you want in your final, top-quality online sequence.

You can either edit each effect to change the render method, or you can set a new default setting, which will be applied to all timewarps and motion effects, using Render settings.

These two options are usually set to VTR-Style and Blended Interpolated, respectively.

Note: **The Render setting is stored with your user profile. It is not set on a per-project basis, but rather is consistently used for all projects in which you'll work.**

Archiving Your Project

After you've told your story, surely to much critical acclaim and enviable Oscar rumblings for Best Editing, there remains some housekeeping to be done. You need to make room on your media drive for your next project by getting rid of the media from the project you've just finished. Don't just output your project and move on to the next; you should archive your project so you can restore it later.

Why not just play the final sequence to tape and move on to the next project? Well, there's an adage that says there are only two certainties in life: taxes and death. It's not wrong, but it's incomplete. The third certainty is that someone higher than you in the pecking order will want to change something in the sequence after you've cleared the media from your system.

If the only material that you've saved from a project is the sequence that you exported to a QuickTime movie or played to tape, it's going to be rather challenging to re-edit that. Sure, you could capture or import the finished sequence into a new project and cut sections out. But what if you have to extend clips to add a minute of time to the total sequence in order to accommodate the sale of the show to another broadcaster? What if you need to change a title from "Frederic" to "Frédéric"?

Archiving compactly prepares the media for long-term storage. It's a little bit of work up front, for the fantastic benefit of being able to restore the project later and continue working with it. If you archived a project with the 1999 release of Media Composer, you could restore it today and play back the media, re-arrange the sequence, update the titles, convert it from 4:3 to 16:9, and output it.

There are lots of techniques for archiving. You'll learn two in this lesson: archiving to videotape and archiving to a folder. Both techniques allow you to selectively archive one or more sequences and the media that relates to them, with the intent being that you can restore the sequence, trim the edits, and revise the effects.

Archive to Folder

Archiving to a folder is ideal for tapeless workflows. It involves exporting all the media as well as the sequence to a folder on a hard drive. You could then copy that folder to an inexpensive external hard drive, perhaps one that you wouldn't use for video editing because it's too slow, although it's fine for archival purposes.

Examples of ways to use the archive to folder method include:

- Archiving to a USB hard disk that could be as large as two or three terabytes (2048–3072 gigabytes). Such a drive could hold many archives.

- Burning the folder to a DVD. A Blu-ray disc can hold approximately 50 gigabytes, so it could be ideal for short-films, commercials, and promos.

- Coping the folder to a network server.

- Uploading it to a very large drop box or cloud storage service.

The possibilities are endless.

Archiving to a folder isn't a magical trick. It's not listed as an explicit feature of Media Composer that you'd find on a menu. The trick in being able to archive to a folder is that it's built-in to the File > Export command. All you need to do is configure an Export properly, and you get the feature.

Some things to keep in mind about the archive to folder technique:

- You can archive (export) sequences, subclips, or master clips.

- You cannot archive (export) an entire project.

If you want to export an entire project, you'll need to repeat the process, or select multiple sequences (or clips) in the bin prior to selecting File > Export. This often isn't a big deal, because despite lots of source material, you often end up with one or two finished sequences. When you archive, you may want only the media referenced by your sequence, not the unused material.

Configuring Export for Archiving to a Folder

To perform an export with the intent of archiving a sequence to a folder, use the following steps:

1. Select one or more sequences in a bin.

2. Choose FILE > EXPORT.

3. Click OPTIONS.

4. Select AAF and configure your AUDIO and VIDEO tabs as shown in Figures 12.9 and 12.10.

Figure 12.9
AAF Video Export options for archive to folder.

Figure 12.10
AAF Audio Export options for archive to folder.

5. Click **SAVE**.

6. Choose a location to export the AAF (sequence data) and media.

7. Click **SAVE** again.

Although Figures 12.9 and 12.10 both indicate Copy All Media, you could also select Consolidate All Media. Consolidating is covered in Lesson 13, "Mastering the Media," but the difference is worth noting now:

■ **Copy all Media:** If a master clip is 30 minutes long and your sequence uses five seconds of it, the entire 30-minute clip is copied.

■ **Consolidate All Media:** If a master clip is 30 minutes long and your sequence uses five seconds of it, only five seconds plus handles are copied. (Handles are an arbitrary extra number of frames at the beginning and ending of each shot.)

Media Composer will export an AAF to the location you specify. The AAF is your sequence. It will then copy (or consolidate) the media files referenced by that sequence into subfolders of the same destination as the AAF. The AAF and the media subfolders are what you need to copy onto a DVD, external hard disk, network device, or whatever kind of device will keep the data in the long term.

There may be times when you have two sequences to export from the same project. Often, one sequence is longer than the other, such as having a director's cut and a studio cut. A director's cut is often longer than a studio cut, because the director often doesn't want to cut any scenes: each scene is equally precious and no director wants to play *Sophie's Choice* on his or her film's scenes. A studio edit tries to come in at about 90–120 minutes (depending on the target audience, children vs. adults); scenes that don't test well in focus groups are removed.

If you were to export both of those sequences using the method described, you'd have two separate AAF files and two media file folders. The media used by the studio edit is the same media also used by the director's edit. You can export, and therefore archive, more efficiently if you use the method described to export the larger sequence first, and then export the shorter sequence using the export settings shown in Figure 12.11.

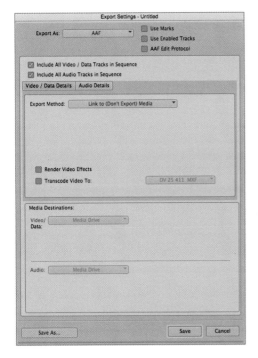

Figure 12.11
Exporting a sequence when the media has already been exported.

In Figure 12.11, you've chosen an export method of Link To. This assumes the media has already been exported and, when you restore (import) the AAF file, it assumes the media has already been imported. You can use this technique provided that the media of the originally exported sequence is a superset of the media used by the second sequence. If the second sequence uses media that wasn't exported by the first sequence, you'll have a problem. The problem is that media won't be available because it was never exported.

To resolve that problem, do one of the following:

- Use Find Bin to locate the few additional clips, and then export them separately with media.

- Export the second sequence in its entirety with consolidated or copied media, instead of relying on linking.

To Restore an Archive to Folder

When your producer finally comes back and asks you to repurpose an older edit, the method for restoring your sequence and media is pretty straightforward. You make a new project, and then import the AAF and related media back into it. If you have additional sequences, you'll import them too. You might not need to use the Relink tool to assist Media Composer in relinking the sequence to the exported media. Relinking is coming up in Lesson 13.

Another great way to archive your sequence is to use the Archive to Videotape feature, covered next.

 First, take a moment to complete Exercise 12, Part 3.

Archive to Videotape

The Archive to Videotape is one of the least known yet most powerful, useful, and elegantly designed features of Media Composer. It uses videotape to archive your footage and enables you to easily restore a sequence from those videotapes. Videotape is a comparatively inexpensive storage medium compared to hard drives, so it's appealing even if your source footage was never recorded to videotape.

The downside of using videotape for archival purposes is that most VTRs introduce some kind of native compression as the video is recorded to tape. Even if your footage is 1:1 (uncompressed) inside Media Composer, the deck may introduce its own compression. For example, Digital Betacam introduces a 2:1 proprietary MPEG2 compression, whereas Betacam SX introduces a 5:1 MPEG2 compression.

Tip: If your videotape format is DV25 or HDV, you might want to think twice about using Archive to Videotape. Your goal in archiving a broadcast-quality sequence is to maintain top quality. If you restore it and there are compression artifacts or a loss of quality, you're likely not benefiting from the archiving process. In those scenarios, consider archiving to a folder, as described in the previous section.

Archive to Videotape has two limitations of which you must be aware:

■ You cannot archive AMA-linked media.

■ You cannot archive progressive media. This includes 24p and 30p media.

How Archive to Videotape Works

Archive to Videotape does a number of clever tricks to ensure archive and restore functionality is reliable and efficient. Essentially, though, it records onto videotapes all the footage that's used by a sequence. The videotapes that you use must be prepared in advance by striping timecode.

Note: The process of striping timecode involves recording to videotape while feeding it black (no video) and silence (no sound), but allowing it to generate timecode. Striping a tape enables an editing system to record footage to the tape with timecode accuracy. You stripe a tape by inserting a blank tape, setting the start timecode, and pressing the Record button when there is no signal going to the VTR.

Here's how to perform an Archive to Videotape, and an explanation of what happens when you select a sequence and choose File > Archive to Videotape:

1. Media Composer asks you to name the archive and identify the start time-code of each videotape, as shown in Figure 12.12.

Figure 12.12
Archive to Video inquires about
your tape resources.

It's important for Media Composer to know the start timecode of each pre-striped tape, so it can lay the footage onto the tape. All the tapes must use the same start timecode, such as 01:00:00:02 or 10:00:00:00.

2. Media Composer then inquires as to the quantity and duration of each tape, as shown in Figure 12.13.

Figure 12.13

How many tapes do you have of each of the following tape durations?

3. Media Composer then examines the sequence (or clip) that you selected. It creates a new "archive sequence" that has all of the footage from each of the tracks separated and lined up onto one video track and a couple audio tracks. You never see or have direct access to this archive sequence.

4. Media Composer splits the archive sequence into durations that match the tapes that you have.

5. Media Composer initiates a *digital cut*, laying the intermediate archive sequences out to tape. As each sequence is laid to tape, Media Composer updates the original sequence, and the original master clips, with the tape name and tape timecodes that indicate the archive location of the clip. For example, the original clip might be from tape 0301BA from timecode 03:01:14:12 - 03:05:21:10, but the archive location of the clip is tape ARCHV001 from timecode 01:01:43:10 onward, which is stored as hidden metadata within the clip or sequence. Because the original sequence (or master clip) has an alternative tape name and timecodes, it can be batch captured from the original tape and timecodes, or it can be restored from the archive metadata.

When you use Archive to Videotape, Media Composer does not archive rendered media, which you can easily re-render. It only outputs original video media, plus handles (if specified), so you can easily restore the sequence's media by using Clip > Restore from Archive.

The Archive to Videotape feature does not encode your sequence and bin data to the videotape. You must back up the bin (.avb file) containing your sequence separately. You need the bin in order to initiate a restore, because the clip in the bin contains the data about the archive, such as the archive tape name and timecodes for each clip in your sequence.

It is recommended that you manually back up any files that have been imported, so you can use the Clip > Batch Import command to restore those later. By using Clip > Batch Import, you can ensure graphics are imported at their full quality as opposed to experiencing the generation loss that occurs when video is laid out to tape and re-ingested from tape.

Review/Discussion Questions

1. What's raster? (See "Understanding Raster" on page 418.)

2. What's the downside of choosing the incorrect raster prior to ingesting media? (See "Understanding Raster" on page 418.)

3. Which media requires more storage space per hour: NTSC Uncompressed 1:1 or DNxHD 220? (See "Table A-5: Resolution Storage Requirements" on page 502.)

4. Why is it useful to generate a source list from the offline project? (See "Generating a Source List" on page 421.)

5. Why would you create an online project? (See "Creating an Online Project" on page 423.)

6. How much storage space at 15:1s would you need to offline edit a documentary having 60 hours of source footage? Assume a typical 10:1 shooting ratio. (See "Table A-5: Resolution Storage Requirements" on page 502.)

7. How much storage space at DNxHD 220X would you need to online edit a documentary having 60 hours of source footage? Assume a typical 10:1 shooting ratio. (See "Table A-5: Resolution Storage Requirements" on page 502.)

8. How do you change a project's format? (See "Understanding Project Format Options" on page 417.)

9. When is it necessary to change a project's format? (See "Understanding Project Format Options" on page 417.)

10. What's the difference between Archiving to a Folder and Archiving to a Videotape? (See "Archiving Your Project" on page 426.)

11. Why would things not work well if you performed an Archive to Videotape and then deleted your media and clips? (See "How Archive to Videotape Works" on page 431.)

Preparing for the Online Editing Stage

In these exercises, you create and configure a clean online project for a show that was offline edited in SD, and will be online edited in HD. Then you bring an offline sequence into the new project, change its format, and pull a source list.

Media Used:
Hell's Kitchen

Duration:
20 minutes

Exercise 12.1: Creating an HD Online Project

Create a project for use in the online editing stage:

1. Select **NEW PROJECT** from the **SELECT USER AND PROJECT** dialog box. The New Project dialog box opens, as shown in Figure EX12.1.

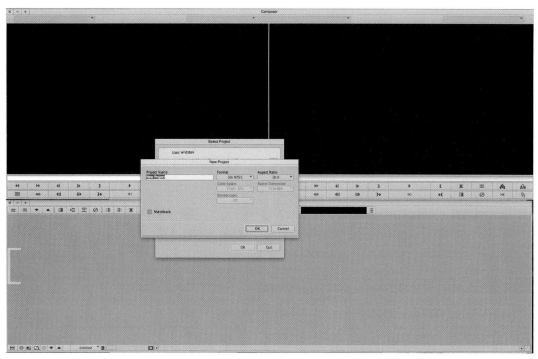

Figure EX12.1
The New Project dialog box.

2. Name the new project **HKS02E09 ONLINE**.

   This project name indicates Hell's Kitchen (HK), Season 2 (S02), Episode 9 (E09). Naming your projects with relevant details such as the production name, season, and episode will help you manage media and projects better, particularly as you approach the final episodes of the season.

3. Choose **1080i 59.94** from the **FORMAT** pop-up menu and click **OK** to close the dialog box.

4. Confirm that the project you created is selected then click **OK** to open the project.

Configuring the Project Settings

Some project settings affect how media is created when it is re-ingested. It's best to set these settings prior to importing, capturing, or relinking material.

To configure your project settings:

1. Click the SETTINGS button in the PROJECT window.

2. Open the AUDIO PROJECT settings and set the following options:
   - Sample Rate: **48kHz**
   - Sample Bit Depth: **24-BIT**
   - Audio File Format: **PCM (MXF)**

   As the audio will be delivered as a finished two-channel mix, you can leave the remaining options alone. Lesson 8, "Working with Multichannel Audio," covers audio formats in more detail. Close the AUDIO PROJECT settings when you are finished.

   Some of the material for this show exists on HDCAM SR tape, while most of it exists on hard disks containing virtual P2 volumes. You need to verify the Capture settings for projects that have tape-based material.

3. Open the CAPTURE settings and set the following options, which were covered in Lesson 2:
   - Preroll method: Standard Timecode.
   - Optimize for batch speed.
   - Eject tape.
   - Log errors to the Console and continue capturing.

   Close the CAPTURE settings when you are finished.

4. Open the DECK settings (via the DECK CONFIGURATION settings) and set the PREROLL to one second.

   Close the two settings dialog boxes when you are finished.

5. Open the MEDIA CREATION settings and set the VIDEO RESOLUTION to **DNxHD 220**.

6. Click APPLY TO ALL and then close the MEDIA CREATION settings.

   The MEDIA CREATION tool lets you specify the default settings for each scenario where media can be created: generating titles, rendering, importing, mixdowns and capturing. Setting them all to DNxHD 220 reduces the likelihood that you might forget to set them later, resulting in some of your media being ingested at a different resolution than the rest.

You've now created an online project and are ready to bring the offline sequence into it.

Bringing the Offline Sequence into the Project

It's time to bring the offline sequence into the new online project, and retrieve the elements that you'll need to conform the online edit.

1. Using Windows Explorer or the Finder, navigate to the STUDENT MATERIALS > LESSON 12 folder.

2. Copy HELLS KITCHEN SEQUENCES.AVB into the newly created online project.

3. Rename the bin SEQUENCES - OFFLINE.

Now that the project is created, you're going to play the part of the offline editor and gather the elements needed for the online.

Pulling a Source List

To determine which tapes and files are needed for the online conform, you need to generate a source list. Begin by pulling a source list for tapes.

To pull a source list for tapes:

1. Select the SEQUENCES - OFFLINE bin.

2. Choose BIN > SET BIN DISPLAY. The Set Bin Display dialog box will appear.

3. Deselect SHOW CLIPS CREATED BY USER from the lower section of the dialog box.

4. Select SOURCES from the upper section of the dialog box.

5. Click OK to close the dialog box and return to the bin.

   The bin now displays only the sources used by the sequence in the project.

6. Select the ICON and NAME columns in the bin.

7. Press CTRL+E or CMD+E to sort the bin by source type and then by name.

8. Choose FILE > PRINT to print a list of sources to a connected printer.

You now have a list of sources required for the online conform.

Pulling an Import Elements List

Although the source list also contains a list of the files imported into the sequence, it does not indicate from where they were imported. To help ensure that the correct version of the graphics is delivered online, you can display the original import file location using the BATCH IMPORT command.

1. Select the final offline sequence in the bin and choose CLIP > BATCH IMPORT.

2. Choose ALL CLIPS from IMPORT TYPE dialog box.

3. The BATCH IMPORT dialog box opens and displays a list of all imported elements.

4. Record the names and file locations of the listed elements.

All of these elements will need to be gathered for the online. This has already been done for this class so you can simply close the dialog box.

In an actual offline to online, additional elements may need to be prepared, including a digital cut or QuickTime export of the offline, a list of fonts used, and so on. You do not gather these elements as part of this exercise.

Exercise 12.2: Setting a Sequence's Format

The offline sequence was cut in a standard definition (SD) project. Sequences and clips created in a project inherit the project's settings, which means the sequence still has an SD format despite being in the new HD online project.

To prepare the sequence for online editing by changing the format:

1. Duplicate the **HK0209** OFFLINE **LOCKED** sequence in the SEQUENCES – OFFLINE bin.

2. Create a SEQUENCES - ONLINE bin.

3. Move the duplicated sequence into the new SEQUENCES - ONLINE bin and rename it **HK0209** ONLINE.

4. Select **HK0209** ONLINE and choose CLIP > MODIFY.

    The MODIFY dialog box opens, as shown in Figure EX12.2.

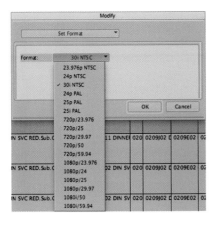

Figure EX12.2
The Modify dialog box.

5. Choose **SET FORMAT** from the modification type pop-up menu.

6. Set the format to **1080i/59.94**.

7. Click **OK** to change the sequence's format. You can confirm that the format has changed by viewing the **FORMAT** column in the bin.

Exercise 12.3: Archiving to a Folder

In this exercise, you archive one of your sequences to a folder on your desktop. The technique involves selecting a sequence and performing an export with the correct settings.

1. Select a sequence in a bin.

2. Choose **FILE > EXPORT**.

   Select your **DESKTOP** as the destination.

3. Select **OPTIONS** and configure the **AUDIO** and **VIDEO EXPORT** options as shown in Figures 12.9 and 12.10.

4. Click **SAVE**.

After the export is complete, you can examine the contents of the folder on your desktop. There is an AAF and a folder containing the MXF media files.

If time allows, create a new project and restore the archive by importing the AAF into a bin.

Lesson 13

Mastering the Media

This lesson introduces techniques for managing media by applying concepts from the previous lesson to use the Consolidate/Transcode and Relink tools.

Media Used: Agent MXZero

Duration: 75 minutes

GOALS

- Understand when and how to use the Media tool
- Learn the conquer and divide technique for locating a corrupt media file
- Understand how the Consolidate/Transcode tool works
- Learn four media management tasks based on Consolidate/Transcode tool
- Differentiate between consolidation from the bin or the Media tool
- Learn how relinking is used to reconnect clips and media files

Understanding the Media Tool

The Media tool provides a window to the contents of the media drive. It's easily organized, sorted, and filtered, like a bin, but it's also easily limited to specific projects or the contents of specific drives. The Media tool doesn't show subclips or sequences, because they exist only within the bins, and not at the media level.

You can use the Media tool to view, delete, or modify the available media files or specific tracks contained in the media file.

Caution: The Media tool will not work in an Interplay environment with shared storage, nor will it work for AMA-Linked media.

An important distinction between the Media tool and a bin is that the Media tool only displays actual media. The clips in a bin appear regardless of the media being online, whereas the content of the Media tool appears only if the media is online. If it's not on the media drive, it's not in the Media tool.

Setting the Media Tool Display

You can set the Media tool to display different types of files from the current or other projects.

To set the Media tool display:

1. Choose TOOLS > MEDIA TOOL. A dialog box appears, as shown in Figure 13.1.

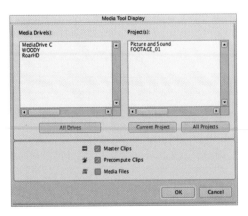

Figure 13.1

Choose Tools > Media Tool and then you can configure the Media tool for specific projects and file types.

2. Select one or more media drives. To include all drives, select ALL DRIVES.

3. Select one or more projects. To include all projects, select ALL PROJECTS.

4. Select one or more file types you want to view (master clips, precompute clips, and media files).

   The Media tool allows you to view master clips, precomputes, and media files.

Technically, master clips are a kind of clip within an Avid bin, which is an .avb file usually found in your project folder. The Media tool is not an Avid bin, although it has been designed to look like one. It's sort of like how science fiction writers often make aliens look more humanoid, instead of having them appear as a spec of dust or bowl of jelly. It's easier for the audience if they can relate the aliens to something they know. For editors, it's easier to see the files in managed media drives when those files look like master clips.

When you select Master Clips, the Media tool will disguise the media files, replacing the original names such as 0209J03A01.C9B8A64F4D93583E.mxf with more familiar names based on the master clips, like *Happy Beagle HDV*.

Precompute clips are just rendered effects. They are effects that have been precomputed, which means processed (rendered) in advance.

You will rarely need to view the undisguised media files; an exception might be for troubleshooting purposes.

Projects List of the Media Tool

The right side of the Media Tool Display window, as shown previously in Figure 13.1, displays a list of projects. When the Media tool opens, it scans the media database and retrieves project names from the database, which is how it's able to populate the list of projects even after the project folders have been deleted. All media files contain the name of their original project.

Media Composer embeds the project names within the metadata of media files as they are created, which occurs during the following scenarios:

- Capturing
- Importing
- Rendering
- Title generating
- Consolidating/transcoding
- Video/audio mixdowns

Note: Each time a managed media file is written, Media Composer embeds the name of the current project into the media file. It's part of the managed media file's metadata. You can copy the media file to another drive, or borrow it for use in another project (File > Open Bin), but even in those situations, the media file will retain the name of the original project.

There is an additional important takeaway message about how this system works: If you see a project in that list, you must have media for it somewhere.

Sorting, Sifting, and Managing Data in the Media Tool

The Media tool provides the same database functionality as a bin, including:

- Sort and sift. For instance, if you sift on the Drive column, you can easily move or copy (consolidate) media files from one drive to another.

- Add, hide, and delete column headings.

- Use saved bin views.

- View clips in Frame or Text view.

Opening Media Tool Clips in the Source Monitor

You can drag master clips from the Media tool into the Source monitor. It's a handy way to verify the contents of a media file prior to deleting it. If you want to keep the clip around long-term, consider dragging it to a bin.

Precomputes are the outcome of rendering. You can't drag precompute files from the Media tool to the bin, and normally you can't load them into the Source monitor either. Without seeing it, you might find it hard to decide if you want to delete the precompute or not. There is a little trick you can use to open precomputes in the Source monitor. It's covered in the sidebar titled "Subsys Monpane Debug Magic."

Orphaned Media Files Have No Master Clip

An *orphaned media file* is a managed media file that doesn't have an associated clip because it has been deleted. Normally, without a clip in a bin, you have no way to get to a media file and it's lost, or "orphaned," but still taking up space and may be referenced by a sequence. You'd either like to recreate its master clip, or if it's genuinely not needed, you'd like to delete it.

Subsys Monpane Debug Magic

You can configure Media Composer to allow the loading of precomputes from the Media tool into the Source monitor. That'll allow you to view the precompute and make an informed decision about whether you want to delete it.

This capability is disabled by default and for good reason: Once you get a clip into the Source monitor, there is a possibility you might edit it into your sequence. If you put it into your sequence, add an effect, and render it, you will have a new precompute built from an existing precompute's metadata. That's not how the Media Composer software has been designed and it's not a scenario that has been tested for long-term stability and durability. You don't want to do something today that might eventually corrupt the sequence after you've put hours, days, or even weeks of additional work into it.

When using this technique, be absolutely mindful that you are overriding a safeguard in order to view precomputes in the Source monitor. You must never edit those precomputes into a sequence.

To override the safeguard and allow loading of precomputes into the Source monitor:

1. Choose TOOLS > CONSOLE.

2. Type **subsys monpane debug** into the CONSOLE tool and press ENTER.

A message should appear in the Console informing you that the monpane is now in Debug mode. You can close the Console tool. The setting will go back to normal after you restart Media Composer.

If you absolutely need to edit with the material in precompute, such as when you don't have the original source material and therefore can't re-render it, there is a safe way to do it. You create a video mixdown of the Source monitor's contents, which will create a new clip and new media file, independent of the precompute. Edit that clip into your sequence.

You can recover or delete orphaned media files using the Media tool in two ways:

■ Press Delete to delete the orphaned media file, as covered in the following section.

■ Recreate the master clip by dragging the orphaned media file back to a bin. When you drag a master clip from the Media tool to the bin, Media Composer will rebuild the master clip using the duplicate metadata embedded in the media file.

Deleting Media

You can delete media using the Media tool, or you can delete it from the bin. You can also delete media that's associated just with a particular sequence, or reverse the scenario and delete all the media except for the media that's needed by a particular sequence.

Deleting Managed Media from a Bin

When deleting a master clip in a bin, you can choose to delete the clip and/or the media, and if you delete the media, you can choose the kind of media. These options are shown in Figure 13.2.

Figure 13.2
Deleting a master clip from a bin.

If you duplicate a clip (which duplicates the clip but not the media file), and you later want to delete the duplicated clip, you would delete the master clip but not associated media files.

If you imported or captured a clip with the wrong settings, you would delete the associate media files but not the clip, and then re-capture or re-import. You'd also use this combination of choices if you wanted to simply delete the media but leave the clip for future reference.

When you include the media, you can choose to delete specific types of media, such as just the audio or just the video. How would you delete a specific track of audio, though? Can you do that from the Delete dialog box shown in Figure 13.2?

Unfortunately, no, you can't choose individual tracks when deleting from a bin, but there is a way: use the Media tool.

Deleting Managed Media from the Media Tool

Deleting items from the Media tool is more comprehensive than deleting from a bin. For example, you can delete media files and precompute clips by media type or just the media for specific tracks. This granular capability makes it possible to delete all of the video at one resolution, or delete tracks you accidentally imported but are not using, as shown in Figure 13.3.

To delete media files:

1. Select one or more media files, master clips, or precompute clips whose media files you want to delete.

2. Press the **DELETE** key to open the **DELETE MEDIA** dialog box (see Figure 13.3).

3. Select the items to delete.

4. Click **OK**. A confirmation dialog box appears, warning that you cannot undo a media deletion.

5. Confirm the items to delete and click **DELETE**.

Figure 13.3
Media objects can be selectively deleted using the Media tool.

The reason this approach works in Media Composer stems from the fact that managed media consists of individual media files per track: one media file for each audio track, and one media file for each video track. Because each media file is a separate file, the Media tool can quickly and selectively delete media associated with one or more specific tracks.

Caution: There is no undo for deleting media. After media has been deleted, the only way to retrieve media associated with a master clip is to ingest the media again, or restore it from an archive.

Deleting Precomputes (Rendered Effects)

You can't easily get back master clip media that you accidentally delete, but what if you delete precomputed media? How can you easily get precomputes back?

Since precomputes are just rendered effects, you can get them back by re-rendering them. Rendering a clip again may be time consuming, but it's easy and doesn't require your intervention, so you might keep this approach in mind on the rare occasion in which you need to free up some space quickly. Delete precomputes, because you can always re-render to recreate them later.

Deleting from a Bin versus the Media Tool

Deleting from a bin is not the same as deleting using the Media tool. If you delete from a bin, you are prompted to choose the specific resolutions of media. This is great for offline vs. online scenarios, where you want to delete the old media, as was shown in Figure 13.2.

To do something similar in the Media tool, you'd need to Custom Sift to hide media files of a particular resolution. Deleting the media from a bin will result in all the associated media files being deleted for the selected resolutions. The Media tool prompts you to choose the specific tracks to delete.

Media Relatives Relate to a Selected Item

With the Avid system, you can identify the media objects (master clips, subclips, and sequences) that share the same media files, regardless of whether the media files are present on the system. Media objects that share the same media files are called *media relatives*.

Identifying media relatives can be useful if you want to know:

- Which master clip a subclip was created from
- All of the master clips, subclips, and precomputes associated with a sequence or project
- Which clips to choose when planning to delete media, but you want to keep all of the media for the sequence online

You can use a bin and the Media tool together to identify media relatives in both places.

To identify media relatives:

1. Open the bin(s) that contains the master clips, subclips, and sequences whose media relatives you want to find.

2. Open the **Media** tool and select **Current Project** and the file type(s).

3. Select the appropriate drives.

Note: Media for clips originally logged or captured in another project will not be displayed if only the current project is selected. That is because their metadata will indicate their original project.

4. Resize and position the bin(s) and the **Media** tool so that you can see them both.

5. If either the bin(s) or the **Media** tool has previously highlighted media objects, deselect them.

6. Click to activate the bin and select one or more master clips, subclips, or sequences.

7. Choose **BIN > SELECT MEDIA RELATIVES**. The media relatives of the selected items are highlighted in the **MEDIA** tool and in all open bins.

Deleting Unused Media for a Project

You can use select media relatives to select and delete media files that were not used in a project. This is useful if you want to delete media from any clips that were not used in order to open drive space.

To identify and delete unused media files:

1. Select **CURRENT PROJECT** and two file types—**MASTER CLIPS** and **PRECOMPUTE CLIPS**—in the **MEDIA TOOL DISPLAY** dialog box.

2. To delete unused precomputes that build up on the drives as a result of changes in rendered effects, select only **PRECOMPUTE CLIPS**.

3. Follow the previous steps to identify media relatives for the sequence.

   The **MEDIA** tool highlights all items that are related to the sequence. If you were to press the **DELETE** key now, you would be deleting all the media that is required for your sequence to play, leaving all the media that is not required. That's the opposite of what you want.

4. With the **MEDIA** tool active, choose **BIN > REVERSE SELECTION**. This reverses the current selection, highlighting all the media files and precomputes that are unrelated to your clips and sequences.

5. Press the **DELETE** key.

Solving the Problem of Corrupt Media Files

Corrupt files cannot be read correctly by Media Composer. Disk failures, electro-magnetic disruption, and saving malfunctions can all lead to corruption. For Media Composer, media files, project files, users, settings, sequences, and all bin contents can all become corrupt.

Danger of corruption is the main reason for backing up projects and settings at the end of the editing day. Its occurrence and location cannot be predicted or totally prevented. Users can only take certain precautions to guard against damage that might be caused by corruption: backing up project information on a regular basis and completing basic system maintenance.

There are some troubleshooting steps you can take to help identify the corruption and recover from it.

Isolating the Corruption

General troubleshooting will typically isolate the presence of corruption.

- Does the problem occur across all clips/sequences/bins or in a specific one?
- Does the problem occur across all users and projects or in a specific one?

Corrupt User Settings

If the problem happens with one user profile but not another, create a new user profile for your use and delete the old, corrupt one.

Corrupt Projects and Settings

Open another project and see if the same behavior exists. Create a new project and a new bin, and see if the same problem exists.

If one project won't open but others will, try deleting MCState, Site_Settings.avs, and Site_attributes from the bad project's folder.

If you determine that a project is in fact corrupt, create a new project, and at the desktop level, copy the bins from the corrupt project into the new project.

A corrupt bin may also result in a project not opening, as discussed in the following section.

Corrupt Bins

- Create a new bin, move clips from the corrupt bin to the new bin, and delete the old bin.
- Did this problem always occur? If not, grab a backup bin from the Avid Attic folder.

A corrupt bin can prevent you from opening the project. The problem stems from a behavior in Media Composer where it automatically opens any bins that were previously open when the project was last used. If one of those bins is corrupt, and Media Composer tries to open it, the corruption may cause Media Composer to crash.

You can tell Media Composer to open the project but not open any previously opened bins by *holding the Alt/Option key down* while opening a project from the Select Project window.

Corrupt Sequences

Before troubleshooting a corrupt sequence, duplicate the sequence and place it in a new bin. This will ensure your original sequence is unaffected while you poke and prod at the duplicate.

- Isolate a specific point where the problem occurs. This might be inconsistent but should generally be around the same area, give or take five seconds.

- Isolate specific tracks on the sequence where the problem occurs by using the audio and video monitors to disable all tracks except for one track at a time.

- Try to cut another source clip or filler into the problem area of the sequence. It may not be sufficient to simply lift; you may need to overwrite filler into its place.

- Try to re-cut the original source clip into the sequence.

Play through the sequence after taking the media temporarily offline. To do this:

1. Exit MEDIA COMPOSER.

2. Rename any related MEDIAFILES FOLDERS so they are hidden from the Avid application. It's recommended to place an "X" at the beginning of the folder name so Media Composer will ignore the contents.

3. Unmount any drives containing AMA-linked media.

    Technically, any change to the spelling or spacing of an OMFI/Avid MediaFiles folder hides the folder from the Avid software, but placing an X at the front is standard. (If the system doesn't let you rename the folder, simply create another folder—give it a meaningful name—and drag the MediaFiles folder into it. The folder is hidden from Media Composer.)

4. Relaunch MEDIA COMPOSER, and play through the problematic sequence.

All media is now offline, and the sequence plays with Media Offline slates. If the sequence now plays without any problems, corrupt media is probably to blame.

Removing Corrupt Media

The first step in determining if corrupt media is the cause of a problem is to "hide" media, as described in the previous section.

If a problem with a clip or sequence goes away after you have hidden the media, media from that drive or drives is probably corrupt. The only way to fix corrupt media is to batch record or re-import the specific media from the clip information, or if you can determine which clip is the problem in the sequence, swap it out for another similar clip.

Conquer and Divide: Locating Corrupted Media

One of the most tedious exercises in an Avid support representative's life is that of isolating a single bad media file from a haystack of thousands. Being able to perform this task rapidly with a deliberate methodology is an exceptionally useful skill. Assume, for example, you have one media file out of 10,000 files that causes a sequence to crash. How do you isolate and remove the offending file? Through a process called *conquer and divide*. With this handy, structured technique, you can quickly isolate a bad media file.

First Step: Divide

Figure 13.4 shows eight media files. One of them, F, is bad. When you divide, you take half the suspect media files and remove them from Media Composer's sight. To do this, you move them into a temporary folder at the root level on your media drive or workspace. (Remember: If the media files are not in \OMFI MediaFiles or \Avid MediaFiles\MXF, Avid will ignore them.)

If dealing with AMA volumes, you can move the items on those volumes into another folder on the same volume.

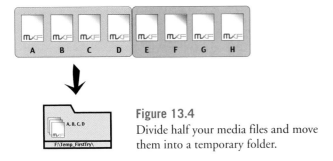

Figure 13.4
Divide half your media files and move them into a temporary folder.

After you've removed half of the media files, try recreating the error in Avid Media Composer. If the problem is still there, you haven't yet found the bad media file. The group of media files that you just removed is probably fine, unless you're experiencing a situation whereby multiple media files are corrupt.

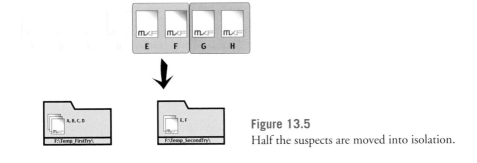

Figure 13.5
Half the suspects are moved into isolation.

Second Step: Repeat

You need to further divide and isolate the remaining media files.

As you have moved more files into isolation, you need to launch Media Composer and see if the problem has been fixed. This second step has resulted in a bad media file, F.mxf, being moved into isolation, so Media Composer will behave properly.

You now know that the corrupt file must have been one of the files in the last batch of moved files. It will be easy to isolate because each time you removed media files, you put them into separate folders. The next step is to determine which exact file is the problem file. You do this by moving half of the most recently files back into the proper media files folder, and then relaunching Media Composer to see whether the problem returns. (See Figure 13.6.)

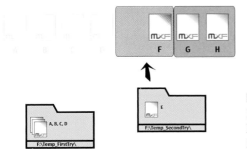

Figure 13.6
Begin to restore half of the previous lot of isolated media files until you identify the problem file.

Conquered

Once you find the bad file, you should consider deleting it. The affected media will need to be replaced, which is easily done using Media Composer's Batch Capture or Batch Import features.

Clearing Rendered Effects

If you want to return effects to their non-rendered state, you can do so by using the Clear Renders command. You may disassociate effects from their render files (precomputes) at a particular point in the timeline, or within a range marked by IN and OUT points. Note that this does *not* delete the precomputes from your drives; it merely breaks the effects connection from the precompute. If you want to reassociate the effect to the precompute, you may do so using the Undo function.

You can also clear all rendered effects except motion effects, or any effects not recognized by the Avid system (effects created with third-party plug-ins not installed on your system). Keep in mind that if you unrender an "unknown" effect, you cannot re-render it on your system since the necessary AVX plug-in isn't installed.

Note: The primary reason for implementing the Clear Renders command originates from the need to work with multi-resolution media in an Interplay environment. When you're editing with the proxy (lo-res) media—and render at that resolution—and then switch to the full-res version, the media switches resolutions, but the precomputes do not. Therefore, you can use the Clear Renders command to disassociate the sequence from its render files, and you can re-render at the higher resolution.

To clear rendered effects:

1. Select all tracks that contain the rendered effects you want to clear. If you want to select a range, mark an **IN** point before the start of the first effect to be cleared; mark an **OUT** point after the last effect to be cleared.

2. Select CLIP > CLEAR RENDERS IN/OUT. (If you didn't select a range, select CLIP > CLEAR RENDERS AT POSITION.) The CLEAR RENDERS dialog box opens, as shown in Figure 13.7.

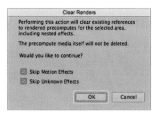

Figure 13.7
The Clear Renders dialog box.

3. Select the appropriate options:
   - SKIP MOTION EFFECTS, if you want to keep all motion effects in the marked range.
   - SKIP UNKNOWN EFFECTS, if you want to keep all effects marked with blank effect icons (third-party effects).

4. Click **OK**.

All rendered effects will be cleared between the IN and OUT points, or at the marked position.

Consolidate Means Copy

Consolidating refers to *copying* media files. When you consolidate media files, the system finds the media files or portions of media files associated with selected clips, subclips, or sequences and copies the referenced frames into a new media file.

Consolidate/Transcode sounds complex and impressive (and it is!), but "consolidate" is just Avid's fancy word for copy. When you're copying media, you are consolidating it. When you consolidate clips, the system finds the media files or portions of media files associated with those sequences, subclips, and master clips and copies the referenced frames into a new media file. *Transcoding* is the same as consolidating, with the added step that media is re-encoded to a different resolution (codec) during the process.

If someone tells you, "Please copy the media for those clips onto this drive," you can reply, "Sure! I'll consolidate them for you."

You will use the Consolidate/Transcode tool to duplicate, copy, and move media. Some editors may be inclined to use the OS X Lion Finder or Windows Explorer to manipulate media files, particularly because that's a common process on other editing systems. But Media Composer has two broad types of media: AMA-linked media and managed media. Managed media is not intended to be manipulated at the file system level, and AMA-linked media would need to be relinked unless the copied clips are in the same location on the other editing system. There is a better way.

The Consolidate/Transcode tool is ideal for copying and moving media. It understands the relationship between clips and media, and it works well for both AMA-linked media and managed media, updating the clips and database files that track the media during the consolidation.

Tip: If you'd like to understand the relationship between clips and media, you should reread the "Deep Dive into Media Files and Clips" section in Lesson 1, "How Workflow Makes, Manages, and Moves Media," on page 37.

Heads Up on Consolidating Master Clips, Subclips, and Sequences

You can consolidate master clips, subclips, or sequences. Before exploring the use of the Consolidate tool for step-by-step media management, it's useful to consider what happens behind the scenes for three common consolidation scenarios:

- Consolidating master clips
- Consolidating subclips
- Consolidating sequences

Consolidating Master Clips

Master clips always point to one or more media files of the same duration. When you consolidate a master clip, Media Composer identifies the associated media files for the selected master clip, and then copies all those frames into new media files.

If Consolidate/Transcode left the new media files as is, they would be orphaned media files that can't be accessed from a bin. To prevent that, Media Composer creates an additional master clip in the same bin as the original master clip. It then connects the clip and the media through the media files database, as shown in Figure 13.8.

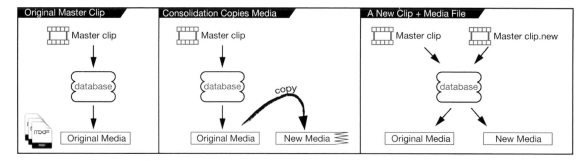

Figure 13.8
The original master clip points to a media file. Frames from that media file are copied into a new media file. A .new master clip is created, and it points to a new media file.

Consolidating Subclips

Subclips point to a range of frames within a media file, instead of pointing to the entire clip, like master clips do. Those frames are typically a subsection, such as a one-minute section of a 40-minute interview.

Note: If the subclip was made with an IN mark at the beginning and an OUT mark at the end of a master clip, the subclip would technically point to the entire media file, which would make it similar to a master clip. It would behave like a master clip in functionality: you couldn't trim earlier than the IN mark, or beyond the OUT mark. Media Composer would still display the subclip icon.

When Media Composer consolidates a subclip, it identifies the specific frames in the media file referenced by the subclip, and copies those frames into a new media file. To prevent creating an orphan clip, it creates a new master clip that's connected to the entire new media file, and to remain consistent, it creates a new subclip that points to the same frames, as shown in Figure 13.9. (Yes, this means your bin will have a new master clip and an additional subclip after consolidating a subclip.)

When you consolidate a subclip, you also have the option of including handles. Handles are additional frames that extend beyond the original range of the subclip. If you've created subclips for an interview and the IN/OUT marks of the subclips are very precise, you could add another 30 frames of handles on each end so you have additional media with which to later create transitions.

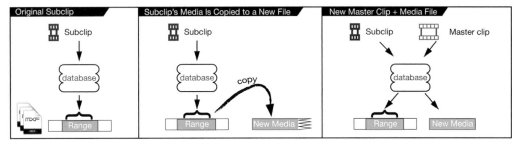

Figure 13.9
Consolidating a subclip. Media referenced by the subclip is copied into a new media file and a master clip is created.

 AVID▶

*In the Avid
Learning Series*

To learn about handles and how useful they are when creating transition effects, refer to *Media Composer 6 Effects Essentials*, part of the Avid Learning Series, and consider taking the corresponding course, MC110, at an Avid Learning Partner.

Consolidating Sequences

A sequence is just a series of subclips. When you consolidate a sequence, Media Composer consolidates every clip in the sequence as though it's a subclip, which it is. Media Composer then duplicates the sequence and links the newly consolidated media to the clips in the duplicated sequence. It also creates new master clips in the bin, so as not to orphan those newly created media files.

The behavior of the consolidation process can be configured, so depending on the options you choose, your results may not be identical to these scenarios, although they'll be similar. See Figure 13.10.

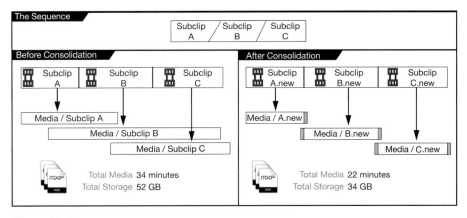

Figure 13.10
Consolidating sequences. Only media referenced by the sequence's clips (plus handles) is copied into new media files.

Consolidating from Bins versus Using the Media Tool

Media Composer can consolidate master clips, subclips, and sequences from a bin, as well as consolidate the items displayed in the Media tool. There are scenarios where it may be preferable to consolidate from the bin as opposed to the Media tool, or vice versa.

Consolidate from the Media Tool When Entire Clips Matter

Recall that the Media tool provides a window to the contents of the media drive. It can be limited to specific projects or the contents of specific drives, and only deals with entire media files, not subclips or sequences.

For those reasons, there are scenarios where it makes sense to consolidate from the Media tool:

■ **When you want to copy all the media referenced by a project.** It's easy to filter the Media tool to display all the media for a specific project, while excluding the media for all other projects.

■ **When you have a significant number of bins.** If you have 100 bins, and you want to copy all the media referenced by the clips in those bins, the Media tool can show it all. Without the Media tool, you would need to open each of the 100 bins and consolidate the contents on a per-bin basis.

■ **When you want to copy a sequence and its entire set of original media, as opposed to just the media referenced by the clips in the sequence.**

Consolidating a sequence from a bin will result in Media Composer copying just the media referenced by the clips in the sequence, which makes it difficult to significantly edit the sequence beyond the existing edits. If you want to move the sequence and all of the media, including the frames well beyond the handles for the timeline, you can use Show Media Relatives to select all the original master clips in the Media tool, and then consolidate those.

Consolidate from Bins When Sequences and Subclips Matter

A master clip in a bin will consolidate the same way a master clip in the Media tool consolidates. The big difference in bins in contrast to the Media tool for consolidation occurs when you consolidate subclips and sequences.

Subclips and sequences point to sections within an original master clip's media file. When they are consolidated, Media Composer only consolidates the referenced frames, instead of the entire media file.

Scenarios where this is useful include:

■ **Promoting subclips to independent master clips.** The frames referenced by the subclip will be placed into a new media file, and a new master clip will be created. If you delete the original master clip and its media file, the frames that were formerly in the subclip will not be offline because they are now independent in a separate media file.

■ **Copying only the media needed to play a specific sequence.** When consolidating a sequence, Media Composer copies the frames referenced by the clips in the sequence into new media files. You can delete the original media files and the sequence still plays, because the frames it needs are now in separate media files.

■ **When there are only a few bins or a few clips.** If you have only a few bins containing master clips, it might be easier to open each bin and consolidate the contents. If you have a sequence and want to copy all the original media, as opposed to the frames actually used in the sequence, you could use Show Reference Clips and consolidate the resulting referenced master clips.

Putting Consolidate to Work

There are five consolidation scenarios that any professional editor should be able to perform:

■ Scenario 1: Move media files from one drive to another.

■ Scenario 2: Centralize media files from many disks onto one disk.

■ Scenario 3: Retain only the media used in a subclip or sequence to clear excess video from your media files to conserve disk space.

■ Scenario 4: Consolidate to change clips' project association to the current project.

■ Scenario 5: Remove an unneeded track from a clip.

Scenario 1: Moving Media

In collaborative workflows, you often need to copy your media from one drive to another, or from one Unity Workspace to another. Other times, you will move media from one location to another. Moving media is the same as copying the media, and then deleting the original media. That's right: The only difference between a copy and a move between two drives is that while they both start with a copy of the media, a move finishes the job by deleting the original media.

Sometimes you may want to *move* media to another drive in order to clear drive space. Since the consolidation process always involves *copying* media, in this process you instruct the system to delete the original media after consolidating.

Here are some reasons for moving media to another drive:

- To make more space available on a specific media drive.

- To move media to a different type of drive, such as moving media from an external media drive to the internal drive of a laptop, so you can edit without requiring the external drive to be connected.

- To move media to a newer drive. This would be advantageous if you are upgrading your media drives to faster or larger media drives.

Note: If a specific clip appears to be causing a **VIDEO_UNDERRUN** or **AUDIO_UNDERRUN** error during playback, consolidating the master clip to a faster drive will frequently eliminate the problem.

To use Consolidate to move media:

1. Open a bin and select the master clips whose media files you want to consolidate.

2. Choose **CLIP > CONSOLIDATE/TRANSCODE**. The **CONSOLIDATE/TRANSCODE** dialog box opens, as shown in Figure 13.11.

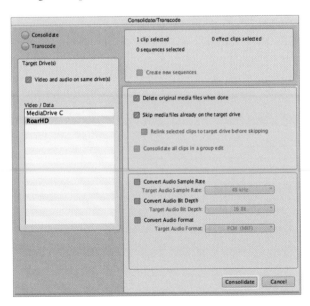

Figure 13.11
Moving media with the Consolidate/Transcode tool.

3. Select the **CONSOLIDATE** option in the upper-left corner.

Note: The Delete Original Media option is unlikely to be available in a Unity
environment.

4. Select DELETE ORIGINAL MEDIA FILES WHEN DONE. Please be aware that
   if you select this option, you may need to relink any additional sequences
   that reference the media you are consolidating.

5. Select SKIP MEDIA FILES ALREADY ON THE TARGET DRIVE if:
   - Some of the media files you are consolidating already exist on the target
     drive.
   - You do not want to affect the media files on the target drive.

6. If you select the option from Step 4 and you previously copied some of the
   media files to the target drive, select RELINK SELECTED CLIPS TO TARGET
   DRIVE BEFORE SKIPPING.

7. If you want to consolidate audio and video to separate drives, deselect the
   video and audio on same drive(s) check box, as shown in Figure 13.12.

8. Select a target disk from the TARGET DRIVE(S) window, as shown in
   Figure 13.12. You can create a drive cue by Shift-clicking multiple drives.

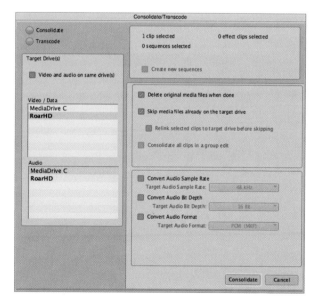

Figure 13.12
Targeting video and audio
drives separately.

The drives are filled in the order of decreasing capacity. Splitting audio
and video is especially important for audio mixers who want to put audio
files on a removable drive for sweetening at a digital audio workstation.

The system will alert you if the disk does not have enough storage space.

9. Convert audio by choosing any of the **AUDIO CONVERSION** options:

  - **CONVERT AUDIO SAMPLE RATE**
  - **CONVERT AUDIO BIT DEPTH**
  - **CONVERT AUDIO FORMAT**

   For example, if your project was edited at 48kHz and 24 bits, you need to convert to 44.1kHz and 16 bits to output tracks to an audio CD.

10. Click **CONSOLIDATE**. When you do so, Media Composer cycles through all the selected clips, copying their media into new media files and connecting the original clips to the new files. When the copy has been completed, Media Composer deletes the original media.

Scenario 2: Copying/Centralizing Media

You can use the Consolidate command with master clips to create backup copies of important media files or duplicate a master clip and its media files for use by another person. When you consolidate media files for a master clip, you create exact copies at full duration of the original media files. Unlike Scenario 1, Scenario 2 retains the copies of the consolidated media files.

For example, you would copy audio media files if you need to send audio to another system for mixing, but you also need to retain it for your use.

To use consolidate to copy media:

1. Open a bin and select the master clips whose media files you want to consolidate.

2. Choose **CLIP > CONSOLIDATE/TRANSCODE**.

   The Consolidate/Transcode dialog box appears, as shown in Figure 13.13.

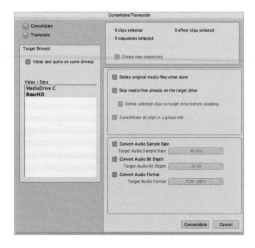

Figure 13.13
Copying media with the Consolidate/Transcode tool.

3. Deselect **DELETE ORIGINAL MEDIA FILES WHEN DONE** because you are copying the media and want to keep the files you are consolidating.

4. Deselect **SKIP MEDIA FILES ALREADY ON THE TARGET DRIVE** because you want to make copies even if some your files are already on the target disk.

5. Select other options, as described in Scenario 1.

   - Target drive(s)
   - Audio conversion options

6. Click **CONSOLIDATE**.

   When you copy media, an additional master clip is created for each media file. This ensures that all media has an associated master clip in a bin, and no media is orphaned on the media drive. But there is one element of uncertainty: Do the original clips point to the original media, or do the original clips point to the new media? When in doubt, Media Composer asks. This is one such situation. The Copying Media Files dialog box appears, as shown in Figure 13.14.

Figure 13.14
The Copying Media Files dialog box is used to specify the relationship between the original clips and the new media files.

7. Select one of the options in the **COPYING MEDIA FILES** dialog box.

   How do you know which of the two options to choose? Your choice depends on which clips you prefer to have an extension. If you choose **KEEP MASTER CLIPS LINKED TO MEDIA ON THE ORIGINAL DRIVE**:

   - The system creates new master clips (with the .new extension) that point to the new consolidated media files on the target disk.
   - The original clips (no extension) point to the original media files on the original disk, just as they did before you started the consolidation.

   This option creates a backup of the master clips and their media files on a separate disk. The connections between clips and media are shown in Figure 13.15.

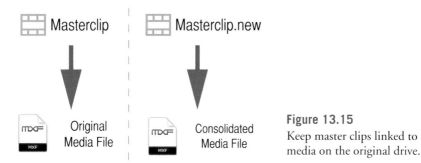

Figure 13.15
Keep master clips linked to media on the original drive.

If you choose RELINK MASTER CLIPS TO MEDIA ON THE TARGET DRIVE:

- The system creates new master clips and appends .old to the clip names. These clips point to the original media files.
- The original clips (those without the .old extension) point to the new consolidated media files on the target disk you chose in the previous dialog box.

This choice also allows you to create a backup of the master clip and its media files on a separate disk. The connections between clips and media are shown in Figure 13.16.

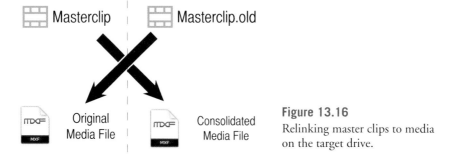

Figure 13.16
Relinking master clips to media on the target drive.

8. Click **OK** to continue the consolidation.

Media Composer duplicates both the media and the master clips. The master clips are in the same bin as the original clips, and either the new master clips or the original master clips are renamed to indicate if they point to the new media or the old media.

 Take a moment to complete Exercise 13, Part 1.

Scenario 3A: Clearing Excess Media by Consolidating Subclips

Consolidating subclips results in the creation of new master clips based on the new duration of the subclips. It's a way to promote the subclips to master clips, giving them all the rights and privileges therein, such as pointing to their own independent media files. This is a powerful way to eliminate unused media and is useful as the basis for a comprehensive capturing/project organization strategy.

You can capture long sections of source material, subclip the usable sections, and then consolidate the subclips to create new master clips. This procedure can save substantial time, particularly when capturing from tape or using workflows that do not involve Avid Media Access (AMA).

A typical scenario might be to capture an entire tape or import an entire file, and then create subclips of the sections of interest. Then consolidate the subclips to promote them to independent master clips, and delete the media associated with the original master clip. The speed of subclipping within Media Composer is much faster than setting marks while shuttling source tapes, and the media files produced by consolidating subclips contain no waste because consolidating a subclip only copies the frames referenced by the subclip, plus some optional handles.

Caution: You should perform this procedure before building your sequence. Otherwise, you will have to relink the sequence to the clips after consolidating.

To use Consolidate to promote subclips to master clips:

1. Create one or more subclips from a master clip. Leave the default names on the subclips.

2. Select all of the subclips and choose **CLIP > CONSOLIDATE/TRANSCODE**.

    The **CONSOLIDATE/TRANSCODE** dialog box appears, as shown in Figure 13.17.

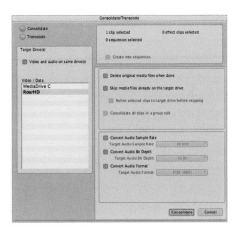

Figure 13.17
Consolidating to promote subclips to master clips and clear excess media.

3. Select **Delete Original Media Files When Done**.

4. Deselect **Skip Media Files Already on the Target Drive** in the Consolidate/Transcode dialog box or the Avid system will not remove the excess media on that disk during the consolidation process.

5. Select other options, as described in Scenario 1.

   - Target drive(s)
   - Audio conversion options

6. Click **OK**.

   A new master clip and subclip is created for each subclip you consolidate. All of the new master clips are automatically named after the original master clip from which they were drawn. Any names that you gave the original subclips do not transfer to the new master clips, but appear on the new subclips.

7. Delete all subclips and the original master clip, including the media files.

8. Optionally, load the new master clips into the Source monitor, and identify and name them.

   The new consolidated master clips will not contain any waste material and will occupy a minimum of drive space.

9. If you have already used the original master clips in a sequence, relink the sequence to the newly created clips.

 Take a moment to complete Exercise 13, Part 2.

Scenario 3B: Clearing Excess Media by Consolidating a Sequence

You can consolidate a sequence in order to delete the excess media you have not used, which is essentially the same as consolidating subclips. Consolidating a sequence is not the same as simply selecting and copying particular media files. Instead, you select the sequence that you want to consolidate, and the system then finds the sections of media files required for playing the sequence. Media Composer then copies the parts of the media file to the target disk that you specify.

When you consolidate a sequence:

- The system creates new media files and master clips that are shorter sections of the original media files and master clips. The new media files and clips are identified by the .new extension.

- Without the new consolidated media files online, you can't play the sequence.

■ The system breaks the old links that connected the sequence to the original media files. The new consolidated media files are not linked to any subclips or sequences except the sequence that you consolidated.

Consolidating a sequence affects it as shown in Figure 13.18.

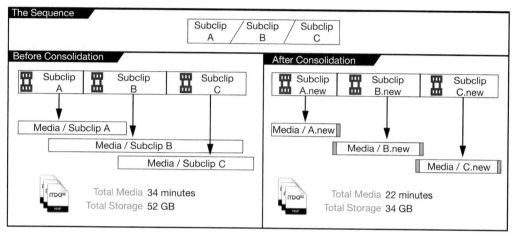

Figure 13.18
Consolidating a sequence results in new media files.

To consolidate a sequence and delete any excess media in the process:

1. Open a bin and select the sequence whose media files you want to consolidate.

2. Choose **CLIP > CONSOLIDATE/TRANSCODE**. The **CONSOLIDATE/TRANSCODE** dialog box appears, as shown in Figure 13.19.

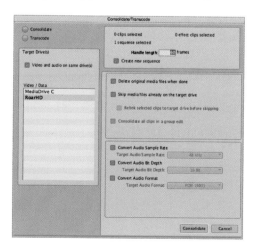

Figure 13.19
Consolidating a sequence to delete excess media.

3. Select **CREATE NEW SEQUENCE** to keep a sequence that links to the old media files.

    You could instead duplicate the sequence before consolidating.

4. Select **DELETE ORIGINAL MEDIA FILES WHEN DONE**.

Tip: Ensure there are no other sequences using the media files in the sequence you are consolidating.

5. Deselect **SKIP MEDIA FILES ALREADY ON THE TARGET DRIVE**.

6. Select other options, as described in Scenario 1.

    -   Target drive(s)
    -   Audio conversion options

    Long sequences at high resolutions may not fit on a single drive even if it is completely empty. You can also select more than one media volume to ensure there will be enough space.

7. Choose a handle length. This is the number of frames the system adds to the ends of the media files it creates for the sequence. The extra footage may be required later for trimming and adjusting effect durations. The Avid system provides a default handle length of 60 frames.

    Adding long handles can take up surprisingly large amounts of drive space. For example, four-second handles on a 200-shot show would result in 26 minutes of media files. At DNxHD 220X, this could require as much as 40GB of space for the handles alone.

8. Select **CONSOLIDATE ALL CLIPS IN A GROUP EDIT** if you are using multi-cam footage, and you want to consolidate the clips from all camera angles, not just the angle you used.

    -   If you are working on the edit and need to copy media to a different drive, select this option.
    -   If you are recapturing for online distribution, deselect this option because you won't need to use all camera angles.

9. Click **OK**.

The system creates new media files and master clips that are shorter sections of the original media files and master clips, and identifies them with a .new extension on their names.

Scenario 4: Using Consolidate to Change Clips' Project Association

It is possible to open bins from one project into another through the File menu. However, clips in those bins and their source and media file references will continue to be associated with their original project. This means that the Media tool will not identify or track media files associated with the clips in the new project. To change the project association of an existing clip, it is necessary to change the project association of the clip's source tape.

To change the project association of a master clip:

1. In the Windows or OS X Lion file hierarchy, move the bins that you want to associate with a project into that project folder.

2. In the Avid system, open the project that now contains those bins. The clips in those bins do not have this project's name association.

3. Select the clips whose project association you want to change.

4. Consolidate the clips to another drive.

The act of consolidating, as you now are quite aware, creates new media files by copying frames from other media files into new media files. When new media files are created, their metadata includes the name of the current project, which is how media files become associated with a project. All the new media files will be associated with the current project. Optionally, you may want to consolidate the new media files back onto the source drive.

Scenario 5: Stripping Out a Track Using Consolidate

Leaving unwanted track lights selected during capturing or logging is a common and fairly serious oversight. For example, capturing a voiceover clip with video selected in the Capture tool at 2:1 compression would consume considerable drive space. You could, of course, use the Media tool to delete just the media for the unwanted track. However, deleting the track before editing this clip into a sequence simplifies editing and avoids the *Media Offline* message.

To strip out a track using subclip and Consolidate:

1. Load the clip with the unwanted track(s) into the Source monitor.

2. Turn off the unwanted track(s) in the **TRACK SELECTOR** panel.

3. Subclip this clip back into the bin.

4. Highlight this newly created subclip in the bin and choose **CLIP > CONSOLIDATE/TRANSCODE**.

5. Select the **CONSOLIDATE** button in the upper-left corner.

6. In the dialog box, do the following, as shown in Figure 13.20.

   - Select **DELETE ORIGINAL MEDIA FILES WHEN DONE**.
   - Deselect **SKIP MEDIA FILES ALREADY ON THE TARGET DRIVE**.
   - Enter **0** for the handle length.
   - Select the target drive.

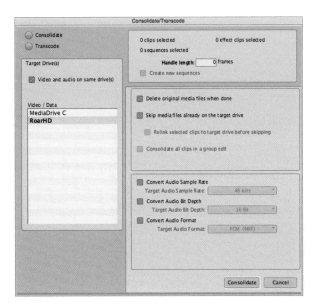

Figure 13.20
Consolidating to strip out
a track from a master clip.

7. Click **OK**.

   The system consolidates your subclip and creates a new subclip and a new
   master clip, both without the unwanted track.

8. Highlight the two subclips and also the original master clip with the
   unwanted track.

9. Press **DELETE**.

   Note: If you have already edited the clip into a sequence, relink the
   sequence to the new master clip.

10. Make sure to check all of the items for deletion in the **DELETE** dialog box.

    You now have a master clip that contains just the track(s) you wanted.

11. Remove the .new extension from the new master clip's name.

Summary of Consolidating Media

The previous sections have focused on use of the Consolidate/Transcode tool for copying media. The Transcode feature is next. Here's a summary of the Consolidate/Transcode tool's consolidation behavior:

- Consolidate means copy.

- Consolidating (copying) an AMA-linked clip will create a duplicate media file in the managed media folder.

- Consolidating AMA-linked clips results in managed media. (Yes, this is just paraphrasing the previous point, but it's important enough that you should read it another way.)

- Consolidating a master clip creates a media file identical to the first.

- Consolidating a subclip creates a media file equal to the length of the subclip.

- A sequence is a series of subclips. Therefore, consolidating a sequence results in new media files of a length equal to the length of the clip in the sequence. (You can add some additional handles, to give you extra frames with which to trim or create a transition.)

- Consolidate copies the media referenced by clips in a bin, but it does not copy the clips themselves, nor the bin.

Note: Consider a situation in which you connect an external drive to your editing system, you consolidate your media onto it, and then you give the drive to another editor to continue editing a sequence. You haven't given the other editor enough: There is no project or bin because the Consolidate tool does not copy either.

Transcode Means Convert

This section covers transcoding. *Transcoding* is a special type of consolidation that lets you change the resolution (codec) of your media during the copy operation.

Transcoding Clips and Sequences

Transcoding lets you change the resolution of the media of your clips and sequences. You can always change the resolution by recapturing, but transcoding is a lot faster and easier.

Note: Transcoding cannot make your footage look any better than it did before you transcoded it. Even though you can take a 15:1s SD sequence and transcode it to 1:1 10-bit HD, it won't look any better. The adage of "garbage in, garbage out" applies here.

Transcoding is a feature of Media Composer that you treat as a technical utility: There is increased flexibility when you can change the media to other resolutions (codecs). It's easier to collaborate and easier to edit on low-power computers or over low-bandwidth connections, both of which were covered in Lesson 4, "Play Together," after you've learned the basics of the tool in this lesson.

See the middle-right pane of the Consolidate/Transcode dialog box for the differences between the transcoding and consolidating, shown in Figure 13.21.

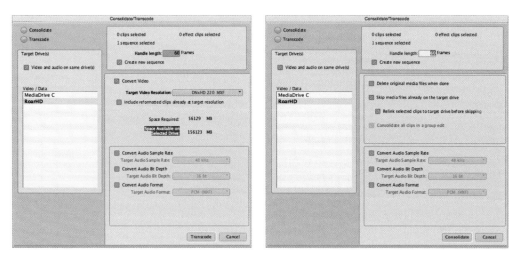

Figure 13.21
The resolution (codec) of media can be changed during transcoding, but not during consolidation.

Transcoding Can Upgrade Your Computer

Transcoding can upgrade your computer and give you a new hard disk and better CPU. It can even clean out the crumbs under your spacebar from last month's Subway sandwich. That's amazing, right? It's not too good to be true, not entirely. What it can do, in all seriousness, is make your computer behave as though you upgraded it, allowing it to breeze through sequences that otherwise might make it stutter.

Consider a scenario in which you have uncompressed HD media. Although this footage may play reasonably well one track at a time, when you begin to layer footage on additional video tracks, your computer struggles to read the two, three, or four uncompressed HD media files at the same time.

Are you thinking, "Oh, I don't cut with four layers of footage. That's a 1990s opening-sequence and I'm beyond that"? If so, think again and look at Figure 13.22.

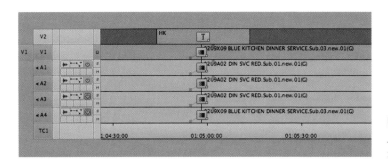

Figure 13.22

A dissolve and a title require reading four media files (streams).

What appears like two streams in Figure 13.22 can actually be four: A title or graphic with alpha requires two media files to be read concurrently (one for the fill, one for the alpha). During a dissolve, both clips on either side of the edit are read concurrently so they can be mixed together. Before you know it, your playback becomes sttteredddd andd ch'ch'chopopopppy.

And it's no wonder! HD 1:1 media is read at approximately 1.1 Gigabits per second (Gb/s). Four media files would require 4.4Gb/s, and most internal hard drives move data at a maximum rate of 3.0Gb/s. (Although newer ones as of mid 2012, supporting SATA 3.0, move it at 6.0Gbs.) In this scenario, the hard drive has become a bottleneck: the files are too big for them to be read quickly.

The solution? Transcode the media. By transcoding the media to another resolution (codec), the media will take less space, which means it can be more easily read from the hard drive. The challenge is in deciding which resolution to use.

There are two approaches:

■ **Choose a resolution that will create a small file but look almost as good as the original.** That would be a DNxHD codec. It would be like taking this book, and making the font smaller so the whole thing fits on fewer pages. The content's there, but the packaging is smaller.

■ **Choose a highly compressed resolution, which will not look good, but will be easily read, even off a slower USB drive.** Afterward, relink the sequence to the original high-quality media. It would be like taking this book and reading just the *Cliff Notes* version. The essentials are there, and it's considerably smaller and quicker to read, but most of the details are missing.

Those workflows are explained in the next sections.

Workflow Example: Convert from HD Uncompressed to Highly Compressed, Then Relink

In this scenario, you have captured uncompressed HD media and now you want to edit from a slow external USB drive using your laptop. You also want all of your media to be available, as opposed to just the media used by a particular sequence.

The workflow is as follows:

1. Set your project format to SD. This will enable the standard definition resolutions.

2. Use the **Consolidate/Transcode** tool as though you are consolidating the master clips, except select **Transcode**.

3. Set the **Resolution** to **15:1s**, as shown in Figure 13.23.

4. Transcode all clips.

5. Edit with the **SD 15:1s** clips.

6. Use **Relink** to reconnect the sequence to the HD 1:1 clips.

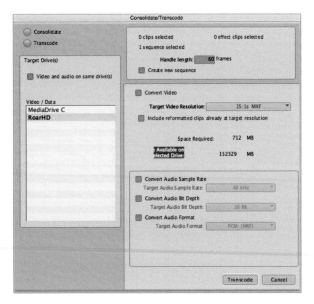

Figure 13.23
Transcoding to 15:1s produces very small media files.

Changing the Resize Algorithm

If you are transcoding genuine SD-originated material (as opposed to HD-down-converted media) to HD media, Avid recommends that you first change the resize algorithm to achieve maximum quality.

When transcoding SD to HD, Media Composer must adjust the frame size for each frame. This resizing process can tax the system. The default resize algorithm, called anti-aliased bi-linear, is lower quality than an alternative, called polyphase. The suggestion, therefore, is that you change to the polyphase algorithm before transcoding.

After making this change, image and render quality will be improved for all resizing operations, including transcode, reformat, resize, and picture-in-picture effects. The only thing that won't be improved is the 3D warp effect. You may, however, see a slight reduction in the number of real-time streams.

To change the resize algorithm through the render settings, select the Advanced (Polyphase) option from the Image Interpolation pull-down menu, as shown in Figure 13.24.

Figure 13.24
Use the advanced resize algorithm to achieve great-looking image enlargements.

Note that releases of Media Composer prior to v3 required the Console tool in order to perform this function. Use of the Console tool is no longer required.

Transcoding Clips or Sequences

This section covers the basic procedure for transcoding media associated with clips and sequences.

To use Transcode:

1. If your target format is different from the current project format, choose the target format in the **PROJECT** window, **FORMAT** tab, and for HD projects, choose a **RASTER TYPE**.

2. In a bin, select the clips or a sequence that you want to transcode.

3. Choose **BIN > CONSOLIDATE/TRANSCODE**. The **CONSOLIDATE/TRANSCODE** dialog box opens.

4. Select **Transcode** in the upper-left corner, as shown in Figure 13.25.

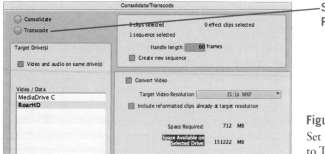

Select Transcode to Convert the Video
Resolution While Consolidating

Figure 13.25
Set the Consolidate tool
to Transcode mode.

5. In the **Target Drive(s)** area, select a drive or drives.

6. Click the **Target Video Resolution** pop-up menu and select a video resolution.

7. Click **Create New Sequence** if you are transcoding a sequence.

   Transcoding will create a new sequence in which the clips are linked to the new media. The original sequence will remain linked to the original media. This option is unavailable if you are transcoding clips.

8. Enter a handle length. This option appears when you select **Create New Sequence.**

9. Choose the appropriate **Audio Conversion** options for the target media.

   When transcoding, set the other options as you would set them when you consolidate media. After you have set the options, the dialog box should look similar to Figure 13.26 for clips.

10. Click the **Transcode** button in the lower-right corner.

    When you transcode media, an additional master clip is created for each media file. This ensures that all media has an associated master clip in a bin and no clips are orphaned.

When transcoding is complete, the following clips/sequences appear in your bin:

- **For transcoded clips**—Both the original and new clips (with a .new extension), shown in Figure 13.27.

- **For a transcoded sequence**—Both the original and new sequence (with a .Transcoded extension), and the clips that are in the sequence with a .new extension. The clips' durations are the durations of the clips in the sequence, plus the handles you gave them.

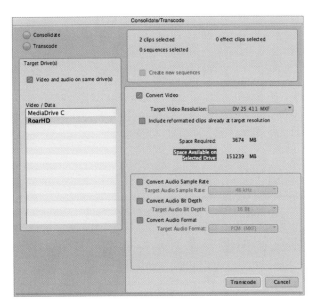

Figure 13.26
Transcoding clips.

Figure 13.27
A bin contains additional clips with a .new suffix after transcoding, as it does with consolidating.

The following two figures illustrate how transcoding a sequence results in new video clips while the audio remains in its original untranscoded form. Both figures represent the same sequence. Figure 13.28 shows the sequence before transcoding.

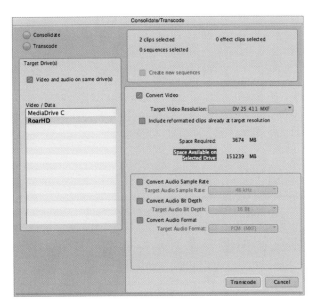

Figure 13.28
Sequence before transcoding.

Figure 13.29 illustrates the same sequence after it was transcoded. Notice that the clips on the video track include the .new suffix, while the audio clips are unaffected.

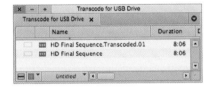

Figure 13.29
Sequence after transcoding: Note the .new suffix on the video clip names.

Figure 13.30 shows the two sequences in the bin after a sequence was transcoded. (The master clips themselves are not shown.) After transcoding a sequence, you should consider renaming it to reflect the new resolution (codec), such as *HD Final Sequence DV25.*

Figure 13.30
A bin after transcoding a sequence: The original sequence and new sequence exist.

Tip: Transcoding does not affect aspect ratio. If you up-convert clips from SD to HD, they will appear stretched when viewed in the 16:9 Source/Record monitors. Therefore, you may want to apply an effect, such as Reformat, Pan and Scan, or Resize, to the transcoded clips in the sequence. Reformatting was covered in Lesson 3, "Advanced Picture Editing."

EXERCISE   *Take a moment to complete Exercise 13, Part 3.*

Relinking Media Files

You use Relink to restore the pointers between the clip or sequence and their associated media files. These links may be broken, for example, when you consolidate or transcode. In Lesson 4, you learned about collaboration techniques that may also require you to relink sequences to media.

In addition, you learned how you can use a three-stage process—unlinking, modifying, and relinking—to add and remove tracks from clips.

Note: Relinking is not the same as reconnecting media in Final Cut Pro. Reconnecting is when you update a clip's metadata to store the file path to a media file. Relinking is when Media Composer re-evaluates metadata using criteria that you specify for media files and clips, and re-establishes the relationships between the clips and media.

Sometimes after you consolidate, transcode, or move material between systems, the clips or sequences lose their link or pointer to the original media files. When a clip becomes unlinked, it displays the "*Media Offline* message." If appropriate media exists online, you can use the Relink command to reestablish the link.

Note: In an Avid Interplay environment, relinking through the Relink dialog box is limited to non-master clips (subclips and sequences).

You can relink master clips to appropriate media files or to source tapes with compatible frame rates, and you can relink based on resolution. Media Composer compares the metadata such as source tape name, timecode information, and channels captured. New links are established to the media files if the search is successful. You can define the relinking process based on specific drives, or all available drives.

Why Is Relink Necessary?

Some reasons why a clip, subclip, or sequence might lose the link to its media:

- The clip was modified.

- The sequence or subclip has been consolidated, transcoded, or decomposed.

- Media was moved to another drive since you last accessed the clip, subclip, or sequence.

- The media's database file is corrupted.

Relinking a Sequence

Relinking a sequence causes Media Composer to cycle through all the clips in the sequence and look for related media files that match the criteria you specify for each clip in the sequence.

To relink a sequence:

1. Confirm that the sequence and the project format are the same. If they are not, change the project's format in the **PROJECT** window.

2. Highlight one or more sequences in a bin.

3. Choose **CLIP > RELINK**. The **RELINK** tool opens, as shown in Figure 13.31.

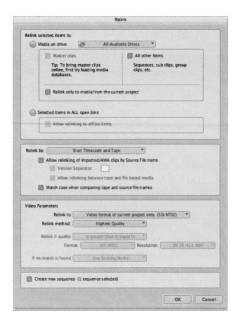

Figure 13.31
The Relink tool.

4. Select **All Other Items**. The system will look for media files that contain the frames it needs.

5. If some of your media originated in a different project, deselect **Relink Only to Media from the Current Project**. Also, if the sequence does not relink to the new clips, try deselecting the option and relinking again.

6. If the sequence still does not relink to the new clips, try deselecting **Match Case When Comparing Tape and Source File Names** and relink again.

7. Select one of the following options from the **Relink Method** menu:

   - **Most Recent (default)**—Relinks to the most recently created clip.

   - **Highest Quality**—Relinks to the highest quality clip. You would choose this option if you captured the same footage at 1:1 and 15:1s.

   - **Most Compressed**—Relinks to the most compressed clip.

   - **Specific Resolution**—Relinks to clips of a specific resolution.

   For example, choose **Most Compressed** to link to the media files that are smallest, but you don't know exactly what resolution it is. Perhaps some files are at 15:1s and some are compressed at the 10:1 resolution (codec). **Most Compressed** will go for the 15:1s files when it finds them, otherwise it will use the 10:1 media, which your hard disk would be able to read more easily than the larger, less compressed files. Choose **Specific Resolution** when you have multiple resolutions (encodings) of the media and you know the specific resolution you want to link to.

If you choose **SPECIFIC RESOLUTION**, choose an option from the **RELINK IF QUALITY** menu and the adjacent **RESOLUTION** menu, as shown in Figure 13.32. You have the option of relinking to the existing media or unlinking if no match is found, as shown in Figure 13.33.

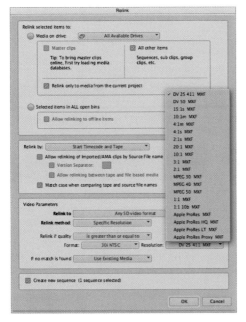

Figure 13.32
Relinking a clip or sequence to a specific media resolution (codec).

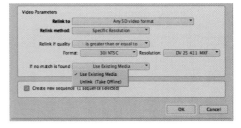

Figure 13.33
Media can be taken offline if no match is found.

If you select **IS GREATER THAN OR EQUAL TO**, lower quality media will be unlinked, ensuring that you do not relink to the wrong media.

8. Select **CREATE NEW SEQUENCE**, as shown in Figure 13.34.

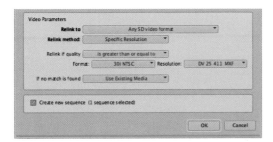

Figure 13.34
Create a new sequence to preserve the original.

This option (selected by default) leaves the original sequence alone and creates a new sequence with a *.relinked* extension. Media is relinked to this new sequence.

9. Use the **Drive** pull-down menu to select the drive you want the sequence relinked to, or select **All Available Drives**.

   Select a specific drive if you want to force the system to link to media on that drive (for example, if the same footage exists on multiple drives).

10. Click **OK**.

The system searches the drives for media files that contain material corresponding to the clip data, particularly the same tape name and the same timecode. If it finds any corresponding media files, their associated clips will no longer display the *Media Offline* message.

This option is often used to change a sequence from one resolution to another.

Relinking Master Clips to Media Files

Sometimes clips in a bin might be unlinked from their media. Your first step to resolve that is to load the media database, as covered in Lesson 4.

If that doesn't bring the media online, you can use the following technique with the Relink tool:

1. Highlight the clips that are showing **Media Offline** in the bin.

2. Choose **Clip > Relink**. The **Relink** dialog box appears, as shown in Figure 13.35.

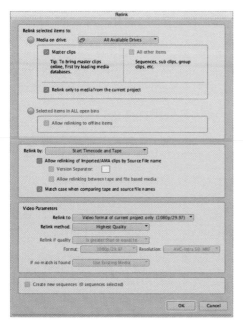

Figure 13.35
Relinking master clips to media files.

3. Select **Master clips**.

4. For other options, refer to "Relinking a Sequence" on page 479.

5. Click **OK**.

Guidelines for Relinking for Tape Media

All relinking is based on identical tape name and timecode of online media in the OMFI MediaFiles or Avid MediaFiles folder.

Rules pertaining to tape name:

■ Each physical tape should have one and only one tape name. Also, each tape name should refer to one and only one physical tape.

■ If a tape was entered as "new" in the Capture tool in a particular project, it is associated with that project. The name of the project is added to the name of the tape, although you may not be able to see it most of the time.

Rules pertaining to timecode:

■ A master clip will not link to media that is even one frame different from its start and end times. Master clips must match exactly.

■ A subclip will relink to media that is longer than the subclip. A subclip expects there to be more media beyond its start and end.

■ A sequence will sometimes relink even when the master clips that were used to edit it will not. Think of a sequence as a collection of subclips and subclips always expect there to be more media on the drives than is used.

Adding and Stripping Out Tracks

In this section, you'll be presented with two opposing scenarios for using unlinking and relinking: adding a track to clips and stripping out a track from clips. First, you'll learn about unlinking and when and why you would use this potentially dangerous feature.

Unlinking Clips from Media

Once a clip has been captured, some data, such as track data, cannot be readily modified, even using the Clip > Modify command. For example, if you forgot to turn a track on during capturing, you can use the Unlink command to separate the clip from its media file (after deleting the media of course), making the system think that it has not been captured. You can then simply modify the tracks.

Caution: Using the Unlink command without first deleting the media files associated with the clip you are unlinking will result in orphaned media files building up on your media drives (unless you plan to immediately relink the clips after modifying them). You can, however, always access them using the Media tool.

Use the Unlink command with caution. Do not use this command on clips that have already been edited into a sequence.

The Unlink command is not normally on any of the menus. It's hidden, to protect those who might otherwise do harm to a sequence or clip by using Unlink without knowing how it works. To reveal it, hold Shift+Ctrl/Cmd and click the Clip menu. It'll appear where the Relink command is normally shown.

Adding Tracks to a Captured Master Clip

You can use the unlink, modify, and relink workflow to add tracks to clips.

1. Select the clip(s) in the bin.

2. Press the **DELETE** key on the keyboard. The **DELETE** dialog box appears.

3. In the **DELETE** dialog box, select the associated media file(s).

4. Click **OK**.

5. Click **DELETE** in response to the prompt.

6. With the clips still selected, press **SHIFT+CTRL/CMD** while choosing **CLIP > UNLINK**. **UNLINK** appears where **RELINK** is usually found in the **CLIP** menu, and it will only appear if you hold **SHIFT+CTRL/CMD** first.

7. Choose **CLIP > MODIFY**.

8. In the **MODIFY** window, choose **SET TRACKS** from the pop-up menu, as shown in Figure 13.36.

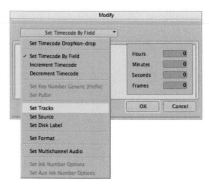

Figure 13.36
Clip > Modify allows you to change many aspects of your clips.

9. Select additional tracks, as shown in Figure 13.37, and click **OK**.

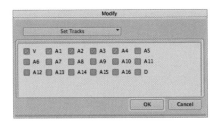

Figure 13.37
Adding tracks.

10. Choose **CLIP > RELINK**, and then select **RELINK OFFLINE MASTER CLIPS TO ONLINE MEDIA FILES**.

11. Click **OK**.

The media is relinked to the master clips. If the clips were edited into a sequence, the media is also relinked to the sequence. You can now batch capture or re-import the modified clip with the proper track selection.

EXERCISE   *Take a moment to complete Exercise 13, Part 4.*

Stripping Out a Track by Using Unlink, Modify, and Relink

In "Scenario 5: Stripping Out a Track Using Consolidate," on page 469 of this lesson, you learned a technique for stripping out a track using subclipping and the Consolidate tool. That method works well for a single clip. If you want to strip out an unwanted track from a batch of clips, however, it's easier to use the process of unlinking, modifying, and relinking.

To strip an unwanted track from one or more master clips:

1. Do the following steps if the media is online:

    a) Open the **MEDIA** tool.

    b) Select the clip(s) with the extraneous track.

    c) Delete the media for the extraneous track.

    d) Close the **MEDIA** tool.

2. Select the clip(s) in the bin.

3. Press **SHIFT+CTRL/CMD** while choosing **CLIP > UNLINK**. The media is offline.

4. Choose **CLIP > MODIFY**.

5. In the **MODIFY** window, choose **SET TRACKS** from the pop-up menu.

6. Deselect the extraneous track and click **OK**.

7. Choose CLIP > RELINK, and select RELINK OFFLINE MASTER CLIPS TO ONLINE MEDIA FILES.

8. Click **OK**.

The media is relinked to the master clips. If the clips were edited into a sequence, the media is also relinked to the sequence.

Review/Discussion Questions

1. The Media tool and bins look identical and you interact with them in a similar way. You can custom-sift, sort, and use custom headings. How do they differ? (See "Understanding the Media Tool" on page 442.)

2. What is the difference between deleting an item from a bin as opposed to deleting it using the Media tool? (See "Understanding the Media Tool" on page 442.)

3. When configuring the Media tool display, Media Composer populates the left-side of the dialog box with a list of projects. Where does it obtain the project names? (See "Projects List of the Media Tool" on page 443).

4. The Media tool allows the display of precomputes, master clips, and media files. How do these three options differ, and when might you use each one? (See "Setting the Media Tool Display" on page 442.)

5. To see all master clips and subclips that are associated with a sequence, what should you do to prepare *before* selecting media relatives? (See "Media Relatives Relate to a Selected Item" on page 448.)

6. How do you isolate the media files in your project that are not in a selected sequence? (See "Media Relatives Relate to a Selected Item" on page 448.)

7. You have accidentally deleted media files using the Media tool. How do you fix this problem? (See "Deleting Managed Media from the Media Tool" on page 446.)

8. You try to open a bin but Media Composer displays a *Fatal Assertion Error*. What do you do? (See "Corrupt Bins" on page 450.)

9. While playing a sequence with a famous studio executive in the room, Media Composer always stops playback and presents an error at roughly the same portion of the sequence. How do you fix the error and explain the situation? (See "Corrupt Sequences" on page 451 and "Conquer and Divide: Locating Corrupted Media" on page 452.)

10. You have rendered all the effects in a scene, but did not notice until afterward that your project's raster setting was incorrect. How do you prepare the clips for re-rendering upon correction of the raster setting? (See "Clearing Rendered Effects" on page 453.)

11. What's the difference between copying files using Windows Explorer or OS X Lion's Finder, in contrast to using Consolidate? (See "Heads Up on Consolidating Master Clips, Subclips, and Sequences" on page 455.)

12. If you were to explain the Consolidate tool to a six-year-old child (or a producer), how would you explain it? (See "Heads Up on Consolidating Master Clips, Subclips, and Sequences" on page 455.)

13. You have a master clip with an IN and OUT mark. You create a subclip from that marked region. You consolidate both the original master clip (which still has the IN mark and OUT mark), and you consolidate the subclip. Is the result of the two Consolidate operations the same? If so, why? If not, how are they different? (See "Consolidating Master Clips" on page 455 and "Consolidating Subclips" on page 456.)

14. Same scenario as question #13, but the IN mark is at the very beginning of the clip, and the OUT mark is at the very end of the clip. You make a subclip and consolidate the subclip, and then consolidate the original master clip. What's the difference in the result? (See "Consolidating Master Clips" on page 455 and "Consolidating Subclips" on page 456.)

15. How does Media Composer choose the frames to consolidate from the source media files when it is consolidating a sequence? (See "Consolidating Sequences" on page 457.)

16. Your assistant editor consolidates a sequence for you. He sets the handle length to 0, despite your clear instructions to set it to 120. What effect will his error have on your ability to continue editing the sequence? (See "Scenario 3B: Clearing Excess Media by Consolidating a Sequence" on page 466.)

17. Give a scenario in which it would be preferable to consolidate from the Media tool. (See "Consolidating from Bins versus Using the Media Tool" on page 458.)

18. Give a scenario in which it would be preferable to consolidate from bins instead of the Media tool. (See "Consolidating from Bins versus Using the Media Tool" on page 458.)

19. What's the difference between configuring Consolidate to move media, as opposed to configuring it to copy media? (See "Scenario 1: Moving Media" on page 459.)

20. You have a master clip of a one-hour interview. There are only three sepa-
    rate one-minute sections that you want; the rest of the master clip is not
    going to be used. Is there a way to preserve just those three separate one-
    minute sections, while deleting the unwanted frames? If so, what's the tech-
    nique? If not, reconsider the answer. (See "Scenario 3A: Clearing Excess
    Media by Consolidating Subclips" on page 465.)

21. You've finished editing a sequence and want to delete everything except for
    the media used by the sequence, plus a second of extra footage on either
    side of each edit. How do you accomplish that? (See "Scenario 3B: Clearing
    Excess Media by Consolidating a Sequence" on page 466.)

22. How does a clip become associated with a project, and how can you alter
    that association? (See "Scenario 4: Using Consolidate to Change Clips'
    Project Association" on page 469).

23. What is the difference between consolidating and transcoding?
    (See "Transcode Means Convert" on page 471.)

24. Why might you consider transcoding when you want to use a slower
    external hard drive? (See "Transcoding Can Upgrade Your Computer"
    on page 472.)

25. After transcoding, your bin contains additional master clips with the .old
    suffix. What does this mean and how did this happen? (See "Scenario 2:
    Copying/Centralizing Media" on page 462.)

26. You'd like to transcode from HD 1:1 10-bit to DNxHD 220X, but the
    Consolidate/Transcode tool only shows resolutions such as 1:1, 2:1, 3:1,
    DV25, and 15:1s. Why is this and how do you fix it so that DNxHD
    220X is available? (See "Transcoding Clips and Sequences" on page 471.)

27. Media Composer doesn't directly link managed media in a bin to media
    files using a file path. It uses the metadata to determine the connections.
    What are some benefits of this system, regarding the use of the Relink tool?
    (See "Relinking Media Files" on page 478.)

28. What are some criteria that you might specify in the Relink tool?
    (See "Relinking a Sequence" on page 479.)

29. Outline the workflow for stripping out an unwanted track from a batch
    of master clips. (See "Adding and Stripping Out Tracks" on page 483.)

30. An inexperienced editor observes you use the Unlink command, and then can't find the same command on his editing system. He asks why it isn't available. How do you explain to the young grasshopper that the command is hidden for his own good? (See "Unlinking Clips from Media" on page 483.)

Exercise 13

Managing Media

The exercises in this lesson are intended to provide you with practice performing media management. You will use the Consolidate/Transcode tool, the Relink tool, and further your knowledge of manipulating the relationships between clips and media files.

Media Used:
Agent MXZero

Duration:
30 minutes

GOALS

- Use the Consolidate tool to duplicate media
- Use the Consolidate tool to transcode media in use by a sequence
- Promote subclips to master clips, so you can delete the media associated with the master clip

Exercise 13.1: Duplicating a Master Clip's Media by Consolidation

In this exercise, you transcode clips from an online to an offline resolution, transcode a sequence, and add the A2 track to a few master clips.

You'll begin this exercise by duplicating a master clip and its media.

1. Open the **Agent MXZero** project.

2. Open the **201 folder > Lesson 13 Selects**.

3. Select the **Lady Chopsticks** clip.

4. Choose **Clip > Consolidate/Transcode**.

5. Configure the **Consolidate/Transcode** tool, as shown in Figure EX13.1.

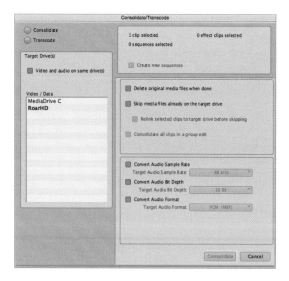

Figure EX13.1
Consolidating a master clip.

Figure EX13.1 shows that **Skip Media Files Already on the Target Drive** has been deselected. If this option was enabled and the target drive was the same as the source drive, nothing would happen because the media is already on the target drive. To ensure the Consolidate/Transcode tool duplicates the media files, you need to deselect this option.

6. Select the target drive and click **Consolidate**. Media Composer duplicates the media and creates a new master clip in the bin that's connected to the new media.

7. Rename the new master clip **Chop Chop**, so it's easier to refer to in subsequent exercises.

Exercise 13.2: Promoting Subclips to Master Clips

You'll now create a couple subclips using the Chop Chop clip, which you created in the Exercise 13.1. Those subclips will share the same media file as Chop Chop, so if you delete the media that's associated with Chop Chop, the subclips will also report *Media Offline*. In this scenario, imagine Chop Chop is an hour in duration, but the two subclips that you'll create are only 30 seconds each. You want to preserve the media used by the subclips, but delete the remaining 59 minutes of media.

You'll use the Consolidate tool to copy the media referenced by the subclips into new media files, after which you can delete Chop Chop's media without losing the video referenced by the subclips.

1. Open **201 folder > Lesson 13 Selects > Chop Chop** into the Source monitor.

2. Create two subclips.

    At 15 seconds into the clip, there is a short section where she licks her lips. This could be saved for a bloopers-reel: subclip it. At the end of the clip, she takes a cigarette from a package: subclip that.

3. Select the two subclips.

4. Choose **Clip > Consolidate / Transcode**.

5. Configure the Consolidate/Transcode tool as shown in Figure EX13.2.

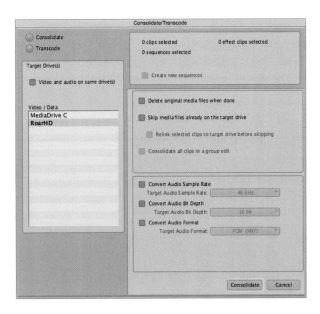

Figure EX13.2

Consolidating a master clip.

Be sure to uncheck Skip Media Files Already on Target Volume and Delete Original Media Files When Done.

6. Click Consolidate. Media Composer copies the frames referenced by the subclips into new media files and creates new master clips for them.

7. Delete Chop Chop's associated media files, but leave the master clip.

8. Open the consolidated clips and confirm their media is still online.

9. Open Chop Chop and confirm the media is offline.

You've now promoted the subclips to independent master clips, which no longer rely on the media of the Chop Chop clip.

Exercise 13.3: Transcoding Clips from an Online to an Offline Resolution

You'll now transcode while consolidating. Transcoding does everything that consolidate does, plus converts the video into a different resolution (codec). You might do this to realize increased performance from your computer when using multiple streams of video concurrently. The more compressed a file is, the quicker it is read off the hard drive.

1. Set the project format to an SD format, as shown in Figure EX13.3.

Figure EX13.3
Set the project format to SD 23.976p.

2. Open the **201 folder > Lesson 13 Selects.**

3. Select the Lady Chopsticks clip.

4. Choose Clip > Consolidate/Transcode.

5. Configure the Consolidate/Transcode tool, as shown in Figure EX13.4.

The 35:1 resolution has been chosen because it offers the best compression. If the project format is not SD, you can't choose 35:1.

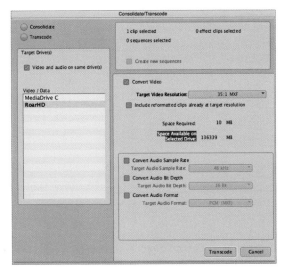

Figure EX13.4
Transcoding a master clip
to the 35:1 resolution.

6. Select the target drive and click **TRANSCODE**. Media Composer duplicates
the media while transcoding it to 35:1. It creates a new master clip in the
bin with the .transcoded suffix.

7. Set the **BIN VIEW** to **FORMAT**, as shown in Figure EX13.5, and compare
the two clips.

Figure EX13.5
The Format bin view allows
comparison of resolution (codec).

8. Compare the image quality of both clips by loading them into the Source
monitor and inspecting them. Be sure you set your **VIDEO QUALITY** setting
to **FULL QUALITY**, and you might consider viewing the images on an external
display or in full-screen mode.

9. Compare the file sizes of the images using **FILE > REVEAL FILE**. As you
learned in Lesson 1, **REVEAL FILE** shows the media file associated with the
master clip.

10. After a media file has been revealed, determine the file sizes by right-clicking
the media file and choosing **GET INFO** (OS X Lion) or **PROPERTIES**
(Windows).

Exercise 13.4: Adding Tracks of Captured Master Clips Using Unlink and Relink

The Lady Chopsticks clip is MOS: It is without sound. There are no audio tracks associated with it. When it's loaded into the Source monitor, only "V1" appears in the source side of the track selector panel.

You will prepare to recapture the clip, but you do not want to have to re-edit the clip into the timeline. By modifying the master clip to support an audio track, and then recapturing the clip, all existing instances of it will have the additional track available.

To add track A2 to the master clip:

1. Open the **201 FOLDER** > **LESSON 13 SELECTS**.

2. Select the **LADY CHOPSTICKS** clip.

3. Press **CMD+SHIFT** (OS X Lion) or **CTRL+SHIFT** (Windows), and choose **CLIP** > **UNLINK**.

   The media is now disassociated from the clip and appears offline.

4. Choose **CLIP** > **MODIFY** > **SET TRACKS** (see Figure 13.36).

5. Add tracks **A1** and **A2**, as shown in Figure EX13.6.

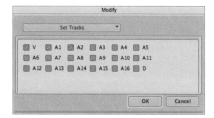

Figure EX13.6
Adding audio tracks to an existing unlinked master clip.

6. Click **OK**. Inspect the **TRACKS** column in the bin's **TEXT** view and confirm the clip now has V1, A1-2.

7. Reconnect the existing video media file to the **LADY CHOPSTICKS** clip. Select **CLIP** > **RELINK**. Leave all the default options and click **OK**.

Media Composer should reconnect the clip to the existing video media. The clip is ready to be recaptured for its audio component.

You've now modified a clip to add additional tracks to it. You've had an opportunity to explore the power of Relink, Consolidate, and the media management tools that have made Media Composer the number one editing system in the world.

Wrapping Up

Over these 13 lessons you've begun a journey to become a better picture and sound editor. The techniques and concepts you've learned will aid to set you apart from many editors, and producers will learn to expect more of you than the average Avid editor. Treat your producers well and your colleagues fairly, and demonstrate your intricate knowledge of Media Composer—the post-production industry will be yours for the taking.

Advanced Media Composer skills don't come easily, and this book is just the beginning of the advanced books in the Avid Learning Series. Now that you have the techniques, you need to put them to use. I tell my students that it's similar to learning to fly an airplane: I can show you what the knobs and dials in the cockpit do, and I can tell you why they matter, but it's not until you sit in the seat on the left (the pilot's seat) and fly that they really begin to make sense. You, like an Airbus pilot, need to get your hours in. The more hours in, the bigger the aircraft you can fly, or the more famous the films you'll get to cut.

If you have questions or comments, or would like to learn more, I encourage you to get in touch. Here are some ways to engage and interact with me:

- Twitter: @splicetraining
- Online videos, including videos demonstrating many of the techniques in this book: http://splicetraining.ca/avidbook
- Email at woody@splicetraining.ca
- Classes are offered in Toronto, Vancouver, and Halifax, as well as occasionally other cities. Get the schedule and sign up online: http://www.splicetraining.ca/mc201

Good luck, and...happy editing!

—Woody

Technical Reference

This appendix is an online editing and archival reference you can use when a project has wrapped up. You'll find many helpful tables in here to expedite your online editing and archiving process.

Table A-1   Available High-Definition Project Formats

Frame Rate	Video Formats
23.976	NTSC 23.976, 720p/23.976, 1080p/23.976
24	NTSC 24p, PAL 24p, 1080/24
25	PAL 25i, PAL 25p, 720p/25, 1080i/50, 1080p/25
30	NTSC 30i, 720p/29.97, 1080i/59.94, 1080p/29.97
50	720p/50
60	720p/59.94

* Although both 24p NTSC and 24p PAL can both switch to 1080p24, you cannot switch between the NTSC and PAL formats due to the difference in frame rate. Note that the letter *i* is used to indicate interlaced formats and the letter *p* indicates progressive formats.

Table A-2   Format Compatibility Between Standard and High Definitions

HD Online	SD Offline	Notes
720p/23.976	23.976p NTSC	You cannot change between these project formats because the edit rates are different.
720p/25	25p PAL or 25i PAL	Change the project format and modify the sequence.
720p/50	25p PAL or 25i PAL	You cannot change between these project formats because the edit rates are different.
720p/59.94	30i NTSC	You cannot change between these project formats because the edit rates are different. Use an NTSC 30i project for offline editing, and then open a new 720p/59.94 project for online editing. Open the desired NTSC 30i bins and modify the final sequence.
1080p/23.976	23.976p NTSC For 23.976p NTSC	For 23.976p NTSC, change the project format and modify the sequence.
1080p/24	24p NTSC or 24p PAL	Change the project format and modify the sequence.
1080p/25	25p PAL or 25i PAL	Change the project format and modify the sequence.
1080p/29.97	30i NTSC	You cannot change between these project formats because the edit rates are different. Use an NTSC 30i project for offline editing, and then open a new 1080p/29.97 project for online editing and open the desired NTSC 30i bins. You do not need to modify the sequence. Duplicate the sequence and then batch capture the duplicated sequence.
1080i/50	25i PAL or 25p PAL	Change the project format and modify the sequence.
1080i/59.94	30i NTSC	Change the project format and modify the sequence.

Table A-3   Rasters at the 1080 HD Format

1080 Format	Rasters
Standard, AVC-Intra, XDCAM HD 50, XDCAM EX	1920×1080
DVCPro HD, XDCAM HD, HDV, AVC Intra 50	1440×1080

Table A-4 Project Types and Purposes

Project Type	Source Footage Transfer
23.976p NTSC	For film-originated or video-originated footage that has been shot at 23.976fps or film-originated footage transferred on digital videotape (such as Digital Betacam).
24p NTSC	For film-originated or other 24fps footage transferred to NTSC videotape.
24p PAL	For film-originated or other 24fps footage transferred to PAL videotape at 25fps.
25i PAL	For PAL video-originated footage (25fps).
25p PAL	For 25fps film footage transferred to PAL videotape.
30i NTSC	For NTSC video-originated or other 30fps footage transferred to NTSC videotape.
720p/23.976	For film-originated material transferred to videotape.
720p/25	For video-originated material that can be captured, edited, and output for HD broadcast. It can also be captured in DVCProHD format.
720p/29.97	For video-originated material. Can be directly captured, edited, and output for HD broadcast.
720p/50	For HDV broadcast (European broadcast).
720p/59.94	For video-originated material. Can be directly captured, edited, and output for HD broadcast.
1080p/23.976	For film-originated footage transferred to videotape.
1080p/24	For film-originated footage transferred to videotape. True 24fps editing.
1080p/25	For film-originated footage transferred to videotape.
1080i/50	For video-originated material. Can be directly captured, edited, and output for HD broadcast.
1080i/59.94	For video-originated material. Can be directly captured, edited, and output for HD broadcast.

Table A-5   Resolution Storage Requirements

Format	Resolution	One Minute of Video Requires
NTSC or PAL	1:1 10-bit	1.54 gigabytes (GB)
	1:1	1.22 gigabytes
1080i/59.94	1:1 10-bit	8.68 gigabytes
	1:1	6.95 gigabytes
	DNxHD 220	1.54 gigabytes
	DNxHD 145	1.00 gigabytes
720p/59.94	1:1 10-bit	3.86 gigabytes
	1:1	3.09 gigabytes
	DNxHD 220	1.54 gigabytes
	DNxHD 145	1.00 gigabytes
1080i/50	1:1 10-bit	7.24 gigabytes
	1:1	5.79 gigabytes
	DNxHD 185	1.28 gigabytes
	DNxHD 120	0.85 gigabytes
1080p/23.976	1:1 10-bit	6.95 gigabytes
	1:1	5.56 gigabytes
	DNxHD 175	1.22 gigabytes
	DNxHD 115	0.81 gigabytes
720p/23.976	1:1 10-bit	3.09 gigabytes
	1:1	2.47 gigabytes
	DNxHD 90	0.61 gigabytes
	DNxHD 60	0.41 gigabytes

* The table includes a subset of the available HD formats. For a complete storage requirement list, refer to the Media Composer Editing documentation.

Table A-6   Delivery Requirements for Offline Elements

Required Element	Notes
Offline project	Although only the final offline sequence is really needed for offline, it is helpful to have the entire project, especially if troubleshooting is required.
Digital cut of final offline	A digital cut of the offline is essential. If there are any questions about title placement, element alignment, or effect design, they can often be answered by examining the offline digital cut. Note: The digital cut should be laid off using sequence timecode to a timecoded tape format such as Beta SP or DVCPRO HD. Do not accept a VHS tape.
The final audio mix	The audio mix can be delivered in a variety of formats. The method of delivery will vary from project to project. Ensure that you and the offline editor agree on the delivery method. Consult Lesson 9, "Fundamentals of Audio Mixing," for advice on sending your mix to Pro Tools.
All required source tapes	The offline editor should double-check that all tapes were packaged and sent to the online.
Non-standard fonts used in offline	Any non-standard fonts should be delivered online.
All online import elements	All graphics, animations, and audio used in the project should be delivered online. Additionally, these elements should meet a graphic delivery requirements spec. This spec is discussed in Table A-9.
List of AVX plug-ins used	If plug-ins were used in the offline, the online editor must know which ones were used so they can be made available online.

Table A-7   Delivery Requirements for Standard-Definition (SD) Still Graphics

Aspect	Requirement	Notes
Frame size: 4×3 square pixel	648×486 (NTSC) 768×576 (PAL)	These are the preferred square pixel sizes for NTSC and PAL. 720×540 can also be used in some situations for both NTSC and PAL.
Frame size: 16x9 square pixel	864×486 (NTSC) 1024×576 (PAL)	These are the preferred sizes for NTSC and PAL.
Frame size: nonsquare pixel	720×486 (NTSC) 720×576 (PAL)	These are the native frame sizes for standard-definition graphics.
Alpha channel	White on black	This is the standard used by all graphics, animation, and compositing packages. The alpha channel must be inverted on import.
Color mode	RGB	Other formats, including CMYK, Indexed, and Grayscale, can cause import errors.
File format	TIFF (.tif), PICT (.pct), or PNG (.png)	These are the three most commonly used graphic formats. The PNG format allows for easy export of layered graphics out of Photoshop.

Table A-8   Additional Delivery Requirements for SD Animation and Video

Aspect	Requirement	Notes
Field ordering	Even, Lower Field First (NTSC) Odd, Upper Field First (PAL) Even, Lower Field First (PAL DV)	Proper field ordering is critical.
Video level	RGB mapping	The other option, 601 Mapping, should be used only when the source requires it (for example, with test patterns).
File format	Avid QuickTime codec	This is the preferred method of delivery.
Frame size (4×3 or 16×9)	720×486 (NTSC) 720×576 (PAL)	The Avid QuickTime codec requires the full ITU-R BT.601 frame size.
Resolution	Uncompressed (1:1)	It is strongly recommended that all SD graphics be uncompressed.

Table A-9   Delivery Requirements for High-Definition (HD) Still Graphics

Aspect	Requirement	Notes
Frame size: 1080-line	1920×1080	High-definition formats natively use square pixels.
Frame size: 720-line	1280×720	High-definition formats natively use square pixels.
Alpha channel	White on black	This is the standard used by all graphics, animation, and compositing packages. The alpha channel must be inverted on import.
Color mode	RGB	Other formats, including CMYK, Indexed, and Grayscale, can cause import errors.
File format	TIFF (.tif), PICT (.pct), or PNG (.png)	These are the three most commonly used graphic formats. The PNG format allows for easy export of layered graphics out of Photoshop.

Table A-10   Additional Delivery Requirements for HD Animation and Video

Aspect	Requirement	Notes
Field ordering: 1080 interlaced	Odd, Upper Field First	Interlaced HD uses field ordering that is opposite of NTSC. If you're using a progressive HD resolution (1080p or 720p), field rendering should *not* be used.
Video level	RGB mapping	The other option, 709 Mapping, should be used only when the source requires it (such as Luma key elements, animated test patterns, preserved highlights, and so on).
File format	Avid DNxHD QuickTime (RGB) or Animation Codec (RGBA)	Avid DNxHD is preferred for RGB animations. If an alpha channel is required, use the Animation codec instead.
Resolution	To match project requirement	Although uncompressed HD is preferred, DNxHD is suitable for most applications and imports much more quickly.

Table A-11   Media Composer SD and HD Formats

SD	HD 1080-Line	HD 720-Line
30i NTSC	1080i/59.94,1080p/59.94	720p/29.97
23.976p NTSC	1080p/23.976	720p/23.976
24p NTSC	1080p/24	Not applicable
25i PAL	1080i/50, 1080p/25	720p/25
25p PAL	1080p/25, 1080i/25	720p/25
24p PAL	1080p/24	Not applicable

INDEX

Avid Learning Series

License Agreement/Notice of Limited Warranty